New Frontiers in Regional Science: Asian Perspectives

Volume 80

This series is a constellation of works by scholars in the field of regional science and in related disciplines specifically focusing on dynamism in Asia.

Asia is the most dynamic part of the world. Japan, Korea, Taiwan, and Singapore experienced rapid and miracle economic growth in the 1970s. Malaysia, Indonesia, and Thailand followed in the 1980s. China, India, and Vietnam are now rising countries in Asia and are even leading the world economy. Due to their rapid economic development and growth, Asian countries continue to face a variety of urgent issues including regional and institutional unbalanced growth, environmental problems, poverty amidst prosperity, an ageing society, the collapse of the bubble economy, and deflation, among others.

Asian countries are diversified as they have their own cultural, historical, and geographical as well as political conditions. Due to this fact, scholars specializing in regional science as an inter- and multi-discipline have taken leading roles in providing mitigating policy proposals based on robust interdisciplinary analysis of multifaceted regional issues and subjects in Asia. This series not only will present unique research results from Asia that are unfamiliar in other parts of the world because of language barriers, but also will publish advanced research results from those regions that have focused on regional and urban issues in Asia from different perspectives.

The series aims to expand the frontiers of regional science through diffusion of intrinsically developed and advanced modern regional science methodologies in Asia and other areas of the world. Readers will be inspired to realize that regional and urban issues in the world are so vast that their established methodologies still have space for development and refinement, and to understand the importance of the interdisciplinary and multidisciplinary approach that is inherent in regional science for analyzing and resolving urgent regional and urban issues in Asia.

Topics under consideration in this series include the theory of social cost and benefit analysis and criteria of public investments, socio-economic vulnerability against disasters, food security and policy, agro-food systems in China, industrial clustering in Asia, comprehensive management of water environment and resources in a river basin, the international trade bloc and food security, migration and labor market in Asia, land policy and local property tax, Information and Communication Technology planning, consumer "shop-around" movements, and regeneration of downtowns, among others.

Researchers who are interested in publishing their books in this Series should obtain a proposal form from Yoshiro Higano (Editor in Chief, higano@jsrsai.jp) and return the completed form to him.

Xiaochun Li • Yunyun Wu

Research on Characteristic Issues in Current Developing Economies

New Application of the Harris – Todaro Model

Springer

Xiaochun Li
Business School
Nanjing University
Nanjing, Jiangsu, China

Yunyun Wu
School of Economics
Nanjing University of Finance and Economics
Nanjing, China

Green Economy Development Institute
Nanjing University of Finance and Economics
Nanjing, China

ISSN 2199-5974 ISSN 2199-5982 (electronic)
New Frontiers in Regional Science: Asian Perspectives
ISBN 978-981-97-7283-4 ISBN 978-981-97-7284-1 (eBook)
https://doi.org/10.1007/978-981-97-7284-1

This Springer imprint is published by the registered company Springer Nature Singapore Pte Ltd.
The registered company address is: 152 Beach Road, #21-01/04 Gateway East, Singapore 189721, Singapore

Contents

Part IV Development Issues

Chapter 1
Introduction

This book utilizes the Harris-Todaro (H-T) model to explore contemporary economic issues in developing countries, with a particular emphasis on China. The H-T model, introduced by American economists J.R. Harris and M.P. Todaro in their paper "Migration, Unemployment and Development: A Two-Sector Analysis" published in 1970, focuses on urban unemployment issues in developing countries and delineates mechanisms for rural-urban labor migration. It posits that the existence of a politically and institutionally determined urban minimum wage at levels higher than that which the free market would allow can, and usually does, lead to urban unemployment. Rural migrants may not always secure employment upon arriving in the city. However, the disparity between urban and rural wages makes the successful location of an urban salaried job so attractive that migrants are willing to take a chance. Rural-urban migration will continue so long as the expected urban wage exceeds the real rural wage. Denoting rural and urban wage rates as "w" and "$\overline{w}_1$ " respectively, and "λ" as the unemployment rate, the H-T model is represented as:

$$w = \frac{\overline{w}_1}{1 + \lambda}$$

This model has attracted attention since its inception, with economists from Europe, America, Japan, Australia, and India conducting in-depth research and extensions. For instance, economists Corden and Findlay (1975) from Australia and America introduced the condition of capital mobility into the model and utilized geometric figures to elucidate the mechanism of the H-T model. Subsequently, economist J.P. Neary (1981) from Ireland further refined the condition of capital mobility, deepening the research. Additionally, American economist Grinols (1991) investigated the situation where rural migrant laborers cannot find formal jobs upon moving to urban areas, suggesting that the unemployed migrant laborers would seek livelihoods in the informal sector of the city, thus extending the model to the urban

X. Li, Y. Wu, *Research on Characteristic Issues in Current Developing Economies*,
New Frontiers in Regional Science: Asian Perspectives 80,
https://doi.org/10.1007/978-981-97-7284-1_1

informal sector and establishing a three-sector model.[1] The utilization of this model reached its peak in the 1990s, focusing primarily on the effects of economic policies on wages and employments in various sectors, international trade, urban unemployment rate, and the status of social welfare during labor migration. After enduring over three decades since its inception, research in this area has gradually faded from the spotlight. Post-2010, however, research utilizing the H-T model experienced a resurgence, with scholars beginning to explore contemporary economic issues in developing countries using this model, injecting unparalleled vitality into this field of study. Unlike earlier research that primarily focused on the internal mechanisms of the H-T model, contemporary economists are concerned with utilizing the H-T model to delve deeper into economic hotspots facing developing economies (such as China). These include the dual agricultural economic structure, producer services, remittances from rural-urban migrants, agricultural pollution, and foreign direct investment (FDI). The shift in research focus is driven by the fact that these contemporary economic challenges were not apparent or significant during the early stages of H-T model research. Methodologically, current research diverges from earlier studies by integrating tools such as constant elasticity of substitution (CES) functions and numerical simulations. This approach aims to provide more precise explanations of present economic issues, combining qualitative and quantitative analyses.

Since September 2003, I have been employed at the Business School of Nanjing University, China, where I have dedicated over 20 years to theoretical economic research on the H-T model. During this time, I have supervised over a hundred bachelor's, master's, doctoral students, and postdoctoral researchers, witnessing the evolution of research on the H-T model as described above. Today, some of my students have taken positions as professional economic researchers in universities, continuing their exploration of the application of the H-T model. I am also grateful for the past 20 years of economic development in China, which has served as a vast laboratory for observing and experiencing rural-urban labor migration, providing my research team and me with abundant inspiration for our work.

This book compiles 13 papers I have authored since 2018, using the H-T model for research and published in various academic journals. These papers, forming the 13 chapters of the book, are organized into four parts: dual agricultural issues, agricultural pollution issues, producer services issues, and development issues. It is worth mentioning that this division is not strictly defined; some papers may "cross boundaries." For example, the Chap. 4, entitled "Rural-urban migrants' remittance and agricultural pollution in the presence of agricultural dualism," could be categorized under both Part I "dual agricultural issues" and Part II "agricultural pollution issues." For convenience in classification, we have placed Chap. 4 in Part II. Below is a brief overview of the rationale behind this division.

[1] Studies on the urban informal sector can be referenced in Fields (1975), Stark (1982), Stiglitz (1982), Quibria (1988), Chaudhuri (1989), Marjit (2003), etc.

1.1 Dual Agricultural Economic Structure

As developing economies reach a certain level of development, rural areas witness the emergence of modern agriculture, resulting in a concentration of land and labor towards modern agriculture. Modern agriculture refers to agricultural sector utilizing modern scientific technologies and capital for production, operation, and management. It relies on the transfer of capital from urban areas and the absorption of land and labor from traditional agriculture to fuel its expansion. Ultimately, modern agriculture absorbs and transforms all land and labor from traditional agriculture, achieving agricultural modernization. However, this process is long-term, and during the development of modern agriculture, rural areas in developing countries often experience prolonged coexistence of traditional agricultural sector and modern agricultural sector. This phenomenon is referred to as "dual agricultural economic structure."

It is essential to note that the dual agricultural economic structure is not entirely identical to the classical urban-rural dual economic structure theory. Both theories involve an "advanced sector" and a "traditional sector," but the main difference lies in the fact that the H-T model considers unemployment in the urban sector of the urban-rural dual economy, whereas explicit unemployment does not exist in the modern agricultural sector of the dual agricultural economy. This is because the H-T model considers factors such as union organizations and government-mandated minimum wage lines in cities, which prevent wage declines, create wage downward rigidity, and result in unemployment. In developing countries, however, government-mandated minimum wage lines in urban areas often do not extend to rural areas, resulting in elastic wages in modern agriculture and hence the absence of unemployment. This distinction implies that certain research findings from traditional urban-rural dualism may not directly apply to the study of the dual agricultural economic structure, underscoring the need to examine various economic phenomena within this specific context.

1.2 Agricultural Pollution

In traditional papers studying environmental issues using the H-T model, the urban sector is often depicted as the polluting sector, while the rural sector is portrayed as the environmentally sensitive sectors. This scenario reflects the situation from the 1990s to the 2010s but does not align with the reality in many developing countries today. Taking China as an example, according to Table 1.1, it is evident that in 2017, the volume of water pollution emissions from agricultural production surpassed those from industrial production. If we continue to study environmental issues based solely on the paradigm of urban pollution impacting rural production, the conclusions drawn will inevitably deviate from economic reality. Therefore, existing research approaches must change.

Table 1.1 Main pollutant emission in wastewater in China in 2017 (10,000 tons) (Communiqué of the Second National Census on Pollution Sources) (https://www.mee.gov.cn/xxgk2018/xxgk/xxgk01/202006/t20200610_783547.html)

	COD emission	Ammonia nitrogen emission	Total nitrogen emission	Total phosphorus emission
National total	2143.98	96.34	304.14	31.54
Industrial source	90.96	4.45	15.57	0.79
Agricultural sources	1067.13	21.62	141.49	21.2
Domestic sources	983.44	69.91	146.52	9.54
Other sources	2.45	0.36	0.56	0.01

COD chemical oxygen demand

My research team and I conducted field investigations in rural areas across various locations in China, including Qixia District in Nanjing City, Jiangsu Province; Lianyungang City in Jiangsu Province; Shouguang City in Shandong Province; Zhoukou City in Henan Province; Jinzhong City in Shanxi Province; and Yangling City in Shaanxi Province. Through these field studies and economic theory analysis, we have identified new pathways of pollution: the excessive use of fertilizers, pesticides, and plastic mulch in agricultural production harms laborers' health by contaminating water sources and air, and adhering to crops, thus causing losses to both agricultural and nonagricultural production. Drawing from this, we have developed a new research approach to agricultural pollution under the background of labor migration.

This part of the book contains three chapters, which reveal the economic impacts of agricultural pollution from three perspectives. I sincerely hope that more scholars will join in research on agricultural pollution in developing countries, conducting more in-depth and comprehensive studies to minimize the economic harm caused by agricultural pollution.

1.3 Producer Services

Producer services are a highly distinctive industry that cannot exist independently in the economy; they must coexist and grow with the industries they serve. However, in our past studies of regional or industrial economies, we often overlooked the existence of producer services. For example, in research on the privatization of mixed-ownership enterprises, conclusions such as "privatization leads to increased unemployment" could be drawn without considering the presence of producer services. However, in the Chinese economy, we have observed that the privatization process has not been accompanied by increased unemployment. One major reason is the existence of producer services in the actual economy. In addition to reducing excess personnel, privatized enterprises tend to outsource services as much as possible to enhance production efficiency, leading to the expansion of producer services. During this process, individuals who lose their jobs through privatization have the opportunity to be employed in producer services.

Under current production technology conditions, producer services are closely intertwined with the industries they serve, making it difficult to envision manufacturing existing independently from producer services within the economy. Based on the experiences of economically developed nations, producer services constitute a substantial portion of the economy, contributing 40–50% to gross domestic product (GDP) through their value added. Therefore, in evaluating the practical relevance of economic theories related to manufacturing, including those based on models like the H-T model, it is pivotal to assess whether they account for the role of producer services. Hence, for research to accurately reflect economic realities, it is essential to consider the presence of producer services.

Of course, this topic may differ for rural economies. When modern agriculture has not yet started in rural areas, traditional agriculture prevails, and agricultural producer services are almost nonexistent. However, as modern agriculture begins and grows in rural areas, there is a market demand for agricultural producer services. Taking China as an example, until the mid-1980s, agricultural production was predominantly carried out through family operations, with little involvement of agricultural producer services. After the mid-1980s, with the transfer of labor between urban and rural areas and the development of modern agriculture, agricultural producer services, represented by mechanized farming, began to emerge. Now, agricultural producer services have developed into various fields such as finance, logistics, warehousing, biological breeding and seedling cultivation, and market development. In economies with a producer services sector, we can offer more meaningful solutions to issues such as privatization, dual agricultural economy, environmental concerns, and income inequality by applying the H-T model.

1.4 Development Issues

In this part, we have included four chapters. These chapters analyze economic development issues in developing countries from four perspectives using the H-T model: the integration of primary, secondary, and tertiary industries in rural areas, the cost of training migrant workers and heterogeneous labor migration, remittances from migrant workers and wage inequality, and FDI and its impact on the environment. Other challenges in development will continue to emerge and require ongoing exploration and research.

Time flies, 54 years have passed, and research on economic issues using the H-T model, especially new economic issues in developing countries, is reaching a climax. This is because the large-scale pattern of the dual urban-rural economy in developing countries considered by the H-T model has not fundamentally changed in today's world, and the problems faced by today's developing economies have undergone significant changes compared to decades ago. There is still much research to be done, but we see that this wave of research results is mainly concentrated in China India and Japan, with contributions from economists in the United States as well. We hope that through this book, more scholars can join our relevant research and contribute wisdom and strength to the smooth development of developing economies and the entry of more developing countries into the ranks of advanced nations.

This book owes a great deal to the generous support of Professor Makoto Tawada, Honorary Professor at Nagoya University in Japan. Professor Tawada was my teacher during my early studies at Nagoya City University in the early 1990s. His continuous encouragement to derive research inspiration from economic realities has been invaluable. Throughout the conception, composition, and subsequent production of this book, he provided invaluable guidance and effective assistance. I extend my heartfelt gratitude to him. I also wish to express my gratitude to the Business School of Nanjing University for its comprehensive support throughout the research and writing process of this book. The school provided a conducive research environment and facilitated the formation of an effective research team, both of which were instrumental in completing this work. The research process for this book was further supported by various projects, including Project No. 17JJD630002 from the Humanities and Social Sciences of the Ministry of Education, China, and Project No. 17SSL074 from the Strategy Consultation on the Double Leads in Jiangsu Province, China. My sincere thanks go out to them. Special thanks are also due to Professor Yoshiro Higano at the University of Tsukuba in Japan for his enthusiastic encouragement and motivation, as well as to Mr. Yutaka Hirachi of Springer Nature Japan for his multifaceted assistance.

Dr. Yunyun Wu, a coauthor of this book, was my colleague in the Department of Economics at the Business School of Nanjing University, where she held the title of "Yuxiu Young Scholar at Nanjing University." She is currently a lecturer in the School of Economics at Nanjing University of Finance and Economics. She has made significant research contributions in recent years and is a rising star in the study of the H-T model. I am grateful for her support and assistance in our collaborative research and in writing this book. Finally, I would like to acknowledge the contributions of the other authors involved in the research and writing of this book, many of whom are current or former members of my research team. They include Dr. Yang Ge, a professor at Nanjing University; Dr. Dianshuang Wang, an associate professor at Anhui University of Finance and Economics; Dr. Zheyu Dong, a lecturer at Ludong University; Dr. Huanan Fu, a lecturer at Shandong Technology and Business University; Dr. Tiantian Jia and Dr. Min Li, both from Nanjing University; and Jing Zhou, a doctoral student at the University of California, Santa Barbara, USA.

Competing Interests No potential conflict of interest was reported by the authors.

References

Chaudhuri TD (1989) A theoretical analysis of the informal sector. World Dev 17(3):351–355. https://doi.org/10.1016/0305-750X(89)90208-8
Corden WM, Findlay R (1975) Urban unemployment, intersectoral capital mobility and development policy. Economica 42(165):59–78. https://doi.org/10.2307/2552986
Fields GS (1975) Rural-urban migration, urban employment and underemployment, and job-search activity in LDCs. J Dev Econ 2(2):165–187. https://doi.org/10.1016/0304-3878(75)90014-0
Grinols EL (1991) Unemployment and foreign capital: the relative opportunity costs of domestic labour and welfare. Economica 58(229):107–121. https://doi.org/10.2307/2554978
Harris JR, Todaro MP (1970) Migration, unemployment and development: a two-sector analysis. Am Econ Rev 60(1):126–142. https://www.jstor.org/stable/1807860
Marjit S (2003) Economic reform and informal wage-a general equilibrium analysis. J Dev Econ 72(1):371–378. https://doi.org/10.1016/S0304-3878(03)00082-8
Neary JP (1981) On the Harris-Todaro model with intersectoral capital mobility. Economica 48(191):219–234. https://doi.org/10.2307/2552914
Quibria MG (1988) Migration, trade unions, and the informal sector: a note on Calvo. Int Econ Rev 29(3):557–563. https://doi.org/10.2307/2526799
Stark O (1982) On modelling the informal sector. World Dev 10(5):413–416. https://doi.org/10.1016/0305-750X(82)90086-9
Stiglitz JE (1982) The structure of labor markets and shadow prices in LDC's. In: Sabot R (ed) Migration and the labour market in developing countries, 1st edn. Routledge, New York. https://doi.org/10.4324/9780429051845

Part I
Dual Agricultural Issues

Chapter 2
Is Human-Capital Investment Necessary to Modernization? The Effect of Rural Polytechnic Training in Dual Agriculture

Abstract In this chapter, we analyze the link between human-capital investment and agricultural modernization in a dualistic agricultural economy. We assume that human-capital investment in the context of agricultural dualism is distinct from that of simple traditional agriculture in that it gives top priority to developing the skills needed for production in the modern agricultural sector. Our aim is to investigate the likely consequences of investments and subsidies that provide polytechnic training to employees in the modern agricultural sector. To this end, we develop a three-sector general equilibrium model with which one can evaluate the effect of rural polytechnic training. Our research indicates that sector investments and government subsidies raise the output of the traditional agricultural sector but conditionally raise the output of the modern agricultural sector. Moreover, sector investments and government subsidies each have greater effects on the development of the traditional sector than they would on that of the modern sector. These, nevertheless, are not conducive to the agricultural modernization.

Keywords Agricultural modernization · Dual agriculture · Government subsidy · Human-capital investment · Rural polytechnic training

2.1 Introduction

The term "dual agriculture" refers to the coexistence of traditional agriculture and modern agriculture in developing countries. Here, traditional agriculture is characterized as small-capital agriculture, such as a family-based system, whereby production and business operations follow traditional practices. Contrastingly, modern agriculture refers to the newly emerged agricultural sector, which is market-oriented and employs modern facilities and technologies to achieve higher productivity than what is found in traditional agriculture (Li and Shen 2012). Transforming traditional agriculture is an important strategic means by which developing countries and regions accelerate their agricultural modernization. However, the modernization of agriculture in a developing economy is a progressive process. For example, some developing countries have started modern agriculture in districts near urban areas

X. Li, Y. Wu, *Research on Characteristic Issues in Current Developing Economies*, New Frontiers in Regional Science: Asian Perspectives 80,
https://doi.org/10.1007/978-981-97-7284-1_2

Table 2.1 Education attainment composition of rural workers (%) (National Bureau of Statistics of China 2018)

	Rural workers		Rural Migrant workers		Local Rural workers	
	2016	2017	2016	2017	2016	2017
Illiterate or semi-illiterate	1.0	1.0	0.7	0.7	1.3	1.3
Elementary school	13.2	13.0	10.0	9.7	16.2	16.0
Junior high school	59.4	58.6	60.2	58.8	58.6	58.5
Senior high school	17.0	17.1	17.2	17.3	16.8	16.8
Junior college or above	9.4	10.3	11.9	13.5	7.1	7.4

Note: The rural workers refer to those who still own rural household registration but engage in nonagricultural industries or work away from their registration areas for over half a year. The local rural workers are rural workers who work within their registered village, whereas the rural migrant workers are rural workers who work outside their registered village

and important transport corridors and have endeavored to develop into remote rural areas far away from urban districts. Overall, the dual agricultural structure is a necessary bridge on the path to agricultural modernization for developing countries.[1] In many emerging economies, such as India, China, and Brazil, the development of the modern agricultural market has already begun to take shape, and the agricultural economy has developed into the dualistic stage.

On the other hand, it is common in developing countries that the human-capital stock in rural areas is inadequate and the quality is low. Take China as an example. According to Table 2.1, most of the rural migrant workers have schooling under the senior middle school level, although they are more educated than local rural workers. Investment in human capital for farmers, according to Schultz (1964), is of primary importance in modernizing agriculture, which should affect the policies of many developing countries. However, Schultz only considers a unitary rural economy without considering the effect of human-capital investments in dual agriculture. In a dualistic agricultural economy, the modern agriculture splits off from traditional agriculture and hence mainly employs labor that is transferred from traditional agriculture. However, the product categories and management patterns of modern agriculture are quite different from those of traditional agriculture, and they require high-skilled labor. Consequently, in developing countries, the primary task for agricultural modernization is improving the quality of the rural population and the level of human capital to meet the production or business operations of modern agriculture. Therefore, the human-capital investments for farmers in dual agriculture are quite different from those in a unitary economy. The limited capital resources should be used to provide polytechnic training to employees in modern agriculture, which should generally focus on specific skills that result in greater efficiencies. It is also known as specific human-capital investment. This kind of human capital is inapplicable in other sectors once labor leaves modern agriculture.

[1] See Li and Xu (2016).

One must therefore ask the following questions. Is the effect of polytechnic training in the modern agricultural sector, as Schultz said, of primary importance in modernizing agriculture? Does the polytechnic training in dual agriculture promote agricultural modernization? Such questions are not divorced from the facts. Many emerging economies provided large financial assistance for rural polytechnic training to develop their agricultural industries. For instance, China's Central Finance allocated 7.09 billion yuan (approximately US$1 = 7.1 yuan, as of October 2019), from 2014 to 2018 to the Cultivation Project of New Professional Farmers to support rural polytechnic training, and the program trained over 16 million professional farmers. There is no doubt that these investments improve farmers' incomes, but the effects on agricultural modernization are still not clear at this point. In addition, numerous empirical studies have shown that human capital significantly enhances the rural economy, but some results have suggested that the promoting effect of human capital is insignificant or even significantly negative (Islam 1995; Knight et al. 1993).

Generally, there are two sources of funds for polytechnic training in the modern agricultural sector: enterprises' self-investments with owned funds and the government subsidies for enterprises' investments.[2] With these investments, which mitigate the pressure to resolve the human-capital issue in modern agriculture, market expectations of the human-capital level and labor efficiency and the wage rate in the modern agricultural sector increase. As a result, labor transfers from the traditional agricultural sector to its modern counterpart. Therefore, the modern agricultural sector gradually expands, and the traditional agricultural sector dwindles, consequently realizing agricultural modernization. In economic practice, however, it is difficult to discern or replicate these mechanisms. This is because a high wage rate both attracts labor and decreases the demand for labor to maximize profits. If the latter plays a decisive role, the result of labor employment contrasts with what we expected. Therefore, the promoting role of human-capital investment in agricultural modernization is ambiguous in a dualistic agricultural economy.

The research literature presents various scenarios whereby the rural sector is divided into modern and traditional agricultural sectors, such as Gupta (1997a, b), Chaudhuri (2006, 2007), and Li and Wu (2018). They involve the liberalization of the labor market, foreign capital investment, production price changes, and environment based on the Harris-Todaro model. However, none of these studies that were previously mentioned has considered human-capital investments. In addition, there is rare theoretical research that embraces modern agriculture in the context of human capital. In related studies, Bhagwati and Srinivasan (1977) studied how education affected the job search processes of individuals, from which they developed the now-famous job ladder model. Djajić (1985) investigated the relationship between vocational training of employees in the production sector and urban unemployment under the assumption of a minimum wage act. Samanta (2003) analyzed the

[2]In developing countries, rural workers are less likely to undertake training. Therefore, this chapter doesn't consider labor's self-investment.

economic effects of the training of urban sector employees under the assumptions of perfect competition in the agricultural sector and imperfect competition in the urban sector. Li and Qian (2011) considered an economy with three sectors, including the urban formal sector, the urban informal sector, and the rural sector, and found that an increase in the human-capital investment of rural-urban migrants reduces the output of the rural sector.

In this chapter, we will analyze whether rural polytechnic training promotes agricultural modernization in a dualistic agricultural economy. According to the economic practice, this chapter investigates two situations: when the modern agricultural sector increases investments in polytechnic training (hereinafter "sector investment") and when the government subsidizes rural polytechnic training (hereinafter "government subsidy"). The main conclusion is that both sector investments and government subsidies raise the output of the traditional agricultural sector but conditionally raise the output of the modern agricultural sector. Moreover, sector investments and government subsidies each have greater effects when promoting the traditional agricultural sector than they would when promoting the modern agricultural sector.

The remainder of this chapter is organized as follows. Section 2.2 systematically established the formal model. Section 2.3 explores the comparative static effects with respect to the sector investment and the government subsidy. Concluding remarks are drawn in Sect. 2.4.

2.2 The Model

We consider a small, open, developing economy consisting of three sectors: one urban sector and two rural sectors. The economy uses labor and capital as production factors, and they do not move internationally. The long-existing institutional obstacles in developing countries have resulted in the stagnation of capital flows between the urban and rural areas. The urban sector (Sector 1) produces import-competing manufacturing commodities. Of the two rural sectors, there is a modern agricultural sector (Sector 2), which uses capital and labor as inputs. However, the other sector within the rural sector, we call it the traditional agricultural sector (Sector 3), which only uses labor to produce export-competing goods. Further, Sector 2 produces a non-traded final commodity. This is because the modern agricultural sector is a newly emerged sector. It is placed in so small scale that just being able to provide for domestic consumption. Such assumption matches the current situation in the developing economy. Suppose commodity 3 is *numeraire*, so that its price equals unity.

2.2.1 *Urban Sector*

The urban sector utilizes labor and sector-specific capital as factors of production. The production function of this sector is

$$X_1 = F^1(L_1, K_1), \tag{2.1}$$

where X_1 is the level of output, L_1 is the level of employment, and K_1 is the capital stock. F^1 is linearly homogeneous and strictly quasi-concave function.

With the condition of maximized profit, we have the formulas as follows:

$$p_1 F_L^1 = \overline{w}_1, \tag{2.2}$$

$$p_1 F_K^1 = r_1. \tag{2.3}$$

In the above equation, $F_L^1 = \partial F^1 / \partial L_1$, $F_K^1 = \partial F^1 / \partial K_1$. $\overline{w}_1$ and r_1 is the urban wage rate and the urban interest rate, respectively. p_1 is the product price in the urban sector, which is fixed world price. The urban wage rate shows downward rigidity because of labor unions and ubiquitous local protectionism, so $\overline{w}_1$ is an exogenous variable.

2.2.2 *Modern Agricultural Sector*

We consider the modern agricultural sector with the following characteristics:

- It is a newly emerged sector and is just being able to provide for domestic consumption. So, the product price is determined endogenously in the domestic market.
- It utilizes labor and sector-specific capital as factors of production.
- It provides polytechnic training for labors to help them develop skills needed for production. We assume the source of funds for polytechnic training is a proportion of enterprises' production.

The production function of this sector is

$$X_2 = F^2(hL_2, K_2), \tag{2.4}$$

and it satisfies all the standard properties satisfied by the production function of the urban sector. h expresses the efficiency of each worker after polytechnic training, that is, the per capita human-capital level in the modern agricultural sector. Here, hL_2 is the human-capital stock. h depends upon the unit cost of training a worker c:

$$h = h(c). \tag{2.5}$$

Here, $h(\cdot)$ satisfies the conditions $h(0) = 1$, $h' > 0$, $h'' < 0$. Let $\varepsilon = h'c/h$ be the elasticity of cost on human-capital level, with the property of $0 < \varepsilon < 1$, by assumption.

The unit cost of training a worker is given by

$$(1-s)c = \frac{\mu P_2 X_2}{L_2} \Leftrightarrow (1-s)cL_2 = \mu P_2 X_2, \tag{2.6}$$

where s is the subsidy rate of training cost per unite of employment and μ $(0 < \mu < 1)$ is the proportion of production used on polytechnic training. p_2 is the product price in the modern agricultural sector.

The equilibrium conditions of the profit-maximizing firm are the following:

$$(1-\mu)p_2 h F_L^2 = w_2, \tag{2.7}$$

$$(1-\mu)p_2 F_K^2 = r_2. \tag{2.8}$$

In the above equation, $F_L^2 = \partial F^2 / \partial hL_2$, $F_K^2 = \partial F^2 / \partial K_2$. w_2 and r_2 is the wage rate and the interest rate in the modern agricultural sector, respectively.

2.2.3 Traditional Agricultural Sector

The traditional agricultural sector uses labor as the only factor of production and the production function is given by

$$X_3 = F^3(L_3), \tag{2.9}$$

where X_3 and L_3 are level of output and employment in the traditional agricultural sector. We assume that $F_L^3 = F'(L_3) > 0$, $F_{LL}^3 = F''(L_3) < 0$.[3]

We assume marginal productivity pricing of labor in the traditional agricultural sector. Let w_3 be the wage rate in the traditional agricultural sector. Hence,

$$F_L^3 = w_3. \tag{2.10}$$

2.2.4 Labor Market

When rural sector was subdivided into the modern and traditional agricultural sectors, rural-urban migrant has a new destination, that is, the modern agricultural sector. Labor is mobile from the traditional agricultural sector to urban areas and the modern agricultural sector. The possible explanations for the transfer of traditional agricultural labor to the modern agricultural sector rather than the urban areas is the relatively low transfer cost and increased time with family. We assume that workers

[3] Similar setting please refer to Gupta (1993).

in the modern agricultural sector are paid on effective labor.[4] Once a traditional agricultural labor has been hired by the modern agricultural sector, he or she will be trained to get specific skills, and then will receive a higher effective wage. Thus, the relationship between the wage rates in the modern and traditional agricultural sectors at the equilibrium point is as follows[5]:

$$w_2 = hw_3. \tag{2.11}$$

On the other hand, there is urban unemployment (L_u) because the wage rate in the urban sector ($\overline{w}_1$) is rigid. Therefore, at the equilibrium point, the wage rate in the traditional agricultural sector equals the expected wage income in urban areas, which is equal to $\overline{w}_1$ multiplied by the probability of finding a job in the urban sector, $L_1/(L_u + L_1)$. Thus, we have

$$w_3 = \overline{w}_1 \frac{L_1}{L_u + L_1} \Leftrightarrow w_3(1 + \lambda) = \overline{w}_1, \tag{2.12}$$

where $\lambda = L_u/L_1$ is the urban unemployment rate. Note that there are two possible choices when laborer flows out from modern agricultural sector: return to the traditional agricultural sector or move to urban areas. In either case, he or she is just an ordinary rural laborer who acts according to Eq. (2.12) because the specific skills acquired in the modern agricultural sector are inapplicable in other sectors.

The full employment condition of labor market can be written as

$$(1 + \lambda)L_1 + L_2 + L_3 = \overline{L}, \tag{2.13}$$

where $\overline{L}$ is the labor endowment in the economy.

2.2.5 *Market Clearing*

We suppose that the social welfare function exhibited by the Cobb-Douglas type such as $U = D_1^{\alpha} D_2^{\beta} D_3^{\gamma}$, when D_1, D_2, and D_3 are the demands for the urban, modern agricultural, and traditional agricultural goods, respectively, and α, β, and γ are positive parameters satisfying $\alpha + \beta + \gamma = 1$. The national income after tax is given by $N = p_1X_1 + p_2X_2 + X_3 - p_2X_2s\mu/(1 - s)$, where the total tax subsidy is $p_2X_2s\mu/(1 - s)$ by Eq. (2.6). Therefore, the total demand for the modern agricultural goods can be expressed by $D_2 = \beta(p_1X_1 + p_2X_2 + X_3 - p_2X_2s\mu / (1 - s))/p_2$. The equilibrium condition of the modern agricultural good market is $D_2 = X_2$. Hence,

[4] The establishment of the wage rate of employees who have a high level of human capital in Eq. (2.5) is in accord with the parameters established by Galor and Moav (2004).

[5] Similar setting please refer to Li and Zhou (2017).

$$\frac{\beta\left[p_1X_1 + \left(1 - \frac{s\mu}{1-s}\right)p_2X_2 + X_3\right]}{p_2} = X_2. \tag{2.14}$$

The general equilibrium setup consists of 14 endogenous variables, L_1, L_2, L_3, λ, r_1, r_2, w_2, w_3, h, c, p_2, X_1, X_2, and X_3, and exactly the same number of independent equations, namely Eqs. (2.1)–(2.14). The solution mechanism is the following. L_1, X_1, and r_1 are solved from Eqs. (2.1)–(2.3). This is a relatively independent part in the model, which we call the urban subsystem and the rest we call the rural subsystem. The endogenous variables in the rural subsystem are all rural variables as well as the urban unemployment rate λ.

2.3 Comparative Statics

We begin the analysis by considering the urban subsystem. Differentiating Eq. (2.2), we obtain:

$$\mathrm{d}L_1 = 0. \tag{2.15}$$

Substituting Eq. (2.15) into Eqs. (2.1) and (2.3), we obtain that the endogenous variables in the urban subsystem are unaffected. Therefore, we should turn to the rural subsystem.[6]

Using Eqs. (2.10), (2.12), and (2.15) and then total differentiation of Eq. (2.13) yields

$$\mathrm{d}L_3 = -\frac{1}{A}\mathrm{d}L_2, \tag{2.16}$$

where $A = 1 - (1 + \lambda)L_1F_{LL}^3/w_3 > 0$. Equation (2.16) simply states that a decrease in L_2 results in more labor employed in the traditional agricultural sector. When laborers move out from the modern agricultural sector, they transfer to urban areas or return to the traditional agricultural sector. Recalling that the special skills acquired in the modern agricultural sector are inapplicable in other sectors. If the released laborers transfer to urban areas, they become the urban unemployment because of the unchanging urban employment. This leads to an increase in the urban unemployment rate, thus reducing the expected urban wage. Thus, most released workers choose to return the traditional agricultural sector until the wage rate in that sector, w_3, equals the expected urban wage again.

[6]Even though the urban sub-system is unaffected, we can examine the social welfare and the urban unemployment by keeping the urban sector. In fact, with an unchanging urban sub-system, we can focus on the rural sub-system.

Substitute Eqs. (2.4) and (2.5) into Eq. (2.6) and make $s = 0$ at the initiation of the subsidy policy. Then, total differentiation of Eq. (2.6), we have

$$\frac{\theta_K^2}{L_2}\mathrm{d}L_2 + \frac{1-\varepsilon\theta_L^2}{c}\mathrm{d}c = \frac{1}{p_2}\mathrm{d}p_2 + \frac{1}{\mu}\mathrm{d}\mu + \mathrm{d}s, \tag{2.17}$$

where $\theta_K^2 = F_K^2 K_2/X_2$, $\theta_L^2 = F_L^2 hL_2/X_2$ are the output elasticities of capital and labor, respectively, $0 < \theta_L^2, \theta_K^2 < 1$, by definition. Similarly, substitute Eqs. (2.5), (2.7), (2.10), and (2.16) into Eq. (2.11) and total differentiation of Eq. (2.11), we have

$$\left(\frac{S_{LL}^2}{L_2} + \frac{S_{LL}^3}{AL_3}\right)\mathrm{d}L_2 + \frac{\varepsilon S_{LL}^2}{c}\mathrm{d}c = -\frac{1}{p_2}\mathrm{d}p_2 + \frac{1}{1-\mu}\mathrm{d}\mu, \tag{2.18}$$

where $S_{LL}^2 = F_{LL}^2 hL_2/F_L^2 < 0$, $S_{LL}^3 = F_{LL}^3 L_3/F_L^3 < 0$.

From Eqs. (2.17) and (2.18), we obtain

$$\mathrm{d}L_2 = -(1-\varepsilon\theta_L^2 + \varepsilon S_{LL}^2)\frac{\mathrm{d}p_2}{cp_2\Delta} + \left(\frac{1-\varepsilon\theta_L^2}{1-\mu} - \frac{\varepsilon S_{LL}^2}{\mu}\right)\frac{\mathrm{d}\mu}{c\Delta} - \frac{\varepsilon S_{LL}^2}{c\Delta}\mathrm{d}s, \tag{2.19}$$

and

$$\mathrm{d}c = \left(\frac{\theta_K^2 + S_{LL}^2}{L_2} + \frac{S_{LL}^3}{AL_3}\right)\frac{\mathrm{d}p_2}{p_2\Delta} + \left[\frac{S_{LL}^2}{L_2\mu} + \frac{S_{LL}^3}{AL_3\mu} - \frac{\theta_K^2}{L_2(1-\mu)}\right]\frac{\mathrm{d}\mu}{\Delta} + \left(\frac{S_{LL}^2}{L_2} + \frac{S_{LL}^3}{AL_3}\right)\frac{\mathrm{d}s}{\Delta}, \tag{2.20}$$

where $\Delta = (1-\varepsilon)S_{LL}^2/cL_2 + (1-\varepsilon\theta_L^2)S_{LL}^3/cAL_3 < 0$.

As the product price in the modern agricultural sector is perfectly flexible, then its market must clear domestically. For the equilibrium in the modern agricultural good market to be Walrasian stable, it requires that

$$Z = \frac{\mathrm{d}(D_2 - X_2)}{\mathrm{d}p_2} < 0,$$

where Z represents the rate of change in the excess demand for the modern agricultural good; and, it must be negative to satisfy the stability of equilibrium. Using Eqs. (2.16), (2.18), (2.19), and (2.20) and simplifying the stability condition, we must have

$$Z = -\frac{(1-\beta)X_2(c\Delta + M - N)}{p_2 c\Delta} < 0, \tag{2.21}$$

where $M = \varepsilon(\theta_L^2 S_{LL}^3 - a\theta_L^3 S_{LL}^2)/AL_3$, $N = (1-\varepsilon)\theta_L^2/L_2 + a(1-\varepsilon\theta_L^2)\theta_L^3/AL_3 > 0$ and $a = X_3/(p_1X_1 + X_3) > 0$. Note that $M > (<)\ 0$ if $a > (<)\ a_1$, where $a_1 = \theta_L^2|S_{LL}^3|/\theta_L^3|S_{LL}^2|$. In developing countries, the value of traditional agricultural output accounts for a sizable proportion of total output value, while the value of manufacturing output accounts for a small proportion. Therefore, we assume a is sufficiently large and, hence, $M > 0$.

In the equilibrium, totally differentiating both side of Eq. (2.14) one obtains

$$\frac{\mathrm{d}p_2}{p_2} = -\frac{\mathrm{d}X_2}{X_2} + a\frac{\mathrm{d}X_3}{X_3} - \frac{\mu\beta}{(1-\beta)}\mathrm{d}s. \tag{2.22}$$

Equation (2.22) shows that, with everything else held constant, government subsidy is negatively related to p_2. This is because with government subsidy, the national income, N, decreases, which tend to reduce the demand of modern agricultural goods and therefore decreases p_2. According to Eq. (2.14), at the initiation of the subsidy policy ($s = 0$), $\beta(p_1X_1 + X_3)$ is the expenditure on modern agricultural goods in the other two sectors, and $(1 - \beta)X_2$ is the corresponding supply. An increase in X_3 augments the demand for modern agricultural goods (because the production of the urban sector is unaffected). Therefore, X_3 is positively related to p_2, and X_2 is negatively related to p_2.

Using Eqs. (2.4), (2.9), (2.18), (2.19), and (2.22) yields

$$\begin{aligned}\mathrm{d}p_2 = &\underbrace{\frac{(1-\beta)X_2}{Zc\Delta}\frac{M}{\mu}\mathrm{d}\mu}_{\text{Human-Capital Investment Effect}} + \underbrace{\frac{(1-\beta)X_2}{Zc\Delta}\frac{N}{1-\mu}\mathrm{d}\mu}_{\text{Production Crowding-Out Effect}} \\ &+ \underbrace{\frac{(1-\beta)X_2}{Zc\Delta}M\mathrm{d}s}_{\text{Investment Subsidy Effect}} + \underbrace{\frac{(1-\beta)X_2}{Zc\Delta}\frac{\beta\mu c\Delta}{1-\beta}\mathrm{d}s.}_{\text{Real Income Effect}}\end{aligned} \tag{2.23}$$

The first component is labeled human-capital investment effect and is derived from Eq. (2.17)—the total differentiation of Eq. (2.6). The first component has two subcomponents. The first subcomponent measures changes in the modern agricultural sector due to an increase in μ. As μ raises, human-capital investment takes up a larger proportion of production, thus improving the productivity of labor and promoting the production in the modern agricultural sector. So, the supply of the modern agricultural goods increases and that is negatively related to p_2. The second subcomponent measures changes in the traditional agricultural sector due to an increase in μ. An increased μ raises the level of human capital in the modern agricultural sector, h. With a raise in h, labor in the modern agricultural sector is paid a higher effective wage rate, so that less labor is demanded by the modern agricultural sector. As previously discussed, a decrease in L_2 increases L_3. An increase in the labor employment would raise the output in the traditional agricultural sector, X_3, inducing in turn an increment in the (derived) demand for modern agricultural goods. Therefore, the second subcomponent is positively related to p_2.

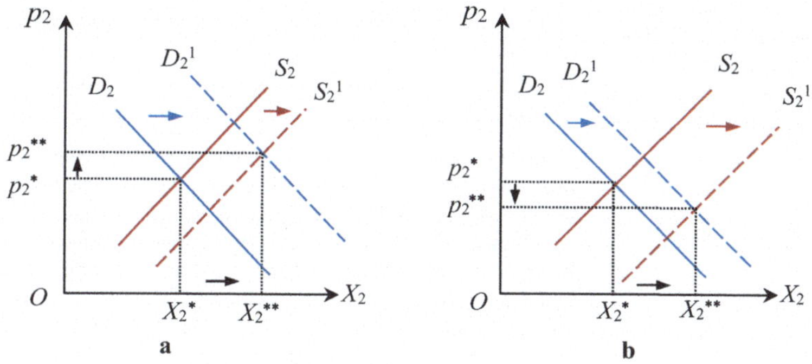

Fig. 2.1 The human-capital investment effects. (**a**) p_2 rises. (**b**) p_2 falls

With the help of Fig. 2.1, we can consider the human-capital investment effect. There, the demand curve D_2 and supply curve S_2 both shift rightward due to an increase in μ. Figure 2.1a represents a situation in which p_2 rises when the demand curve makes a larger move than the supply curve; Fig. 2.1b represents a situation in which p_2 falls when the demand curve makes a smaller move than the supply curve. In case a is sufficiently large, the entire human-capital investment effect on p_2 is positive.

The second component, labeled production crowding-out effect, is derived from Eq. (2.18)—the total differentiation of Eq. (2.11). As μ raises, it reduces the proportion of production be used for input factors, $1 - \mu$, thereby causing an outflow of input factors. When labor move out from the modern agricultural sector into the traditional agricultural sector, the resulting increase in the employment expands the output in the traditional agricultural sector, X_3, and therefore raises the demand of modern agricultural goods. As for the effects on X_2, it depends on the comparison effect between productivity-enhancing of labor and factor outflow. If the elasticity of cost on human-capital level, ε, is big enough, the same capital used for training labor has a greater effect on production than that used for hiring labor, therefore, the production crowding-out effect increases X_2. On the other hand, given a small enough value of ε, the factor outflow effect covers the productivity-enhancing effect, and then X_2 decreases. In any case, the entire production crowding-out effect on p_2 is positive.

The third component, labeled investment subsidy effect, measures changes in p_2 due to changes in human-capital investment with government subsidies. Like the first component, the third component is also derived from Eq. (2.17), thus, they affect p_2 in the same direction but in different sizes.

The last component, labeled real income effect, is derived from Eq. (2.22)—the total differentiation of Eq. (2.14). As s raises, it increases the total tax subsidy and decreases the real national income, thus reducing the demand of modern agricultural goods. Therefore, the real income effect on p_2 is negative.

Table 2.2 Effects of sector investment [see Eqs. (2.40)–(2.47) in Appendix]

	dL_1	dX_1	dL_2	dh	dc	dX_2	dL_3	dX_3	dU
$d\mu$	0	0	–	+	+	[+]	+	+	[+]
	dr_1	dr_2	dw_2	dw_3	dp_2	$d\lambda$	$dX_2/X_2 - dX_3/X_3$		
$d\mu$	0	\	\	–	\	+	–		

Notes: '+' and '–' mean that the changes of μ make the endogenous variables change in the same and opposed directions, respectively; '0' means that the changes of μ have no impacts on endogenous variables; '\' means the changes of μ have ambiguous impacts on endogenous variables; '[+]' mean that the changes of μ make the endogenous variables change in the same direction under specific conditions

2.3.1 The Economic Influence of Sector Investment

We will analyze the effect of sector investment first. When $ds = 0$, substituting Eq. (2.23) in Eqs. (2.4), (2.9), (2.19) and (2.20), we obtain[7]

$$\frac{dp_2}{d\mu} = \frac{(1-\beta)X_2}{Zc\Delta}\left(\frac{M}{\mu} + \frac{N}{(1-\mu)}\right) > 0, \tag{2.24}$$

$$\frac{dX_2}{d\mu} = \frac{X_2\theta_L^2(1-\beta)X_2}{Zp_2c\Delta}\left[\frac{\varepsilon\left(a\theta_L^3 - S_{LL}^3\right)}{AL_3}\frac{1}{\mu} + \left(\frac{a\varepsilon\theta_L^3}{AL_3} - \frac{1-\varepsilon}{L_2}\right)\frac{1}{(1-\mu)}\right], \tag{2.25}$$

$$\frac{dX_3}{d\mu} = \frac{F_L^3(1-\beta)X_2}{Ap_2Zc\Delta}\left[\frac{\varepsilon\left(\theta_L^2 - S_{LL}^2\right)}{\mu} + \frac{1}{(1-\mu)}\right] > 0, \tag{2.26}$$

$$\frac{dX_2/X_2}{d\mu} - \frac{dX_3/X_3}{d\mu} = -\frac{(1-\beta)X_2}{p_2Zc\Delta}G < 0, \tag{2.27}$$

where $G = \left[M + \frac{\varepsilon(1-a)\theta_L^3\left(\theta_L^2 - S_{LL}^2\right)}{AL_3}\right]\frac{1}{\mu} + \frac{1}{(1-\mu)}\left[\frac{(1-\varepsilon)\theta_L^2}{L_2} + \frac{\left(1 - a\varepsilon\theta_L^2\right)\theta_L^3}{AL_3}\right] > 0.$

Substituting these results into the model, we obtain the effects of sector investment on endogenous variables. To summarize, we obtain Table 2.2 and Proposition 1.

Proposition 1 *Sector investment raises the output of the traditional agricultural sector, but raises the output of the modern agricultural sector if* $\varepsilon > \varepsilon_1$.[8] *Moreover, it results in a greater increase in the scale of the traditional sector than that of the modern sector.*

As mentioned above, the human-capital investment effect increases X_2, X_3, and p_2, while the production crowding-out effect increases X_3 and p_2. So, sector

[7] See Eqs. (2.34)–(2.36), and (2.40)–(2.42) in Appendix.

[8] $\varepsilon_1 = \mu AL_3/\left[\mu AL_3 - (1-\mu)S_{LL}^3 L_2 + a\theta_L^3 L_2\right],\ 0 < \varepsilon_1 < 1.$

Fig. 2.2 Effects of sector investment on X_2 and p_2

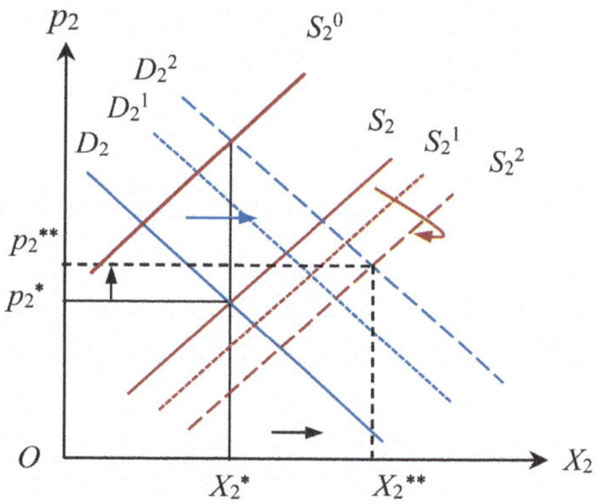

investment increases X_3 and p_2. The effect of sector investment on X_2 and p_2 can be illustrated by Fig. 2.2. Let curve D_2 and curve S_2 represent the demand curve and supply curve for the modern agricultural good, respectively, by which the initiate equilibrium pair (p_2^*, X_2^*) is determined. With a raise in μ, curve D_2 and curve S_2 shift rightward to the curves D_2^1 and S_2^1 by the human-capital investment effect, respectively; the curve D_2^1 shifts rightward to the curve D_2^2 by the production crowding-out effect, while the curve S_2^1 shifts rightward or leftward depending on the parameters of the system. When $\varepsilon > (<) \varepsilon_2$, the production crowding-out effect increases (decreases) X_2.[9] At the new equilibrium, the price and output in the modern agricultural sector is p_2^{**} and X_2^{**}, respectively. Sector investment raises X_2 only when the supply curve does not shift leftwards over S_2^0, that is $\varepsilon > \varepsilon_1$. However, p_2^{**} bigger than p_2^*. According to Eq. (2.22), when $\mathrm{d}p_2/\mathrm{d}\mu > 0$, $a[(\mathrm{d}X_3/X_3)/\mathrm{d}\mu] - (\mathrm{d}X_2/X_2)/\mathrm{d}\mu > 0$. Therefore, even if X_2 raises, sector investment results in a greater expansion in the traditional agricultural sector than in the modern agricultural sector.

Generally, with human-capital training for urban-rural migrant, rural labor tends to flow out from rural areas, thereby reducing the output and profit of the rural sector (see Li and Qian 2011). However, in this chapter, with sector investment, laborers tend to return traditional agricultural sector, thereby promoting the traditional agricultural sector. This is because with a higher human-capital level, laborer in the modern agricultural sector bolster his or her bargaining power and is paid a higher effective wage rate. This causes the modern agricultural sector to reduce employment.[10] As previously discussed, when labors leave the modern agricultural sector, most of them choose to return traditional agricultural sector, raising the scale of traditional agricultural sector. These results indicate that sector investment is accompanied by a decreased employment in the modern agricultural sector, an increased

[9] $\varepsilon_2 = AL_3/\left(AL_3 + a\theta_L^3 L_2\right)$, $\varepsilon_1 < \varepsilon_2 < 1$.

[10] Li and Qian (2011) considers the human-capital investment in the urban sector, where wage rate is institutionally set at a level higher than the market clearing rate and hence an increase in human-capital level cannot raise the wage rate.

employment, and an expansion of production in the traditional agricultural sector, which is quite different from agricultural modernization.

2.3.2 *The Economic Influence of Government Subsidy*

We will now analyze the effect of government subsidy. Similarly, when $d\mu = 0$, substituting Eq. (2.23) in Eqs. (2.4), (2.9), (2.19), and (2.20), we obtain[11, 12]

$$\frac{dp_2}{ds} = \frac{(1-\beta)X_2}{Zc\Delta}\left(M + \frac{\beta\mu c\Delta}{1-\beta}\right), \tag{2.28}$$

$$\frac{dX_2}{ds} = \frac{X_2\theta_L^2(1-\beta)X_2}{Zp_2c\Delta}\left[\frac{\varepsilon\left(a\theta_L^3 - S_{LL}^3\right)}{AL_3} + \left(\frac{\varepsilon S_{LL}^3}{AL_3} - \frac{(1-\varepsilon)}{L_2}\right)\frac{\beta\mu}{1-\beta}\right], \tag{2.29}$$

$$\frac{dX_3}{ds} = \frac{F_L^3(1-\beta)X_2}{Ap_2Zc\Delta}\left[\left(1 - \frac{\beta\mu}{1-\beta}\right)\varepsilon\left(\theta_L^2 - S_{LL}^2\right) + \frac{\beta\mu}{1-\beta}\right] > 0, \tag{2.30}$$

$$\frac{dX_2/X_2}{ds} - \frac{dX_3/X_3}{ds} = -\frac{(1-\beta)X_2}{p_2Zc\Delta}Q < 0, \tag{2.31}$$

where

$$Q = \left(1 - \frac{\beta\mu}{1-\beta}\right)\left[M + \frac{(1-a)\varepsilon\theta_L^3\left(\theta_L^2 - S_{LL}^2\right)}{AL_3}\right] + \frac{\beta\mu}{1-\beta} \times \left[\frac{(1-\varepsilon)\theta_L^2}{L_2} + \frac{\left(1 - a\varepsilon\theta_L^2\right)\theta_L^3}{AL_3}\right] > 0.$$

To summarize, we obtain Table 2.3 and Proposition 2.

Proposition 2 *Government subsidy (1) raises the output of the traditional agricultural sector, (2) raises the output of the modern agricultural sector if* $\varepsilon > \varepsilon_3$,[13] *and (3) increases the scale of the traditional sector more than that of the modern sector.*

As mentioned above, like the human-capital investment effect, the investment subsidy effect increases p_2, X_2, and X_3. However, with government subsidy, the real income effect decreases the national income, *N*, and then the consumptions of each

[11] See Eqs. (2.37)–(2.39) and (2.48)–(2.50).

[12] According to Eq. (2.14) at the initiation when $s = 0$, we have $\beta(p_1X_1 + X_3) = (1 - \beta)p_2X_2$. Because the modern agricultural sector was recently established, $p_2X_2 < p_1X_1 + X_3$, and then $\beta < (1 - \beta)$. Because $0 < \mu < 1$ and $0 < \beta / (1 - \beta) < 1$, $1 - \mu\beta/(1 - \beta) > 0$.

[13] $\varepsilon_3 = \beta\mu AL_3/\left[\beta\mu AL_3 + (1-\beta)L_2a\theta_L^3 - (1-\beta-\beta\mu)L_2S_{LL}^3\right]$, $\varepsilon_1 > \varepsilon_3 > 0$.

Table 2.3 Effects of government subsidy [see Eqs. (2.48)–(2.55) in Appendix]

	dL_1	dX_1	dL_2	dh	dc	dX_2	dL_3	dX_3	dU
ds	0	0	–	+	+	[+]	+	+	[+]
	dr_1	dr_2	dw_2	dw_3	dp_2	$d\lambda$	$dX_2/X_2 - dX_3/X_3$		
ds	0	\	\	–	\	+	–		

Notes: '+' and '–' mean that the changes of s make the endogenous variables change in the same and opposed directions, respectively; '0' means that the changes of s have no impacts on endogenous variables; '\' means the changes of *s* have ambiguous impacts on endogenous variables; '[+]' mean that the changes of s make the endogenous variables change in the same direction under specific conditions

good, D_i. Note that $D_2 = X_2$ in equilibrium, so the real income effect decreases X_2. Moreover, because the balance of trade equilibrium requires that $p_1D_1 + D_3 = p_1X_1 + X_3$, the real income effect decreases X_3 (with unchanging X_1). According to Eq. (2.30), the entire effect of government subsidy on X_3 is positive. As for the effects of government subsidy on p_2 and X_2 depending on the comparison between the investment subsidy effect and the real income effect. Note that when $\varepsilon > \varepsilon_3$, *the contraction effect of government subsidy on* X_2 *will not outweigh the promotion effect.* However, even if X_2 raises, it has a greater effect in promoting the traditional agricultural sector than it would in promoting the modern agricultural sector.

Above all, both sector investment and government subsidy, which try to promote the modern agricultural sector, not only improves the traditional agricultural sector, but also may have negative consequences for the modern sector. This, nevertheless, is not conducive to what we expected: modernizing agriculture. Besides, we find that government subsidy is better with respect to the production of modern agriculture, because it requires a smaller value of ε ($\varepsilon_1 > \varepsilon_3$) to raise the output in the modern agricultural sector. However, sector investment is better with respect to the improvement of human capital, because it leads to a faster growth in human capital than government subsidy, which is given by $dc/d\mu - dc/ds > 0$.[14]

Finally, we consider the social welfare. Recalling the social welfare function, $U = D_1^{\alpha}D_2^{\beta}D_3^{\gamma}$ and using Eqs. (2.15), (2.25), (2.26), (2.28), and (2.29), we have

$$\frac{dU}{d\mu} = \frac{U(1-\beta)X_2}{p_2Zc\Delta}\left\{\begin{array}{c}\left[a\theta_L^2\theta_L^3 - a(1-\beta)\theta_L^3S_{LL}^2 - \beta\theta_L^2S_{LL}^3\right]\dfrac{\varepsilon}{\mu AL_3} \\ \left[\dfrac{a\theta_L^3\left(1-\beta+\varepsilon\beta\theta_L^2\right)}{AL_3} - \dfrac{(1-\varepsilon)\beta\theta_L^2}{L_2}\right]\dfrac{1}{(1-\mu)}\end{array}\right\}, \tag{2.32}$$

[14] See Eq. (2.56) in Appendix.

$$\frac{\mathrm{d}U}{\mathrm{d}s} = \frac{U(1-\beta)X_2}{Zp_2c\Delta} \times \left\{ \begin{array}{l} \frac{\varepsilon}{AL_3}\left[\beta\theta_L^2\left(a\theta_L^3 - S_{LL}^3\right) + a(1-\beta)\theta_L^3\left(\theta_L^2 - S_{LL}^2\right)\right] \\ +\frac{\mu\beta}{(1-\beta)}\left[\frac{(1-\varepsilon)\left[(1-\beta)S_{LL}^2 - \theta_L^2\right]}{L_2} + \frac{\left[1-\beta\left(1-\theta_L^2\varepsilon\right)\right]S_{LL}^3}{AL_3}\right] \end{array} \right\}. \quad (2.33)$$

Because sector investment increases p_2 and X_3, it improves social welfare when X_2 increases. Note that when $\beta \to 0$, $\mathrm{d}U/\mathrm{d}\mu > 0$. Because the modern agricultural sector is newly emerged, the value of this sector accounts for a small proportion of total output value. Therefore, we assume the value of β is small enough and, hence $\mathrm{d}U / \mathrm{d}\mu > 0$ even if X_2 decreases. As for government subsidy, it also improves social welfare when the value of β is small enough.

2.4 Concluding Remarks

In this chapter, we examine the economic effects of rural polytechnic training. We find that in the agricultural dualism context, polytechnic training in the modern agricultural sector does not always positive contribute to agricultural modernization. There is a greater increase in the scale of the traditional agricultural sector, although the scale of the modern agricultural sector may expand. In particular, it may result in a decline in the production of the modern agricultural sector when the elasticity of cost on human-capital level, ε, is small enough. These results are not conducive to agricultural modernization. For the first time, such conclusions are generalized in the H-T model, which have great practical significance in that they remind the related departments of the induced expansion in traditional agriculture due to rural polytechnic training.

When we include polytechnic training in human-capital investment, the conclusion in this chapter revises the opinion in Schultz (1964) that investment in human capital for farmers is of primary importance in modernizing agriculture. Once this consideration is combined with the agricultural dualism context, there are far-reaching implications for our understanding of the relationship between human-capital investments and agricultural modernization.

Competing Interests

Funding This work was supported by the Humanities and Social Sciences of the Ministry of Education, China, Project No. 17JJD630002.

Disclosure Statement No potential conflict of interest was reported by the authors.

Appendix

Substituting Eq. (2.23) into Eqs. (2.4), (2.19), and (2.20), we obtain the effects of s and μ on the production of the modern agricultural sector:

$$\frac{dL_2}{d\mu} = -\frac{(1-\beta)X_2}{p_2 Zc\Delta}\left[\frac{\varepsilon\left(\theta_L^2 - S_{LL}^2\right)}{\mu} + \frac{1}{(1-\mu)}\right] < 0, \tag{2.34}$$

$$\frac{dc}{d\mu} = \frac{(1-\beta)X_2}{p_2 Z\Delta}\left[\left(\frac{\theta_L^2 - S_{LL}^2}{L_2} + \frac{a\theta_L^3 - S_{LL}^3}{AL_3}\right)\frac{1}{\mu} + \frac{1}{(1-\mu)}\left(\frac{1}{L_2} + \frac{a\theta_L^3}{AL_3}\right)\right] > 0, \tag{2.35}$$

$$\frac{dX_2}{d\mu} = \frac{X_2\theta_L^2(1-\beta)X_2}{Zp_2 c\Delta}\left[\frac{\varepsilon\left(a\theta_L^3 - S_{LL}^3\right)}{AL_3}\frac{1}{\mu} + \left(\frac{a\varepsilon\theta_L^3}{AL_3} - \frac{1-\varepsilon}{L_2}\right)\frac{1}{(1-\mu)}\right], \tag{2.36}$$

$$\frac{dL_2}{ds} = -\frac{(1-\beta)X_2}{p_2 Zc\Delta}\left[\left(1 - \frac{\beta\mu}{1-\beta}\right)\varepsilon\left(\theta_L^2 - S_{LL}^2\right) + \frac{\beta\mu}{1-\beta}\right] < 0, \tag{2.37}$$

$$\frac{dc}{ds} = \frac{(1-\beta)X_2}{p_2 Z\Delta}\left[\frac{\theta_L^2}{L_2} + \frac{a\theta_L^3}{AL_3} + \frac{\beta\mu\theta_K^2}{(1-\beta)L_2} - \left(1 - \frac{\beta\mu}{1-\beta}\right)\left(\frac{S_{LL}^2}{L_2} + \frac{S_{LL}^3}{AL_3}\right)\right]$$
$$> 0, \tag{2.38}$$

$$\frac{dX_2}{ds} = \frac{X_2\theta_L^2(1-\beta)X_2}{Zp_2 c\Delta}\left[\frac{\varepsilon\left(a\theta_L^3 - S_{LL}^3\right)}{AL_3} + \left(\frac{\varepsilon S_{LL}^3}{AL_3} - \frac{(1-\varepsilon)}{L_2}\right)\frac{\beta\mu}{1-\beta}\right]. \tag{2.39}$$

Substituting the above results into the model, we can obtain the following:

$$\frac{dL_3}{d\mu} = \frac{(1-\beta)X_2}{Ap_2 Zc\Delta}\left[\frac{\varepsilon\left(\theta_L^2 - S_{LL}^2\right)}{\mu} + \frac{1}{(1-\mu)}\right] > 0, \tag{2.40}$$

$$\frac{dX_3}{d\mu} = \frac{F_L^3(1-\beta)X_2}{Ap_2 Zc\Delta}\left[\frac{\varepsilon\left(\theta_L^2 - S_{LL}^2\right)}{\mu} + \frac{1}{(1-\mu)}\right] > 0, \tag{2.41}$$

$$\frac{dX_2/X_2}{d\mu} - \frac{dX_3/X_3}{d\mu} = -\frac{(1-\beta)X_2}{p_2 Zc\Delta}G < 0, \tag{2.42}$$

$$\frac{dw_3}{d\mu} = \frac{F_{LL}^3(1-\beta)X_2}{Ap_2 Zc\Delta}\left[\frac{\varepsilon\left(\theta_L^2 - S_{LL}^2\right)}{\mu} + \frac{1}{(1-\mu)}\right] < 0, \tag{2.43}$$

$$\frac{d\lambda}{d\mu} = -\frac{(1+\lambda)F_{LL}^3(1-\beta)X_2}{w_3 Ap_2 Zc\Delta}\left[\frac{\varepsilon\left(\theta_L^2 - S_{LL}^2\right)}{\mu} + \frac{1}{(1-\mu)}\right] > 0, \tag{2.44}$$

$$\frac{dw_2}{d\mu}=\frac{w_2(1-\beta)X_2}{p_2Zc\Delta}\left\{\begin{array}{l}\frac{1}{\mu}\left[\varepsilon\left(\theta_L^2-S_{LL}^2\right)\left(\frac{1}{L_2}+\frac{S_{LL}^3}{AL_3}\right)+\frac{\varepsilon\left(a\theta_L^3-S_{LL}^3\right)}{AL_3}\right]\\+\frac{1}{(1-\mu)}\left(\frac{\varepsilon}{L_2}+\frac{S_{LL}^3}{AL_3}+\frac{a\varepsilon\theta_L^3}{AL_3}\right)\end{array}\right\}, \tag{2.45}$$

$$\frac{dr_2}{d\mu}=\frac{r_2(1-\beta)X_2}{p_2Zc\Delta}\left\{\begin{array}{l}\frac{1}{\mu}\left(M+\frac{\varepsilon S_{KL}^2\left(a\theta_L^3-S_{LL}^3\right)}{AL_3}\right)\\+\frac{1}{(1-\mu)}\left[c\Delta+M+S_{KL}^2\left(\frac{a\varepsilon\theta_L^3}{AL_3}-\frac{1-\varepsilon}{L_2}\right)\right]\end{array}\right\}, \tag{2.46}$$

$$\frac{dU}{d\mu}=\frac{U(1-\beta)X_2}{p_2Zc\Delta}\left\{\begin{array}{l}\left[a\theta_L^2\theta_L^3-a(1-\beta)\theta_L^3S_{LL}^2-\beta\theta_L^2S_{LL}^3\right]\frac{\varepsilon}{\mu AL_3}\\\left[\frac{a\theta_L^3\left(1-\beta+\varepsilon\beta\theta_L^2\right)}{AL_3}-\frac{(1-\varepsilon)\beta\theta_L^2}{L_2}\right]\frac{1}{(1-\mu)}\end{array}\right\}, \tag{2.47}$$

$$\frac{dL_3}{ds}=\frac{(1-\beta)X_2}{Ap_2Zc\Delta}\left[\left(1-\frac{\beta\mu}{1-\beta}\right)\varepsilon\left(\theta_L^2-S_{LL}^2\right)+\frac{\beta\mu}{1-\beta}\right]>0, \tag{2.48}$$

$$\frac{dX_3}{ds}=\frac{F_L^3(1-\beta)X_2}{Ap_2Zc\Delta}\left[\left(1-\frac{\beta\mu}{1-\beta}\right)\varepsilon\left(\theta_L^2-S_{LL}^2\right)+\frac{\beta\mu}{1-\beta}\right]>0, \tag{2.49}$$

$$\frac{dX_2/X_2}{ds}-\frac{dX_3/X_3}{ds}=-\frac{(1-\beta)X_2}{p_2Zc\Delta}Q<0, \tag{2.50}$$

$$\frac{dw_3}{ds}=\frac{F_{LL}^3(1-\beta)X_2}{Ap_2Zc\Delta}\left[\left(1-\frac{\beta\mu}{1-\beta}\right)\varepsilon\left(\theta_L^2-S_{LL}^2\right)+\frac{\beta\mu}{1-\beta}\right]<0, \tag{2.51}$$

$$\frac{d\lambda}{ds}=-\frac{(1+\lambda)F_{LL}^3(1-\beta)X_2}{w_3Ap_2Zc\Delta}\left[\left(1-\frac{\beta\mu}{1-\beta}\right)\varepsilon\left(\theta_L^2-S_{LL}^2\right)+\frac{\beta\mu}{1-\beta}\right]>0, \tag{2.52}$$

$$\frac{dw_2}{ds}=\frac{w_2(1-\beta)X_2}{p_2Zc\Delta}\times\left[\begin{array}{l}\left[\varepsilon\left(\theta_L^2-S_{LL}^2\right)\left(\frac{1}{L_2}+\frac{S_{LL}^3}{AL_3}\right)+\frac{\varepsilon\left(a\theta_L^3-S_{LL}^3\right)}{AL_3}\right]\left(1-\frac{\mu\beta}{(1-\beta)}\right)\\+\left(\frac{\varepsilon}{L_2}+\frac{\varepsilon a\theta_L^3}{AL_3}+\frac{S_{LL}^3}{AL_3}\right)\frac{\mu\beta}{(1-\beta)}\end{array}\right], \tag{2.53}$$

$$\frac{dr_2}{ds}=\frac{r_2(1-\beta)X_2}{p_2Zc\Delta}\left\{\begin{array}{l}\left[M+\frac{\varepsilon S_{KL}^2\left(a\theta_L^3-S_{LL}^3\right)}{AL_3}\right]\\+\left[S_{KL}^2\left(\frac{\varepsilon S_{LL}^3}{AL_3}-\frac{(1-\varepsilon)}{L_2}\right)+c\Delta\right]\frac{\mu\beta}{(1-\beta)}\end{array}\right\}, \tag{2.54}$$

$$\frac{\mathrm{d}U}{\mathrm{d}s}=\frac{U(1-\beta)X_2}{Zp_2c\Delta} \times\left\{\begin{array}{l}\frac{\varepsilon}{AL_3}\left[\beta\theta_L^2\left(a\theta_L^3-S_{LL}^3\right)+a(1-\beta)\theta_L^3\left(\theta_L^2-S_{LL}^2\right)\right] \\ +\frac{\mu\beta}{(1-\beta)}\left[\frac{(1-\varepsilon)\left[(1-\beta)S_{LL}^2-\theta_L^2\right]}{L_2}+\frac{\left[1-\beta\left(1-\theta_L^2\varepsilon\right)\right]S_{LL}^3}{AL_3}\right]\end{array}\right\}, \tag{2.55}$$

$$\frac{\mathrm{d}c}{\mathrm{d}\mu}-\frac{\mathrm{d}c}{\mathrm{d}s}=\frac{(1-\beta)X_2}{p_2Z\Delta}R>0, \tag{2.56}$$

where

$$G=\left[M+\frac{\varepsilon(1-a)\theta_L^3\left(\theta_L^2-S_{LL}^2\right)}{AL_3}\right]\frac{1}{\mu}+\frac{1}{(1-\mu)}\left[\frac{(1-\varepsilon)\theta_L^2}{L_2}+\frac{\left(1-a\varepsilon\theta_L^2\right)\theta_L^3}{AL_3}\right]>0,$$

$$Q=\left(1-\frac{\beta\mu}{1-\beta}\right)\left[M+\frac{(1-a)\varepsilon\theta_L^3\left(\theta_L^2-S_{LL}^2\right)}{AL_3}\right]+\frac{\beta\mu}{1-\beta} \times\left[\frac{(1-\varepsilon)\theta_L^2}{L_2}+\frac{\left(1-a\varepsilon\theta_L^2\right)\theta_L^3}{AL_3}\right]>0,$$

and

$$R=\left(\frac{\theta_L^2-S_{LL}^2}{L_2}+\frac{a\theta_L^3-S_{LL}^3}{AL_3}\right)\frac{1-\mu}{\mu}+\frac{a\theta_L^3}{(1-\mu)AL_3}+\frac{(1-\beta)-\mu\theta_K^2(1-\mu)\beta}{(1-\mu)(1-\beta)L_2} -\left(\frac{S_{LL}^2}{L_2}+\frac{S_{LL}^3}{AL_3}\right)\frac{\beta\mu}{1-\beta}>0.$$

Data Availability Statement

These data were derived from the following resources available in the public domain:

1. National Bureau of Statistics of China (2018), Survey Report on the Monitoring of Chinese Migrant Workers. (in Chinese) Available at http://www.stats.gov.cn/tjsj/zxfb/201804/t20180427_1596389.html
2. data about the Cultivation Project of New Professional Farmers issued by the Ministry of Agriculture and Rural Affairs of PRC (in Chinese) Available at http://www.moa.gov.cn/govpublic/SCYJJXXS/201909/t20190906_6327427.html

References

Bhagwati JN, Srinivasan TN (1977) Education in a 'job ladder' model and the fairness-in-hiring rule. J Public Econ 7(1):1–22. https://doi.org/10.1016/0047-2727(77)90034-2

Chaudhuri S (2006) Labor market reform, welfare and urban unemployment in a small open economy. Keio Econ Stud 43(2):1–17. https://doi.org/10.2139/ssrn.929167

Chaudhuri S (2007) Foreign capital, welfare and urban unemployment in the presence of agricultural dualism. Jpn World Econ 19(2):149–165. https://doi.org/10.1016/j.japwor.2005.08.001

Djajić S (1985) Human-capital, minimum wage and unemployment: a Harris-Todaro model of a developed open economy. Economica 52(208):491–508. https://doi.org/10.2307/2553881

Galor O, Moav O (2004) From physical to human capital accumulation: inequality and the process of development. Rev Econ Stud 71(4):1001–1026. https://doi.org/10.1111/0034-6527.00312

Gupta MR (1993) Rural-urban migration, informal sector and development policies: a theoretical analysis. J Dev Econ 41(1):137–151. https://doi.org/10.1016/0304-3878(93)90040-T

Gupta MR (1997a) Informal sector and informal capital market in a small open less-developed economy. J Dev Econ 52(2):409–428. https://doi.org/10.1016/S0304-3878(96)00445-2

Gupta MR (1997b) Foreign capital and the informal sector: comments on Chandra and Khan. Economica 64(254):353–363. https://doi.org/10.1111/1468-0335.00083

Islam N (1995) Growth empirics: a panel data approach. Q J Econ 110(4):1127–1170. https://doi.org/10.2307/2946651

Knight M, Loayza N, Villanueva D (1993) Testing the neoclassical theory of economic growth: a panel data approach. Int Monet Fund S Pap 40(3):512–541. https://doi.org/10.2307/3867446

Li X, Qian X (2011) Economic analysis on the urban-rural disparity in human capital in China. S Afr J Econ 79(2):146–160. https://doi.org/10.1111/j.1813-6982.2011.01277.x

Li X, Shen Q (2012) A study on urban private capital and the transfer of labor in the modern agriculture sector. J Econ Policy Reform 15(2):135–152. https://doi.org/10.1080/17487870.2012.672833

Li X, Wu Y (2018) Environment and economy in the modern agricultural development. Asia-Pac J Account E 25(1-2):163–176. https://doi.org/10.1080/16081625.2016.1246191

Li X, Xu Y (2016) Unemployment, wage inequality and international factor movement in the presence of agricultural dualism. Rev Dev Econ 20(2):415–425. https://doi.org/10.1111/rode.12235

Li X, Zhou Y (2017) Economic and environmental effects of rural-urban migrant training. In: Li X (ed) Labor transfer in emerging economies. Springer, Singapore, pp 37–55. https://doi.org/10.1007/978-981-10-3569-2_3

National Bureau of Statistics of China (2018) Survey Report on the monitoring of Chinese migrant workers. (in Chinese) Available at http://www.stats.gov.cn/tjsj/zxfb/201804/t20180427_1596389.html (accessed 4 Dec 2019)

Samanta S (2003) Training, unemployment and fiscal subsidy: a Harris Todaro approach. https://doi.org/10.2139/ssrn.471981

Schultz TW (1964) Transforming traditional agriculture. Yale University Press, New Haven

Chapter 3
International Factor Mobility and Environment in a Dual Agricultural Economy

Abstract The purpose of this study is to investigate the environmental implications of international factor movements in developing countries under agricultural dualism. Utilizing a general equilibrium model that incorporates a modern agricultural sector at different stages, we examine the effects of international factor movements on the environment. At the beginning of the modern agricultural sector, international labor movement has no influence on the environment in developing countries. Additionally, if the share of modern agricultural capital in the economy reaches a certain threshold, international capital inflow improves the environment, while capital outflow harms it. Conversely, when the modern agricultural capital share remains below this threshold, capital inflow leads to environmental harm, whereas capital outflow contributes to environmental improvement. However, after the popularization of modern agriculture, both international labor and capital movements affect the environment in a similar manner: factor inflow adversely affects the environment, whereas outflow enhances it. Consequently, the compatibility of international factor movement with environmental protection in a developing country becomes plausible.

Keywords Dual agriculture · Environment · International factor movement · Modern agriculture

3.1 Introduction

Many emerging economies, such as India, China, and Brazil, have taken modern agriculture as an impetus and vigorously promoted it. Here, "modern agriculture" refers to the newly emerged agricultural sector, which is market-oriented and employing modern facilities and technologies to achieve higher productivity than is found in traditional agriculture (Li and Shen 2012). The fundamental difference between modern agriculture and traditional agriculture is that the former requires a certain level of capital investment, whereas the latter is characterized as small-capital agriculture. In developing countries, long-existing institutional obstacles have

X. Li, Y. Wu, *Research on Characteristic Issues in Current Developing Economies*, New Frontiers in Regional Science: Asian Perspectives 80,
https://doi.org/10.1007/978-981-97-7284-1_3

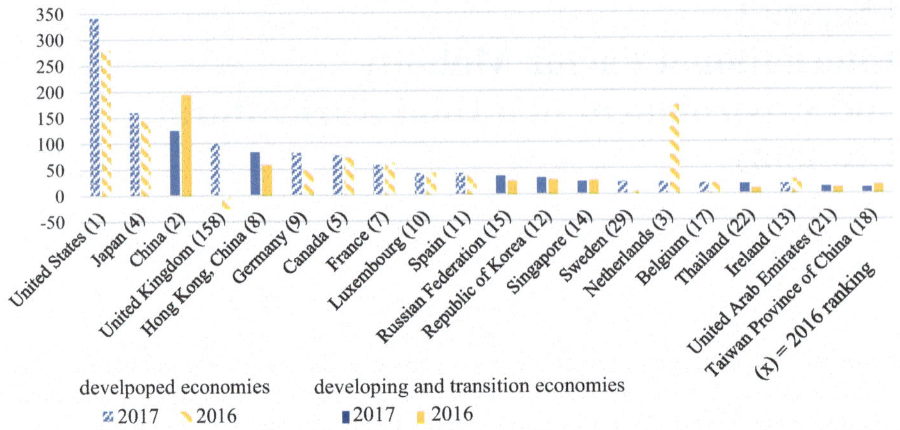

Fig. 3.1 FDI outflows, top 20 home economies, 2016 and 2017 (billions of dollars) (United Nations Conference on Trade and Development 2018) (https://unctad.org/publication/world-investment-report-2018)

resulted in the stagnation of capital flows between the urban and rural sectors. Given that the capital necessary for development primarily originates from urban areas, the progression of modern agriculture is a gradual and continuous process that from nil and from small to large.[1] Moreover, dual agricultural structure is an inevitable phenomenon during the development of modern agriculture in most developing countries.

On the other hand, many developing countries, especially emerging economies, have increasingly focused on international factor movements. This is because emerging economies represent the most dynamic region globally, leading to frequent occurrences of international factor movement within these regions. Foreign direct investment (FDI) continues to stand as the largest external source of finance for developing economies. Moreover, as these economies grow rapidly, there is a noticeable trend of enterprises from developing countries expanding into overseas markets and investing abroad (see Fig. 3.1). For instance, data from the World Investment Report (2018) reveals that China, among developing countries, ranks as the largest recipient of FDI and the second largest globally; conversely, it also emerges as the largest investing country among developing nations and the third largest globally. Regarding international migration, a significant portion of the labor force in developing countries has migrated to other nations. Nevertheless, as indicated in Table 3.1, less developed regions and low-income countries also serve as recipients of migrant workers.

Among the various effects of international factor movements in developing countries, our primary concern lies with their potential to cause environmental

[1]For example, in early 2018, China released a package of policies under the "No 1 central document", charting the roadmap for rural vitalization and proposing to realize modernization of agriculture and rural areas by 2050. This is a development plan spanning 32 years.

Table 3.1 International migration, 2000 and 2017 (International Migration Report 2017) (https://desapublications.un.org/publications/international-migration-report-2017-highlights)

Major area, region, country, or area of destination	Number of international migrants (thousands)		International migrants as percentage of total population	
	2000	2017	2000	2017
WORLD	**172,604**	**257,715**	**2.8**	**3.4**
More developed regions	103,418	145,984	8.7	11.6
Less developed regions	69,186	111,732	1.4	1.8
Least developed countries	10,073	14,442	1.5	1.4
Less developed regions, excl. least developed countries	59,155	97,331	1.4	1.8
High-income countries	100,405	164,847	9.6	14.1
Middle-income countries	64,042	81,440	1.4	1.4
Low-income countries	7733	10,915	1.8	1.6
Sub-Saharan Africa	13,717	22,976	2.0	2.2

destruction. These nations often grapple with significant environmental pollution, exacerbated by the transfer of pollution-intensive industries from developed to developing countries as part of economic globalization. In efforts to stimulate economic growth and job creation, developing countries may relax pollution controls measures for certain industries, potentially exacerbating environmental issues further due to international factor movements. Moreover, numerous studies highlight that urban manufacturing production generates environmental pollutants, which degrade the environment and have negative repercussions on agricultural production, as agricultural production depends on environmental quality.[2] Given this scenario, it is reasonable to consider that the presence and development of modern agriculture significantly impact the economic structure, as well as the urban and rural structure in a developing country, thereby playing a significant role in environmental outcomes. This drives us to question whether environmental protection and international factor movements can coexist harmoniously in a developing country characterized by agricultural dualism.

Various articles have introduced the concept of dual agriculture into theoretical analysis by dividing the rural sector into the modern and traditional agricultural sectors. Examples include Chaudhuri (2006, 2007), Gupta (1997a, b), Nag and Banerjee (2014), and Li and Wu (2018). While Chaudhuri (2007) focused on international capital inflow, national welfare, and unemployment rate in the presence of agricultural dualism; Li and Wu (2018) investigated the environmental and economic effects of policies intended to promote modern agriculture. However, these studies did not explicitly examine the relationship between international factor movements and the environment. Similarly, research has been conducted on the

[2]Related studies include Copeland and Taylor (1999), Rapanos (2007), Tawada and Sun (2010), and Kondoh and Yabuuchi (2012).

environmental and economic impacts of international factor movements.[3] Notably, Li et al. (2014) focused on the international skilled and unskilled labor movement, agricultural product price change, and environmental problems; Kondoh and Yabuuchi (2012) investigated the effects of increased inflow of foreign workers on environmental stock in the presence of a pollution abatement equipment sector; Tawada and Sun (2010) considered the effect of factor endowment expansion on the environment. Despite capturing the economic structure of developing countries with dual economy, these studies did not analyze the setting of agricultural dualism.

None of the existing literature has endeavored to combine the three factors—environmental problem, international factor movement, and dual agriculture—into a unified framework. Nevertheless, this issue is based on the needs of policy. The developing economies are now confronting a new situation, in which faster and more complex flows of international factors, more serious environmental problems, and dual agriculture occur simultaneously. In the absence of studies that consider all these three issues simultaneously, this chapter makes a positive contribution to the academic field.

The purpose of this study is to investigate the impact of international factor movements on the environment in a dual agricultural economy. We developed a three-sector model and categorized the development of modern agriculture into beginning and popularization stages. Our main findings suggest that at the beginning of modern agricultural development, international labor movement has no influence on the environment in developing countries. Furthermore, if the modern agricultural capital share in the economy reaches a certain level, international capital inflow improves the environment whereas capital outflow harms the environment; otherwise, capital inflow harms the environment whereas capital outflow improves the environment. However, after the popularization of modern agriculture, international labor movement and international capital movement affect the environment in the same direction: factor inflow harms the environment, while outflow improves the environment. These findings diverge significantly from those of other authors, such as Tawada and Sun (2010), Kondoh and Yabuuchi (2012), Li et al. (2014), Jorgenson (2006), Jorgenson et al. (2007), Cole et al. (2011), and Shahbaz et al. (2015). We highlight the crucial role played by dual agriculture in shaping the relationship between international factor movements and the environment.

The rest of this chapter is organized as follows: Sects. 3.2 and 3.3 deal with the beginning case and the popularization case, respectively, while Sect. 3.4 presents our conclusion.

[3] Beladi and Rapp (1993), Beladi and Frasca (1999), Daitoh (2008), Tsakiris et al. (2008), and Tawada and Sun (2010) have focused on the environmental issues within the framework of general equilibrium analysis. Additionally, Kar and Guha-Khasnobis (2006), Yabuuchi (2007), Beladi et al. (2008), Chaudhuri and Banerjee (2010), and Chaudhuri and Gupta (2014) have paid attention to the influences of international factor movements on the economy.

3.2 At the Beginning of Modern Agricultural Development

Since the capital required for development primarily originates from urban areas, the beginning of modern agriculture typically occurs in districts near urban areas and vital transportation routes (Li and Xu 2016). Consequently, we can characterize the modern agriculture sector at the beginning of development with the following attributes:

- Concentration on high-value-added agricultural products that necessitate significant capital inputs.
- Limited supply of land factor due to geographic restrictions.[4]
- Wage rate heavily influenced by the urban sector, as workers in these areas find it convenient to transfer into urban employment opportunities.

3.2.1 *The Model*

We consider a small open developing economy with three sectors: the urban sector, the modern agricultural sector, and the traditional agricultural sector. The economy uses three factors to produce: these are labor, L; capital, K; and land, T. The urban sector uses labor and capital to produce import-competing goods, X_1. The modern agricultural sector uses labor capital and land to produce importable goods, X_2.[5] The traditional agricultural sector uses labor and land to produce export-competing goods, X_3. We assume that only the production by the urban sector causes emissions of pollutants that harm the environment. The harmful substances emitted, such as waste gas, waste residue, and waste water, pollute the atmosphere, rivers, and, hence, water and soil for agricultural use. This results in a decline in the production efficiency of the agricultural sectors. Let $\overline{E}$ to represent the environment endowment when there is no pollution in the economy. δ is the pollution that the urban sector discharges in producing one unit of goods. Thus, the environmental quality of the economy can be represented as[6]

[4] At the beginning of development, the modern agricultural sector primarily concentrates in districts near urban areas and important transportation routes. Land availability for the modern agricultural sector is limited, and land mobility is not a prominent feature. Moreover, allowing for land mobility between traditional and modern agriculture would overly complicate calculations, detracting from the research focus.

[5] At the beginning of development, due to limited land supply and small-scale production, products from the modern agricultural sector may be in short supply, necessitating reliance on imports.

[6] The formulation of Eq. (3.1), which describes the relationship between urban sector production and the environment, can also be found in studies by Copeland and Taylor (1999), Tawada and Sun (2010), and Li et al. (2014).

$$e = \frac{\overline{E} - \delta X_1}{\overline{E}}, \tag{3.1}$$

where $0 \leq e \leq 1$, and, when $e = 1$, the environment is in the best condition. It worsens when e decreases.

Considering the pollution in the economy, under the condition that the markets are perfectly competitive, we could obtain the following:

$$a_{L1}\overline{w} + a_{K1}r = p_1, \tag{3.2}$$

$$\frac{a_{L2}\overline{w}}{e^{\varepsilon_2}} + \frac{a_{K2}r}{e^{\varepsilon_2}} + \frac{a_{T2}\tau_2}{e^{\varepsilon_2}} = p_2, \tag{3.3}$$

$$\frac{a_{L3}w}{e^{\varepsilon_3}} + \frac{a_{T3}\tau_3}{e^{\varepsilon_3}} = 1, \tag{3.4}$$

where a_{ij} ($i = L, K, T; j = 1, 2, 3$) represents the factor i used in producing a unit product in the jth sector without consideration of the pollution in the economy. e^{ε_j} ($j = 2, 3$) express the externalities generated by environmental pollution on the production efficiency of the modern agricultural sector and the traditional agricultural sector, respectively, with the property $0 < \varepsilon_2, \varepsilon_3 < 1$. At the beginning of development, the modern agricultural sector faces the same labor market with the urban sector.[7] Thus, $\overline{w}$ is the wage rate in the urban and the modern agricultural sectors, which is downwardly rigid due to some political and institutional considerations. w is the wage rate in the traditional agricultural sector, which is flexible. We assume that capital moves freely between the urban sector and the modern agricultural sector, so that r is the interest rate of capital in the urban and the modern agricultural sectors. τ_j ($j = 2, 3$) is the land rental in the jth sector. Suppose the traditional agricultural good is *numeraire*, so that its price equals unity. p_j ($j = 1, 2$) represent the product prices of the urban sector and the modern agricultural sector, respectively, which are both fixed world prices.

Labor is mobile from the traditional agricultural sector to the urban sector and the modern agricultural sector. We use L_{U1} to represent the unemployment in the urban and the modern agricultural sectors and μ_1 to denote the labor unemployment rate in these two sectors; hence, $\mu_1 = L_{U1}/a_{L1}X_1 + a_{L2}X_2$. According to the Harris-Todaro model, the labor allocation mechanism between sectors can be shown as follows:

$$w = \frac{a_{L1}X_1 + a_{L2}X_2}{a_{L1}X_1 + a_{L2}X_2 + L_{U1}}\overline{w} \Leftrightarrow (1 + \mu_1)w = \overline{w}. \tag{3.5}$$

[7] Given the convenience for workers in the modern agricultural sector to transfer into the urban sector, the wage rate in the modern agricultural sector should fall below the urban wage rate. Otherwise, attracting laborers to the sector would prove challenging.

It is supposed that land is immobile between sectors at the beginning of the modern agricultural development.[8] Then, the clearing conditions of the three factors—labor, capital, and land—could be shown as follows:

$$a_{L1}X_1 + \frac{a_{L2}X_2}{e^{\varepsilon_2}} + \frac{a_{L3}X_3}{e^{\varepsilon_3}} + \mu_1\left(a_{L1}X_1 + \frac{a_{L2}X_2}{e^{\varepsilon_2}}\right) = \overline{L} + L^* = L, \tag{3.6}$$

$$a_{K1}X_1 + \frac{a_{K2}X_2}{e^{\varepsilon_2}} = \overline{K} + K^* = K, \tag{3.7}$$

$$\frac{a_{T2}X_2}{e^{\varepsilon_2}} = T_2, \tag{3.8}$$

$$\frac{a_{T3}X_3}{e^{\varepsilon_3}} = T_3, \tag{3.9}$$

where $\overline{L}$ and $\overline{K}$ are the domestic endowments of labor and capital, while L^* and K^* are international transfer of labor and capital, which may be positive or negative, respectively.[9] T_2 and T_3 are fixed and the land employed in the modern agricultural sector and the traditional agricultural sector, respectively.

This completes the description of the model in the beginning case, which consists of nine equations [Eqs. (3.1)–(3.9)] in nine endogenous variables, e, w, r, τ_2, τ_3, μ_1, X_1, X_2, and X_3 with exogenous variables and parameters given by $\overline{E}$, $\overline{w}$, p_1, p_2, L, K, T_2, T_3, δ, ε_2, and ε_3.

3.2.2 *Analysis*

The Effect for International Capital Movement

From Eq. (3.2), we obtain the equilibrium value of r. Thus, international factor movements would not affect the interest rate. Then, from Eq. (3.3), we learn that the land rental in the modern agricultural sector (τ_2) is positively related to the environment quality (e). And, from Eq. (3.1), it is easy to verify that an increase in the output of urban sector will directly reduce the environment quality. Differentiating Eq. (3.8) and then also (3.7), we obtain[10]

$$\lambda_{K1}\widehat{X}_1 + \lambda_{K2}\left(S_{KT}^2 - S_{TT}^2\right)\widehat{\tau}_2 = \widehat{K}, \tag{3.10}$$

where "^" represents the proportional change, for example, $\widehat{X}_1 = \mathrm{d}X_1/X_1$, λ_{ij} is the allocative share of factor i in the jth sector, for example, $\lambda_{K1} = a_{K1}X_1/K$, and S_{ij}^h is the

[8] Refer to Footnote 4.

[9] Positive values of L^* and K^* represent inflows of labor and capital, respectively, while negative values indicate outflows of labor and capital, respectively.

[10] Refer to the Appendix for detailed derivations.

partial elasticity of substitution between factors i and j in the hth sector, for example, $S^2_{KT} = (\tau_2/aK2)(\partial a_{K2}/\partial \tau_2)$, $S^h_{ij} > 0(i \neq j)$ and $S^h_{ij} < 0(i = j)$.

Eq. (3.10) indicates that international capital inflows have two effects on the environment: one linked to the output of the urban sector and the other related to the land rental in the modern agricultural sector. There is, first of all, an "extent of the urban sector" effect. As the stock of capital is augmented, with everything else held constant, the urban output raise, inducing environmental damage. A second channel through which international capital inflow affects the environment involves a "relative factor price" effect. To specify this mechanism, note that, for a rigid wage rate and given land supply, the resulting increase in the capital relative to land tends to raise the rental rate on land relative to the interest rate, which indicate greater incentive of the modern agricultural sector to compete for labor and capital with the urban sector. Thus, production factors transfer from the pollution urban sector to the non-pollution modern agricultural sector, inducing environment improvement. The consequence is that the environmental quality is pulled in two different directions by the capital inflow. By the same token, the environmental quality is pulled in two different directions by the capital outflow. This is reflected in the following relationship[11]

$$\frac{\widehat{e}}{\widehat{\overline{K}}} = \begin{cases} >0, & \text{if} \lambda_{K2}/\lambda_{K1} > k^0, \\ <0, & \text{if} \lambda_{K2}/\lambda_{K1} < k^0, \end{cases} \tag{3.11}$$

where $k^0 = 1/\left[ab\left(S^2_{KT} - S^2_{TT}\right)\right] > 0$, $a = \delta X_Y/(\overline{E} - \delta X_1) > 0$, $b = \varepsilon_2/\theta_{T2} > 0$ and θ_{ij} is the distributive share of factor i in the jth sector, for example, $\theta_{T2} = \tau_2 a_{T2}/(e^{\varepsilon_2} p_2)$. Thus, we can obtain Proposition 1.

Proposition 1 *Consider a small, open developing country with a modern agricultural sector at the beginning of development. Inflow of international capital improves the environment in the developing countries whereas outflow harms the environment iff* $\lambda_{K2}/\lambda_{K1} > k^0$.

The effects of international capital inflow on the environment in our framework operate through two main channels—an "extent of the urban sector" effect and a "relative factor price" effect. The consequence depends on the comparison of these two effects. Note that, as urban capital flow to the modern agricultural sector, even though urban production harms the environment, the environmental gain from the second effect can be large enough to leave a net positive balance on environment, when the ratio $\lambda_{K2}/\lambda_{K1}$ above k^0. Therefore, capital inflow improves the environment in the developing countries, which is different from much of the literature on this

[11] We assume that $\left(S^2_{KT} - S^2_{TT}\right)\lambda_{K2} b \neq \lambda_{K1}/a$ to ensure the stability of equilibrium in the capital market.

subject.[12] This is mainly because, by incorporating the modern agricultural sector, we can not only consider the effects of international capital inflow into the urban sector but also analyze the effects of capital inflow into the modern agricultural sector. These results are of great significance for governments in developing countries to figure out appropriate policies of environmental protection and utilization of international capital. Conversely, we can analyze the situation in which capital flows out of the developing countries.

The Effect for International Labor Movement

In contrast to international capital movement, international labor movement creates different effects. Both the "extent of the urban sector" effect and the "relative factor price" effect failed. On the one hand, an increase in the labor force expands the outputs in the traditional agricultural sector. The case is similar to the labor outflows. Most of the labor outflows come from the traditional agricultural sector. On the other hand, changes in labor force cannot affect the wage-interest ratio in the urban and modern agricultural sectors because their wage rates are downwardly rigid. Therefore, international labor movement neither harms nor benefits the environment because it does not influence the urban sector and the modern agricultural sector. This is visualized by differentiating Eqs. (3.7) and (3.8) with respect to L

$$\left[(S_{KT}^2 - S_{TT}^2)\lambda_{K2}b - \frac{\lambda_{K1}}{a}\right]\widehat{e} = 0 \ when\ \widehat{K} = 0 \Leftrightarrow \frac{\widehat{e}}{\widehat{L}} = 0. \tag{3.12}$$

And then, we consider the traditional agricultural sector, and obtain[13]

$$\widehat{w}/\widehat{L} < 0, \widehat{r}_3/\widehat{L} > 0, \widehat{X}_3/\widehat{L} > 0, \widehat{\mu}_1/\widehat{L} > 0 \tag{3.13}$$

Thus, we can obtain Proposition 2.

Proposition 2 *Consider a small, open developing country with a modern agricultural sector at the beginning of development. International movement labor does not affect the environment; however, labor inflow raises the output and the land rental in the traditional agricultural sector but lowers its wage rate, whereas raises the unemployment rate; conversely, labor outflow decreases the output and the land rental in the traditional agricultural sector but raises its wage rate, whereas lowers the unemployment rate.*

---

[12] Additional references include Jorgenson (2006), Jorgenson et al. (2007), Tawada and Sun (2010), Cole et al. (2011), and Shahbaz et al. (2015).

[13] Refer to the Appendix for detailed derivations.

3.3 After the Popularization of Modern Agricultural Development

As modern agriculture progresses, it extends into remote rural areas that are distant from urban districts. Consequently, after the popularization of modern agricultural sector, the influence of the urban sector diminishes, while the influence of the traditional agricultural sector grows, and the wage rate in the modern agricultural sector becomes flexible. Additionally, the products of the modern agricultural sector are no longer limited to those with high added value but encompass a wide range of agricultural products. In other words, modern and traditional agricultural goods become indistinguishable.

3.3.1 *The Model*

The relationship between the production of the three sectors and the pollution in the economy is the same as before, shown as Eq. (3.1). The wage rate for labor in the urban sector is still downwardly rigid and exogenous. The wage rates for labor in the two agricultural sectors are flexible. There is perfect mobility of land between the two agricultural sectors. Hence, under the condition that the markets are perfectly competitive, we obtain

$$a_{L1}\overline{w} + a_{K1}r = p_1, \tag{3.14}$$

$$\frac{a_{L2}w_2}{e^{\varepsilon_2}} + \frac{a_{K2}r}{e^{\varepsilon_2}} + \frac{a_{T2}\tau}{e^{\varepsilon_2}} = 1, \tag{3.15}$$

$$\frac{a_{L3}w_3}{e^{\varepsilon_3}} + \frac{a_{T3}\tau}{e^{\varepsilon_3}} = 1, \tag{3.16}$$

where w_2 and w_3 are flexible and represent the wage rates for the modern and the traditional agricultural sectors, respectively. In general, $w_2 > w_3$ is established, otherwise modern agriculture will be unable to attract labor factors needed to develop. τ is the land rental in the agricultural sectors. We use L_{U2} to denote the unemployment in the urban sector, and μ_2 to denote the labor unemployment rate in the urban sector; hence, $\mu_2 = L_{U2}/(a_{L1}X_1)$. In the labor market equilibrium, on the one hand, the wage rate in the traditional agricultural sector equals the expected wage income in the urban sector, which is based on the Harris-Todaro model. On the other hand, the wage rate in the traditional agricultural sector equals the wage rate in the modern agricultural sector, which is based on the Lewis model.[14] Thus, the labor allocation mechanism can be shown as

[14] Farmers will compare the wage rate offered by traditional production with that of working in the modern agricultural sector. As long as the latter exceeds the former, farmers will transfer to the modern agricultural sector. The transfer will stop only when wage rates are equal.

$$w_3 = \frac{a_{L1}X_1}{a_{L1}X_1 + L_{U2}}\overline{w} \Leftrightarrow w_3(1+\mu_2) = \overline{w}, \tag{3.17}$$

and

$$w_3 = w_2 = w. \tag{3.18}$$

Eq. (3.17) represents the labor transfer equilibrium between the urban and the traditional agricultural sectors, and Eq. (3.18) denotes the labor transfer equilibrium between the two agricultural sectors.

The market clearing conditions of production factors are as the following equations:

$$a_{L1}X_1 + \frac{a_{L2}X_2}{e^{\varepsilon_2}} + \frac{a_{L3}X_3}{e^{\varepsilon_3}} + \mu_2 a_{L1}X_1 = L, \tag{3.19}$$

$$a_{K1}X_1 + \frac{a_{K2}X_2}{e^{\varepsilon_2}} = K, \tag{3.20}$$

$$\frac{a_{T2}X_2}{e^{\varepsilon_2}} + \frac{a_{T3}X_3}{e^{\varepsilon_3}} = T_2 + T_3 = T. \tag{3.21}$$

where T represents the endowments of land in the economy.

Now, the general equilibrium model in the popularization case has been constructed. It consists of nine equations: Eq. (3.1) and Eqs. (3.14)–(3.21). Nine endogenous variables are determined: w_2, w_3, r, τ, μ_2, e, X_1, X_2, and X_3. The solution mechanism is the following: w_2, w_3, (or w), r, and τ in terms of e are solved from Eqs. (3.14)–(3.16) and (3.18), which we call the price subsystem. Then, the rest determine the values of μ_2, e, X_1, X_2, and X_3, which we call the quantity subsystem.

3.3.2 *Analysis*

Here, we examine the environmental effects of international factor movements after the popularization of modern agricultural development. As adopting modern methods in production, each worker in the modern sector can manage more land than in the traditional sector. Thus, we assume that the modern agricultural sector is relatively land-intensive, while the traditional agricultural sector is relatively labor-intensive (e.g., $a_{T2}/a_{L2} > a_{T3}/a_{L3}$). Furthermore, the modern agricultural sector has strong antipollution ability (e.g., $\varepsilon_2 < \min\{\varepsilon_3\theta_{T2}/\theta_{T3}, \varepsilon_3\theta_{L2}/\theta_{L3}\}$).

We begin the analysis by considering the price subsystem. Differentiating Eqs. (3.15) and (3.16) by using (3.18), we obtain[15]

[15] Refer to the Appendix for detailed derivations.

$$\frac{\widehat{w}}{\widehat{e}} = \frac{\varepsilon_2\theta_{T3} - \varepsilon_3\theta_{T2}}{\theta_{L2}\theta_{T3} - \theta_{T2}\theta_{L3}} > 0, \tag{3.22}$$

$$\frac{\widehat{\tau}}{\widehat{e}} = \frac{\varepsilon_3\theta_{L2} - \varepsilon_2\theta_{L3}}{\theta_{L2}\theta_{T3} - \theta_{T2}\theta_{L3}} < 0. \tag{3.23}$$

Eqs. (3.22) and (3.23) show that the agricultural wage rate is positively related to the environment quality, while the land rental is negatively related to the environment quality. To understand these results, observe that, this expression for (a_{L2} w + a_{K2} r + a_{T2} τ)/(a_{L3} w + a_{T3} τ) is the relative price of good 3 in terms of good 2 without consideration of the pollution, which is equal to $e^{\varepsilon_3}/e^{\varepsilon_2}$ as given by Eqs. (3.15) and (3.16). When $\varepsilon_3/\varepsilon_2$ is bigger than θ_{T3}/θ_{T2} and θ_{L3}/θ_{L2}, as e decreases, indicating a declining $e^{\varepsilon_3}/e^{\varepsilon_2}$, for a unaltered r, the wage rate of labor which is used more intensively in the production of good 3 increases, while the rental of land which is used more intensively in the production of good 2 decreases (according to the Stolper-Samuelson theorem).

Then, we consider the quantity subsystem. Differentiating Eqs. (3.19)–(3.21) by using (3.17), (3.22), and (3.23), we obtain the effects of international factor movements on the environment[16]

$$\frac{\widehat{e}}{\widehat{K}} = \frac{\lambda_{T2}\lambda_{L3} - \lambda_{L2}\lambda_{T3}}{\Delta} < 0, \tag{3.24}$$

$$\frac{\widehat{e}}{\widehat{L}} = \frac{\lambda_{K2}\lambda_{T3}}{\Delta} < 0, \tag{3.25}$$

where

$$\begin{aligned}\Delta = & -\frac{(1+\mu_2)\lambda_{L1}\lambda_{K2}\lambda_{T3}}{a} - \frac{\lambda_{K1}(\lambda_{L3}\lambda_{T2} - \lambda_{L2}\lambda_{T3})}{a} \\ & + \frac{\left[(1+\mu_2)\lambda_{L1}\lambda_{T3} + (\lambda_{L3}\lambda_{T2}S_{TL}^2 + \lambda_{L3}\lambda_{T3}S_{TL}^3) - (\lambda_{L2}\lambda_{T3}S_{LL}^2 + \lambda_{L3}\lambda_{T3}S_{LL}^3) + (\lambda_{L3}\lambda_{T2} - \lambda_{L2}\lambda_{T3})S_{KT}^2\right]\lambda_{K2}(\varepsilon_3\theta_{T2} - \varepsilon_2\theta_{T3})}{\theta_{L2}\theta_{T3} - \theta_{T2}\theta_{L3}} \\ & + \frac{\left[(\lambda_{L2}\lambda_{T3}S_{LT}^2 + \lambda_{L3}\lambda_{T3}S_{LT}^3) - (\lambda_{T2}\lambda_{L3}S_{TT}^2 + \lambda_{L3}\lambda_{T3}S_{TT}^3) - (\lambda_{L3}\lambda_{T2} - \lambda_{L2}\lambda_{T3})S_{KL}^2\right]\lambda_{K2}(\varepsilon_3\theta_{L2} - \varepsilon_2\theta_{L3})}{\theta_{L2}\theta_{T3} - \theta_{T2}\theta_{L3}} \\ < & \ 0.\end{aligned}$$

Thus, we can obtain Proposition 3.

Proposition 3 *Consider a small, open developing country with a modern agricultural sector after the popularization of development. Inflows of international capital and labor harm the environment in the developing countries, whereas outflows benefit the environment.*

After the popularization of modern agricultural development, inflows of international capital harm the environment, which is different from Proposition 1. The reason for the difference is as follows. When international capital inflows into a

[16] Refer to the Appendix for detailed derivations.

developing country, capital available to the urban sector increases, expanding the urban production and inducing environmental damage. This is the same in the beginning case and the popularization case. Nevertheless, as to the increases in the capital utilized in the modern agricultural sector, results are different in the two cases. In the beginning case, because the modern agricultural sector competes directly with the urban sector for the labor and capital factors in the same factor markets, international capital inflows into the modern agricultural sector results in a positive effect on the environment. In the popularization case, however, the modern agricultural sector competes directly with the traditional agricultural sector for the labor and land factors in the same factor markets. Note that after the popularization of development, modern agricultural sector is land-intensive relative to the traditional agricultural sector and has strong antipollution ability. Therefore, when international capital inflows into the modern agricultural sector, it causes the substitution of capital to labor. Some of the displaced laborers move into the urban sector, resulting in a negative influence on the environment. Conversely, we can consider the situation in which capital flows out of the developing countries.

By the same token, the impacts of international labor movement on the environment are quite different in the beginning and the popularization cases. In the beginning case, international labor movement can cause neither factor mobiles nor changes in production by changing the wage-interest ratio between the urban sector and the modern agricultural sector. Therefore, international labor movement does not impact the environment in the beginning case. However, in the popularization case, international labor movement affects the factor inputs in the urban sector through the substitution of capital and land in the economy. When labor flow out from a developing country, most of the labor outflows come from the agricultural sectors. This causes an increase in the agricultural wage rate. At this time, the wage gap between the expected urban wage and the agricultural wage reduces—so that the amount of labor transfer into the urban sector decreases—then the growth of the urban sector slows down, leading to environmental improvement. Conversely, we can examine the situation in which labor inflow of the developing countries.[17]

3.4 Conclusion

This chapter constructs a general equilibrium model under economic dualism and agricultural dualism. We investigate the impact that the international capital and labor movements have on the environment of developing countries under the development of modern agriculture. Through the results of the chapter, we see that under different stages of modern agriculture, the degree and direction of the impacts

[17] Kondoh and Yabuuchi (2012) suggest that international immigration improves the environment if pollution abatement equipment is sufficiently effective, while Li et al. (2014) found that inflows of skilled labor deteriorate the environment, whereas inflows of unskilled labor improve it.

that international factor movements have on the environment differ, and it is possible for the international factor movement to be compatible with environmental protection in a developing country. In particular, international capital inflow improves the environment in developing countries when the modern agricultural capital share in the economy increases to a certain level. For the first time, such conclusions are generalized in the study of the relation between international capital inflow and the environment.

The differences between this chapter and the aforementioned articles are that:

- We consider the three issues facing developing countries—international factor movements, environmental problems, and agricultural dualism—in one framework. This is what some developing countries are now confronting during the course of economic development.
- We consider the impact of international factor movements on the environment in two stages of modern agricultural development—the beginning stage and the popularization stage. Such an analysis is more in line with the economic reality of developing countries and facilitates their choice of economic development policies at different stages of modern agriculture development.

Competing Interests

Funding This work was supported by Yuxiu Postdoctoral School of Nanjing University and the Humanities and Social Sciences of the Ministry of Education, China, Project No. 17JJD630002.

Disclosure Statement No potential conflict of interest was reported by the authors.

Appendix

In this appendix, we derive various mathematical expressions presented in the main text.

Eq. (3.11)

An increase in the output of urban sector equal to $\widehat{X}_1$ then creates environmental damage [obtained by differentiating Eq. (3.1)] given by

$$\widehat{e} = -u\widehat{X}_1. \tag{3.26}$$

Notice that by Eq. (3.2), as wage rate is downwardly rigid, interest rate r will be unaffected to guarantee zero profit. Then, turn to the modern agricultural sector. Substituting the unaffected r into Eq. (3.3) and then differentiating it, we obtain

$$\widehat{\tau}_2 = b\widehat{e}. \tag{3.27}$$

Substituting Eqs. (3.26) and (3.27) into Eq. (3.10) yields

$$\left[-\frac{\lambda_{K1}}{a} + \lambda_{K2}\left(S_{KT}^2 - S_{TT}^2\right)b\right]\widehat{e} = \widehat{K}. \tag{3.28}$$

Thus, we have Eq. (3.11) in the text.

Eq. (3.13)

Totally differentiating Eqs. (3.4), (3.5), (3.6), and (3.9), one obtains

$$\begin{bmatrix} \theta_{L3} & \theta_{T3} & 0 \\ S_{TL}^3 & S_{TT}^3 & 1 \\ A & \lambda_{L3}S_{LT}^3 & \lambda_{L3} \end{bmatrix} \begin{bmatrix} \widehat{w} \\ \widehat{\tau}_3 \\ \widehat{X}_3 \end{bmatrix} = \begin{bmatrix} 0 \\ 0 \\ 1 \end{bmatrix} \widehat{L} + \begin{bmatrix} \varepsilon_3 \\ \varepsilon_3 \\ B \end{bmatrix} \widehat{e}, \tag{3.29}$$

where $A = \lambda_{L3}S_{LL}^3 - (1+\mu_1)(\lambda_{L1}+\lambda_{L2}) < 0$ and $B = (1+\mu_1)\left[\lambda_{L1}/a - \left(S_{LT}^2 - S_{LL}^2\right)\lambda_{L2}b\right] + \lambda_{L3}\varepsilon_3$. Solving Eq. (3.29), we obtain $\widehat{w}/\widehat{L} < 0, \widehat{\tau}_3/\widehat{L} > 0, \widehat{X}_3/\widehat{L} > 0$, and then $\widehat{\mu}_1/\widehat{L} > 0$ by Eq. (3.5). Thus, we have Eq. (3.13) in the text.

Eqs. (3.22) and (3.23)

Differentiating Eqs. (3.15) and (3.16) by using (3.18), we obtain

$$\begin{bmatrix} \theta_{L2} & \theta_{T2} \\ \theta_{L3} & \theta_{T3} \end{bmatrix} \begin{bmatrix} \widehat{w} \\ \widehat{\tau} \end{bmatrix} = \begin{bmatrix} \varepsilon_2 \\ \varepsilon_3 \end{bmatrix} \widehat{e}. \tag{3.30}$$

Solving the set of equations given by Eq. (3.30), we have Eqs. (3.22) and (3.23) in the text.

Eqs. (3.24) and (3.25)

Differentiating Eqs. (3.19)–(3.21) by using (3.17), (3.22), and (3.23), we obtain the effects of international factor movements on the environment

$$\begin{bmatrix} \lambda_{L2} & \lambda_{L3} & G_1 \\ \lambda_{K2} & 0 & G_2 \\ \lambda_{T2} & \lambda_{T3} & G_3 \end{bmatrix} \begin{bmatrix} \widehat{X}_2 \\ \widehat{X}_3 \\ \widehat{e} \end{bmatrix} = \begin{bmatrix} 1 \\ 0 \\ 0 \end{bmatrix} \widehat{L} + \begin{bmatrix} 0 \\ 1 \\ 0 \end{bmatrix} \widehat{K}, \tag{3.31}$$

where

$$G_1 = -\frac{(1+\mu_2)\lambda_{L1}}{a} - (\lambda_{L2}\varepsilon_2 + \lambda_{L3}\varepsilon_3) + \frac{\left[(1+\mu_2)\lambda_{L1} - \lambda_{L2}S_{LL}^2 - \lambda_{L3}S_{LL}^3\right](\varepsilon_3\theta_{T2} - \varepsilon_2\theta_{T3})}{\theta_{L2}\theta_{T3} - \theta_{T2}\theta_{L3}} + \frac{\left(\lambda_{L2}S_{LT}^2 + \lambda_{L3}S_{LT}^3\right)(\varepsilon_3\theta_{L2} - \varepsilon_2\theta_{L3})}{\theta_{L2}\theta_{T3} - \theta_{T2}\theta_{L3}},$$

$$G_2 = -\frac{\lambda_{K1}}{a} - \lambda_{K2}\varepsilon_2 + \frac{\lambda_{K2}\left[S_{KT}^2(\varepsilon_3\theta_{L2} - \varepsilon_2\theta_{L3}) - S_{KL}^2(\varepsilon_3\theta_{T2} - \varepsilon_2\theta_{T3})\right]}{\theta_{L2}\theta_{T3} - \theta_{T2}\theta_{L3}},$$

and

$$G_3 = -(\varepsilon_2\lambda_{T2} + \varepsilon_3\lambda_{T3}) - \frac{\left(\lambda_{T2}S_{TL}^2 + \lambda_{T3}S_{TL}^3\right)(\varepsilon_3\theta_{T2} - \varepsilon_2\theta_{T3})}{\theta_{L2}\theta_{T3} - \theta_{T2}\theta_{L3}} + \frac{\left(\lambda_{T2}S_{TT}^2 + \lambda_{T3}S_{TT}^3\right)(\varepsilon_3\theta_{L2} - \varepsilon_2\theta_{L3})}{\theta_{L2}\theta_{T3} - \theta_{T2}\theta_{L3}}.$$

Solving the set of equations given by Eq. (3.31), we have Eqs. (3.24) and (3.25) in the text.

References

Beladi H, Frasca R (1999) Pollution control under an urban binding minimum wage. Ann Reg Sci 33:523–533. https://doi.org/10.1007/s001680050119

Beladi H, Rapp J (1993) Urban unemployment and the backward incidence of pollution control. Ann Reg Sci 27:153–163. https://doi.org/10.1007/BF01581943

Beladi H, Chaudhuri S, Yabuuchi S (2008) Can international factor mobility reduce wage inequality in a dual economy? Rev Int Econ 16:893–903. https://doi.org/10.1111/j.1467-9396.2008.00751.x

Chaudhuri S (2006) Labor market reform, welfare and unemployment in a small open economy. Keio Econ Stud 43(2):1–17. https://doi.org/10.2139/ssrn.929167

Chaudhuri S (2007) Foreign capital, welfare and urban unemployment in the presence of agricultural dualism. Jpn World Econ 19(2):149–165. https://doi.org/10.1016/j.japwor.2005.08.001

Chaudhuri S, Banerjee D (2010) Foreign capital inflow, skilled–unskilled wage inequality and unemployment of unskilled labour in a fair wage model. Econ Model 27:477–486. https://doi.org/10.1016/j.econmod.2009.10.015

Chaudhuri S, Gupta MR (2014) International factor mobility, informal interest rate and capital market imperfection: a general equilibrium analysis. Econ Model 37:184–192. https://doi.org/10.1016/j.econmod.2013.09.034

Cole MA, Elliott RJ, Zhang J (2011) Growth, foreign direct investment, and the environment: evidence from Chinese cities. J Reg Sci 51(1):121–138. https://doi.org/10.1111/j.1467-9787.2010.00674.x

Copeland B, Taylor M (1999) Trade, spatial separation, and the environment. J Int Econ 47:137–168. https://doi.org/10.1016/S0022-1996(98)00020-8

Daitoh I (2008) Environmental protection and trade liberalization in a small open dual economy. Rev Dev Econ 12:728–736. https://doi.org/10.1111/j.1467-9361.2008.00455.x

Gupta MR (1997a) Informal sector and informal capital market in a small open less-developed economy. J Dev Econ 52(2):409–428. https://doi.org/10.1016/S0304-3878(96)00445-2

Gupta MR (1997b) Foreign capital and the informal sector: comments on Chandra and Khan. Economica 64(254):353–363. https://doi.org/10.1016/S0304-3878(96)00445-2

Jorgenson AK (2006) The transnational organization of production and environmental degradation: a cross-national study of the effects of foreign capital penetration on water pollution intensity, 1980–1995. Soc Sci Q 87(3):711–730. https://doi.org/10.1111/j.1540-6237.2006.00405.x

Jorgenson AK, Dick C, Mahutga MC (2007) Foreign investment dependence and the environment: an ecostructural approach. Soc Probl 54(3):371–394. https://doi.org/10.1525/sp.2007.54.3.371

Kar S, Guha-Khasnobis B (2006) Foreign capital, skill formation, and migration of skilled workers. J Policy Reform 9:107–123. https://doi.org/10.1080/13841280600772010

Kondoh K, Yabuuchi S (2012) Unemployment, environmental policy, and international migration. J Int Trade Econ Dev 21(5):677–690. https://doi.org/10.1080/09638199.2010.535613

Li X, Shen Q (2012) A study on urban private capital and the transfer of labor in the modern agriculture sector. J Econ Policy Reform 15:135–152. https://doi.org/10.1080/17487870.2012.672833

Li X, Wu Y (2018) Environment and economy in the modern agricultural development. Asia-Pac J Account E 25(1–2):163–176. https://doi.org/10.1080/16081625.2016.1246191

Li X, Xu Y (2016) Unemployment, wage inequality and international factor movement in the presence of agricultural dualism. Rev Dev Econ 20(2):415–425. https://doi.org/10.1111/rode.12235

Li X, Xu Y, Wang D (2014) Environment and labor movement of skilled labor and unskilled labor between sectors. Econ Model 38:367–371. https://doi.org/10.1016/j.econmod.2014.01.018

Nag RN, Banerjee R (2014) Agricultural dualism, wage inequality and development policies. Int J Sustain Agric Res 1(1):1–18. http://www.conscientiabeam.com/archive/70/03-2014/1

Rapanos VT (2007) Environmental taxation in a dualistic economy. Environ Dev Econ 12:73–89. https://doi.org/10.1017/S1355770X06003391

Shahbaz M, Nasreen S, Abbas F, Anis O (2015) Does foreign direct investment impede environmental quality in high-, middle-, and low-income countries? Energy Econ 51:275–287. https://doi.org/10.1016/j.eneco.2015.06.014

Tawada M, Sun S (2010) Urban pollution, unemployment and national welfare in a dualistic economy. Rev Dev Econ 14:311–322. https://doi.org/10.1111/j.1467-9361.2010.00554.x

Tsakiris N, Hatzipanayotou P, Michael MS (2008) Pollution, capital mobility and tax policies with unemployment. Rev Dev Econ 12:223–236. https://doi.org/10.1111/j.1467-9361.2007.00383.x

United Nations Conference on Trade and Development (2018) World Investment Report 2018: Investment and New Industrial Policies. https://unctad.org/publication/world-investment-report-2018

United Nations, Department of Economic and Social Affairs, Population Division (2017) International Migration Report 2017: Highlights(ST/ESA/SER.A/404). https://desapublications.un.org/publications/international-migration-report-2017-highlights

Yabuuchi S (2007) Unemployment and international factor movement in the presence of skilled and unskilled labor. Rev Dev Econ 11:437–449. https://doi.org/10.1111/j.1467-9361.2007.00368.x

Chapter 4
Rural Dual Economics, Subsidy Policy, and the Income Inequality Between Skilled and Unskilled Workers

Abstract This chapter builds a general-equilibrium model with three sectors to study the effects of several modern-agricultural factor price subsidy policies on the income inequality between skilled and unskilled labor. We find that all types of price subsidies, including those on skilled labor, unskilled labor, and capital, enlarge the income inequality if capital is sector-specific, but they decrease this gap if capital moves freely between sectors. Moreover, to what extent the income gap would be altered depends on the ratio of factor income to total output, and we also find that the urban unemployment decreases under certain conditions regardless of capital mobility.

Keywords Modern agriculture · Factor price subsidy policy · Income inequality · Rural dual economics · Labor migration

4.1 Introduction

Most countries, regardless of their respective development, have experienced increasing income inequity between skilled labor and unskilled labor. According to the Heckcher-Ohlin-Samuelson (HOS) theory, if developing countries export goods whose production is highly reliant upon unskilled labor, the demand for unskilled workers will increase, the wages for unskilled workers will also increase and shrinks the skilled and unskilled wage gap. However, it is a totally different story in the case of China, India, developing Southern African countries, and elsewhere (Atolia 2007; Beyer et al. 1999; Harrison and Hanson 1999; Kijima 2006; Xu and Li 2008; Zhu and Trefler 2005), which generally export such products. China is an example of this practice. According to the research of Yu (2012), income inequity in China has experienced a sharp increase. The relative wage rate between skilled and unskilled workers increased from 1.17 in 1995 to 2.06 in 2006, recording an average of 5.6% growth on a year-to-year basis. Although it decreased slightly, the relative wage rate remained high, at approximately 1.78, from 2007 to 2010.

In addition, modern agriculture refers to agriculture that is market-oriented and uses modern science and technology to manage and produce. Compared with

X. Li, Y. Wu, *Research on Characteristic Issues in Current Developing Economies*, New Frontiers in Regional Science: Asian Perspectives 80,
https://doi.org/10.1007/978-981-97-7284-1_4

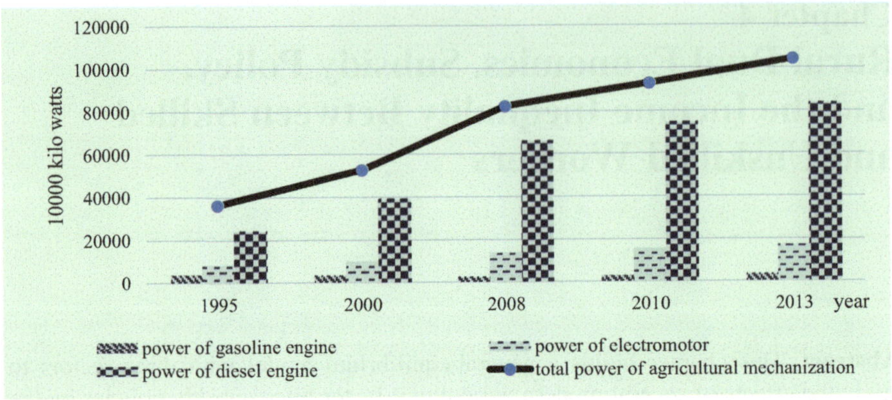

Fig. 4.1 The growth of the total power of mechanization in China: 1995–2013 (2015 China Agricultural statistical yearbook)

developed countries, the level of modern agriculture in developing countries is low, and they therefore make every effort to develop modern agriculture. For example, in China, the fiscal expenditures made by the Chinese government on the "three agricultural aspects," agricultural development, rural development, and rural laborers, have increased year by year. Eliminating the impacts of price change, the total amount was only 1.536 billion RMB in 1985, and it rose to 12,387.6 billion RMB in 2012, indicating an annual increase in expenditures on the "three agricultural aspects" of 17.7%. With regard to the developing level of modern agriculture, mechanization has increased much. The total power consumed by agricultural mechanization was 28,707.7 million kw in 1990, which rose to 103,906.8 million kw in 2013 with an annual growth rate of 5.8% (Fig. 4.1). To promote the development of modern agriculture, the Chinese government has formulated a variety of subsidy policies, including wage subsidy policies to increase the rural farmer's income directly, production input factor subsidies, and other subsidy policies to spread advanced cultivation technology.[1]

Nevertheless, subsidizing the factor price is an important measure to develop modern agriculture. Promoting the development and growth of a new sector will result in a corresponding influence on the economy. Given the circumstance of such a large income gap, it is important to study how price-subsidy policies in modern agriculture would affect wage inequality.

Modern agriculture has been used as a producing sector in the general-equilibrium system since the early 1990s. Typical studies include Gupta (1997a, b), Chaudhuri (2006, 2007), Li and Shen (2012), Li et al. (2014), and Li and Xu (2016). They combined modern agriculture in static general-equilibrium models when analyzing how different economic elements, such as inflow of foreign

[1] Please refer to He et al. (2015).

capital, liberalization of labor markets, subsidy policies on modern agriculture, etc., would affect social welfare, unemployment, and self-development. They divided workers into urban groups and rural ones, or separated by different sectors. However, as a matter of fact, the labor in their studies was homogeneous. There are two big problems in this assumption of homogeneity: It can neither reflect the complexity of labor in the real economy nor analyze the problem of income inequity between skilled labor and unskilled labor.

Numerous theoretical works have explored the topic of income inequity: Marjit and Kar (2005), Yabuuchi and Chaudhuri (2007), Beladi et al. (2010), Chaudhuri and Banerjee (2010), Gupta and Dutta (2010), and Li and Xu (2016). However, while all such studies researched the effects of various elements on income inequity from different perspectives, they had a couple of things in common: First, they ignored the development of modern agriculture in developing countries, and second, most of their research was only on the traditional agricultural sector in the subject rural area. In the model of Li and Xu (2016) with two urban sectors and two rural ones (including a modern agricultural sector in a rural area), they researched the effects of international flow of the factors on unemployment and income inequity, but they ignored the effects of agriculture subsidy policies.

Thus, the existing theoretical literature concerning wage inequity between skilled labor and unskilled labor in developing countries, specifically within the framework of labor migration, does not consider the modern agricultural sector. Nor did it study the effects of subsidy policies on the development of modern agriculture on wage inequality, which represents a shortcoming in the existing literature. This chapter develops a static general-equilibrium model with three sectors, including a modern agricultural one in a rural area to investigate the effects of modern agricultural subsidy policies on the wage inequality between skilled labor and unskilled labor in two cases of capital mobility and immobility. We have found that, regardless of which factor the government subsidizes in its price-subsidy policy, it enlarges the wage inequality in the case where capital is sector-specific, while decreasing this gap in the case where capital is mobile between the urban sector and the modern agricultural sector. Moreover, to what extent the income gap would change depends on the ratio of factor income to total output. We also find that the urban unemployment decreases under certain conditions regardless of whether capital is mobile.

The rest of the chapter is organized as follows. We establish a basic model in Sect. 4.2. In Sect. 4.3, we analyze the effects of price subsidy policies on wage inequality in two cases of capital mobility and immobility. The case where capital cannot flow between the urban sector and the modern agricultural sector means that capital has sector specificity, and the case of capital mobility means that capital can move between the urban sector and the modern agricultural sector without restriction. In Sect. 4.4, we state our conclusion.

4.2 Basic Model

A small open economy has three sectors: the urban sector (sector 1), the modern agriculture sector (sector 2), and the traditional agricultural sector (sector 3). We assume that there are three inputs: skilled labor, unskilled labor, and capital, all of which have fixed endowments. The urban sector employs skilled labor, unskilled labor, and capital to produce manufacturing product X_1, Considering that the modern agricultural sector produces agricultural goods by using modern management and advanced machines and equipment. The modern agricultural sector employs skilled, unskilled labor, and capital as input factors to produce agricultural product X_2. The traditional agricultural sector uses one factor—unskilled labor—to produce agricultural product X_3. Skilled labor moves perfectly between the urban sector and the modern agricultural sector with flexible wages,[2] and this flexibility ensures full employment of skilled workers. The wage rate of unskilled labor in the urban sector has downward rigidity and is higher than the unskilled wage rate in other sectors. It is because workers in the urban sector are often protected by minimum wage laws and other institutional elements. Unskilled workers move perfectly between the two agricultural sectors with flexible wages and no unemployment.

The three product markets are completely competitive. Production functions exhibit constant returns to scale with positive and diminishing marginal productivity to each factor. The following symbols will be used for formal presentation of the model:

$\overline{K_i}$	Endowment of capital in sector i in the case where capital is sector-specific, $i = 1, 2$
$\overline{K}$	Endowment of capital
$\overline{S}$	Endowment of skilled labor (in physical unit)
$\overline{L}$	Endowment of unskilled labor (in physical unit)
X_i	Level of output of the ith sector, $i = 1, 2, 3$
P_i	Relative price of the ith commodity, $i = 1, 2$, exogenously given
a_{SX_i}	Skilled labor-output ratio in sector i, $i = 1, 2$
a_{LX_i}	Unskilled labor-output ratio in sector i, $i = 1, 2, 3$
a_{KX_i}	Capital-output ratio in sector i, $i = 1, 2$
w_i^s	Wage rate of skilled labor in sector i, $i = 1, 2$
$\overline{w}_1$	Wage rate of unskilled labor in sector 1
w_i	Wage rate of unskilled labor in sector i, $i = 2, 3$
r_i	Return on capital of K in sector i, $i = 1, 2$
θ_{J_i}	Distributive share of the Jth input in the ith sector, $J = S, L, K$; $i = 1, 2, 3$
L_{uu}	Urban unemployment of unskilled labor
" $\wedge$ "	Proportionate change

[2]In developing countries, the marginal productivity of skilled labor is higher than the marginal productivity of unskilled labor, so the wage rate of skilled labor is much higher than the rigid wage rate of unskilled labor. Thus, the wage rate of skilled labor is perfectly flexible. The same hypothesis can be found in Yabuuchi and Chaudhuri (2007).

Under the condition that the markets are perfectly competitive, we could obtain that

$$w_1^s a_{SX_1} + \overline{w}_1 a_{LX_1} + r_1 a_{KX_1} = P_1, \quad (4.1)$$

$$w_2^s a_{SX_2} + w_2 a_{LX_2} + r_2 a_{KX_2} = P_2, \quad (4.2)$$

$$w_3 a_{LX_3} = 1. \quad (4.3)$$

We first consider the economy where capital is specific to each sector, so we suppose that $\overline{K}_1$ and $\overline{K}_2$ are given and fixed. The market-clearing conditions of the three factors, skilled labor, unskilled labor and capital, could be shown as follows:

$$a_{SX_1} X_1 + a_{SX_2} X_2 = \overline{S}, \quad (4.4)$$

$$a_{LX_1} X_1 + a_{LX_2} X_2 + a_{LX_3} X_3 + L_{uu} = \overline{L}, \quad (4.5)$$

$$a_{KX_1} X_1 = \overline{K_1}, \quad (4.6)$$

$$a_{KX_2} X_2 = \overline{K_2}. \quad (4.7)$$

The rural-urban Harris-Todaro migration equilibrium condition of unskilled labor is expressed as

$$w_3 = \frac{a_{LX_1} X_1}{a_{LX_1} X_1 + L_{uu}} \overline{w_1}. \quad (4.8)$$

In the skilled labor market equilibrium, the wage rate in the urban sector equals the wage rate in the modern agricultural sector. In the unskilled labor market equilibrium, the wage rate in the traditional agricultural sector equals the wage rate in the modern agricultural sector. Therefore, we have

$$w_1^s = w_2^s, \quad (4.9)$$

$$w_2 = w_3. \quad (4.10)$$

Our basic theoretical model has been established. In this general-equilibrium model, there are ten endogenous variables, namely, w_1^s, w_2^s, w_2, w_3, r_1, r_2, X_1, X_2, X_3, L_{uu}, and the same number of independent equations, namely, Eqs. (4.1)–(4.10); P_1, P_2, S, L, K, and $\overline{w}_1$ are exogenous variables. First, w_3 and w_2 are solved from Eqs. (4.3) and (4.10). Then, w_1^s, w_2^s, r_1, r_2, X_1, X_2 are simultaneously solved from Eqs. (4.1), (4.2), (4.4), (4.6), (4.7), and (4.9). Finally, L_{uu} is solved from Eq. (4.8) and X_3 is determined by Eq. (4.5). According to Eq. (4.3), we find that the wages in sector 3 are affected only by the price of its product; in other words, the government's subsidy policies do not influence the wages in sector 3 if its product price does not change. According to Eq. (4.10), the wages in sector 2 are influenced by sector 3 and does not change the general equilibrium. Therefore, the main task for us is to analyze the effects of subsidy policies on the wages for skilled labor.

4.3 Analysis and Discussion

4.3.1 *Capital Specificity*

A Wage Subsidy Policy on Skilled Labor in the Modern Agricultural Sector

We analyze the effects of a wage subsidy policy on skilled labor in the modern agricultural sector, and assume the subsidy rate is v_s.

Equation (4.2) can be rewritten as follows:

$$w_2^s(1-v_s)a_{SX_2}+w_2a_{LX_2}+r_2a_{KX_2}=P_2. \tag{4.2'}$$

Differentiating Eqs. (4.1), (4.2), (4.4), (4.6), and (4.7), and considering the initial value of subsidy rate is zero, the following expressions are respectively derived:

$$\hat{r}_1=-\frac{\theta_{S_1}}{\theta_{K_1}}\hat{w}_1^s, \tag{4.11}$$

$$\theta_{s_2}\hat{w}_2^s+\theta_{k_2}\hat{r}_2=\theta_{s_2}v_s\hat{v}_s, \tag{4.12}$$

$$S_1\hat{X}_1+S_2\hat{X}_2+\left(S_1\varepsilon^1_{Sw_1^s}+S_2\varepsilon^2_{Sw_2^s}-\frac{\theta_{S_1}}{\theta_{K_1}}S_1\varepsilon^1_{Sr_1}\right)\hat{w}_1^s+S_2\varepsilon^2_{Sr_2}\hat{r}_2=0, \tag{4.13}$$

$$\hat{X}_1+\left(\varepsilon^1_{Kw_1^s}-\frac{\theta_{S_1}}{\theta_{K_1}}\varepsilon^1_{Kr_1}\right)\hat{w}_1^s=0, \tag{4.14}$$

$$\hat{X}_2+\varepsilon^2_{Kw_2^s}\hat{w}_2^s+\varepsilon^2_{Kr_2}\hat{r}_2=0. \tag{4.15}$$

Here, $\varepsilon^i_{JP_j}(i=1,2,3;\ J=S,L,K,\ P_j=w_s,w,r)$ can measure the degree of substitution between factors in sector i. For example, $\varepsilon^1_{Kw_1^s}=\frac{\partial(a_{KX_1})}{\partial w_1^s}\frac{w_1^s}{(a_{KX_1})}$, which is the elasticity of required capital per unit output to the wage rate of skilled labor w_1^s in sector 1. Without loss of generality, we assume that $\varepsilon^i_{Jp_J}<0,\ \varepsilon^i_{Jp_{-J}}>0$.[3]

Using Eqs. (4.12)—(4.15), we calculate the effect of $\hat{v}_s$ on $\hat{w}_1^s$

[3]The same hypothesis can be found in Chaudhuri and Banerjee (2010).

$$\frac{\widehat{w}_1^s}{\widehat{v}_s} = \frac{-S_2\theta_{S_2}v_s\left(\varepsilon_{Kr_2}^2 - \varepsilon_{Sr_2}^2\right)}{\theta_{S_2}S_2\left(\varepsilon_{Sr_2}^2 - \varepsilon_{Kr_2}^2\right) + \theta_{K_2}\left(S_2\varepsilon_{Kw_2^s}^2 + S_1C - B\right)} > 0,$$

where $B = S_1\varepsilon_{Sw_1^s}^1 + S_2\varepsilon_{Sw_2^s}^2 - \frac{\theta_{S_1}}{\theta_{K_1}}S_1\varepsilon_{Sr_1}^1 < 0$, $C = \varepsilon_{Kw_1^s}^1 - \frac{\theta_{S_1}}{\theta_{K_1}}\varepsilon_{Kr_1}^1 > 0$. Then we obtain the variation of income inequality affected by wage subsidy policy related to skilled labor in the modern agricultural sector as follows:

$$\frac{\overset{\wedge}{w_1^s - w_3}}{\overset{\wedge}{v_s}} = \frac{-w_1^sS_2\theta_{S_2}v_s\left(\varepsilon_{Kr_2}^2 - \varepsilon_{Sr_2}^2\right)}{\left(w_1^s - w_3\right)\left[\theta_{S_2}S_2\left(\varepsilon_{Sr_2}^2 - \varepsilon_{Kr_2}^2\right) + \theta_{K_2}\left(S_2\varepsilon_{Kw_2^s}^2 + S_1C - B\right)\right]} > 0. \quad (4.16)$$

We find that the wage subsidy policy on skilled labor in the modern agricultural sector does not affect unskilled wages, while it increases the wages of skilled labor, and enlarges the skilled-unskilled wage gap. This is because, after the wages are subsidized, the demand for skilled labor in sector 2 increases, which leads to higher nominal wages to attract more skilled labor, and in turn skilled labor is released from sector 1 to sector 2. A decrease in skilled labor raises the skilled labor wage rate w_1^s and lowers the marginal return of capital r_1 in sector 1. Meanwhile, the inflow of skilled labor raises the marginal return of capital r_2 and the unskilled wage rate w_2 in sector 2. A higher unskilled labor wage rate in sector 2 attracts unskilled labor to transfer from sector 3 to sector 2. Considering the constant returns to scale in sector 3, a decrease in unskilled labor lowers the level of output in the same proportion, and unskilled labor wages remain constant. In this process, an increase in skilled labor in sector 2 lowers the skilled wage rate v_l, and according to Eq. (4.16), we find that the skilled labor wage rate in the new equilibrium is higher than the initial level. From the analysis above, we know that the skilled labor wage subsidy policy raises the level of output in sector 2 because it absorbs skilled labor from sector 1 and unskilled labor from sector 3. As a result, the skilled-unskilled wage gap becomes larger.

A Wage Subsidy Policy on Unskilled Labor in the Modern Agricultural Sector

If we assume the subsidy rate is v_l, Eq. (4.2) can be rewritten as follows:

$$w_2^s a_{SX_2} + w_2(1 - v_l)a_{LX_2} + r_2 a_{KX_2} = P_2. \quad (4.2'')$$

Completely differentiating Eq. (4.2″), we yield

$$\theta_{s_2}\overset{\wedge}{w_1^s} + \theta_{k_2}\overset{\wedge}{r_2} = \theta_{L_2}v_l\overset{\wedge}{v_l}. \quad (4.12')$$

Using Eqs. (4.12′), (4.13)– (4.15), we calculate the effect of $\widehat{v}_l$ on $\widehat{w}_1^s$

$$\frac{\hat{w}_1^s}{\hat{v}_l} = \frac{S_2\theta_{L_2}v_l\left(\varepsilon_{Sr_2}^2 - \varepsilon_{Kr_2}^2\right)}{\theta_{S_2}S_2\left(\varepsilon_{Sr_2}^2 - \varepsilon_{Kr_2}^2\right) + \theta_{K_2}\left(S_2\varepsilon_{Kw_2^s}^2 + S_1C - B\right)} > 0.$$

So, we calculate the influence of unskilled wage rate subsidies on the skilled-unskilled wage ratio, and have

$$\frac{\hat{w_1^s - w_3}}{\hat{v}_l} = \frac{w_1^s S_2\theta_{L_2}v_l\left(\varepsilon_{Sr_2}^2 - \varepsilon_{Kr_2}^2\right)}{\left(w_1^s - w_3\right)\left[\theta_{S_2}S_2\left(\varepsilon_{Sr_2}^2 - \varepsilon_{Kr_2}^2\right) + \theta_{K_2}\left(S_2\varepsilon_{Kw_2^s}^2 + S_1C - B\right)\right]} > 0. \quad (4.17)$$

The wage subsidy policy on unskilled labor in sector 2 lowers the unit cost of unskilled employment in the urban sector. Sector 2 attracts unskilled labor by increasing the unskilled wage rate, which results in the migration of unskilled labor from sector 3 to sector 2. Due to the imbalance of Eq. (4.8), where its left side is larger than its right side, meaning urban unemployed workers find jobs in the rural sector. The inflow of unskilled labor increases wages w_2^s for skilled labor and interest rate r_2. Meanwhile, a_{LX_2} also increases.[4] In other words, unskilled labor increases much more rapidly than output, which leads to decreasing marginal output on unskilled labor. This trend continues until sector 2 and 3 share the same unskilled wage rate. At the same time, skilled workers move from sector 1 to sector 2 due to higher wages in sector 2. When w_1^s equals w_2^s, this process stops. Wage rate for unskilled labor in sector 2 returns to its initial level in the new equilibrium, meanwhile the skilled wage rate increases due to higher marginal productivity of skilled labor. Therefore, the skilled-unskilled wage gap becomes increasingly larger.

Interest Subsidy Policy on Capital in the Modern Agricultural Sector

We assume the subsidy rate is v_k, then Eq. (4.2) can be rewritten as follows:

$$w_2^s a_{SX_2} + w_2 a_{LX_2} + r_2(1 - v_k)a_{KX_2} = P_2. \quad (4.2''')$$

Completely differentiating Eq. (4.2‴), we yield

$$\theta_{S_2}\hat{w}_2^s + (1 - v_k)\theta_{K_2}\hat{r}_2 = \theta_{K_2}v_k\hat{v}_k. \quad (4.12'')$$

Now, solving Eqs. (4.12″), (4.13)–(4.15) simultaneously, we obtain the effect of $\hat{v}_k$ on $\hat{w}_1^s$

[4] $\hat{a}_{LX_2} = \hat{L}_2 - \hat{X}_2 = \varepsilon_{Lw_2^s}^2\hat{w}_2^s + \varepsilon_{Lr_2}^2\hat{r}_2 > 0$, so, in sector 2, unskilled labor increases faster than output.

$$\frac{\overset{\wedge}{w_1^s}}{\overset{\wedge}{v_k}} = \frac{S_2\theta_{K_2}v_k\left(\varepsilon_{Sr_2}^2 - \varepsilon_{Kr_2}^2\right)}{\theta_{S_2}S_2\left(\varepsilon_{Sr_2}^2 - \varepsilon_{Kr_2}^2\right) + \theta_{K_2}\left(S_2\varepsilon_{Kw_2^s}^2 + S_1C - B\right)} > 0.$$

So, we calculate the influence of the capital interest rate subsidy on the skilled-unskilled wage ratio, and we obtain

$$\frac{\overset{\wedge}{w_1^s - w_3}}{\overset{\wedge}{v_k}} = \frac{w_1^s S_2\theta_{K_2}v_k\left(\varepsilon_{Sr_2}^2 - \varepsilon_{Kr_2}^2\right)}{\left(w_1^s - w_3\right)\left[\theta_{S_2}S_2\left(\varepsilon_{Sr_2}^2 - \varepsilon_{Kr_2}^2\right) + \theta_{K_2}\left(S_2\varepsilon_{Kw_2^s}^2 + S_1C - B\right)\right]} > 0. \quad (4.18)$$

Under the circumstance of fixed capital, sector 2 cannot absorb more capital by increasing the nominal interest rate. Just like subsidies for product costs, sector 2 will use higher wage rates to attract more skilled and unskilled labor. Therefore, subsidizing capital interest plays the same role as a wage rate subsidy. Thus, the methods we use and the results we obtain are similar. Therefore, it is unnecessary to repeat the process.

Furthermore, the skilled-unskilled wage gap becomes larger no matter which factors the government subsidizes. However, there is a difference in the speed at which it changes. We assume that the three factors share the same subsidy rate, v. Using Eqs. (4.16)–(4.18), we obtain

$$\left(\frac{\overset{\wedge}{w_1^s - w_3}}{\hat{v}}\right)^s - \left(\frac{\overset{\wedge}{w_1^s - w_3}}{\hat{v}}\right)^l$$

$$= \frac{v w_1^s S_2\left(\varepsilon_{Kr_2}^2 - \varepsilon_{Sr_2}^2\right)\left(\theta_{L_2} - \theta_{S_2}\right)}{\left(w_1^s - w_3\right)\left[\theta_{S_2}S_2\left(\varepsilon_{Sr_2}^2 - \varepsilon_{Kr_2}^2\right) + \theta_{K_2}\left(S_2\varepsilon_{Kw_2^s}^2 + S_1C - B\right)\right]} \begin{cases} > 0, & \text{if } \theta_{S_2} > \theta_{L_2} \\ < 0, & \text{if } \theta_{S_2} < \theta_{L_2} \end{cases},$$

$$\left(\frac{\overset{\wedge}{w_1^s - w_3}}{\hat{v}}\right)^s - \left(\frac{\overset{\wedge}{w_1^s - w_3}}{\hat{v}}\right)^k$$

$$= \frac{w_1^s S_2\left(\varepsilon_{Kr_2}^2 - \varepsilon_{Sr_2}^2\right)v\left(\theta_{K_2} - \theta_{S_2}\right)}{\left(w_1^s - w_3\right)\left[\theta_{S_2}S_2\left(\varepsilon_{Sr_2}^2 - \varepsilon_{Kr_2}^2\right) + \theta_{K_2}\left(S_2\varepsilon_{Kw_2^s}^2 + S_1C - B\right)\right]} \begin{cases} > 0, & \text{if } \theta_{S_2} > \theta_{K_2} \\ < 0, & \text{if } \theta_{S_2} < \theta_{K_2} \end{cases},$$

$$\left(\frac{\overset{\wedge}{w_1^s - w_3}}{\hat{v}}\right)^l - \left(\frac{\overset{\wedge}{w_1^s - w_3}}{\hat{v}}\right)^k$$

$$= \frac{w_1^s S_2\left(\varepsilon_{Kr_2}^2 - \varepsilon_{Sr_2}^2\right)v\left(\theta_{K_2} - \theta_{L_2}\right)}{\left(w_1^s - w_3\right)\left[\theta_{S_2}S_2\left(\varepsilon_{Sr_2}^2 - \varepsilon_{Kr_2}^2\right) + \theta_{K_2}\left(S_2\varepsilon_{Kw_2^s}^2 + S_1C - B\right)\right]} \begin{cases} > 0, & \text{if } \theta_{L_2} > \theta_{K_2} \\ < 0, & \text{if } \theta_{L_2} < \theta_{K_2} \end{cases}.$$

The reason why we have these results is that the income share of the factor influences the amount of subsidies sector 2 could receive, which then affects to what extent the skilled-unskilled wage gap would vary. If skilled and unskilled labor have the same subsidy rate, v, Eqs. (4.2′) and (4.2″) will be rewritten as, $\theta_{S_2} + \theta_{L_2} + \theta_{K_2} = 1 + v\theta_{S_2}$ and $\theta_{S_2} + \theta_{L_2} + \theta_{K_2} = 1 + v\theta_{L_2}$. If $\theta_{S_2} > \theta_{L_2}$, we will have $v\theta_{S_2} > v\theta_{L_2}$, which suggests that the government pays more to sector 2 for subsidizing skilled wage rates, compared with the case of unskilled wage rates. More payment means buying more production inputs. Given sector-specific capital, more subsidies will be used to hire more skilled or unskilled workers, which have a positive impact on raising the skilled wage rate.

Price subsidies to different factors lead to different rates of change in the skilled-unskilled wage gap, which are affected by the income share of factors. The above three formulas show that subsidizing the factor with a larger income share results in a higher rate of change in the skilled and unskilled wage gap, and vice versa. The government should subsidize the factor prices with a smaller income share, if they decide to develop modern agriculture while retaining the slow varying rate of the skilled and unskilled wage gap.

To sum up, we arrive at the following Proposition 1.

Proposition 1 *In the case where capital is sector-specific, no matter which factor in sector 2 the government subsidizes on price, its output increases, and the skilled-unskilled wage gap becomes larger; subsidizing the factors with a larger income share loads to a higher rate of change in the skilled-unskilled wage gap, and* vice versa.

The above cases of sector-specific capital can be proven in the real economy. Taking China as an example: Chinese modern agriculture is still in its early phase, and the farmer's scale of cultivation is small. The capital used in planting mainly comes from the farmer's own savings with few urban industrial or commercial capital directly injected into the modern agriculture (Li 2012; Yang et al. 2011). Thus, it can be seen that there is urban sector-specific capital and modern agricultural sector-specific capital. Therefore, the phenomena of income inequality correspond to the situations of sector-specific capital. After 2013, the government began to "encourage and guide industrial and commercial capital to invest in rural areas to develop modern planting and breeding industries suited for commercialized management, and introduce modern factors of production and operation models into agriculture."[5] Urban industrial and commercial capital began to be injected into rural areas on a relatively large scale for the development of more large-scale modern agriculture. It can be speculated that the capitals flowing from cities to rural areas will become increasingly larger and larger in the next few years, and the model of sector-specific capital will no longer be applicable.

[5] See Central Committee of the Communist Party of China (2013).

4.3.2 Mobile Capital Case

In this section, we offer a similar analysis to the previous section, but in the case where capital moves freely between the urban sector and modern agricultural sector. The two sectors share the same interest rate in the equilibrium, so we have

$$w_1^s a_{SX_1} + \overline{w}_1 a_{LX_1} + r a_{KX_1} = P_1, \tag{4.1l}$$

$$w_2^s a_{SX_2} + w_2 a_{LX_2} + r a_{KX_2} = P_2, \tag{4.2l}$$

$$a_{KX_1} X_1 + a_{KX_2} X_2 = \overline{K}. \tag{4.6l}$$

We have nine equations, from Eqs. (4.3)–(4.5), (4.8)–(4.10), (4.1^l), (4.2^l), and (4.6^l), which determine nine endogenous variables, namely, w_1^s, w_2^s, w_2, w_3, r, X_1, X_2, X_3, and L_{uu}. P_1, P_2, $\overline{S}$, $\overline{L}$, $\overline{K}$, and $\overline{w}_1$ are given exogenously. w_2 and w_3 are found from Eqs. (4.3) and (4.10). w_1^s, w_2^s, and r are solved from Eqs. (4.4), (4.9), and (4.6^l), and L_{uu} is then found from Eq. (4.8). Finally, X_3 is solved from Eq. (4.5).

Because capital per skilled labor in two sectors influences the mobility of factors and plays an important role in the following discussion, we make the following assumption

$$\frac{K_1}{S_1} < \frac{K_2}{S_2} \Leftrightarrow K_1 S_2 < K_2 S_1 \Leftrightarrow \theta_{K_1}\theta_{S_2} < \theta_{K_2}\theta_{S_1}.$$

This is similar to the assumption in Beladi et al. (2008) and in Li and Xu (2016).[6] It means that capital per skilled labor in the modern agricultural sector is higher than that in the urban sector. This assumption is reasonable in the early developing stages of modern agriculture. Compared with capital, skilled labor is much more lacking in that period. That is why we have this result.

A Wage Subsidy Policy on Skilled Labor in the Modern Agricultural Sector

Equation (4.2) in the basic model can be rewritten as follows:

$$w_2^S (1 - v_s^l) a_{SX_2} + w_2 a_{LX_2} + r a_{KX_2} = P_2. \tag{4.2'1}$$

Differentiating Eqs. (4.1^l), $(4.2'^l)$, and (4.9), we have the following expressions:

[6]Beladi et al. (2008) assume that the amount of capital corresponding to unit skilled labor in the agricultural sector is higher than that in the urban sector. Li and Xu (2016) assume that the amount of capital corresponding to unit skilled labor in the modern agriculture sector is higher than that in the urban sector.

$$\hat{r} = -\frac{\theta_{S_1}}{\theta_{K_1}} \hat{w_1^s}, \tag{4.19}$$

$$\frac{\hat{w_1^s}}{\hat{v_s^l}} = \frac{\theta_{K_1}\theta_{S_2}v_s}{\theta_{K_1}\theta_{S_2} - \theta_{S_1}\theta_{K_2}} < 0.$$

Because the unskilled wage rate does not change, the skilled and unskilled wage gap becomes

$$\frac{\widehat{(w_1^s - w_3)}}{\hat{v_s^l}} = \frac{w_1^s\theta_{K_1}\theta_{S_2}v_s^l}{(w_1^s - w_3)[\theta_{K_1}\theta_{S_2} - \theta_{K_2}\theta_{S_1}]} < 0. \tag{4.20}$$

From Eq. (4.20), we know that subsidizing the wage rate for skilled labor decreases the rate itself, and shrinks the skilled and unskilled wage gap in the new equilibrium. But why does it change in this way?

After subsidizing wage rates for skilled workers, sector 2 increases this rate to absorb more skilled labor from sector 1. With the outflow of skilled labor, marginal productivity of capital in sector 1 decreases, and capital partially moves from sector 1 to sector 2.

We know that $a_{SX_i}^i (i = 1, 2)$ is an equation of w_i^s,w_i, and r. Total differentiating $a_{SX_i}^i$, we get

$$\hat{a}_{SX_i}^i = \varepsilon_{Sw_i^s}^i \hat{w_i^s} + \varepsilon_{Sw_i}^i \hat{w_i} + \varepsilon_{Sr}^i \hat{r} = \varepsilon_{Sw_i^s}^i \hat{w_i^s} + \varepsilon_{Sr}^i \hat{r}. \tag{4.21}$$

From Eqs. (4.19) and (4.21), we obtain

$$\hat{a}_{SX_i} = \hat{S_i} - \hat{X_i} = \left(\varepsilon_{Sw_i^s}^i - \frac{\theta_{S_1}}{\theta_{K_1}}\varepsilon_{Sr}^i\right)\hat{w_i^s}. \tag{4.22}$$

Total differentiating a_{KX_i}, $i = 1, 2$ in the same way, we have

$$\hat{a}_{KX_i} = \hat{K_i} - \hat{X_i} = \left(\varepsilon_{Kw_i^s}^i - \frac{\theta_{S_1}}{\theta_{K_1}}\varepsilon_{Kr}^i\right)\hat{w_i^s}. \tag{4.23}$$

Comparing with the right side of Eqs. (4.22) and (4.23), $\left(\varepsilon_{Sw_i^s}^i - \frac{\theta_{S_1}}{\theta_{K_1}}\varepsilon_{Sr}^i\right) < 0$, $\left(\varepsilon_{Kw_i^s}^i - \frac{\theta_{S_1}}{\theta_{K_1}}\varepsilon_{Kr}^i\right) > 0$. Therefore, we get

$$\left(\hat{S_i} - \hat{X_i}\right)\left(\hat{K_i} - \hat{X_i}\right) < 0. \tag{4.24}$$

Equation (4.24) means that the decreasing rate of output in sector 1 lies between that of capital and of skilled labor. The changing rate of output in sector 2 is between that of capital and of skilled labor.

Completely differentiating Eq. (4.4), we obtain

$$\hat{S}_1 = -\frac{S_2}{S_1}\hat{S}_2 . \tag{4.25}$$

Completely differentiating $K_1 + K_2 = \overline{K}$, we obtain

$$\hat{K}_1 = -\frac{K_2}{K_1}\hat{K}_2 . \tag{4.26}$$

From Eqs. (4.25) and (4.26), we have

$$\frac{\left(\hat{K}_1 / \hat{S}_1\right)}{\left(\hat{K}_2 / \hat{S}_2\right)} = \frac{K_2 S_1}{K_1 S_2}.$$

Considering $K_1 S_2 < K_2 S_1$, we have

$$\left(\hat{K}_1 / \hat{S}_1\right) > \left(\hat{K}_2 / \hat{S}_2\right) \begin{cases} 1 > \left(\hat{K}_1 / \hat{S}_1\right) > \left(\hat{K}_2 / \hat{S}_2\right) > 0, (a_1) \\ \left(\hat{K}_1 / \hat{S}_1\right) > 1 > \left(\hat{K}_2 / \hat{S}_2\right) > 0, (a_2) \\ \left(\hat{K}_1 / \hat{S}_1\right) > \left(\hat{K}_2 / \hat{S}_2\right) > 1, (a_3) \end{cases} .$$

Considering the transferring forms, $(a_1)$and (a_3) cannot achieve equilibrium,[7] and we obtain the reasonable one of factor migration: $\left(\hat{K}_1 / \hat{S}_1\right) > 1 > \left(\hat{K}_2 / \hat{S}_2\right) > 0.$ It indicates that in sector 1, capital decreases faster than skilled labor, while in sector 2, capital increases faster than skilled labor. Combined with Eqs. (4.24) and (4.25),

---

[7]We use (a_1) as an example for illustration, if $1 > \left(\hat{K}_1 / \hat{S}_1\right) > \left(\hat{K}_2 / \hat{S}_2\right) > 0$, we have $0 > \hat{K}_1 > \hat{X}_1 > \hat{S}_1, 0 < \hat{K}_2 < \hat{X}_2 < \hat{S}_2$, and so we can obtain $a_{KX_1} > 0, a_{KX_2} < 0, a_{SX_1} < 0, a_{SX_2} > 0$, so the capital interest in sector 1 declines, the wage rate of skilled labor rises, but the capital interest rises and the wage rate of skilled labor declines in sector 2. Capital will flow from sector 1 to sector 2, and skilled labor will transfer from sector 2 to sector 1, the original flow pattern of factors will be changed, so the flow pattern of factors described by the inequality $1 > \left(\hat{K}_1 / \hat{S}_1\right) > \left(\hat{K}_2 / \hat{S}_2\right) > 0$ is unsustainable. Elimination is the reason.

we obtain $\hat{K}_1 < \hat{X}_1 < \hat{S}_1$, $\hat{K}_2 < \hat{X}_2 < \hat{S}_2$, and get $a_{KX_1} < 0$, $a_{SX_1} > 0$, $a_{KX_2} < 0$ and $a_{SX_1} > 0$. Skilled wage rates in sector 1 and 2 decrease due to subsidizing the rate in sector 2. In the new equilibrium, the two sectors have the same wage rate, which is lower than the initial value.

From the above analysis, we know that the major reason why the skilled wage rate decreases is that the increasing rate of skilled labor is more than that of output in sector 2, and the decreasing rate of skilled labor is less than that of output in sector 1. Consequently, with decreasing marginal productivity of skilled labor in the two sectors, the wage rate in the new equilibrium is lower than initial level.

A Wage Subsidy Policy on Unskilled Labor in the Modern Agricultural Sector

We assume the subsidy rate is v_l^l and Eq. (4.2) can be rewritten as follows:

$$w_2^s a_{SX_2} + w_2(1 - v_l)a_{LX_2} + r a_{KX_2} = P_2. \tag{4.2''1}$$

Differentiating Eq. (4.2$''^l$), we obtain

$$\frac{\widehat{w_1^s - w_3}}{\hat{v}_l^l} = \frac{w_1^s \theta_{K_1}\theta_{L_2}v_l}{\left(w_1^s - w_3\right)\left[\theta_{K_1}\theta_{S_2} - \theta_{S_1}\theta_{K_2}\right]} < 0. \tag{4.27}$$

We find that subsidizing the wage rate for unskilled labor also decreases the rate for skilled labor, and shrink wage inequality. Sector 2 attracts more unskilled workers by raising wages after a subsidy policy. Unskilled labor in sector 3 and the unemployed move to sector 2. The inflow of unskilled labor raises marginal productivity of skilled workers and capital, and absorbs skilled labor and capital from sector 1. Just like the above analysis, we obtain $\left(\hat{K}_1 / \hat{S}_1\right) > 1 > \left(\hat{K}_2 / \hat{S}_2\right) > 0$, with $\hat{K}_1 < \hat{X}_1 < \hat{S}_1 < 0$ and $0 < \hat{K}_2 < \hat{X}_2 < \hat{S}_2$, which means that the increasing rate of skilled labor is higher than that of output in sector 2, and the decreasing rate of skilled labor is less than that of output in sector 1. Therefore, the marginal productivity of skilled labor in the two sectors declines, and the wage rate in the new equilibrium is lower than the initial level.

An Interest Subsidy Policy in the Modern Agricultural Sector

We assume that the subsidy rate is v_k^l, and Eq. (4.2) can be rewritten as

$$w_2^S a_{SX_2} + w_2 a_{LX_2} + r(1 - v_k)a_{KX_2} = P_2. \tag{4.2'''1}$$

After differentiating Eq. (4.2′″^{l}), we obtain

$$\frac{\overset{\wedge}{w_1^s}}{\overset{\wedge}{v_k^l}} = \frac{\theta_{K_1}\theta_{K_2}v_k^l}{\theta_{K_1}\theta_{S_2} - \theta_{S_1}\theta_{K_2}} < 0.$$

In addition, we calculate the influence of subsidy policy on the skilled and the unskilled wage rate gap

$$\frac{\overset{\wedge}{w_1^s - w_3}}{\overset{\wedge}{v_k^l}} = \frac{w_1^s\theta_{K_1}\theta_{K_2}v_k^l}{(w_1^s - w_3)[\theta_{K_1}\theta_{S_2} - \theta_{K_2}\theta_{S_1}]} < 0. \tag{4.28}$$

Similarly, we obtain the relationship that $\left(\overset{\wedge}{K_1} / \overset{\wedge}{S_1}\right) > 1 > \left(\overset{\wedge}{K_2} / \overset{\wedge}{S_2}\right) > 0$, and we have $\overset{\wedge}{K_1} < \overset{\wedge}{X_1} < \overset{\wedge}{S_1} < 0$ and $0 < \overset{\wedge}{K_2} < \overset{\wedge}{X_2} < \overset{\wedge}{S_2}$, which means that in sector 1, capital decreases more rapidly than skilled labor, while in sector 2, it increases more slowly than skilled labor. As a result, the marginal productivity of capital in the two sectors increases, while that of skilled labor decreases. In the new equilibrium, skilled labor has the same level of wage rate in sector 1 and 2, which is lower than the initial level.

After studying three types of subsidy policy, we find that, no matter which factor the government decides to subsidize with regard to price, it decreases the skilled and unskilled wage gap. However, the changing rates are largely different among three factors. If we assume that subsidy rate for each element is the same,v^l, using Eqs. (4.20), (4.27), and (4.28), we can calculate the different influence on wage inequality as follows

$$\left(\frac{\overset{\wedge}{w_1^s - w_3}}{\overset{\wedge}{v^l}}\right)^s - \left(\frac{\overset{\wedge}{w_1^s - w_3}}{\overset{\wedge}{v^l}}\right)^l = \frac{v^l w_1^s\theta_{K_1}}{(w_1^s - w_3)} \frac{(\theta_{S_2} - \theta_{L_2})}{(\theta_{K_1}\theta_{S_2} - \theta_{K_2}\theta_{S_1})}\begin{cases} >0, & \text{if } \theta_{S_2} < \theta_{L_2} \\ <0, & \text{if } \theta_{S_2} > \theta_{L_2} \end{cases},$$

$$\left(\frac{\overset{\wedge}{w_1^s - w_3}}{\overset{\wedge}{v^l}}\right)^s - \left(\frac{\overset{\wedge}{w_1^s - w_3}}{\overset{\wedge}{v^l}}\right)^k = \frac{v^l w_1^s\theta_{K_1}}{(w_1^s - w_3)} \frac{\theta_{S_2} - \theta_{K_2}}{(\theta_{K_1}\theta_{S_2} - \theta_{K_2}\theta_{S_1})}\begin{cases} >0, & \text{if } \theta_{S_2} < \theta_{K_2} \\ <0, & \text{if } \theta_{S_2} > \theta_{K_2} \end{cases},$$

$$\left(\frac{\overset{\wedge}{w_1^s - w_3}}{\overset{\wedge}{v^l}}\right)^l - \left(\frac{\overset{\wedge}{w_1^s - w_3}}{\overset{\wedge}{v^l}}\right)^k = \frac{v^l w_1^s\theta_{K_1}}{(w_1^s - w_3)} \frac{\theta_{L_2} - \theta_{K_2}}{(\theta_{K_1}\theta_{S_2} - \theta_{K_2}\theta_{S_1})}\begin{cases} >0, & \text{if } \theta_{L_2} < \theta_{K_2} \\ <0, & \text{if } \theta_{L_2} > \theta_{K_2} \end{cases}.$$

We find that the shrinking rate of wage inequality is affected by the income share of factors. The rate is greater if the factor with the price subsidy has a larger income share, and vice versa. Then the government may choose the factor with a larger share of income to subsidize if eliminating wage inequality is their first and major priority.

Therefore, we have the following Proposition 2.

Proposition 2 *In the case where capital is mobile between the urban sector and the modern agricultural sector, no matter what type of factor government decides to subsidize on price, it shrinks the skilled and unskilled wage gap; subsidizing the factor with a larger income share shrinks the wage gap at a faster rate, and* vice versa.

If we subsidize the modern agriculture good price, the effect just like subsidizing on the price of the input factor, enlarges the income inequality in the case of sector-specific capital, while it decreases this gap in the case where capital is mobile between two sectors.

4.3.3 Urban Unemployment

According to Eq. (4.8), we have

$$\widehat{L}_{uu} = \frac{(\overline{w}_1 - w_3)L_1}{w_3 L_{uu}} \widehat{L}_1. \tag{4.29}$$

The substitution of capital and unskilled labor σ^1_{LK} can be written as $\sigma^1_{LK} = \frac{\widehat{a_{LX_1}} - \widehat{a_{KX_1}}}{\widehat{r_1} - \widehat{\overline{w}_1}}$, so that we have $\widehat{L}_1 = \sigma^1_{LK}\widehat{r}_1$. Based on the Eqs. (4.11) and (4.29), we have

$$\widehat{L}_{uu} = -\frac{(\overline{w}_1 - w_3)L_1}{w_3 L_{uu}} \frac{\theta_{S_1}}{\theta_{K_1}} \sigma^1_{LK} \widehat{w^s_1}. \tag{4.30}$$

If capital is sector-specific, all types of price subsidies will increase w^s_1, so according to the Eq. (4.30), the effect of a subsidy policy on urban unemployment depends on the value of σ^1_{LK}. When $\sigma^1_{LK} > 0$, the subsidy policy will decrease urban unemployment, and when $\sigma^1_{LK} < 0$, the subsidy policy will increase urban unemployment.

If we consider the case where capital is mobile between sectors, we rewrite the Eq. (4.29) as $\widehat{L}_{uu} = \frac{(\overline{w}_1 - w_3)L_1}{w_3 L_{uu}}\left(\sigma^1_{LK}\widehat{r} + \widehat{K}_1\right)$, so we have $\widehat{L}_{uu} = \frac{(\overline{w}_1 - w_3)L_1}{w_3 L_{uu}}\widehat{r}\left(\sigma^1_{LK} + \varphi^1_{Kr}\right)$, where $\varphi^1_{Kr} = \frac{dK_1}{dr}\frac{r}{K_1} < 0$, which is the price elasticity of demand for capital, thus we have $\widehat{L}_{uu} = -\frac{(\overline{w}_1 - w_3)L_1}{w_3 L_{uu}}\frac{\theta_{S_1}}{\theta_{K_1}}\left(\sigma^1_{LK} + \varphi^1_{Kr}\right)\widehat{w^s_1}$. When $\sigma^1_{LK} + \varphi^1_{Kr} > 0$, the subsidy policy will increase urban unemployment, and when $\sigma^1_{LK} + \varphi^1_{Kr} < 0$, the subsidy policy will decrease urban unemployment.

4.4 Conclusion

Developing countries often face a dilemma between developing modern agriculture and eliminating income inequality. Modern agriculture in developing countries employs unskilled and skilled labor, which affects their wage level, and income inequality. This chapter adopts modern agriculture into the model, and analyzes the effects of different subsidy policies to factor price on income inequality. The result is that in the case where capital is sector-specific, no matter which factor in sector 2 the government subsidizes on price, its output increases and the skilled-unskilled wage gap becomes larger; subsidizing the factor with a larger income share causes a higher changing rate in the skilled unskilled wage gap, and vice versa. In the case where capital is mobile between the urban sector and the modern agricultural sector, no matter what type of factor the government decides to subsidize on price, it shrinks the skilled and unskilled wage gap; subsidizing the factor with a larger income share shrinks the wage gap at a faster rate, and vice versa. We also find that urban unemployment decreases under certain conditions regardless of whether capital flows freely. Therefore, when deciding which subsidy policy to use, governors should consider the impacts of capital mobility, and take effective measures to gradually reduce capital mobility barriers. However, they should take income share of the different factors into consideration. Based on different capital mobility conditions, and the relationships among these income shares, governors could choose the most suitable policy with the most controllable level of income inequality.

Competing Interests No potential conflict of interest was reported by the authors.

References

Atolia M (2007) Trade liberalization and rising wage inequality in Latin America: reconciliation with HOS theory. J Int Econ 71(2):467–494. https://doi.org/10.1016/j.jinteco.2006.06.005

Beladi H, Chaudhuri S, Yabuuchi S (2008) Can international factor mobility reduce wage inequality in a dual economy? Rev Int Econ 16(5):893–903. https://doi.org/10.1111/j.1467-9396.2008.00751.x

Beladi H, Chakrabarti A, Marjit S (2010) Skilled-unskilled wage inequality and urban unemployment. Econ Inq 48(4):997–1007. https://doi.org/10.1111/j.1465-7295.2009.00247.x

Beyer H, Rojas P, Vergara R (1999) Trade liberalization and wage inequality. J Dev Econ 59(1): 103–123. https://doi.org/10.1016/S0304-3878(99)00007-3

Central Committee of the Communist Party of China (2013) Decision of the Central Committee of the Communist Party of China on some major issues concerning comprehensively deepening the reform. People's Daily. http://en.people.cn/90785/8525422.html. Accessed 9 Jan

Chaudhuri S (2006) Labor market reform, welfare and urban unemployment in a small open economy. Keio Econ Stud 43(2):1–17. https://doi.org/10.2139/ssrn.929167

Chaudhuri S (2007) Foreign capital, welfare and urban unemployment in the presence of agricultural dualism. Jpn World Econ 19(2):149–165. https://doi.org/10.1016/j.japwor.2005.08.001

Chaudhuri S, Banerjee D (2010) Foreign capital inflow, skilled–unskilled wage inequality and unemployment of unskilled labour in a fair wage model. Econ Model 27:477–486. https://doi.org/10.1016/j.econmod.2009.10.015

Gupta MR (1997a) Informal sector and informal capital market in a small open less-developed economy. J Dev Econ 52(2):409–428. https://doi.org/10.1016/S0304-3878(96)00445-2
Gupta MR (1997b) Foreign capital and the informal sector: comments on Chandra and Khan. Economica 64(254):353–363. https://doi.org/10.1111/1468-0335.00083
Gupta MR, Dutta PB (2010) Skilled-unskilled wage inequality: a general equilibrium analysis. Res Econ 64(4):247–263. https://doi.org/10.1016/j.rie.2010.07.001
Harrison A, Hanson G (1999) Who gains from trade reform? Some remaining puzzles. J Dev Econ 59(1):129–154. https://doi.org/10.1016/S0304-3878(99)00008-5
He ZW, Cao J, Luo YH (2015) Handbook on agriculture subsidy policy in China. Jindun Publishing House, Beijing. (in Chinese) ISBN: 9787508277578
Kijima Y (2006) Why did wage inequality increase? Evidence from urban India 1983-99. J Dev Econ 81(1):97–117. https://doi.org/10.1016/j.jdeveco.2005.04.008
Li QS (2012) Analysis of capital supply and demand in the development of modern agriculture. Jiangsu Agric Sci 40(5):409–411. https://doi.org/10.15889/j.issn.1002-1302.2012.05.034. (in Chinese)
Li X, Shen Q (2012) A study on urban private capital and the transfer of labor in the modern agriculture sector. J Econ Policy Reform 15(2):135–152. https://doi.org/10.1080/17487870.2012.672833
Li X, Xu Y (2016) Unemployment, wage inequality and international factor movement in the presence of agricultural dualism. Rev Dev Econ 20(2):415–425. https://doi.org/10.1111/rode.12235
Li X, Xu Y, Wang D (2014) Environment and labor movement of skilled labor and unskilled labor between sectors. Econ Model 38:367–371. https://doi.org/10.1016/j.econmod.2014.01.018
Marjit S, Kar S (2005) Emigration and wage inequality. Econ Lett 88(1):141–145. https://doi.org/10.1016/j.econlet.2005.02.003
Xu B, Li W (2008) Trade, technology, and China's rising skill demand. Econ Transit 16:59–84. https://doi.org/10.1111/j.1468-0351.2007.00314.x
Yabuuchi S, Chaudhuri S (2007) International migration of labour and skilled-unskilled wage inequality in a developing economy. Econ Model 24(1):128–137. https://doi.org/10.1016/j.econmod.2006.06.006
Yang G, Hu L, Wang W (2011) Moderate scale of farmers' cultivated land management and its performance: an empirical analysis based on questionnaire survey of rural households in 6 counties in Hubei province. Resour Sci 33(3):505–512. (in Chinese)
Yu MC (2012) Trade in intermediate goods, technology spillovers, and wage gap in developing countries: a theoretic framework. J Int Trade 8:14–21. (in Chinese)
Zhu SC, Trefler D (2005) Trade and inequality in developing countries: a general equilibrium analysis. J Int Econ 65(1):21–48. https://doi.org/10.1016/j.jinteco.2003.11.005

Part II
Agricultural Pollution Issues

Chapter 5
Rural-Urban Migrants' Remittance and Agricultural Pollution in the Presence of Agricultural Dualism

Abstract This chapter established an open general-equilibrium model to study the effect of the change of rural-urban migrants' remittances rate on agricultural pollution. We found that the increase of migrants' remittances rate would not influence on the output of agricultural pollution factor production sector or the agricultural pollution in the capital specific case. However, in the mobile capital case, the increase in the rural-urban migrants' remittances rate will decrease the output of the agricultural pollution factor production sector and then decrease the agricultural pollution. In addition, we investigated the numerical characteristics of the effects of the change in the rural-urban migrants' remittances rate on the relevant variables, and we also found that the increase of the migrants' remittances rate would increase the national income and improve the level of gross national welfare under certain conditions, no matter in the capital specific case or in the mobile capital case.

Keywords Migrants' remittance · Agricultural pollution · Modern agriculture · Agricultural dualism

5.1 Introduction

Rural-urban migrants' remittance (hereinafter referred to as "RUMs' remittances") refer to the part of wages income sent back to their hometown by the migrant workers who were employed in region outside their hometown in order to subsidize the family consumption. It is a widespread phenomenon in developing countries with typical urban-rural dual economic characteristics such as China. The RUMs' remittances mentioned in this article are the income transfer of migrant workers who are employed across regions within a country, which is different from the transnational migrants' remittance caused by transnational employment. There have been many studies on the economic effects of the transnational migrants' remittance, for instance, Lundahl (1985), Djajic (1986), Kirwan and Holden (1986), Taylor and Wyatt (1996), Quibria (1997), Djajic (1998), Kar and Beladi (2004), Pradhan et al. (2008), Ball et al. (2013), and Mauricio and Jose (2016). mainly considered the economic effects of migrants' remittances on the income distribution, poverty

X. Li, Y. Wu, *Research on Characteristic Issues in Current Developing Economies*, New Frontiers in Regional Science: Asian Perspectives 80,
https://doi.org/10.1007/978-981-97-7284-1_5

reduction, national welfare, investment, agricultural production, and the economy development of the labor source countries.

However, as a typical rural-urban dual economy and the economic and social disequilibrium between Chinese provinces has triggered massive migration streams since the late 1980s (Gries et al. 2015), this phenomenon means that the migrants' remittance in China mainly comes from the rural-urban migrant workers rather than the transnational migrant workers. Estimated by some scholars that the Chinese RUMs' remittances reached US$367.41 billion in 2016,[1] which was larger than the central fiscal expenditure on agriculture, rural areas, and farmers in the same year (i.e., US$277.65 billion or RMB 1844.2 billion).[2] This is a huge amount of funds inflow for rural areas, which will undoubtedly have important influences on agricultural production, agricultural pollution, and the rural economy. And the effects of the RUMs' remittances on the economy have attracted the attention and have produced a series of research literatures such as Li and Shen (2012), Li and Zhou (2015), Li and Wang (2015), and Wu and Li (2020). In this chapter, we will take the relationship between RUMs' remittances and agricultural pollution as the research object, and constructs a general equilibrium model to investigate the impact of the change of migrant workers' remittances rate on agricultural pollution and other variables.

Although there have been many studies on migrants' remittance, none of them investigated the possible impact of migrants' remittance on the environmental pollution except Li and Zhou (2015). Different from this article, what they studied was an urban-rural dual closed economy with agricultural unitary structure and analyzed the effect of migrant workers' remittances on industrial pollution rather than on agricultural pollution. However, agricultural pollution has replaced industrial pollution gradually and became the primary pollution source for many developing countries, such as China. Taking water pollution of China as an example, Fig. 5.1a shows that the emission of industrial pollution source and agricultural pollution source of chemical oxygen demand (COD) in wastewater from 2011 to 2015, while Fig. 5.1b shows the emission of industrial pollution source and agricultural pollution source of ammonia nitrogen in wastewater from 2011 to 2015. From Fig. 5.1, we can find that the emission of agricultural sources is far greater than that of emission industrial sources, no matter the emission of COD or ammonia nitrogen in wastewater. The problem of agricultural pollution has also attracted the attention of the Chinese government in order to decrease the agricultural pollution and ensure the safety of agricultural ecological environment, Ministry of Agriculture and Aural Affairs of China formulated and issued two documents in 2015, namely "action plan for zero growth of fertilizer use by 2020" and "the action plan for zero growth of pesticide use by 2020," respectively.[3] And agricultural

[1] For the detailed estimation process, please refer to Wu and Li (2020).

[2] January 23, 2017, Ministry of Finance of the People's Republic of China: Financial Revenue and Expenditure in 2016, http://gks.mof.gov.cn/tongjishuju/201701/t20170123_2526014.htm.

[3] http://www.moa.gov.cn/nybgb/2015/san/201711/t20171129_5923401.htm.

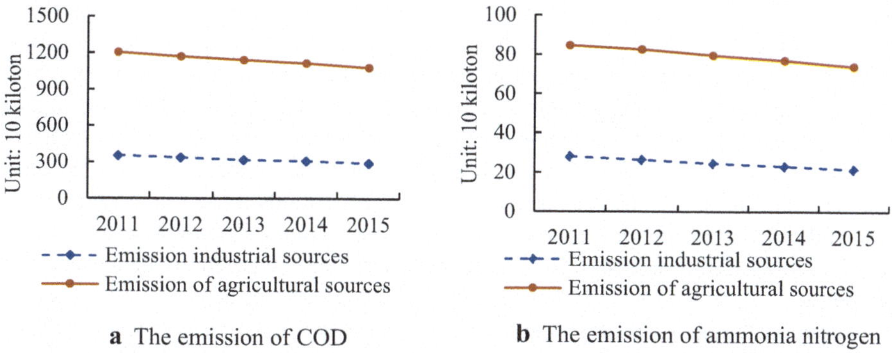

Fig. 5.1 The emission of industrial pollution source and agricultural pollution source of chemical oxygen demand (COD) and ammonia nitrogen in wastewater (China Environmental Statistics Yearbook in 2012–2016). (**a**) The emission of COD. (**b**) The emission of ammonia nitrogen

pollution in economic development is also a concern topic, such as Braden et al. (1991), Hammer (1992), Martínez and Albiac (2004), and Taheripour et al. (2008), where Taheripour et al. (2008) evaluated the welfare impacts of alternative policies for reducing agricultural nitrogen pollution in an open economy by using a general equilibrium approach. They found that removing the distortions and imposing nitrogen reduction subsidies and/or output taxes can reduce nitrogen pollution and enhance national welfare.

Agricultural pollution is mainly caused by the input factors that can cause pollution in the agricultural production process (hereinafter referred to as "Z"), such as pesticides, fertilizers, agricultural films, and catalysts. It is worth noting that the transmission path of agricultural pollution is different from that of industrial pollution in C-T mode (Copeland and Taylor 1999), and they pointed out that industrial pollution directly damages agricultural production through medias such as land, atmosphere, and water. Many scholars such as Tawada and Sun (2010), Chao et al. (2012), and Kondoh and Yabuuchi (2012) had studied the effects of industrial pollution on economic in the C-T framework. As input factors, agricultural pollution factors will not only directly affect agricultural production, but also affect agricultural workers' health capital through agricultural pollution such as harmful residues of agricultural products and water pollution, and then indirectly affect agricultural production. Therefore, the impact of agricultural pollution on production is reflected in the impact of agricultural pollution on the endogenous factors in the production process, which is also the main difference between the agricultural pollution path studied in this chapter and the C-T model.

In addition, the setting of agricultural unitary structure has been increasingly unable to fully reflect the reality of agricultural development in many developing countries. For example, China, India, Brazil, and other emerging economies are vigorously promoting the development of modern agriculture in recent years, and their agricultures have changed from the former unitary traditional agriculture to the dual agricultural structure of modern agriculture and traditional agriculture.

Therefore, the long-term coexistence of traditional agriculture and modern agriculture is an inevitable stage of agricultural development for many developing countries. This dual structure of agriculture has been adopted by some researches, with typical studies including Gupta (1997a, b) and Chaudhuri (2006, 2007). In fact, as a kind of transfer payment from the urban areas to the rural areas, RUMs' remittances not only subsidize migrant workers' household and then enhance the living standards of rural residents, but also provide considerable funds for agricultural production and rural economic development, which will also impact the input structure and quantity of agricultural factors in agricultural production and then on the agricultural pollution.

Based on the above analysis, in order to investigate the environmental effects of the RUMs' remittances in the presence of agricultural pollution, we establish a three-sector general equilibrium model which includes the modern agricultural sector, the traditional agricultural sector, and agricultural pollution factor production sector to investigate the effects of the changes in the RUMs' remittances rate on agricultural pollution both in the capital specific case and mobile capital case.

The rest of this chapter is organized as follows: In Sect. 5.2, we established an open general-equilibrium model as the basic analysis framework of this chapter. In Sect. 5.3, we analyzed the effects of the changes of the RUMs' remittances rate on agricultural pollution both in the capital-specific case and in the mobile capital case, respectively. In Sect. 5.4, we used relevant economic data from China in 2017 to calibrate the parameters of the model and perform numerical simulations in order to examine whether the model constructed in this chapter correctly explains the effects of the changes of the RUMs' remittances on agricultural pollution and national welfare, etc. Lastly, we stated the conclusion in Sect. 5.5.

5.2 Model

We consider a small open developing economy with three sectors which are modern agricultural sector (the sector 1), traditional agriculture sector (the sector 2), and agricultural pollution factor production sector (the sector Z), where the agricultural pollution factor production sector is located in urban areas and the other two sectors are located in rural areas. Among them, the modern agricultural sector employs labor, capital, and agricultural pollution factor to produce export-competing product X_l; the traditional agricultural sector employs labor and agricultural pollution factor to produce export-competing product X_2; and the agricultural pollution factor production sector inputs labor and capital to produce intermediate input factor for the modern agricultural sector and the traditional agricultural sector. All the markets are perfectly competitive, and the factors endowment are exogenously given. We assume labor can move among the three sectors above freely, while the capital also perfectly mobile between the modern agriculture sector and the agricultural pollution factor production sector in the mobile capital case, but capital is specific to the modern agriculture sector and the agricultural pollution factor production sector in the capital specific case.

In addition, we define h as the impact of agricultural pollution factors on workers' health capital (i.e., labor productivity), and the concrete form is $h = (1 + Z)^{\varepsilon}$, where the parameters ε is in the ranges of $(-1, 0]$. We also define k as the total rural-urban migrants' remittances. Because the rural-urban migrants' remittances are equivalent to a kind of transfer payment from urban areas to rural areas, it will produce positive externalities to the modern agricultural sector and traditional agricultural sector. Then, we use the functions $g_1(k) = (1 + k)^{\sigma_1}$ and $g_2(k) = (1 + k)^{\sigma_2}$ to express the externality generated by k on the sector 1 and the sector 2, where the parameters σ_1 and σ_2 (we assume $\sigma_1 > \sigma_2$) are in the range of [0, 1), and with the properties $g_i \geq 1$, $g_i' > 0$, and $g_i'' < 0$.

Thus, the production function of the above three sectors are as follows:

$$Z = F^Z(hL_Z, K_Z),$$

$$X_1 = g_1(k)F^1(hL_1, K_1, Z_1),$$

$$X_2 = g_2(k)F^2(hL_2, Z_2).$$

where, F^Z, F^1, and F^2 are production functions increasing with each factor, satisfying linear homogeneity, and are quasi-concave.[4] Variables X_i, ($i = 1, 2$), and Z indicate the output of modern agricultural sector, traditional agricultural sector, and the urban sector, respectively; L_i, ($i = 1, 2, Z$) indicate their respective quantity of labor; K_1 and K_Z are the capital utilized by the sector 1 and the sector Z, respectively.

We first consider an economy where capital is specific to the sector 1 and the sector Z. Under the conditions that the markets are perfectly competitive, in the capital-specific case, the following conditions can be obtained by the zero profit conditions:

$$hw_1 a_L^1 + r_1 a_K^1 + P_Z a_Z^1 = g_1 P_1, \tag{5.1}$$

$$hw_2 a_L^2 + P_Z a_Z^2 = g_2, \tag{5.2}$$

$$h\overline{w} a_L^Z + r_Z a_K^Z = P_Z. \tag{5.3}$$

where a_i^j ($i = L, K, Z; j = 1, 2, Z$) are the functions of factor prices which represent the quantity of the i-th factor used in the j-th sector to produce one unit of output without the rural-urban migrants' remittances k in the economy. We set the price of product X_2 to unit 1 and take it as the numeraire. Thus, the P_Z and P_1 are the relative prices of the product Z and product X_1 to the price of product X_2, respectively, which are determined by the world market and then are exogenous. Variables r_1 and r_Z are the return rate on capital in the sector 1 and the sector Z, respectively; w_1 and w_2

[4]The formations of X_1 and X_2 follow Copeland and Taylor (1999).

indicate the wages of the modern agriculture sector and the traditional agricultural sector which are flexible. Due to the minimum wage law and other reasons, the wage of unit labor in the agricultural pollution factor production sector is given as $\overline{w}$.

We assume the rural-urban migrants send a proportion of their income μ $(0 \leq \mu \leq 1)$ to their hometown to subsidize their family members and then define k as the total rural-urban migrants' remittances. Thus, we can obtain the following equation:

$$k = \mu h \overline{w} Z a_L^Z. \tag{5.4}$$

At present, for the vast majority of developing countries, the process of agricultural modernization is still in its infancy. Compared with the traditional agricultural sector, the scale of modern agricultural sector is still relatively small, so the modern agricultural sector cannot absorb the labor transferred from the traditional agricultural sector fully. Moreover, compared with traditional agriculture, modern agricultural sector is more dependent on capital input. And according to the viewpoint of Li and Wu (2018), we assume that the absorption of labor by the modern agricultural sector is constrained by capital in this sector. Thus, we set the relationship between employed labor and capital in the sector 2 as follows:

$$Y_1 a_L^1 = Y_1 a_K^1. \tag{5.5}$$

Therefore, the wage rate in the modern agricultural sector exceeds that in the traditional sector, and it is determined by the following (similar settings please refer to Gupta 1994 and Li and Wu 2018): $w_1 = w_1(w_2, K_1)$. If $K_1 = 0$, the modern agricultural sector will degenerate into the traditional agricultural sector, and then the wages are equal. And if $K_2 > 0$, we assume $w_1 > w_2$, because the capital using improves labor efficiency, causing a higher marginal productivity of labor.

We use L_U to represent the unemployment in the urban sector and define λ as the unemployment rate in the urban sector, hence $\lambda = hL_U / Za_L^Z$. Considering agricultural pollution, the actual effective wages in the three sectors are hw_1, hw_2, and $h\overline{w}$, respectively. Thus, the labor allocation mechanism which is based on Harris and Todaro (1970) can be shown as follows[5]:

$$w_2 \left[(1 + \lambda) Z a_L^Z + Y_1 a_L^1 \right] = \overline{w} Z a_L^Z + w_1 Y_1 a_L^1. \tag{5.6}$$

We define L as the labor endowment in the economy, then the market-clearing condition of labor is as follows:

[5]For the research on the equilibrium of H-T labor transfer among the three sectors with unequal wages, please also refer to Grinols (1991), Gupta (1993, 1997a), Li and Shen (2012), Li and Wu (2018), etc.

$$(1+\lambda)Za_L^Z + Y_1a_L^1 + Y_2a_L^2 = hL. \tag{5.7}$$

The capital market-clearing conditions in the capital-specific case are

$$Y_1a_K^1 = K_1, \tag{5.8}$$

$$Za_K^Z = K_Z. \tag{5.9}$$

In the two equations above, K_1 and K_Z indicate the capital input of sector 1 and Z, respectively, which are given in the capital-specific case.

In the mobile capital case, capital perfectly mobile between the sector 1 and the sector Z, so the equations $r_1 = r_Z = r$ are hold in equilibrium. Thus, Eqs. (5.1) and (5.3) can be rewritten as follows:

$$hw_1a_L^1 + ra_K^1 + P_Za_Z^1 = g_1P_1, \tag{5.1*}$$

$$h\overline{w}a_L^Z + ra_K^Z = P_Z, \tag{5.3*}$$

In addition, we define K as the capital endowments in the economy; thus, the capital market-clearing condition in the mobile capital case is

$$Y_1a_K^1 + Za_K^Z = K. \tag{5.10}$$

So far, our basic theoretical model has been established. Among them, Eqs. (5.1)–(5.9) describe the behaviors of economic entities in the capital-specific case, which has nine endogenous variables, X_1, X_2, Z, k, r_1, r_Z, w_1, w_2, and λ, and seven exogenous variables, $\overline{w}$, P_1, P_Z, θ, K_1, K_Z, and L. Eqs. (5.1*), (5.2), (5.3*), (5.4)–(5.7), and (5.10) describe the behaviors of economic entities in the mobile-specific case, which has eight endogenous variables, X_1, X_2, Z, k, r, w_1, w_2, and λ, and six exogenous variables, $\overline{w}$, P_1, P_Z, θ, K, and L.

5.3 Comparative Static Analysis

5.3.1 Capital-Specific Case

By differentiating the Eqs. (5.3) and (5.9), we will yield $\widehat{Z}/\widehat{\mu} = 0, \widehat{r}_Z/\widehat{\mu} = 0$ by using Cramer's rule. The symbol "$\dot{\Lambda}$" indicates the percentage of change in the relevant variables.

Then we will yield $\widehat{k}/\widehat{\mu} > 0$, $\widehat{w}_2/\widehat{\mu} = \frac{\sigma_2}{\theta_{L2}} \frac{k}{1+k} \frac{\widehat{k}}{\widehat{\mu}} > 0$ and the following matrix equations by differentiating the remaining seven equations and substituting the equations $\widehat{Z}/\widehat{\mu} = 0, \widehat{r}_Z/\widehat{\mu} = 0$ into the seven total differential equations:

$$\begin{pmatrix} 0 & 0 & \theta_{L1} & \theta_{K1} & 0 \\ 1 & 0 & S_{KL}^{1} & S_{KK}^{1} & 0 \\ 0 & 0 & (S_{LL}^{1}-S_{KL}^{1}) & (S_{LK}^{1}-S_{KK}^{1}) & 0 \\ -(w_1-w_2)X_1a_L^1 & 0 & -\left[(w_1-w_2)S_{LL}^{1}+w_1\right]X_1a_L^1 & -(w_1-w_2)X_1a_L^1S_{LK}^{1} & w_2\lambda Za_L^Z \\ X_1a_L^1 & X_2a_L^2 & X_1a_L^1S_{LL}^{1} & X_1a_L^1S_{LK}^{1} & \lambda Za_L^Z \end{pmatrix}\begin{pmatrix} \widehat{X}_1 \\ \widehat{X}_2 \\ \widehat{w}_1 \\ \widehat{r}_1 \\ \widehat{\lambda} \end{pmatrix} = \begin{pmatrix} \sigma_1\frac{k}{1+k} \\ 0 \\ 0 \\ -\frac{1}{\theta_{L2}}\sigma_2\frac{k}{1+k}\left[(1+\lambda)w_2Za_L^Z+w_2Y_1a_L^1\right] \\ -\frac{1}{\theta_{L2}}\sigma_2\frac{k}{1+k}Y_2a_L^2S_{LL}^2 \end{pmatrix}\widehat{\mu}. \tag{5.11}$$

where θ_{ij} $(i = L, K, Z; j = 1, 2, Z)$ indicates the distributive share of the i-th input in the j-th sector; $S_{ij}^t = \left(\partial a_i^t/\partial P_j\right)\left(P_j/a_i^t\right)$, $(t = 1, 2, Z; i, j = L, K, Z)$, and with the properties: $S_{ii}^t < 0$, if $i \neq j$, $S_{ij}^t > 0$.

We define "Δ" as the determinant of the coefficient matrix of the equation system (5.11). Thus, we can yield the following inequality:

$$\Delta = w_2\lambda Za_L^Z Y_2 a_L^2\left[\theta_{L1}\left(S_{LK}^1 - S_{KK}^1\right) + \theta_{K1}\left(S_{KL}^1 - S_{LL}^1\right)\right] > 0. \tag{5.12}$$

Solving Eq. (5.11) by using Cramer's rule, we can obtain Table 5.1 as follows (please refer to the Appendix 1 for details of the calculation procedure):

Summarizing the results in Table 5.1, we arrive at the following proposition.

Proposition 1 *In the capital-specific case, the changes of the RUMs' remittances rate have no effect on the agricultural pollution, and the increase of RUMs' remittances rate will enhance the output level of the modern agriculture.*

Proposition 1 shows that the increase of the RUMs' remittances rate will not impact the agricultural pollution in the capital-specific case, which is different from the conclusion of Li and Zhou (2015), who thought that the increase of migrant workers' remittances rate would worsen environmental pollution in the short term. The economic mechanism of the results in Table 5.1 and proposition 1 are as follows: Because the nominal wage of sector Z is rigid, the labor demand of sector

Table 5.1 The changes of RUMs' remittances rate on variables in the capital-specific case

	$\widehat{X}_1$	$\widehat{X}_2$	$\widehat{Z}$	$\widehat{k}$	$\widehat{w}_1$	$\widehat{w}_2$	$\widehat{r}_1$	$\widehat{r}_Z$	$\widehat{\lambda}$
$\widehat{\mu}$	+	\	0	+	+	+	+	0	\

Note: '+' and '−' mean that the changes of RUMs' remittances rate μ induce the endogenous variables change in the same and opposed directions, respectively; '0' means that the changes of μ have no influence on endogenous variables; and '\' means that the changes of μ induce the endogenous variables change are uncertain

Z is unchanged too, and in the capital-specific case, the capital input of sector Z is also unchanged, and then the output level Z and the return on capital r_Z of sector Z are unchanged. Therefore, the increase of RUMs' remittances rate has increased the total rural-urban migrants' remittances k. The increase of total remittances will become the driving force for rural labor to continue to transfer to the urban sector, so that the labor supply in the rural sector has a downward trend, and then will increase the wages (i.e., w_1 and w_2) of labor in the modern agricultural sector and the traditional agricultural sector. Although the decline of labor supply in the agricultural sector will have a negative impact on agricultural production, the increase of the rural-urban migrants' remittances enhances the positive externalities of the RUMs' remittances to modern agricultural sector and traditional agricultural sector. Therefore, the specific effects of the increase of the RUMs' remittances rate on the output level of the modern agricultural sector and the traditional agricultural sector depend on whether the positive externalities of the increase of remittance k to the productions of the modern agricultural sector and the traditional agricultural sector are greater than the negative effects of the decrease of rural labor on the productions of the two agricultural sectors. Because the positive externality of the rural-urban migrants' remittances k to the modern agricultural sector is greater than that to the traditional agricultural sector ($\sigma_1 > \sigma_2$), the increase of the RUMs' remittances rate is more likely to enhance the output level of the modern agricultural sector, while the impact on the output level of the traditional agricultural sector is ambiguous under the existing conditions. And if the positive externalities of the increase of remittance k to the production of the traditional agricultural sector is greater than the negative effects of the decrease of rural labor on the production of the traditional agricultural sector, the increase of the RUMs' remittances rate will enhance the output level of the traditional agricultural sector too.

5.3.2 Mobile Capital Case

Differentiating the Eqs. (5.3*) and (5.4), the following expressions are, respectively, derived:

$$\hat{r} = -\varepsilon \frac{Z}{1+Z} \frac{\theta_{LZ}}{\theta_{KZ}} \hat{Z}, \tag{5.13}$$

$$\hat{k} = \frac{1}{\theta_{KZ}} \left(\theta_{KZ} + \varepsilon \frac{Z}{1+Z} \theta_{KZ} + \varepsilon \frac{Z}{1+Z} S_{LL}^{Z} \right) \hat{Z} + \hat{\mu}. \tag{5.14}$$

We can yield the following matrix equations by differentiating the Eqs. (5.1*), (5.2), (5.5)–(5.7), and (5.10) and substituting the Eqs. (5.13) and (5.14) into the six total differential equations:

$$\begin{pmatrix} C_1 & 0 & 0 & \theta_{L1} & 0 & 0 \\ C_2 & 0 & 0 & 0 & \theta_{L2} & 0 \\ C_3 & Y_1 a_K^1 & 0 & Y_1 a_K^1 S_{KL}^1 & 0 & 0 \\ C_4 & 0 & 0 & (S_{LL}^1 - \delta S_{KL}^1) & 0 & 0 \\ C_5 & -(w_1 - w_2) Y_1 a_L^1 & 0 & -\left[(w_1 - w_2) S_{LL}^1 + w_1\right] Y_1 a_L^1 & (w_1 - w_2) Y_1 a_L^1 & \lambda w_2 Z a_L^Z \\ C_6 & Y_1 a_L^1 & Y_2 a_L^2 & Y_1 a_L^1 S_{LL}^1 & Y_2 a_L^2 S_{LL}^2 & \lambda Z a_L^Z \end{pmatrix} \begin{pmatrix} \widehat{Z} \\ \widehat{Y}_1 \\ \widehat{Y}_2 \\ \widehat{w}_1 \\ \widehat{w}_2 \\ \widehat{\lambda} \end{pmatrix}$$
$$= \begin{pmatrix} \sigma_1 \frac{k}{1+k} \\ \sigma_2 \frac{k}{1+k} \\ 0 \\ 0 \\ 0 \\ 0 \end{pmatrix} \widehat{\mu}. \tag{5.15}$$

where,

$$C_1 = \varepsilon \frac{Z}{1+Z} \frac{(\theta_{L1}\theta_{KZ} - \theta_{LZ}\theta_{K1})}{\theta_{KZ}} - \sigma_1 \frac{k}{1+k} \frac{1}{\theta_{KZ}}$$
$$\times \left(\theta_{KZ} + \varepsilon \frac{Z}{1+Z} \theta_{KZ} + \varepsilon \frac{Z}{1+Z} S_{LL}^Z\right),$$

$$C_2 = \varepsilon \frac{Z}{1+Z} \theta_{L2} - \sigma_2 \frac{k}{1+k} \frac{1}{\theta_{KZ}} \left(\theta_{KZ} + \varepsilon \frac{Z}{1+Z} \theta_{KZ} + \varepsilon \frac{Z}{1+Z} S_{LL}^Z\right),$$

$$C_3 = Z a_K^Z + \varepsilon \tfrac{Z}{1+Z} \tfrac{1}{\theta_{KZ}} \left[Y_1 a_K^1 (\theta_{KZ} S_{KL}^1 - \theta_{LZ} S_{KK}^1) - Z a_K^Z S_{KK}^Z\right], C_4 = \varepsilon \tfrac{Z}{1+Z} \tfrac{1}{\theta_{KZ}} \left[\theta_{KZ} (S_{LL}^1 - S_{KL}^1) - \theta_{LZ} (S_{LK}^1 - S_{KK}^1)\right],$$

$$C_5 = (w_1 - w_2) Y_1 a_L^1 + \varepsilon \frac{Z}{1+Z} \frac{1}{\theta_{KZ}} (w_1 - w_2) Y_1 a_L^1 \left[(\theta_{LZ} S_{LK}^1 - \theta_{KZ} S_{LL}^1) + S_{LL}^Z\right],$$

$$C_6 = (1+\lambda) Z a_L^Z - \varepsilon \frac{Z}{1+Z}$$
$$\times \left[(1+\lambda) Z a_L^Z (1 - S_{LL}^Z) + Y_1 a_L^1 (1 - S_{LL}^1) + Y_2 a_L^2 (1 - S_{LL}^2)\right] - \varepsilon \frac{Z}{1+Z} \frac{\theta_{LZ}}{\theta_{KZ}}$$
$$\times \left((1+\lambda) Z a_L^Z S_{LK}^Z + Y_1 a_L^1 S_{LK}^1\right).$$

Solving Eq. (5.15) by using Cramer's rule, we can obtain Table 5.2 (please refer to the Appendix 2 for details of the calculation procedure).

Summarizing the results in Table 5.2, we arrive at the following proposition.

Proposition 2 *In the mobile capital case, the increase of the RUMs' remittances rate will decrease the agricultural pollution, and increase the output level of the modern agricultural sector if the absolute value of parameter ε is small enough.*

Table 5.2 The changes of RUMs' remittances rate on variables in the mobile capital case

	$\widehat{X}_1$	$\widehat{X}_2$	$\widehat{Z}$	$\widehat{k}$	$\widehat{w}_1$	$\widehat{w}_2$	$\widehat{r}$	$\widehat{\lambda}$
$\widehat{\mu}$	(+)	\	–	\	(−)	(−)	–	(+)

Note: '+' and '−' mean that the changes of the RUMs' remittances rate μ induces the endogenous variables change in the same and opposed directions, respectively; '\' means that the changes of μ on endogenous variables are uncertain; and the bracket indicates that certain conditions are required for the establishment of the conclusion, that is, conditional establishment

Proposition 2 shows that the increase of the RUMs' remittances rate will decrease agricultural pollution and then enhance the environmental level in the mobile capital case, which is consistent with the conclusions of Li and Zhou (2015) in the long term. The results of Table 5.2 show us that in the mobile capital case, the increase of the RUMs' remittances rate will reduce the output of sector Z and thus reduce agricultural pollution, and enhance the output level of the modern agricultural sector, but the impact on the output of the traditional agricultural sector is uncertain. The economic mechanisms are as follows: the rise of RUMs' remittances rate improves the external environment of agricultural production, and will also give greater play to the role of capital in production. Therefore, compared with before the rise of RUMs' remittances rate, capital becomes relatively abundant, and then r decreases. Because the capital price r will decrease and the nominal wage of sector Z is rigid, the sector Z will replace labor with capital, and the employment of the sector Z will decrease. If the positive impact of the increase of capital input in the sector Z on production is less than the negative impact of the decrease of labor employment on production in the sector Z, the output of the sector Z will decrease. The decline of labor demand in sector Z will increase the urban unemployment rate and reduce the expected wage level of the city, resulting in the return of labor from the city to the rural sector, and then reduce the wage level of modern agricultural sector and traditional agricultural sector. And because of the decrease of labor employment in sector Z, the impact of the increase of the RUMs' remittances rate on the total amount of the rural-urban migrants' remittance is uncertain. The RUMs' remittances have the positive externalities to modern agricultural sector and traditional agricultural sector, and the positive externalities to modern agricultural sector is large enough, the output level of the modern agricultural sector will increase.

5.4 Parameter Calibration, Estimation, and Numerical Simulation

5.4.1 Calibration and Estimation of Parameters

The above theoretical model analysis provides the influence directions of the change in the RUMs' remittances rate on the agricultural pollution. In this section we will investigate the numerical characteristics of the effects of the change in the RUMs' remittances rate on the agricultural pollution, the output levels of the above three sectors and the national welfare both in the capital-specific case and the mobile capital case. Therefore, we first calibrate the parameters of the model based on the China's macroeconomic data, then simulate the model based on the calibrated parameters, and finally conduct sensitivity analysis to test the robustness of the numerical simulation results.

We set up the production functions in the modern agricultural sector, traditional agricultural sector, and the agricultural pollution factor production sector as Cobb-Douglas form, the specific forms are as follows:

$$X_1 = (1+k)^{\sigma_1}(1+Z)^{\varepsilon\alpha_1}L_1^{\alpha_1}Z_1^{\alpha_2}K_2^{1-\alpha_1-\alpha_2},$$

$$X_2 = (1+k)^{\sigma_2}(1+Z)^{\varepsilon\beta}L_2^{\beta}Z_2^{1-\beta},$$

$$Z = (1+Z)^{\varepsilon\gamma}L_Z^{\gamma}K_Z^{1-\gamma},$$

where, parameter α_1 is the output elasticities of labor in the modern agricultural sector and α_2 is the output elasticities of agricultural pollution factor in the modern agricultural sector; parameters β and γ are the output elasticities of labor in the traditional agricultural sector and the agricultural pollution factor production sector, respectively. Parameters σ_1 and σ_2 represent the externalities of the rural-urban migrants' remittances to the production of modern and traditional agricultural sectors, respectively, and the initial value of agricultural production effects of the RUMs' remittances on modern agriculture and traditional agriculture are set as $g_1 = 1.2$ and $g_2 = 1.1$, respectively. The parameter ε is the impact coefficient of agricultural pollution factor on health capital of workers in agricultural productions.

According to China Statistical Yearbook and provincial statistical yearbook, due to the availability of data, we take the data in 2017 as the benchmark data. Based on the criteria of China's National Bureau of statistics for the division of four regions in China's economy, the first industry of 10 provinces in the eastern region is expressed as the sector 1,[6] while the other 23 provinces are expressed as the sector 2, and we take the pesticide and fertilizer industries. Etc. as the agricultural pollution factor production sector. And then according to the 2017 statistical yearbook data of China's provinces, we estimated that the value-added of sector 1 and sector 2 were 2099.16 billion yuan and 4110.79 billion yuan, respectively; the number of employees of sector 1 and sector 2 were 54.71 million and 154.73 million, respectively, while the effective wage level of sector 1 and sector 2 were 16,778.24 yuan and 13,429.53 yuan, respectively.

[6]The 10 provinces and cities in the eastern region are Beijing, Tianjin, Hebei, Shanghai, Jiangsu, Zhejiang, Fujian, Guangdong, and Hainan. China's National Bureau of statistics mainly has two standards for the division of China's economic regions, namely, three regional standards and four regional standards. This chapter adopts the latest four regional standards, namely, the eastern region, the central region, the western region, and the northeast region.

Table 5.3 The results of the calibration of the parameters

Parameter	α_1	α_2	β	γ	σ_1	σ_2	ε
Calibration value	0.507	0.189	0.811	0.397	0.025	0.013	−0.025

The agricultural pollution factor production sector defined in this chapter mainly includes the factors input in the agricultural production process, which will have adverse effects on human health, water resources, and soil, namely, pesticides, fertilizers, and agricultural film. In view of the availability of data, we take the data of value-added of industries, employment, and wages of relevant departments in China Statistical Yearbook (2017) as well as the data of pesticide and fertilizer industries in Chinese industry Statistical Yearbook (2017) as the raw data. We calculate the employment number of the pesticide and chemical fertilizer industry is about 1.948 million and the value-added of pesticide and chemical fertilizer industry is about 297.08 billion yuan.[7] Combining the two estimated data above with the average wage of urban employees in 2017, we can estimate the factor output elasticity of the sector Z.

As for the interest rate, the benchmark one-to-five-year lending rate announced by China's central bank in 2017 is 4.75%. And due to the lower limit and the maximum floating coefficient of bank's loan interest rate are 0.9 times and 2.3 times of the benchmark interest rate, respectively, we assume the interest rate level of agricultural pollution factor production sector is 1.6 times of the benchmark interest rate, that is, 7.6%. Generally speaking, the financing conditions of the rural sector are more difficult than those of the urban sector, thus the interest rate level of the rural sector is higher than that of the urban sector. Therefore, it is reasonable to consider that the interest rate in the sector 1 is higher than that of sector Z, which is setting as 9.6% in the capital-specific case. In addition, following the model set in the previous article, the price of sector 2 is set to 1, and the relative price of sector 1 and sector Z are compared with that of sector 1, respectively.

Based on the economic data above, we first calibrated the parameters in the mobile capital case. The results are shown in Table 5.3.

5.4.2 *Numerical Simulation*

In this section, we will carry out the numerical simulation based on the parameters which were calibrated in the previous section and investigate the numerical characteristics of the effects of the change in the RUMs' remittances rate on the agricultural pollution and the output levels of the above three sectors both in the capital-specific case and the mobile capital case.

[7]Please refer to Li et al. (2020) for detailed calculation logic.

Capital-Specific Case

The numerical simulation results of the model in the capital-specific case are shown in Fig. 5.2. According to the Fig. 5.2, the increase of the RUMs' remittances rate μ will not impact the output level of the sector Z and then the agricultural pollution level in the capital-specific case, which is consistent with the conclusion of the Proposition 1. At the same time, the increase of the RUMs' remittances rate μ will enhance the output level of the sector 1 and the total RUMs' remittances rate, which are also consistent with the conclusions of the Proposition 1. In addition, although we cannot determine the effect of the change in the RUMs' remittances rate on the output level of the sector 2 according to the previous theoretical analysis, we find that the increase of RUMs' remittances rate will also improve the output level of the sector 2 according to the numerical simulation results which is based on the macroeconomic data of China in 2017. This means the positive externalities of the increase of remittance k to the production of the traditional agricultural sector is indeed greater than the negative effects of the decrease of rural labor on the production of the traditional agricultural sector in China.

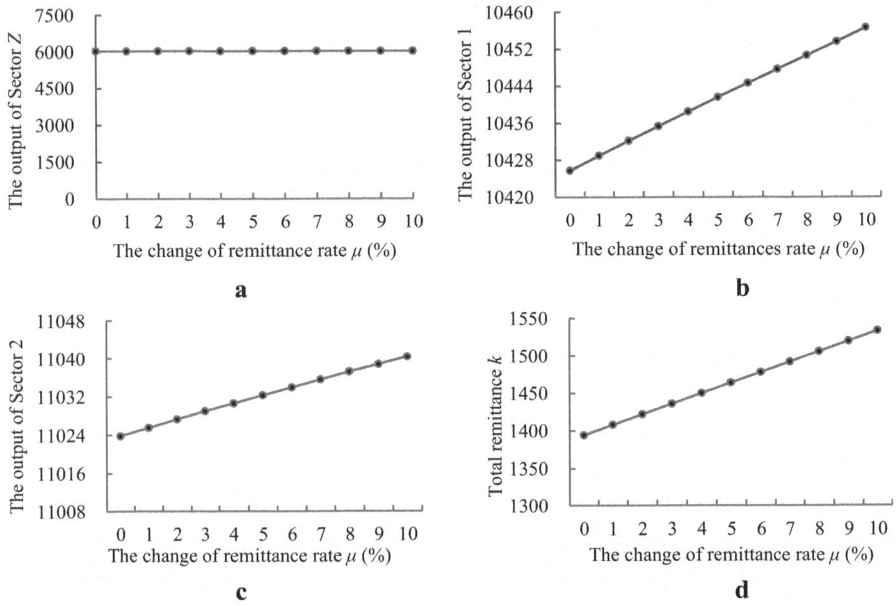

Fig. 5.2 The economic effects of the change of the RUMs' remittances rate, where $\sigma_1 = 0.0251$ and $\sigma_2 = 0.0131$

Mobile Capital Case

The numerical simulation results of the model in the mobile capital case are shown in Fig. 5.3. According to Fig. 5.3, the increase of the RUMs' remittances rate μ will decrease the output level of the sector Z and then the agricultural pollution level in the mobile capital case, which are consistent with the conclusion of the Proposition 2. At the same time, the increase of the RUMs' remittances rate μ will enhance the output level of the sector 1. In addition, although we cannot determine the effects of the change of the RUMs' remittances rate on the output level of sector 2 or the total remittance according to the previous theoretical analysis, we can find that the increase of the RUMs' remittances rate will also enhance the output level of sector 2 and the total remittance according to the numerical simulation results based on the macroeconomic data of China in 2017. This numerical simulation result shows that the negative effect which resulted from the decline output of the sector Z on the total remittance is less than the positive effect of the increase of the RUMs' remittances rate on the total amount of the rural-urban migrants' remittances.

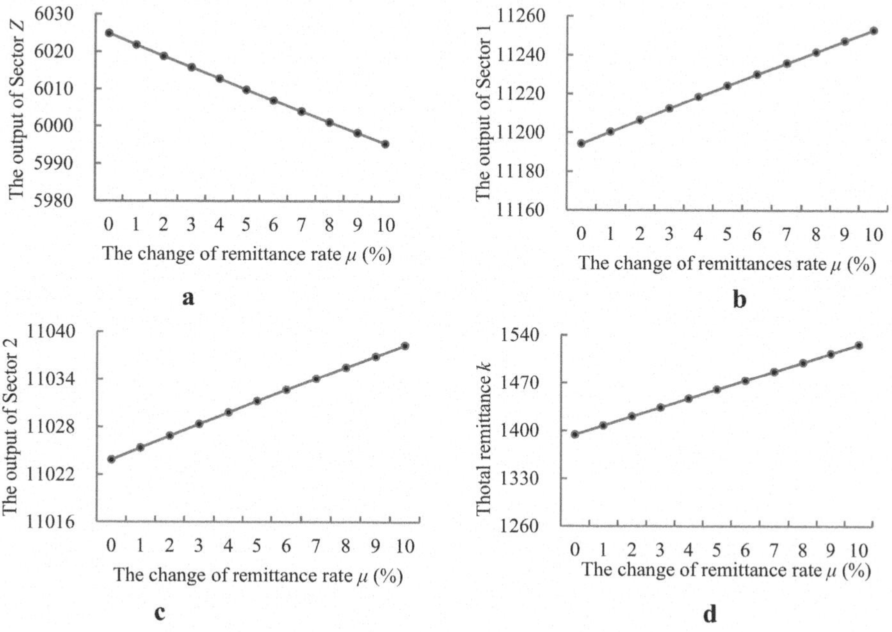

Fig. 5.3 The economic effects of the change of the RUMs' remittances rate, where $\sigma_1 = 0.0251$ and $\sigma_2 = 0.0131$

5.4.3 The Sensitivity Test

In the benchmark model, the initial value of agricultural production effects of the RUMs' remittances on modern agriculture and traditional agriculture are set as $g_1 = 1.2$ and $g_2 = 1.1$, respectively, and then the calibration values of the parameters σ_1 and σ_2 are 0.0251 and 0.0131, respectively. Because the above initial assignment has certain subjectivity, we will examine whether different initial values of g_i $(i = 1,2)$ will change the conclusions of the previous conclusion and the numerical characteristics of the effects of the rural-urban migrants' remittances on agricultural pollutions and the output levels of the three sectors. We select $g_1 = 1.15$, $g_2 = 1.05$ (i.e., $\sigma_1 = 0.0193$ and $\sigma_2 = 0.0067$), and $g_1 = 1.25$, $g_2 = 1.15$ (i.e., $\sigma_1 = 0.0308$ and $\sigma_2 = 0.0193$), respectively, and make numerical simulation by the same method again. The results of the model re-simulation in the capital-specific case and the mobile capital case are shown in Figs. 5.4, 5.5, 5.6 and 5.7.

According to the numerical simulation results of Figs. 5.4, 5.5, 5.6 and 5.7, we can find that the different initial values of the parameters σ_1 and σ_2 will not have a substantial impact on the conclusions and numerical characteristics of this chapter, which fully show that the numerical simulation results are stable.

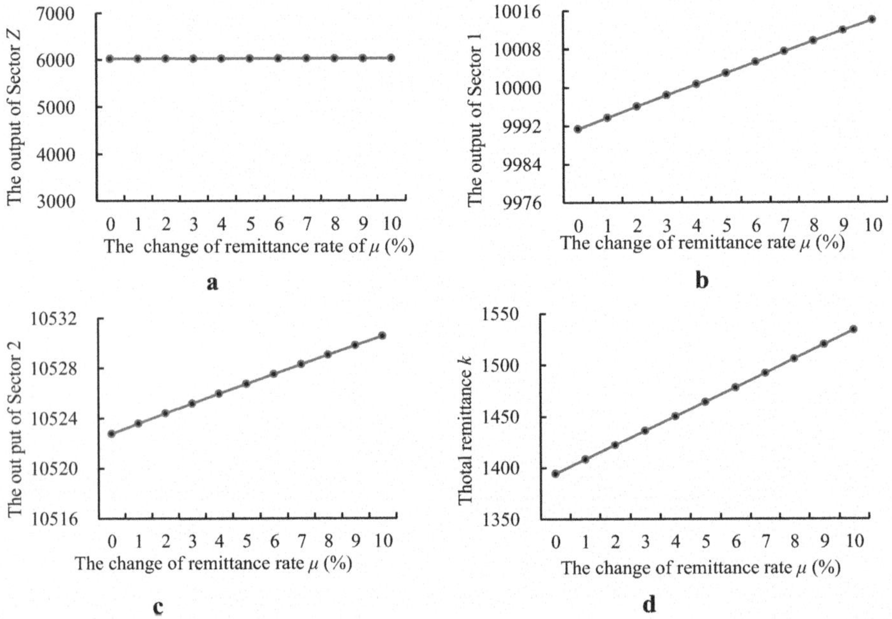

Fig. 5.4 The economic effects of the change of the RUMs' remittances rate in the capital-specific case, where $\sigma_1 = 0.0193$ and $\sigma_2 = 0.0067$

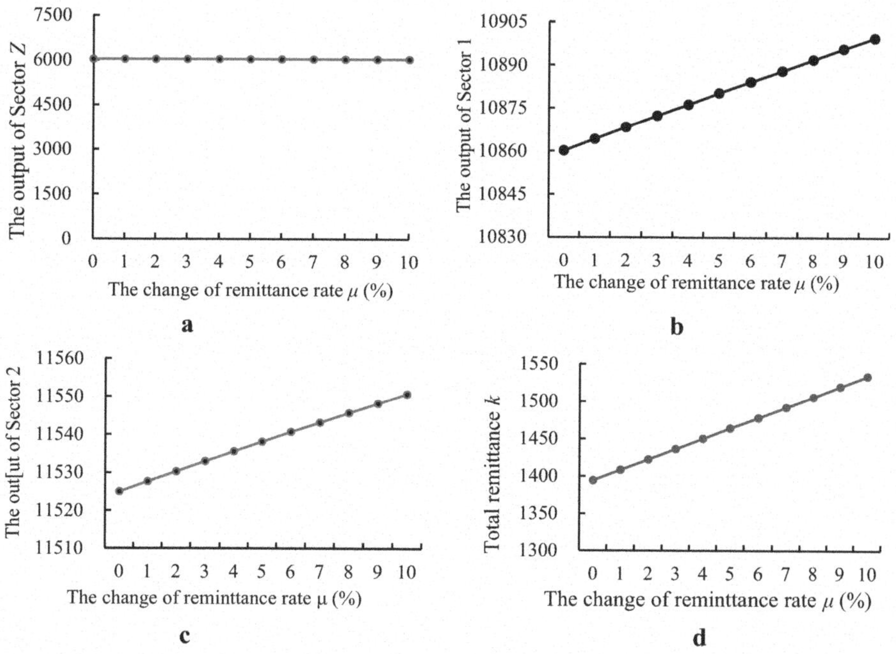

Fig. 5.5 The economic effects of the change of the RUMs' remittances rate in the capital-specific case, where $\sigma_1 = 0.0308$ and $\sigma_2 = 0.0193$

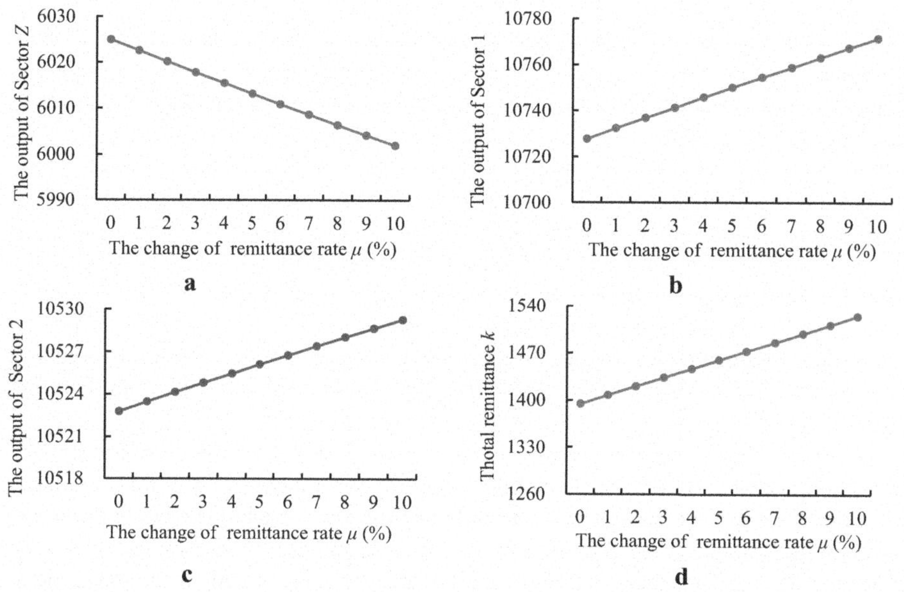

Fig. 5.6 The economic effects of the changes of the RUMS' remittances rate in the mobile capital case, where $\sigma_1 = 0.0193$ and $\sigma_2 = 0.0067$

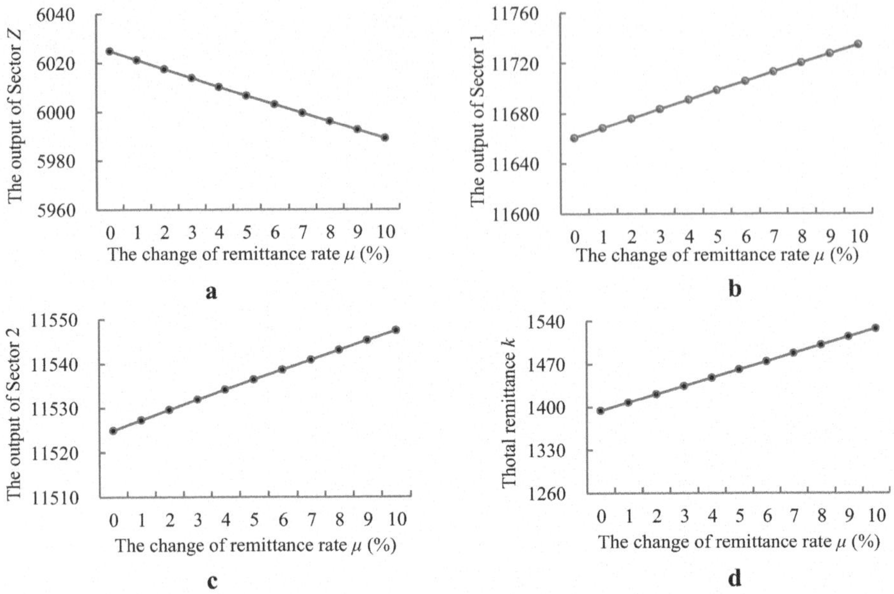

Fig. 5.7 The economic effects of the change of the RUMs' remittances rate in the mobile capital case, where $\sigma_1 = 0.0308$ and $\sigma_2 = 0.0193$

5.4.4 *National Welfare Effect*

We now turn our attention to the national welfare effect of the change of the RUMs' remittances rate on the basis of the analysis in the previous section. According to the nature of indirect effect function $v(p, y)$, the effect level of representative consumers are only related to the income level y and the product price p. Due to we consider a small economy with dual economic characteristics in this chapter, the products' prices of the three sectors are exogenously given. That is, the utility level of representative consumer is only related to the income level y in the model, and then the higher the income level, the higher the effect level. Hence, to investigate the effect of the change of the RUMs' remittances rate on national welfare, we simply focus on the national income, which is denoted as $Y = P_1X_1 + P_2X_2$. And the numerical characteristics of the effects of the change of the RUMs' remittances rate on national income in the capital-specific case and the mobile capital case are shown in Fig. 5.8.

The numerical simulation results in Fig. 5.8 show that the increase of the RUMs' remittances rate will increase the national income under certain conditions, no matter in the capital-specific case or in the mobile capital case. In addition, we find that the effect of the change in the RUMs' remittances rate on national income in the mobile capital case is greater than that in the capital-specific case by comparing the slope of the two national income curves in Fig. 5.8. Thus, we can obtain Proposition 3.

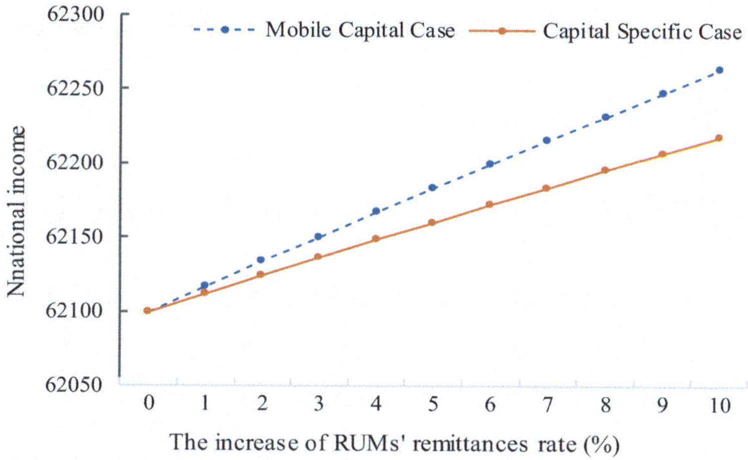

Fig. 5.8 The national income effects of the increase of the RUMs' remittances rate, where $\sigma_1 = 0.0251$ and $\sigma_2 = 0.0131$

Proposition 3

- *The increase of the RUMs' remittances rate will increase the national income and then the national welfare level under certain conditions based on the relevant macroeconomic data of China in 2017, no matter in the capital-specific case or in the mobile capital case.*
- *The effect of the change in the RUMs' remittances rate on national income in the mobile capital case is greater than that in the capital-specific case.*

In addition, we also select $g_l = 1.15$, $g_2 = 1.05$ (i.e., $\sigma_1 = 0.0193$ and $\sigma_2 = 0.0067$) and $g_1 = 1.25$, $g_2 = 1.15$ (i.e. $\sigma_1 = 0.0308$ and $\sigma_2 = 0.0193$), respectively, and make numerical simulation by the same method again to study the numerical characteristics of the effects of the rural-urban migrants' remittances on the national income and whether the numerical simulation results are stable. The results of the re-simulation of the model in the capital-specific case and the mobile capital case are shown in Figs. 5.9 and 5.10. Comparing the results in Figs. 5.8, 5.9 and 5.10, we find that the different initial values of the parameters and will not have a substantial impact on the numerical characteristics of this chapter, which fully show that the effects of the change of the RUMs' remittances rate on the national income and then the national welfare are stable too.

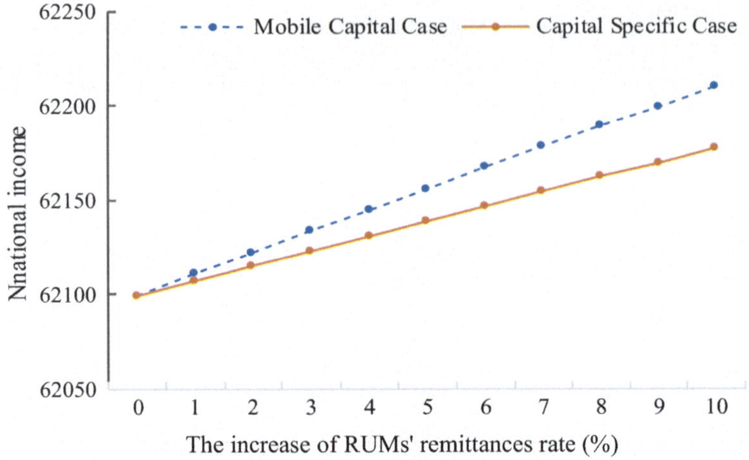

Fig. 5.9 The national income effects of the increase of the RUMs' remittances rate, where $\sigma_1 = 0.0193$ and $\sigma_2 = 0.0067$

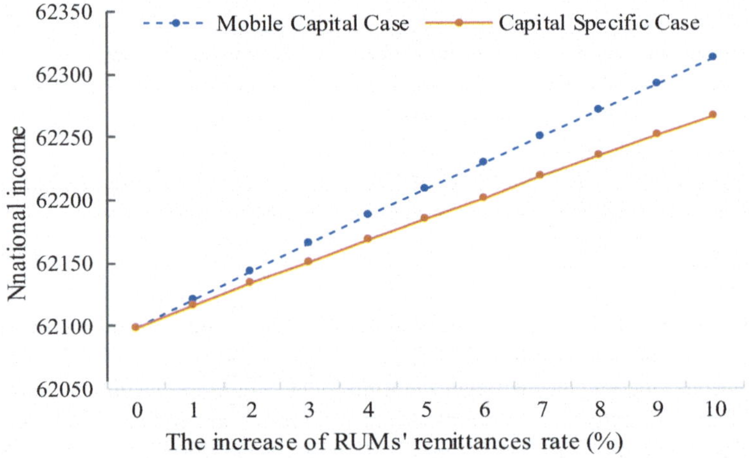

Fig. 5.10 The national income effects of the increase of the RUMs' remittances rate, where $\sigma_1 = 0.0308$ and $\sigma_2 = 0.0193$

5.5 Conclusion

The path of agricultural pollution is different from industrial pollution. We explored the effect of the change of the RUMs' remittances rate on agricultural pollution in an open general-equilibrium framework which contains three sectors. And there are two differences between this article and the existing literature:

- We investigated the effect of the change of the remittances rate on agricultural pollution rather than the industrial pollution, and then the transmission path of agricultural pollution in the chapter is different from them.
- Different from the existing literature set the agricultural sector as a unitary structure, our model set the agricultural sector as dual agricultural structure in which traditional agriculture and modern agriculture coexist, and this setting is more consistent with the agricultural structure of many developing economies.

We can draw the following conclusions through the previous theoretical analysis: Firstly, in the capital-specific case, the increase of the RUMs' remittances rate has no influence on the output level of agricultural pollution factor production sector and so as to the agricultural pollution. Secondly, in the mobile capital case, the increase of the RUMs' remittances rate will decrease the output level of agricultural pollution factor production sector and then the agricultural pollution. There are also some differences between our research conclusions on the effects of the change in the RUMs' remittances rate on environmental pollution and those of Li and Zhou (2015). They thought that the increase of the RUMs' remittances rate would aggravate the environmental pollution in the short term, while it would decrease the environmental pollution in the long term, that is, the effect of the change in the RUMs' remittances rate on industrial pollution is different between the capital-specific case and the mobile capital case. This chapter found that the increase of the RUMs' remittances rate will not increase agricultural pollution, but will decrease agricultural pollution in the mobile capital case.

We also investigated the numerical characteristics of the effects of the change of the RUMs' remittances rate on the output of the modern agricultural sector, and the agricultural pollution factor production sector, etc., and the results of numerical simulation also verify the relevant conclusions of the model in the previous sections. In addition, according to the numerical simulation analysis based on the macroeconomic data of China in 2017, we have obtained some new findings that are not confirmed in the theoretical analysis. And we also find that the increase of the RUMs' remittances rate will enhance the national income and then to the national welfare level both in the capital-specific case and the mobile capital case. The theoretical analysis and numerical simulation analysis of this chapter show that for the developing economies like China, which have the characteristics of dual structure of agriculture and rural-urban dual economy at the same time, the policies that encourage migrant workers to improve the RUMs' remittances rate are beneficial both to the improvement of agricultural sector production and national welfare and then to decrease agricultural pollution.

The consumption of the rural-urban migrants' remittances in rural areas can not only have externalities on the production of the agricultural sector, but also promote the improvement of labor human capital, which will influence on the agricultural economy and agricultural pollution.[8] Therefore, analyzing the economic and

---

[8]We thank one of the anonymous reviewers for his/her professional advice.

environmental effects of migrant workers' remittances from the perspective of the role of migrant workers' remittances on labor human capital in the agricultural sector may also be an important direction of future research.

Competing Interests

Funding This work was supported by the Humanities and Social Sciences of the Ministry of Education, China, Project No. 17JJD630002.

Disclosure Statement No potential conflict of interest was reported by the authors.

Appendix 1

Solving Eq. (5.11) by using Cramer's rule, we can yield the following results:

$$\Delta_{X_1} = -\sigma_1 \frac{k}{1+k} w_2 \lambda Z a_L^Z Y_2 a_L^2 \left(S_{KL}^1 S_{LK}^1 - S_{KK}^1 S_{LL}^1\right) > 0, \tag{5.16}$$

$$\begin{aligned}\Delta_{X_2} = {} & \frac{1}{\theta_{L2}} \frac{k}{1+k} \lambda Z a_L^Z Y_1 a_L^1 \left(S_{KK}^1 - S_{LK}^1\right)\left(\sigma_1 w_1 \theta_{L2} - \theta_{L1} \sigma_2 w_2\right) + \frac{\sigma_2}{\theta_{L2}} \frac{k}{1+k} \lambda Z a_L^Z w_2 Y_1 a_L^1 \theta_{K1} \left(S_{KL}^1 - S_{LL}^1\right) \\ & + \frac{\sigma_2}{\theta_{L2}} \frac{k}{1+k} \lambda Z a_L^Z \left[\theta_{L1}\left(S_{KK}^1 - S_{LK}^1\right) - \theta_{K1}\left(S_{KL}^1 - S_{LL}^1\right)\right]\left(w_2 Y_2 a_L^2 S_{LL}^2 - (1+\lambda) w_2 Z a_L^Z\right),\end{aligned} \tag{5.17}$$

$$\Delta_{w_1} = \sigma_1 \frac{k}{1+k} w_2 \lambda Z a_L^Z Y_2 a_L^2 \left(S_{LK}^1 - S_{KK}^1\right) > 0, \tag{5.18}$$

$$\Delta_{r_1} = \sigma_1 \frac{k}{1+k} w_2 \lambda Z a_L^Z Y_2 a_L^2 \left(S_{KL}^1 - S_{LL}^1\right) > 0, \tag{5.19}$$

$$\begin{aligned}\Delta_\lambda = {} & \frac{\sigma_2}{\theta_{L2}} \frac{k}{1+k} \left[(1+\lambda) w_2 Z a_L^Z + w_2 Y_1 a_L^1\right] Y_2 a_L^2 \left[\theta_{L1}\left(S_{KK}^1 - S_{LK}^1\right) - \theta_{K1}\left(S_{KL}^1 - S_{LL}^1\right)\right] \\ & - \sigma_1 \frac{k}{1+k} w_1 Y_1 a_L^1 Y_2 a_L^2 \left(S_{KK}^1 - S_{LK}^1\right).\end{aligned} \tag{5.20}$$

In view of Eqs. (5.16)–(5.20) and combine with Eq. (5.12), it is clear that the changes of RUMs' remittances rate μ will not impact the output Z of the agricultural pollution factor production sector, and will makes the endogenous variables k, r_1, w_1, and w_2 change in the same direction. In addition, because the inequality $\left(S_{KL}^1 S_{LK}^1 - S_{KK}^1 S_{LL}^1\right) < 0$ is hold, then the changes of the RUMs' remittances rate μ will also make the output of the sector 1 changes in the same direction. However, the effects of the changes of the RUMs' remittances rate μ on the output of the sector 2 and the unemployment rate λ are uncertain.

Appendix 2

The determinant of square matrix in Eq. (5.15) is

$$\Omega = \frac{1}{\theta_{KZ}} \times \left\{ \begin{array}{l} \varepsilon \dfrac{Z}{1+Z} \left[\begin{array}{l} \theta_{LZ}\theta_{L2}\lambda w_2 Z a_L^Z X_2 a_L^2 X_1 a_K^1 \left[\theta_{K1}\left(S_{LL}^1 - S_{KL}^1\right) + \theta_{L1}\left(S_{KK}^1 - S_{LK}^1\right) \right] \\ +\theta_{L1}\theta_{L2}\lambda w_2 X_2 a_L^2 Z a_L^Z Z a_K^Z S_{KK}^Z \end{array} \right] \\ -\sigma_1 \dfrac{k}{1+k} \theta_{L2}\lambda w_2 Z a_L^Z X_2 a_L^2 X_1 a_K^1 \left(S_{KL}^1 - S_{LL}^1\right) \left(\theta_{KZ} + \varepsilon \dfrac{Z}{1+Z}\theta_{KZ} + \varepsilon \dfrac{Z}{1+Z} S_{LL}^Z \right) \end{array} \right\}.$$

According to the expression of determinant Ω, if the absolute value of the parameter ε is sufficiently small,[9] we will yield $\Omega < 0$.

Solving matrix equations by Cramer's rule (5.15), we can induce the following results:

$$\Omega_{X_1} = \sigma_1 \frac{k}{1+k}\frac{1}{\theta_{KZ}} \theta_{L2} w_2 \lambda Z a_L^Z Y_2 a_L^2 \left\{ \begin{array}{l} \varepsilon \dfrac{Z}{1+Z} \left(\begin{array}{l} \theta_{LZ} Y_1 a_K^1 \left(S_{KL}^1 S_{LK}^1 - S_{LL}^1 S_{KK}^1\right) \\ +Z a_K^Z S_{KK}^Z \left(S_{KL}^1 - S_{LL}^1\right) \end{array} \right) \\ -\theta_{KZ} Z a_K^Z \left(S_{KL}^1 - S_{LL}^1\right) \end{array} \right\}, \tag{5.21}$$

$$\begin{aligned} \Omega_{X_2} = {} & \varepsilon \frac{Z}{1+Z}\sigma_1 \frac{k}{1+k}\frac{1}{\theta_{KZ}} \lambda Z a_L^Z Y_1 a_K^1 \left(S_{LL}^1 - S_{KL}^1\right) \left[w_2 Y_2 a_L^2 S_{LL}^2 - (w_1 - w_2) Y_1 a_L^1\right] \left[\theta_{L1}\theta_{KZ} - \theta_{LZ}\theta_{K1} - \theta_{L2}\theta_{KZ}\right] \\ & + \varepsilon \frac{Z}{1+Z}\frac{k}{1+k} \lambda Z a_L^Z \left[\begin{array}{l} \sigma_2 \theta_{L1} w_2 Y_2 a_L^2 S_{LL}^2 + \sigma_2 \theta_{L1} w_2 Y_1 a_L^1 \\ +(\sigma_1\theta_{L2} - \sigma_2\theta_{L1}) w_1 Y_1 a_L^1 \end{array} \right] \frac{1}{\theta_{KZ}} Y_1 a_K^1 \left[\left(\theta_{KZ} S_{KL}^1 - \theta_{LZ} S_{KK}^1\right) + \left(\theta_{LZ} S_{LK}^1 - \theta_{KZ} S_{LL}^1\right) \right] \\ & + \sigma_1 \frac{k}{1+k} \theta_{L2}\lambda Z a_L^Z \left(S_{LL}^1 - S_{KL}^1\right) \left\{ \begin{array}{l} \varepsilon \dfrac{Z}{1+Z}\dfrac{1}{\theta_{KZ}} w_2 Y_1 a_L^1 Y_1 a_K^1 \left[\left(\theta_{KZ} S_{KL}^1 - \theta_{LZ} S_{KK}^1\right) + \left(\theta_{LZ} S_{LK}^1 - \theta_{KZ} S_{LL}^1\right) \right] \\ \qquad - \varepsilon \dfrac{Z}{1+Z} w_2 Y_1 a_K^1 Y_1 a_K^1 Y_2 a_L^2 S_{LL}^2 \\ + \varepsilon \dfrac{Z}{1+Z}\dfrac{1}{\theta_{KZ}} w_2 (w_1 - w_2) Y_1 a_L^1 Y_1 a_K^1 S_{KL}^1 \left[\left(\theta_{KZ} S_{KL}^1 - \theta_{LZ} S_{KK}^1\right) + \left(\theta_{LZ} S_{LK}^1 - \theta_{KZ} S_{LL}^1\right) \right] \\ - w_1 Y_1 a_L^1 Z a_K^Z + (1+\lambda) w_2 Y_1 a_K^1 Z a_L^Z - (w_1 - w_2) Y_1 a_L^1 Y_1 a_K^1 \\ - \varepsilon \dfrac{Z}{1+Z}\dfrac{1}{\theta_{KZ}} (w_1 - w_2) Y_1 a_L^1 \left(Y_1 a_K^1 S_{LL}^Z - Z a_K^Z S_{KK}^Z\right) \\ + \varepsilon \dfrac{Z}{1+Z}\dfrac{1}{\theta_{KZ}} w_2 (1+\lambda) Z a_L^Z Y_1 a_K^1 S_{LL}^Z + \varepsilon \dfrac{Z}{1+Z}\dfrac{1}{\theta_{KZ}} w_2 Y_1 a_L^1 Z a_K^Z S_{KK}^Z \\ - \varepsilon \dfrac{Z}{1+Z}\dfrac{1}{\theta_{KZ}} w_1 Y_1 a_L^1 Y_1 a_K^1 \left[\left(\theta_{KZ} S_{KL}^1 - \theta_{LZ} S_{KK}^1\right) + \left(\theta_{LZ} S_{LK}^1 - \theta_{KZ} S_{LL}^1\right) \right], \end{array} \right\} \end{aligned} \tag{5.22}$$

[9] According to the definition and form setting of function h in Sect. 5.2, it is reasonable that the absolute value of parameter ε will be sufficiently small. This is also confirmed by the results of parameter calibration based on China's economic data in Sect. 5.4 of this chapter.

$$\Omega_Z = \sigma_1 \frac{k}{1+k}\theta_{L2}\lambda w_2 Z a_L^Z Y_1 a_K^1 Y_2 a_L^2 \left(S_{KL}^1 - S_{LL}^1\right) > 0, \tag{5.23}$$

$$\Omega_{w_1} = -\varepsilon \frac{Z}{1+Z}\frac{1}{\theta_{KZ}}\sigma_1 \frac{k}{1+k}\theta_{L2}\lambda w_2 Z a_L^Z Y_2 a_L^2 Y_1 a_K^1 \left[\left(\theta_{KZ}S_{KL}^1 - \theta_{LZ}S_{KK}^1\right) + \left(\theta_{LZ}S_{LK}^1 - \theta_{KZ}S_{LL}^1\right)\right] > 0, \tag{5.24}$$

$$\Omega_{w_2} = \varepsilon \frac{Z}{1+Z}\frac{1}{\theta_{KZ}}\left[\begin{array}{l} \frac{k}{1+k}\lambda w_2 Z a_L^Z Y_1 a_K^1 Y_2 a_L^2 \left(S_{LL}^1 - S_{KL}^1\right)\left(\sigma_1\theta_{L2}\theta_{KZ} + \sigma_2\theta_{LZ}\theta_{K1}\right) \\ -\sigma_2 \frac{k}{1+k}\theta_{LZ}\theta_{L1}\lambda w_2 Z a_L^Z Y_2 a_L^2 Y_1 a_K^1 \left(S_{LK}^1 - S_{KK}^1\right) \end{array}\right] > 0, \tag{5.25}$$

$$\begin{aligned} \Omega_\lambda = {} & \varepsilon \frac{Z}{1+Z}\frac{1}{\theta_{KZ}}\left[\left(\sigma_2\theta_{L1}w_1 - \sigma_1\theta_{L2}w_1\right) - \sigma_2\theta_{L1}w_2\right]\frac{k}{1+k}Y_1 a_L^1 Y_2 a_L^2 Y_1 a_K^1\left[\left(\theta_{LZ}S_{LK}^1 - \theta_{KZ}S_{LL}^1\right) + \left(\theta_{KZ}S_{KL}^1 - \theta_{LZ}S_{KK}^1\right)\right] \\ & + \varepsilon \frac{Z}{1+Z}\frac{k}{1+k}\frac{1}{\theta_{KZ}}(w_1 - w_2)Y_1 a_L^1 Y_2 a_L^2\left[\sigma_2\left(\theta_{L1}\theta_{KZ} - \theta_{LZ}\theta_{K1}\right) - \sigma_1\theta_{L2}\theta_{KZ}\right]Y_1 a_K^1\left(S_{LL}^1 - S_{KL}^1\right) \\ & + \varepsilon \frac{Z}{1+Z}\sigma_1 \frac{k}{1+k}\theta_{L2}Y_2 a_L^2 Y_1 a_K^1\left(S_{LL}^1 - S_{KL}^1\right)\frac{1}{\theta_{KZ}}(w_1 - w_2)Y_1 a_L^1\left[\left(\theta_{LZ}S_{LK}^1 - \theta_{KZ}S_{LL}^1\right) + \left(\theta_{KZ}S_{KL}^1 - \theta_{LZ}S_{KK}^1\right)\right] \\ & + \sigma_1 \frac{k}{1+k}\theta_{L2}Y_2 a_L^2\left(S_{LL}^1 - S_{KL}^1\right)\left\{\begin{array}{l} (w_1 - w_2)Y_1 a_L^1 Z a_K^Z + (w_1 - w_2)Y_1 a_L^1 Y_1 a_K^1 \\ +\varepsilon \frac{Z}{1+Z}\frac{1}{\theta_{KZ}}(w_1 - w_2)Y_1 a_L^1 Y_1 a_K^1\left[\left(\theta_{LZ}S_{LK}^1 - \theta_{KZ}S_{LL}^1\right) + \left(\theta_{KZ}S_{KL}^1 - \theta_{LZ}S_{KK}^1\right)\right] \\ +\varepsilon \frac{Z}{1+Z}\frac{1}{\theta_{KZ}}(w_1 - w_2)Y_1 a_L^1\left(Y_1 a_K^1 S_{LL}^Z - Z a_K^Z S_{KK}^Z\right) \end{array}\right\}. \end{aligned} \tag{5.26}$$

In view of Eqs. (5.21)–(5.26) and combining the Eqs. (5.13) and (5.14) in the sector 3.1, it is clear that the increase of the RUMs' remittances rate μ will decrease the output of the sector Z and so as to the agricultural pollution, and the increase of the RUMs' remittances rate will also decrease return rate on capital r. In addition, if the absolute value of the parameter ε is sufficiently small, it can be obtained that the increase of the RUMs' remittances rate μ will also enhance the output of the sector 1, and increase the urban unemployment rate λ. However, the effects of the change of the RUMs' remittances rate μ on the output of the sector 2 is uncertain.

References

Ball CP, Lopez C, Reyes J (2013) Remittance, inflation and exchange rate regimes in small open economies. World Econ 36(4):487–507. https://doi.org/10.1111/twec.12042

Braden JB, Larson RS, Herricks EE (1991) Impact targets versus discharge standards in agricultural pollution management. Am J Agric Econ 73(2):388. https://doi.org/10.2307/1242722

Chao CC, Laffargue JP, Sgro PM (2012) Environmental control, wage inequality and national welfare in a tourism economy. Int Rev Econ Financ 22(1):201–207. https://doi.org/10.1016/j.iref.2011.10.013

Chaudhuri S (2006) Labor market reform, welfare and urban unemployment in a small open economy. Keio Econ Stud 43(2):1–17. https://doi.org/10.2139/ssrn.929167

Chaudhuri S (2007) Foreign capital, welfare and urban unemployment in the presence of agricultural dualism. Jpn World Econ 19(2):149–165. https://doi.org/10.1016/j.japwor.2005.08.001

Copeland B, Taylor M (1999) Trade, spatial separation, and the environment. J Int Econ 47:137–168. https://doi.org/10.1016/S0022-1996(98)00020-8

Djajic S (1986) International migration, remittances and welfare in a dependent economy. J Dev Econ 21(2):229–234. https://doi.org/10.1016/0304-3878(86)90059-3

Djajic S (1998) Emigration and welfare in an economy with foreign capital. J Dev Econ 56(2): 433–445. https://doi.org/10.1016/S0304-3878(98)00073-X
Gries T, Kraft M, Simon M (2015) Explaining inter-provincial migration in China. Pap Reg Sci 95(4):709–731. https://doi.org/10.1111/pirs.12156
Grinols EL (1991) Unemployment and foreign capital: the relative opportunity costs of domestic labour and welfare. Economica 58(229):107–121. https://doi.org/10.2307/2554978
Gupta MR (1993) Rural-urban migration, informal sector and development policies: a theoretical analysis. J Dev Econ 41(1):137–151. https://doi.org/10.1016/0304-3878(93)90040-T
Gupta MR (1994) Foreign capital, income inequality and welfare in a Harris-Todaro model. J Dev Econ 45(2):407–414. https://doi.org/10.1016/0304-3878(94)90040-X
Gupta MR (1997a) Informal sector and informal capital market in a small open less-developed economy. J Dev Econ 52(2):409–428. https://doi.org/10.1016/S0304-3878(96)00445-2
Gupta MR (1997b) Foreign capital and the informal sector: comments on Chandra and Khan. Economica 64(254):353–363. https://doi.org/10.1111/1468-0335.00083
Hammer DA (1992) Designing constructed wetlands systems to treat agricultural nonpoint source pollution. Ecol Eng 1(1):49–82. https://doi.org/10.1016/0925-8574(92)90025-W
Harris J, Todaro M (1970) Migration, unemployment and development: a two-sector analysis. Am Econ Rev 60(1):126–142. https://www.jstor.org/stable/1807860
Kar S, Beladi H (2004) Skill formation and international migration: welfare perspective of developing countries. Jpn World Econ 16(1):35–54. https://doi.org/10.1016/j.japwor.2002.10.001
Kirwan F, Holden D (1986) Emigrants' remittances, non-traded goods and economic welfare in the source country. J Econ Stud 13(2):52–58. https://doi.org/10.1108/eb002623
Kondoh K, Yabuuchi S (2012) Unemployment, environmental policy, and international migration. J Int Trade Econ Dev 21(5):677–690. https://doi.org/10.1080/09638199.2010.535613
Li X, Shen Q (2012) A Study on urban private capital in the modern agriculture sector and the transfer of labour. J Econ Policy Reform, 15(02):135–152. https://doi.org/10.1080/17487870.2012.672833
Li X, Wang D (2015) The impacts of rural–urban migrants' remittances on the urban economy. Ann Reg Sci 54:591–603. https://doi.org/10.1007/s00168-015-0668-y
Li X, Wu Y (2018) Environment and economy in the modern agricultural development. Asia Pac J Account Econ 25(1–2):163–176. https://doi.org/10.1080/16081625.2016.1246191
Li X, Zhou J (2015) Environmental effects of remittance of rural–urban migrant. Econ Model 47: 174–179. https://doi.org/10.1016/j.econmod.2015.02.023
Li X, Fu H, Wu Y (2020) Pollution mitigation, unemployment rate and wage inequality in the presence of agricultural pollution. China Econ Rev 61:101425. https://doi.org/10.1016/j.chieco.2020.101425
Lundahl M (1985) International migration, remittances and real incomes: effects on the source country. Scand J Econ 87(4):647–657. https://doi.org/10.2307/3439977
Martínez Y, Albiac J (2004) Agricultural pollution control under Spanish and European environmental policies. Water Resour Res 40(10):W10501.1–W10501.12. https://doi.org/10.1029/2004WR003102
Mauricio G, Jose G (2016) Remittances: A key factor for economic change and the reduction of poverty in Latin America. The Case of Guatemala (Book). 289–305. https://doi.org/10.4018/978-1-4666-8820-9.ch014
Pradhan G, Upadhyay M, Upadhyaya K (2008) Remittances and economic growth in developing countries. Eur J Dev Res 20:497–506. https://doi.org/10.1080/09578810802246285
Quibria MG (1997) International migration, remittances and income distribution in the source country: a synthesis. Bull Econ Res 49(1):29–46. https://doi.org/10.1111/1467-8586.00025
Taheripour F, Khanna M, Nelson CH (2008) Welfare impacts of alternative public policies for agricultural pollution control in an open economy: a general equilibrium framework. Am J Agric Econ 90(3):701–718. https://doi.org/10.1111/j.1467-8276.2008.01139.x
Tawada M, Sun S (2010) Urban pollution, unemployment and national welfare in a dualistic economy. Rev Dev Econ 14:311–322. https://doi.org/10.1111/j.1467-9361.2010.00554.x

Taylor JE, Wyatt TJ (1996) The shadow value of migrant remittance, income and inequality in a household-farm economy. J Dev Stud 32(6):899–912. https://doi.org/10.1080/00220389608422445

Wu Y, Li X (2020) Rural-Urban Migrants' Remittances and Wage Inequality: evidence from China. Agric Econ (Czech), 66(3):129–139. https://doi.org/10.17221/53/2019-AGRICECON

Chapter 6
Private Mitigation, Unemployment Rate, and Wage Inequality in the Presence of Agricultural Pollution

Abstract This chapter establishes a small open general-equilibrium model to investigate the effects of changes in consumers' unit private mitigation expenditure on the unemployment rate and urban-rural wage inequality, among other factors. We find that in the capital-specific case, an increase in unit private mitigation expenditure not only increases the urban unemployment rate but also expends urban-rural wage inequality. In the capital movable case, the conclusions are exactly opposite to those of the capital-specific case. Furthermore, under certain conditions, an increase in unit private mitigation expenditure may improve national income. According to parameter calibration and numerical simulation results using relevant macroeconomic data from China in 2017, we also find that the effects of changes in unit private mitigation expenditure on the urban unemployment rate are greater than those on the urban-rural wage inequality; the degree of influence of changes in unit private mitigation expenditure on the unemployment rate in the capital movable case is greater than that in the capital-specific case, but the degree of influence of changes in unit private mitigation expenditure on urban-rural wage inequality in the capital movable case is smaller than that in the capital-specific case.

Keywords Agricultural pollution · Private mitigation · Wage inequality · Unemployment

6.1 Introduction

In developing countries, agricultural pollution has gradually replaced industrial pollution and become the primary source of pollution. Taking water pollution as an example, according to the data from China's Environmental Statistics Yearbook 2016, in 2015, the chemical oxygen demand (COD) emissions of major pollutants in wastewater reached 22.235 million tons, of which 10.685 million tons were from agricultural sources and 2.934 million tons from industrial sources. Agricultural pollution emissions were 3.64 times h0000000000igher than industrial pollution emissions. Additionally, the emission of ammonia nitrogen in wastewater was 2.299 million tons, with 0.726 million tons originating from agricultural sources and 0.215

X. Li, Y. Wu, *Research on Characteristic Issues in Current Developing Economies*, New Frontiers in Regional Science: Asian Perspectives 80,
https://doi.org/10.1007/978-981-97-7284-1_6

million tons from industrial sources, making agricultural pollution emissions 3.35 times higher than industrial pollution emissions. Agricultural pollution is mainly caused by factors that can lead to pollution in the production process (hereinafter referred to as "Z"), such as pesticides, fertilizers, agricultural films, and catalysts. It is noteworthy that the transmission path of agricultural pollution differs from industrial pollution. Copeland and Taylor (1999) have pointed out that industrial pollution damages agricultural production through media such as land, atmosphere, and water. Since then, many scholars such as Tawada and Sun (2010), Chao et al. (2012), Kondoh and Yabuuchi (2012), and Li and Wu (2018) have studied the effects of industrial pollution on the economy within this framework.

According to the data from China Environmental Statistics Yearbook 2016, the use of pesticides, plastic films, and fertilizers in China reached 1.79 million tons, 1.46 million tons, and 60.226 million tons, respectively, in 2015. Additionally, the application intensity of chemical fertilizer in China in 2015 was 361 kg/ha, which is much higher than the 225 kg/ha environmental safety application limit recognized by developed countries. It is 2.6 times that of the United States and 2.5 times that of the European Union.[1] Thus, agricultural pollution not only impacts the agricultural sector but also affects the industry and other sectors. The natural response of laborers to agricultural pollution is to repair the damage through pollution alleviating consumption.[2] This private mitigation behavior inevitably influences the urban unemployment rate and urban-rural wage inequality. When agricultural laborers' health is affected by agricultural pollution, private mitigation expenditure will influence pollution factor input, potentially affecting the value created and wage income of agricultural laborers, and thus the urban unemployment rate and urban-rural wage inequality will change.

At present, the economic theoretical research literature on environmental pollution mainly analyzes the national welfare effects of pollution reduction or control policies, such as pollution tax, pollution emission permit, and so on. Chao et al. (2000) developed a general equilibrium model to examine the optimal level of environmental preservation in terms of its costs and benefits for both closed and open economies. They found that the optimal preservation policy for a closed economy is to tax the general population and use the tax revenue to compensate affected workers; but for a small open economy, free trade in resources can meet whatever shortage of domestic productive resources that may occur, thereby leading to a higher optimal level of environmental preservation. Martínez and Albiac (2004) analyzed the effectiveness of nonpoint source pollution control policies and emission reduction measures in Spain. Their research findings questioned the reliance of the Water Framework Directive on water pricing as a pollution control instrument

[1] March 18, 2015, "Circular on the issuance of 'the Action Plan for Zero Increase in Fertilizer Use by 2020′ and 'the Action Plan for Zero Increase in Pesticide Use by 2020′," Ministry of Agriculture and Rural Affairs of the People's Republic of China, http://www.moa.gov.cn/govpublic.

[2] For analysis of consumer behavior in the presence of private mitigation, see Courant and Porter (1981), Shibata and Winrich (1983), Bartik (1988), McKitrick and Collinge (2002), and Hotte and Winer (2012).

for reaching good status for all waters because higher water prices close to full recovery cost advocated by the directive appear to be inefficient as an emission control instrument. Another important result is that abatement measures based on input taxes and standards on nitrogen appear to be more suitable than the National Irrigation Plan subsidies designed to promote irrigation investments. Taheripour et al. (2008) assessed the welfare effects of alternative policies to reduce agricultural pollution in open economies within the framework of a general equilibrium model, arguing that eliminating distortions caused by income tax and agricultural subsidies and implementing reduced nitrogen subsidies and/or export taxes could improve welfare and reduce nitrogen pollution. Chiroleu-Assouline et al. (2011) analyzed the effects of environmental pollution tax on income inequality of heterogeneous labor. Sun et al. (2012) evaluated the increases of agricultural nonpoint source (NPS) pollution in China for the period 2000–2008 by surveying the literature on water and soil pollution from fertilizers and pesticides, and assessing the surplus nitrogen balance within provinces. They found that the main causes for NPS pollution were excessive inputs of nitrogen fertilizer and pesticides, which were partly the result of inadequate agricultural extension services and the rapid expansion of intensive livestock production with little waste management, and put forward relevant policy suggestions. Baumgärtner et al. (2017) studied how the distribution of income among members of society, and income inequality in particular, affects social willingness to pay (WTP) for environmental public goods.

Additionally, some theoretical literature studies the economic effects of private pollution mitigation. Hotte and Winer (2008) studied the nature of individual demands for environmental regulation and for trade openness in the general equilibrium of a small open economy where the environment is an input to production. They found that when private mitigation is possible at a cost, trade polarizes the interests of the rich and poor with respect to the stringency of regulation. Then, Hotte and Winer (2012) further analyzed the demands by individuals of varying incomes for regulation of the environment and of trade, and the implications of these demands for equilibrium public policy choices in a small open economy producing two tradable goods, one of which is polluting, where more stringent environmental control reduces income. They believed that the differential ability of individuals to privately mitigate the consequences of domestic pollution for their health at a cost is a key characteristic of the analysis throughout. They found that when citizens can choose between mitigating the health consequences of domestic pollution privately and reducing pollution through public policy, the same polarization of interests underlies equilibrium policy choices in both democratic and autocratic regimes.

However, the economic theoretical literature studying the effects of changes in unit private mitigation expenditure on the urban unemployment rate and urban-rural wage inequality is rare and this is an inevitable issue for developing countries in their development. In fact, in the presence of agricultural pollution, private mitigation expenditure is an inevitable expenditure for laborers. If the pressure of private mitigation expenditure is high, the agricultural sector will substitute labor for agricultural pollution factors in agricultural production to decrease the pressure of private mitigation expenditure. This behavior will inevitably affect the transfer of urban-rural labor, and subsequently, the urban unemployment rate and urban-rural wage inequality. Therefore, the purpose of this chapter is to analyze the effects of changes in consumers' unit private mitigation expenditure on the urban unemployment rate and urban-rural wage inequality in the presence of agricultural pollution. To achieve these goals, we establish a three-sector general-equilibrium model, and analyze how the urban unemployment rate and urban-rural wage inequality will be affected under both conditions of capital-specific and capital movable when the expenditure of unit private mitigation changes. We found that the effects of changes in unit private mitigation expenditure on the urban unemployment rate and urban-rural wage inequality in the two cases are opposite. In the capital-specific case, an increase in unit private mitigation expenditure will not only increase the urban unemployment rate but also exacerbate urban-rural wage inequality. Conversely, in the capital movable case, the conclusions are exactly opposite to those of the capital-specific case. Additionally, under certain conditions, an increase in unit private mitigation expenditure may improve national income. Furthermore, according to the parameter calibration and numerical simulation results of the relevant macroeconomic data of China in 2017, we found that the effect of changes in unit private mitigation expenditure on the urban unemployment rate is greater than that on urban-rural wage inequality. The influence degree of changes in unit private mitigation expenditure on the unemployment rate in the capital movable case is greater than that in the capital-specific case, but the influence degree of changes in unit private mitigation expenditure on urban-rural wage inequality in the capital movable case is smaller than that in the capital-specific case. These conclusions appear for the first time in relevant theoretical research. In addition, this chapter first proposes that increasing unit private mitigation expenditure in the capital mobility case can not only decrease the urban unemployment rate and narrow urban-rural wage inequality but also enhance national income, meaning that developing countries should encourage individuals to increase unit private mitigation expenditures.

The rest of the chapter is organized as follows. We establish a basic model in Sect. 6.2. In Sect. 6.3, we analyze the effects of changes in unit private mitigation expenditure on the urban unemployment rate and urban-rural wage inequality in two cases: capital-specific and capital movable. The case where capital cannot move between sectors means that capital has sector specificity, while the case of capital movable means that capital can move between the urban industrial sector and the agricultural pollution factor sector without restriction. In Sect. 6.4, we use relevant economic data from China in 2017 to calibrate the parameters of the model. Then, we use the calibrated parameters to perform numerical simulations to examine whether the model constructed in this chapter correctly explains the impacts of changes in consumer unit private mitigation expenditure on the urban unemployment rate and urban-rural wage inequality. In Sect. 6.5, we state our conclusion.

6.2 Model

This chapter considers a small open developing economy with three sectors which are the agricultural sector, the urban industrial sector, and the agricultural pollution factor production sector. Among them, the agricultural sector employs labor L_A and agricultural pollution factor Z to produce exportable agricultural product A; the industrial sector employs labor L_M and capital K_M to produce importable industrial product M; and the agricultural pollution factor production sector utilizes labor L_Z and capital K_Z to produce agricultural pollution factor Z, which is the intermediate goods used as input in the agricultural sector. While the agricultural pollution factor is essential for agricultural production, it can also have detrimental health effects on consumers. We assume labor transfers from the agricultural sector to the urban industrial sector and the agricultural pollution factor production sector. All markets are perfectly competitive, and factor endowments are exogenously given.

In addition, this chapter defines h as the effect of the agricultural pollution factor on human capital in agricultural production. The specific form of h is as follows:

$$h = Z^{\varepsilon}, \tag{6.1}$$

where the parameter ε is in the range of $[-1, 0]$.

Under the condition of perfectly competitive markets and according to the zero-profit conditions, we obtain the following equations:

$$ha_L^A w + P_Z a_Z^A = 1, \tag{6.2}$$

$$ha_L^M \overline{w} + r_M a_K^M = P_M, \tag{6.3}$$

$$ha_L^Z \overline{w} + r_Z a_K^Z = P_Z, \tag{6.4}$$

where a_{ij} ($i = L, K, Z$; $j = A, M, Z$) is the amount of the i-th factor used in the j-th sector to produce a unit of output such as $a_L^A = hL_A/A$, $a_Z^A = Z/A$, $a_L^M = hL_M/M$, $a_K^Z = K_Z/Z$; P_M and P_Z are the relative prices of industrial sector and agricultural pollution factor production sector products to agricultural products, respectively, and are determined by the world market, thus exogenous in this chapter's model; r_M and r_Z indicate the interest rates in the industrial sector and the pollution factor production sector, respectively. Due to minimum wage laws and other factors, the wages of unit labor in the urban industrial sector and the pollution factor production sector are given as $\overline{w}$, while the wage of unit labor in the agricultural sector is flexible and recorded as w.

Agricultural pollution damages people's health, where $(1-h)\ L_A$ indicates the total labor capacity lost in the agricultural sector. μ represents the unit private mitigation expenditure of labor, so $\mu(1-h)\ L_A$ is the gross expenditure of rural labors' pollution alleviates. If the pollution factor income $P_Z\ Z$ is greater than the total expenditure of rural labors' private mitigation, the agricultural sector will continue to increase the use of the agricultural pollution factor; if $P_Z\ Z$ is less than the total expenditure, the agricultural sector will reduce the input of the agricultural pollution factor. In equilibrium, the following condition is established:

$$P_Z Z = \frac{\mu(1-h)}{h} A a_L^A. \tag{6.5}$$

We define L_U as the unemployment in the industrial sector and the pollution factor production sector and λ as the unemployment rate of labor in the two sectors, hence $\lambda = L_U / \left(M a_L^M + Z a_L^Z\right)$. Considering agricultural pollution, the actual effective wages in rural and urban sectors are hw and $h\overline{w}$, respectively. Because the sizes of h in rural and urban sectors are equal, the unit labor wage level remains the basis of labor transfer. Thus, the allocation mechanism based on the Harris and Todaro (1970) model can be expressed as

$$\overline{w} = (1+\lambda)w. \tag{6.6}$$

Let L be the endowment of labor, the market clearing condition of labor can be expressed as

$$\left(M a_L^M + Z a_L^Z\right)(1+\lambda) + A a_L^A = hL. \tag{6.7}$$

In the capital-specific case, the capital input in the industrial sector and the agricultural pollution factor production sector are defined as K_M and K_Z, respectively. Therefore, the capital market clearing conditions are

$$M a_K^M = K_M, \tag{6.8}$$

$$Z a_K^Z = K_Z. \tag{6.9}$$

Since capital flows freely between the industrial sector and the pollution factor production sector in the capital movable case, equation $r_M = r_Z = r$ holds, and Eqs. (6.3) and (6.4) can be rewritten as

$$h a_L^M \overline{w} + r a_L^M = P_M, \tag{6.3*}$$

$$h a_L^Z \overline{w} + r a_K^Z = p_Z. \tag{6.4*}$$

And, the capital market-clearing condition is as follows:

$$M a_K^M + Z a_K^Z = K, \tag{6.10}$$

where K is the endowment of capital in the economy, with $K = K_M + K_Z$.

At this point, the model of this chapter is built. Among them, Eqs. (6.1)–(6.9) are models of the capital-specific case, with nine endogenous variables h, w, λ, P_Z, A, M, Z, r_M, and r_Z and six exogenous variables $\overline{w}$, P_M, μ, K_M, K_Z, and L. Eqs. (6.1), (6.2),

(6.3*), (6.4*), (6.5)–(6.7), and (6.10) are models of the capital movable case with eight endogenous variables h, w, λ, P_Z, A, M, Z, and r and five exogenous variables $\overline{w}$, P_M, μ, K, and L.

6.3 Comparative Static Analysis

6.3.1 Capital-Specific Case

Equations (6.1)–(6.9) fully describe the short-term behavior of the economic entity, so differentiating Eqs. (6.1)–(6.9) can yield the following matrix equation:

$$\begin{bmatrix} 0 & 0 & \varepsilon\theta_{LA} & \theta_{LA} & 0 & 0 & \theta_{ZA} & 0 \\ 0 & 0 & \varepsilon\theta_{LM} & 0 & \theta_{KM} & 0 & 0 & 0 \\ 0 & 0 & \varepsilon\theta_{LZ} & 0 & 0 & \theta_{KZ} & -1 & 0 \\ -1 & 0 & 1-\varepsilon S_{LL}^{A}+\frac{\varepsilon}{1-h} & -S_{LL}^{A} & 0 & 0 & 1-S_{LZ}^{A} & 0 \\ 0 & 0 & 0 & 1+\lambda & 0 & 0 & 0 & \lambda \\ Aa_L^A & (1+\lambda)Ma_L^M & B & Aa_L^A S_{LL}^A & (1+\lambda)Ma_L^M S_{LK}^M & (1+\lambda)Za_L^Z S_{LK}^Z & Aa_L^A S_{LZ}^A & \lambda\left(Ma_L^M+Za_L^Z\right) \\ 0 & 1 & \varepsilon S_{KL}^{M} & 0 & S_{KK}^{M} & 0 & 0 & 0 \\ 0 & 0 & 1+\varepsilon S_{KL}^{Z} & 0 & 0 & S_{KK}^{Z} & 0 & 0 \end{bmatrix} \begin{bmatrix} \widehat{A} \\ \widehat{M} \\ \widehat{Z} \\ \widehat{w} \\ \widehat{r}_M \\ \widehat{r}_Z \\ \widehat{P}_Z \\ \widehat{\lambda} \end{bmatrix} = \begin{bmatrix} 0 \\ 0 \\ 0 \\ 1 \\ 0 \\ 0 \\ 0 \\ 0 \end{bmatrix} \widehat{\mu}. \tag{6.11}$$

Among them $B = (1+\lambda)Za_L^Z + (1+\lambda)\varepsilon\left(Ma_L^M S_{LL}^M + Za_L^Z S_{LL}^Z\right) + \varepsilon Aa_L^A S_{LL}^A - \varepsilon\left[(1+\lambda)\left(Ma_L^M + Za_L^Z\right) + Aa_L^A\right] > 0$; "^" indicates the rate of change of the variables, so $\widehat{w}$, $\widehat{p}_Z$, $\widehat{r}_M$, $\widehat{r}_Z$, $\widehat{A}$, $\widehat{M}$, $\widehat{Z}$, $\widehat{\lambda}$, and $\widehat{\mu}$ are the rate of change of related variables; θ_{ij} $(i = L, K, Z; j = A, M, Z)$ indicates the distributive share of the i-th input in the j-th sector, and the form of θ_{ij} are as follows: $\theta_{LA} = hwhL_A/A$; $\theta_{LZ} = P_Z Z/A$; $\theta_{LM} = h\overline{w}hL_M/P_M M$; $\theta_{KM} = r_M K_M/P_M M$; $\theta_{LZ} = h\overline{w}hL_Z/P_Z Z$; $\theta_{KZ} = r_Z K_Z/P_Z Z$; S_{ij} $(i = L, K, Z; j = A, M, Z)$ measures the substitution elasticity between elements i in department j, such as $S_{LL}^A = \left(\partial a_L^A/\partial hw\right)\left(hw/a_L^A\right) < 0$, $S_{LK}^M = \left(\partial a_L^M/\partial r_M\right)\left(r_M/a_L^M\right) > 0$, and, similarly, $S_{KK}^M < 0$, $S_{KK}^Z < 0$, $S_{LZ}^A > 0$, $S_{LK}^Z > 0$.

Define the determinant of the coefficient matrix in Eq. (6.11) as Δ and we obtain $\Delta < 0$ by stability (please refer to Appendix 1 for the details of the calculation). Solving Eq. (6.11) by using Cramer's rule, we can get Table 6.1 as follows (please refer to the Appendix 2 for details of the calculation procedure):

Summarizing the results in Table 6.1, we arrive at the following proposition.

Proposition 1 *In the capital-specific case, the increase of per unit private mitigation expenditure will increase the urban unemployment rate λ and expand the urban-rural wage inequality.*

The increase of μ alleviates the negative effect of using pollution factor Z in the agricultural sector on labor, which makes the agricultural sector willing to use pollution factor Z instead of labor and then reduce the demand for labor. Thus, the

Table 6.1 Summary of results in the capital-specific case

	$\widehat{A}$	$\widehat{M}$	$\widehat{Z}$	$\widehat{r}_M$	$\widehat{r}_Z$	$\widehat{P}_Z$	$\widehat{w}$	$\widehat{\lambda}$	$\widehat{\overline{w}} - \widehat{w}$
$\widehat{\mu}$	–	+	+	+	+	+	–	+	+

Note: Symbols "+" and "–" indicate that the change of remittance rate Mu has the same and opposite effects on the corresponding variables, respectively

labor demand curve of the agricultural sector tends to move to the left, which leads to the decrease of wage w in the agricultural sector and the expansion of the urban-rural wage inequality. But the effect of the increase of unit private mitigation expenditure on the output of the agricultural sector is ambiguous. In addition, the increase of demand for pollution factor Z in agricultural sector will promote the expansion of production scale of the sector Z, thus increasing the demand for labor and capital in the sector Z, so r_Z will rise; because of the widening of the urban-rural wage inequality, the attraction of the urban sectors to the rural labor will be enhanced, the labors in sector A tend to shift to sector M and sector Z. The result of this trend is that sector M and sector Z more likely increase labor employment and thus output. In addition, part of the labor transferred from the industrial sector joins the unemployed, and the urban unemployment rate λ rises.

6.3.2 *Capital Movable Case*

At beginning, to simplify the analysis, we make the following assumption.

Assumption 1 *The* per capital *of urban industrial sector M is equal to that of the pollution factor production sector Z, that is, the equality* $Ma_K^M/Ma_L^M = Ma_K^Z/Ma_L^Z$ *is hold.*

Differentiating Eqs. (6.1), (6.2), (6.3*), (6.4*), (6.5)–(6.7), and (6.10) can yield the following matrix equation:

$$\begin{bmatrix} 0 & 0 & \varepsilon\theta_{LA} & \theta_{LA} & 0 & \theta_{ZA} & 0 \\ 0 & 0 & \varepsilon\theta_{LM} & 0 & \theta_{KM} & 0 & 0 \\ 0 & 0 & \varepsilon\theta_{LZ} & 0 & \theta_{KZ} & -1 & 0 \\ -1 & 0 & 1-\varepsilon S_{LL}^A + \dfrac{\varepsilon}{1-h} & -S_{LL}^A & 0 & 1-S_{LZ}^A & 0 \\ 0 & 0 & 0 & 1+\lambda & 0 & 0 & \lambda \\ Aa_L^A & (1+\lambda)Ma_L^M & B & Aa_L^A S_{LL}^A & C & Aa_L^A S_{LZ}^A & \lambda(Ma_L^M + Za_L^Z) \\ 0 & Ma_K^M & F & 0 & G & 0 & 0 \end{bmatrix} \begin{bmatrix} \widehat{A} \\ \widehat{M} \\ \widehat{Z} \\ \widehat{w} \\ \widehat{r} \\ \widehat{P}_Z \\ \widehat{\lambda} \end{bmatrix} = \begin{bmatrix} 0 \\ 0 \\ 0 \\ 1 \\ 0 \\ 0 \\ 0 \end{bmatrix} \widehat{\mu}. \qquad (6.12)$$

where $C = (1+\lambda)\left(Ma_L^M S_{LK}^M + Za_L^Z S_{LK}^Z\right) > 0$, $F = Za_K^Z + \varepsilon\left(Ma_K^M S_{KL}^M + Za_K^Z S_{KL}^Z\right)$, $G = Ma_K^M S_{KK}^M + Za_K^Z S_{KK}^Z < 0$.

Define the determinant of the coefficient matrix in Eq. (6.12) as Ω and we obtain $\Omega > 0$ by stability (please refer to Appendix 3 for the details of the calculation).

Table 6.2 Summary of results in the capital mobility case

	$\widehat{A}$	$\widehat{M}$	$\widehat{Z}$	$\widehat{r}$	$\widehat{P_Z}$	$\widehat{w}$	$\widehat{\lambda}$	$\widehat{\overline{w}} - \widehat{w}$
$\widehat{\mu}$	−	−	+	+	−	+	−	−

Note: Symbols "+" and "−" indicate that the change of remittance rate μ has the same and opposite effects on the corresponding variables, respectively

Solving Eq. (6.12) by using Cramer's rule, we can get Table 6.2 as follows (please refer to the Appendix 4 for details of the calculation procedure):

Summarizing the results in Table 6.2, we arrive at the Proposition 2:

Proposition 2 *In the capital movable case, the increase of the unit private mitigation expenditure μ will narrow the urban-rural wage inequality and reduce the urban unemployment rate λ.*

As for the changes of the urban unemployment rate and the urban-rural wage inequality, the conclusion of Proposition 2 is contrary to that of Proposition 1. The main reason is that Proposition 2 is obtained under the condition of capital movable, while Proposition 1 is obtained under the condition of capital-specific used in the sector M and the sector Z. The rise of μ makes the agricultural sector may willing to use pollution factor Z instead of labor and the increased in the demand for the pollution factor Z in the agricultural sector increased, and the sector Z may employ more capital and labor to increase production, so the interest rate r rises. The interaction between the increasing in the demand of the pollution factor Z in the agricultural sector and the increasing supply of the sector Z may result in the price P_Z unchanged.

In addition, the increasing in the demand for the pollution factor Z in the agricultural sector not only replace some labor and then reduce the labor use in the agricultural sector, but also decrease h, which will decrease the output of the agricultural sector A and increase the wage of the agricultural sector A and then narrow the urban-rural wage inequality. In the labor market, the labor released by the agricultural sector will increase unemployment; but the rise in the capital interest rate r tends to make the sector M and the sector Z use more labor to replace capital, and the increasing in the demand for the pollution factor Z also decrease h, the sector M and the sector Z will also employ more labor to maintain the stability of production, so that the urban unemployment rate λ is more likely to decrease.

6.3.3 National Welfare Analysis

We now turn our attention to the national welfare effect of the change of private mitigation expenditure of consumers on the basis of the analysis in the previous section. Because this chapter considers a small open economy with dual economic characteristics, the price of agricultural and industrial products is exogenously given.

According to the nature of indirect effect function $v(P_M, Y)$, where Y is defined as national income. The effect level of representative consumers is related to the income level and the price of products, because the prices of products in the agricultural sector and the industry sector are given, then the higher the income level, the higher the effect level. Hence, to investigate the effect of the change of private mitigation expenditure of consumers on national welfare, we simply focus on the national income. Moreover, since private mitigation expenditure is an inevitable passive consumption of consumers, this part of expenditure should be deducted from national income, so the national income equation for welfare analysis in this chapter is denoted as $Y = h^2wL + rK - \mu(1-h)L$. And then we can get (please refer to the Appendix 5 for details of the calculation procedure)

$$\frac{\widehat{Y}}{\widehat{\mu}} = \frac{\lambda\varepsilon A a_L^A M a_K^M}{Y\widehat{\mu}}\{[(2hw+\mu)\theta_{ZA}\theta_{KM} - hw\theta_{LA}\theta_{KM}]hL - \theta_{LM}\theta_{ZA}rK\}.$$

In the mobile capital case, if $K/L > k_0$, ($k_0 = h\theta_{KM}[(2hw + \mu) - hw\theta_{LA}/\theta_{ZA}]/r\theta_{LM}$) is hold, we can yield $\widehat{Y}/\widehat{\mu} > 0$. Therefore, in the mobile capital case, the increase of private mitigation expenditure will increase national income and improve national welfare. Generally speaking, the increase of passive consumption expenditure will reduce the utility of consumers, but we find that under certain conditions, the increase of passive private mitigation expenditure will increase national income and improve national welfare. This is because the increase of private mitigation expenditure has the effects of improving effective labor and increasing output. Then, we can find that private mitigation should be encouraged in the case of capital mobility, because this can not only narrow the urban-rural wage inequality and decrease the urban unemployment rate, but also improve national income and improve national welfare if the per capita capital of the whole society reaches a certain level (e.g., $K/L > k_0$).

6.4 Parameter Calibration, Estimation, and Numerical Simulation

6.4.1 *Calibration and Estimation of Parameters*

The above theoretical model analysis gives the influence direction of private mitigation expenditure changes on the urban unemployment rate and the urban-rural wage inequality. In this section, we will investigate the numerical characteristics of the theoretical model about the effects of the change of consumers' unit private mitigation expenditure on the urban unemployment rate and the urban-rural wage inequality, therefore this section first calibrates the parameters of the model with the relevant macroeconomic data of China in 2017, then simulates the model based on the calibrated parameters, and finally conducts sensitivity analysis to test the robustness of the numerical simulation results.

We set up the production functions of three sectors as a Cobb-Douglas form:

$$A = (hL_A)^{\alpha_1} Z^{\alpha_2},$$

$$M = (hL_M)^{\beta_1} K_M^{\beta_2},$$

$$Z = (hL_Z)^{\gamma_1} K_Z^{\gamma_2},$$

where, α_1, α_2, β_1, β_2, γ_2, and γ_1 are the respective output elasticities of associated factors in the three departments. The above parameters satisfy the properties $\alpha_1 + \alpha_2 = 1, \beta_1 + \beta_2 = 1, \gamma_1 + \gamma_2 = 1$, h is the external effect function of agricultural pollution factors on labor force, and according to the previous model, we assume the specific form is $h = Z^{\varepsilon}$, $\varepsilon \in (-1, 0)$ indicates the externality parameter of the pollution factor.

Based on three strata of industry in the China Statistical Yearbook (2017) issued by the National Bureau of Statistics of China, we take the primary industry as the rural agricultural sector in this chapter, take the pesticide, fertilizer industries, etc. as the agricultural pollution sector, and the remaining sectors in secondary and tertiary industries are regarded as the urban industry sector.

In the primary industry, the value-added was 6209.95 billion yuan, the number of employed labors was 209.44 million, and the per capita disposable income of rural households was 13,432 yuan, which is defined as the effective labor wage level hw of the rural agricultural sector, thus the nominal wage w of unit labor in the rural agricultural sector is 15,802.35 yuan. We can then calculate the output elasticity in the rural agricultural sector.

The agricultural pollution factor production sector defined in this chapter mainly includes the factors input in the agricultural production process, which will have adverse effects on human health, water resources, and soil, namely, pesticides, fertilizers, agricultural film, and so on. In view of the availability of data, this chapter takes the data of value-added of industries, employment, and wages of relevant departments in China Statistical Yearbook (2017) as well as the data of pesticide and fertilizer industries in Chinese industry Statistical Yearbook (2017) as raw data to estimate the factor output elasticity of agricultural pollution factor Z department. The calculation logics are as follows: we first calculated the proportion of sales output value of pesticide and chemical fertilizer industry to total sales output value of industrial departments in 2017, and then multiply this ratio by the employment number of the industrial sector in 2017 as the estimated data of the employment number of the pesticide and chemical fertilizer industry, which is about 1.948 million. At the same time, multiplying the ratio of industrial value-added to industrial sales output value by the sales output value of pesticide and chemical fertilizer industry as the estimated data of the value-added of pesticide and chemical fertilizer industry, which is about 297.08 billion yuan. Combining the two estimated data above with the average wage of urban employees in 2017, we can estimate the factor output elasticity of the agricultural pollution factor production sector. In addition, according to the factor output elasticity of the agricultural sector, the value-added of primary industry and the number of employees in the primary industry in 2017, we also can calculate the usage quantity of pollution factor Z in sector A, and then estimate the labor input in sector Z based on the estimated output elasticity of factor Z in the sector A.

In 2017, the value-added of China's secondary and tertiary industries was 33,274.27 billion yuan and 42,591.21 billion yuan, respectively, and the number of employed labors in secondary and tertiary industries was 218.24 million and 348.72 million, respectively. This chapter takes the value-added of the secondary and tertiary industries and the number of employed persons minus the value-added of sector Z and the number of employed persons, respectively, as the basic data of sector M, while the average employment wage of urban units in 2017 was 74,318 yuan, which is defined as the effective labor wage level $h\overline{w}$ of sector M, thus the nominal wage $\overline{w}$ of unit labor in sector M is 87,432.94 yuan, and then the factor output elasticity of factors in sector M can be obtained.

As for the capital price, according to benchmark one-to-five-year lending rate announced by China's central bank in 2017, it could represent as 6.75%. Generally speaking, the added value of agricultural products is lower than that of industrial products. Therefore, from the perspective of capital for profit, the prospects of comprehensive investment in agricultural pollution factor input sector are lower than that of urban industrial sector. In addition, compared with the urban industrial sector, agricultural pollution factor production sector is generally smaller in scale, capital is relatively scarce, and the financing conditions of agricultural pollution factor sector are comparable to those of industrial sector. For difficulties, the capital price of agricultural pollution factor department is higher than that of industrial sector M, which is also more in line with the reality of China. Therefore, it is reasonable to consider that the interest rate in the sector Z is higher than that of sector M, which is setting as $1.5 * 6.75\% = 10.125\%$. At the same time, the initial assignment value of h is 0.85, and the calibration value of parameters is calculated based on this.

In addition, following the model set in the previous article, the price of sector A product is set to 1, and the relative price of sector M and sector Z product is compared with that of sector A product, respectively.

Based on the above economic data, in the capital-specific case we first calibrated the parameters of the factor output elasticity of each sector, the unit private mitigation expenditure μ, and the effect of the agricultural pollution factor on human capital ε. The results are shown in Table 6.3.

For the capital movable case, the main difference to the capital-specific case is that the equilibrium capital prices of each department are equal when the capital market is cleared. Therefore, when calibrating the capital movable situation, the interest rates of sector M and sector Z is set as 6.75%. But the calibration results of the relevant parameters are same to the capital-specific case which are also shown in Table 6.3.

Table 6.3 The results of the calibration of the parameters

Parameter	α_1	α_2	β_1	β_2	γ_2	γ_1	μ	ε
Calibration value	0.385	0.615	0.559	0.441	0.487	0.513	12.155	−0.014

Table 6.4 The numerical simulation results in the capital-specific case

	λ_i (%)	$\lambda_i - \lambda_0$	$CR\lambda_i$	w_i	$w_i - w_0$	$\overline{w} - w_0$	$CRWI_i$
1.00 μ	5.4947	0	0	15,788.375	0	71,644.566	0
1.01 μ	5.4950	0.0003	0.0055	15,788.344	−0.031	71,644.566	0.000043
1.02 μ	5.4953	0.0006	0.0109	15,788.314	−0.061	71,644.566	0.000085
1.03 μ	5.4956	0.0009	0.0164	15,788.285	−0.09	71,644.566	0.000126
1.04 μ	5.4958	0.0011	0.0200	15,788.256	−0.119	71,644.566	0.000166
1.05 μ	5.4961	0.0014	0.0255	15,788.228	−0.147	71,644.566	0.000205
1.06 μ	5.4964	0.0017	0.0309	15,788.200	−0.175	71,644.566	0.000244
1.07 μ	5.4966	0.0019	0.0346	15,788.173	−0.202	71,644.566	0.000282
1.08 μ	5.4969	0.0022	0.0400	15,788.146	−0.229	71,644.566	0.000320
1.09 μ	5.4972	0.0025	0.0455	15,788.120	−0.255	71,644.566	0.000356
1.10 μ	5.4974	0.0027	0.0491	15,788.095	−0.280	71,644.566	0.000391

Note: 1. The subscript ordinal "i"($i = 0, 1, 2, \ldots 10.$) indicates the corresponding variable value when the percentage increase rate of parameter μ is "i". For example, λ_o and λ_2 represent the corresponding value of variable λ when the value of parameter μ increases by 0% and 2%, respectively. And the variables with a subscript as zero means the benchmark variables

2. "$CR\lambda_i$" means the percentage change rate of λ, and $CR\lambda_i = \frac{(\lambda_i - \lambda_0)^*}{\lambda_0} 100\%$

3. "$CRWI_i$" means the percentage change rate of the wage inequality, and $CRWI_i = \frac{(w_i - w_0)^*}{(\overline{w} - w_0)} 100\%$

6.4.2 Numerical Simulation

In this section, we will use the parameters, which were calibrated based on the China's macroeconomic data in 2017, to conduct numerical simulation and investigate the numerical characteristics of the theoretical model about the effects of unit private mitigation expenditure on the urban unemployment rate and the urban-rural wage inequality. At the same time, in the end of this section, we will simulate the effect of the change of unit private mitigation expenditure on national income in the capital movable case.

Capital-Specific Case

The numerical simulation results in the capital-specific case are shown in Table 6.4. Table 6.4 shows the numerical characteristics of the effects of the change of unit private mitigation expenditure on urban unemployment rate and urban-rural wage inequality, which calibrated and simulated by the relevant macroeconomic data of China in 2017. In capital-specific situation, the increase of unit private mitigation expenditure will not only increase the urban unemployment rate and deteriorate the employment environment of workers in urban areas, but also reduce the wage level in the agricultural sector, thus widening the urban-rural wage inequality. This trend is consistent with the conclusion of Proposition 1 in Sect. 6.3.1. As can be seen from the data in column 4 of Table 6.4, if the growth rate of unit private mitigation expenditure μ increases from 1% to 10% in the capital-specific case, it will increase the urban unemployment rate by 0.0055% to 0.0491%, respectively. And the data in column 8 of Table 6.4 shows that if the growth rate of parameter μ increases from 1% to 10% in the specific capital case, it will lead to the expand of the urban-rural wage inequality by 0.000043% to 0.000391%, respectively. Moreover, we can find that in the specific capital case the effect of the changes of unit private mitigation expenditure on urban-rural wage inequality is far less than that of the urban unemployment rate by comparing the data in columns 4 and 8 of Table 6.4.

Capital Mobility Case

The numerical simulation results of the model in the capital mobility case are shown in Table 6.5.

Table 6.5 shows the numerical characteristics of the impact of the change of unit private mitigation expenditure on urban unemployment rate and urban-rural wage inequality, which calibrated and simulated by the relevant macroeconomic data of China in 2017. The increase of per unit private mitigation expenditure in the capital mobility case will not only reduce urban unemployment rate, but also increase wage level of agricultural sector, thus narrowing the urban-rural wage inequality. This changing trend is just contrary to the conclusion in the capital-specific case. As can be seen from the data in column 4 of Table 6.5, if the growth rate of unit private mitigation expenditure μ increases from 1% to 10% in the capital movable case, it will decrease the urban unemployment rate by 2.280,4% to 24.831,0%, respectively.

Table 6.5 The numerical simulation results in the capital movable case

	λ_i (%)	$\lambda_i - \lambda_0$	$CR\lambda_i$	w_i	$w_i - w_0$	$\overline{w} - w_0$	$CRWI_i$
1.00 μ	4.7054	0	0	15,767.175	0	71,665.766	0
1.01 μ	4.5981	−0.1073	−2.2804	15,767.180	0.005	71,665.766	−0.000007
1.02 μ	4.4888	−0.2166	−4.6032	15,767.184	0.009	71,665.766	−0.000013
1.03 μ	4.3775	−0.3279	−6.9686	15,767.189	0.014	71,665.766	−0.000020
1.04 μ	4.2641	−0.4413	−9.3786	15,767.194	0.019	71,665.766	−0.000027
1.05 μ	4.1486	−0.5568	−11.8332	15,767.200	0.025	71,665.766	−0.000035
1.06 μ	4.0309	−0.6745	−14.3346	15,767.205	0.030	71,665.766	−0.000042
1.07 μ	3.9110	−0.7944	−16.8827	15,767.210	0.035	71,665.766	−0.000049
1.08 μ	3.7887	−0.9167	−19.4819	15,767.216	0.041	71,665.766	−0.000057
1.09 μ	3.6641	−1.0413	−22.1299	15,767.222	0.047	71,665.766	−0.000066
1.10 μ	3.5370	−1.1684	−24.8310	15,767.227	0.052	71,665.766	−0.000073

Note: Here "*i*" has the same meaning as "*i*" in Table 6.4

And the data in column 8 of Table 6.5 shows that if the growth rate of parameter μ increases from 1% to 10% in the capital movable case, it will lead to narrowing of the urban-rural wage inequality by 0.000007% to 0.000073%, respectively. Moreover, we can find that the effect of the changes of the parameter μ on urban-rural wage inequality is also far less than that of urban unemployment rate by comparing the data in columns 4 and 8 of Table 6.5.

In general, the model of capital-specific case is more in line with the short-term economic situation, and the model of capital mobility case is more in line with the long-term situation. Thus, we can get Proposition 3 by comparing the numerical simulation results of columns 4 and 8 in Table 6.4 and Table 6.5.

Proposition 3 *According to the parameter calibration and numerical simulation results of the relevant macroeconomic data of China in 2017, two conclusions can be obtained as follows:*

- *The effect of the change of unit private mitigation expenditure on the urban unemployment rate is greater than that of the urban-rural wage inequality.*
- *The influence degree of the change of unit private mitigation expenditure on the unemployment rate in the capital movable case is greater than that of the capital-specific case, but the influence degree of the change of unit private mitigation expenditure on the urban-rural wage inequality in the capital movable case is smaller than that of the capital-specific case.*

Sensitivity Test

In this section, we will examine whether different initial values of the effects of agricultural pollution on human capital will affect the conclusions of this chapter and the numerical characteristics of the impact of private mitigation expenditure on urban unemployment rate and urban-rural wage inequality. In the benchmark model, the initial value of human capital effect of agricultural pollution is $h_0 = 0.85$ and the calibration value of the parameters ε is -0.014. Because the above initial assignment has certain subjectivity, we will select $\varepsilon = -0.012$ and $\varepsilon = -0.016$, respectively, and make numerical simulation by the same method to investigate the numerical characteristics of the effects of unit private mitigation expenditure on urban unemployment rate and urban-rural wage inequality. The results of the re-simulation of the model under two kinds of capital liquidity between sectors are shown in Tables 6.6, 6.7, 6.8 and 6.9.

According to the numerical simulation results of Tables 6.6, 6.7, 6.8 and 6.9, we can find that the different initial values of the parameters ε will not have a substantial impact on the conclusions and numerical characteristics of this chapter, which fully shows that the numerical simulation results and model conclusions of Proposition 3 is stable.

Table 6.6 The numerical simulation results in the capital-specific case while $\varepsilon = -0.016$

	λ_i (%)	$\lambda_i - \lambda_0$	$CR\lambda_i$	w_i	$w_i - w_0$	$\overline{w} - w_0$	CRWI_i
1.00 μ	5.4925	0	0	16,072.225	0	72,931.368	0
1.01 μ	5.4928	0.0003	0.0055	16,072.196	−0.029	72,931.368	0.000040
1.02 μ	5.4931	0.0006	0.0109	16,072.167	−0.058	72,931.368	0.000080
1.03 μ	5.4933	0.0008	0.0146	16,072.139	−0.086	72,931.368	0.000118
1.04 μ	5.4936	0.0011	0.0200	16,072.111	−0.114	72,931.368	0.000156
1.05 μ	5.4939	0.0014	0.0255	16,072.085	−0.140	72,931.368	0.000192
1.06 μ	5.4941	0.0016	0.0291	16,072.058	−0.167	72,931.368	0.000229
1.07 μ	5.4944	0.0019	0.0346	16,072.033	−0.192	72,931.368	0.000263
1.08 μ	5.4946	0.0021	0.0382	16,072.008	−0.217	72,931.368	0.000298
1.09 μ	5.4948	0.0023	0.0419	16,071.983	−0.242	72,931.368	0.000332
1.1 μ	5.4951	0.0026	0.0473	16,071.959	−0.266	72,931.368	0.000365

Note: Here "*i*" has the same meaning as "*i*" in Table 6.4

Table 6.7 The numerical simulation results in the capital movable case while $\varepsilon = -0.016$

	λ_i (%)	$\lambda_i - \lambda_0$	$CR\lambda_i$	w_i	$w_i - w_0$	$\overline{w} - w_0$	CRWI_i
1.00 μ	4.8373	0	0	16,051.372	0	72,952.221	0
1.01 μ	4.7322	−0.1051	−2.1727	16,051.373	0.001	72,952.221	−0.0000014
1.02 μ	4.6252	−0.2121	−4.3847	16,051.375	0.003	72,952.221	−0.0000041
1.03 μ	4.5163	−0.3210	−6.6359	16,051.377	0.005	72,952.221	−0.0000069
1.04 μ	4.4054	−0.4319	−8.9285	16,051.379	0.007	72,952.221	−0.0000096
1.05 μ	4.2924	−0.5449	−11.2645	16,051.381	0.009	72,952.221	−0.0000123
1.06 μ	4.1774	−0.6599	−13.6419	16,051.383	0.011	72,952.221	−0.0000151
1.07 μ	4.0602	−0.7771	−16.0647	16,051.385	0.013	72,952.221	−0.0000178
1.08 μ	3.9407	−0.8966	−18.5351	16,051.388	0.016	72,952.221	−0.0000219
1.09 μ	3.8190	−1.0183	−21.0510	16,051.39	0.018	72,952.221	−0.0000247
1.10 μ	3.6950	−1.1423	−23.6144	16,051.393	0.021	72,952.221	−0.0000288

Note: Here "*i*" has the same meaning as "*i*" in Table 6.4

National Welfare Effect

The numerical characteristics of the effect of unit private mitigation expenditure on national income in the capital movable case are shown in Table 6.10. And the results of the re-simulation of the model which based on the different initial values of the parameter ε are shown in Tables 6.11 and 6.12.

According to the numerical simulation results of Table 6.10, we can find that in the capital movable case the increase of unit private mitigation expenditure will not only decrease the urban unemployment rate and narrow the urban-rural wage inequality, but also enhance the national income. In addition, according to the

Table 6.8 The numerical simulation results in the capital-specific case while $\varepsilon = -0.012$

	λ_i (%)	$\lambda_i - \lambda_0$	$CR\lambda_i$	w_i	$w_i - w_0$	$\overline{w} - w_0$	CRWI$_i$
1.00 μ	5.4981	0	0	15,372.082	0	69,757.357	0
1.01 μ	5.4984	0.0003	0.0055	15,372.050	−0.032	69,757.357	0.000046
1.02 μ	5.4987	0.0006	0.0109	15,372.018	−0.064	69,757.357	0.000092
1.03 μ	5.4990	0.0009	0.0164	15,371.987	−0.095	69,757.357	0.000136
1.04 μ	5.4993	0.0012	0.0218	15,371.957	−0.125	69,757.357	0.000179
1.05 μ	5.4996	0.0015	0.0273	15,371.927	−0.155	69,757.357	0.000222
1.06 μ	5.4999	0.0018	0.0327	15,371.898	−0.184	69,757.357	0.000264
1.07 μ	5.5002	0.0021	0.0382	15,371.869	−0.213	69,757.357	0.000305
1.08 μ	5.5004	0.0023	0.0418	15,371.840	−0.242	69,757.357	0.000347
1.09 μ	5.5007	0.0026	0.0473	15,371.813	−0.269	69,757.357	0.000386
1.10 μ	5.5010	0.0029	0.0527	15,371.785	−0.297	69,757.357	0.000426

Note: Here "*i*" has the same meaning as "*i*" in Table 6.4

Table 6.9 The numerical simulation results in the capital movable case while$\varepsilon = -0.012$

	λ_i (%)	$\lambda_i - \lambda_0$	$CR\lambda_i$	w_i	$w_i - w_0$	$\overline{w} - w_0$	CRWI$_i$
1.00 μ	4.5089	0	0	15,350.432	0	69,779.007	0
1.01 μ	4.3981	−0.1108	−2.4574	15,350.441	0.009	69,779.007	−0.000013
1.02 μ	4.2852	−0.2237	−4.9613	15,350.450	0.018	69,779.007	−0.000026
1.03 μ	4.1702	−0.3387	−7.5118	15,350.459	0.027	69,779.007	−0.000039
1.04 μ	4.0530	−0.4559	−10.1111	15,350.468	0.036	69,779.007	−0.000052
1.05 μ	3.9335	−0.5754	−12.7614	15,350.478	0.046	69,779.007	−0.000066
1.06 μ	3.8116	−0.6973	−15.4650	15,350.487	0.055	69,779.007	−0.000079
1.07 μ	3.6874	−0.8215	−18.2195	15,350.497	0.065	69,779.007	−0.000093
1.08 μ	3.5607	−0.9482	−21.0295	15,350.507	0.075	69,779.007	−0.000107
1.09 μ	3.4315	−1.0774	−23.8950	15,350.516	0.084	69,779.007	−0.000120
1.10 μ	3.2996	−1.2093	−26.8203	15,350.526	0.094	69,779.007	−0.000135

Note: Here "*i*" has the same meaning as "*i*" in Table 6.4

numerical simulation results of Tables 6.11 and 6.12, the different initial values of the parameter ε will not have a substantial impact on the conclusion and numerical characteristic of national income analysis in the preceding article, which fully shows that the conclusion and the numerical simulation results about the effect of unit private mitigation expenditure on national income is stable too.

Table 6.10 The numerical simulation results in the capital movable case while $\varepsilon = -0.014$

	1.00 μ	1.01 μ	1.02 μ	1.03 μ	1.04 μ	1.05 μ	1.06 μ	1.07 μ	1.08 μ	1.09 μ	1.10 μ
Y	454,409.073	458,238.974	462,118.957	465,949.089	469,779.334	473,659.667	477,490.134	481,370.681	485,201.370	489,082.137	492,963.001
CRY_i	0.000	0.843	1.697	2.540	3.382	4.236	5.079	5.933	6.776	7.630	8.484

Note: 1. Here "i" has the same meaning as "i" in Table 6.4 to Table 6.9

2. "CRY_i" means the percentage change rate of Y, and $CRY_i = \frac{Y_i - Y_0}{Y_0} * 100\%$

Table 6.11 The numerical simulation results in the capital movable case while $\varepsilon = -0.012$

	$1.00\ \mu$	$1.01\ \mu$	$1.02\ \mu$	$1.03\ \mu$	$1.04\ \mu$	$1.05\ \mu$	$1.06\ \mu$	$1.07\ \mu$	$1.08\ \mu$	$1.09\ \mu$	$1.10\ \mu$
Y	463,995.703	467,879.394	471,813.137	475,696.990	479,630.892	483,514.908	487,448.965	491,383.105	495,267.349	499,201.634	503,135.998
CRY_i	0.000	0.837	1.685	2.522	3.370	4.207	5.055	5.903	6.740	7.588	8.435

Note: Same as Table 6.10

Table 6.12 The numerical simulation results in the capital movable case while $\varepsilon = -0.016$

	$1.00\ \mu$	$1.01\ \mu$	$1.02\ \mu$	$1.03\ \mu$	$1.04\ \mu$	$1.05\ \mu$	$1.06\ \mu$	$1.07\ \mu$	$1.08\ \mu$	$1.09\ \mu$	$1.10\ \mu$
Y	446,636.983	450,463.248	454,239.701	458,066.276	461,893.001	465,669.900	469,496.915	473,324.073	477,151.378	480,928.844	484,756.424
CRY_i	0.000	0.857	1.702	2.559	3.416	4.261	5.118	5.975	6.832	7.678	8.535

Note: Same as Table 6.10

6.5 Conclusion

Private mitigation is people's instinctive response to environmental pollution. The level of consumers spend on the unit private mitigation is not only affected by the level of economic development, but also has an impact on economic development. This chapter is different from the previous theoretical articles on the effects of environmental pollution on wage inequality and unemployment rate, which focus on agricultural pollution rather than industrial pollution. The conclusion of this chapter is first obtained in the field of theoretical economics. In addition, we used related economic data from China in 2017 to calibrate the parameters of the model, and then we used the calibrated parameters to perform numerical simulations and carried out a sensitivity analysis to test the robustness of the model's conclusions, the results verify the validity of the theoretical model. Compared with previous studies, this chapter mainly has the following three differences:

- This chapter analyzes the economic effects of agricultural pollution on the urban unemployment rate and the urban-rural wage inequality by focusing on the impact of agricultural pollution on labor health, that is, human capital.
- We consider the role of private mitigation in the study of urban unemployment and urban-rural wage inequality, and it is the first time that the propositions of the effects of private mitigation on the urban unemployment rate and the urban-rural wage inequality are obtained.
- On the basis of theoretical analysis, the model is calibrated and simulated by using relevant economic data, which not only obtains the impact directions the changes of unit private mitigation expenditure on the urban unemployment and the urban-rural wage inequality, but also measures the numerical characteristics of the corresponding impact effect.

This chapter explored these three perspectives not only for academic considerations, but also for practical problems which are faced by developing countries in economic development. That is to say, private mitigation has become an inevitable expenditure for every labor in developing countries in the presence of environmental pollution.

At the same time, under certain conditions, the increase of unit private mitigation expenditure may improve national welfare. Thus, this study is a useful attempt to explore the mechanisms between national welfare and private mitigation in this new economic operating environment. In addition, this chapter first proposes that increasing the unit private mitigation expenditure in the capital mobility case can not only decrease the urban unemployment rate and narrow the urban-rural wage inequality, but also enhance the national income, which means that developing countries should encourage individuals to increase unit private mitigation expenditures.

Competing Interests

Funding This work was supported by the Humanities and Social Sciences of the Ministry of Education, China, Project No. 17JJD630002.

Disclosure Statement No potential conflict of interest was reported by the authors.

Appendix

Appendix 1

The determinant of square matrix in Eq. (6.11) is

$$\begin{aligned}
\Delta = {} & \lambda(1+\lambda)\varepsilon\theta_{LA}Ma_L^M S_{KK}^Z S_{KK}^M + \lambda(1+\lambda)\theta_{KM}\theta_{LA}S_{KK}^Z Za_L^Z \\
& + \lambda(1+\lambda)\varepsilon\theta_{KM}\theta_{LA}S_{KK}^Z\left(Ma_L^M S_{LL}^M + Za_L^Z S_{LL}^Z\right) \\
& + \lambda\varepsilon\theta_{KM}\theta_{LA}Aa_L^A S_{KK}^Z S_{LL}^A - \lambda\varepsilon\theta_{KM}\theta_{LA}Aa_L^A S_{KK}^Z \\
& - \lambda(1+\lambda)\theta_{KM}\theta_{LA}\left(1+\varepsilon S_{KL}^Z\right)Za_L^Z S_{LK}^Z \\
& - \lambda(1+\lambda)\varepsilon\theta_{LA}\theta_{LM}Ma_L^M S_{LK}^M S_{KK}^Z + \lambda(1+\lambda)\theta_{KM}\theta_{ZA}\left(Ma_L^M + Za_L^Z\right)\left(\varepsilon S_{KK}^Z - \theta_{KZ}\right) \\
& + \lambda\theta_{LA}\theta_{KM}Aa_L^A S_{KK}^Z\left(1 - \varepsilon S_{LL}^A + \frac{\varepsilon}{1-h}\right) + \lambda\theta_{LA}\theta_{KM}Aa_L^A\left(\varepsilon S_{KK}^Z - \theta_{KZ}\right) \\
& - \lambda\theta_{KM}Aa_L^A S_{LL}^A\left(\varepsilon S_{KK}^Z - \theta_{ZA}\theta_{KZ}\right) - \lambda\theta_{KM}\theta_{KZ}\theta_{ZA}Aa_L^A\left(1+\varepsilon S_{KL}^Z\right)S_{LL}^A \\
& + \lambda\varepsilon\theta_{KM}Aa_L^A S_{KK}^Z S_{LL}^A\left(\theta_{LA} + \theta_{LZ}\theta_{ZA}\right).
\end{aligned}$$

Since the sign of Δ cannot be directly determined, we will use dynamic adjustment to decide its sign. In the established model, the dynamic adjustment process of the model is as follows:

$$\dot{A} = d_1\left(1 - ha_L^A w - P_Z a_Z^A\right), \tag{6.13}$$

$$\dot{M} = d_2\left(P_M - ha_L^M \overline{w} - r_M a_K^M\right), \tag{6.14}$$

$$\dot{Z} = d_3\left(P_Z - ha_L^Z \overline{w} - r_Z a_K^Z\right), \tag{6.15}$$

$$\dot{w} = d_4\left(\left(Ma_L^M + Za_L^Z\right)(1+\lambda) + Aa_L^A - hL\right). \tag{6.16}$$

$$\dot{r}_M - d_5\left(Ma_K^M - K_M\right), \tag{6.17}$$

$$\dot{r}_Z = d_6\left(Za_K^Z - K_Z\right), \tag{6.18}$$

$$\dot{P} = d_7\left(P_Z Z - \frac{\mu(1-h)}{h} A a_L^A\right), \tag{6.19}$$

$$\dot{\lambda} = d_8(\overline{w} - (1+\lambda)w), \tag{6.20}$$

where '.' represents differentiation with respect to time and d_j ($j = 1, 2, \ldots, 8$) is the positive coefficient measuring the speed of adjustment and $d_j > 0$. In the product market, according to the Marshall adjustment process, when the price that the demander is willing to pay is not equal to the price that the supplier is willing to accept, the market adjusts the quantity of the product; in the factor market, because the factor endowment is exogenously given, the market adjusts the factor price to make the factor demand equal to the factor supply.

The determinant of the Jacobian matrix of Eqs. (6.13–6.20) is

$$|J|_1 = d_1 \ldots d_8 P_M \begin{vmatrix} 0 & 0 & -\varepsilon\theta_{LA} & -\theta_{LA} & 0 & 0 & -\theta_{ZA} & 0 \\ 0 & 0 & -\varepsilon\theta_{LM} & 0 & -\theta_{KM} & 0 & 0 & 0 \\ 0 & 0 & -\varepsilon\theta_{LZ} & 0 & 0 & -\theta_{KZ} & 1 & 0 \\ -1 & 0 & 1-\varepsilon S_{LL}^A + \frac{\varepsilon}{1-h} & -S_{LL}^A & 0 & 0 & 1-S_{LZ}^A & 0 \\ 0 & 0 & 0 & 1+\lambda & 0 & 0 & 0 & \lambda \\ Aa_L^A & (1+\lambda)Ma_L^M & B & Aa_L^A S_{LL}^A & (1+\lambda)Ma_L^M S_{LK}^M & (1+\lambda)Za_L^Z S_{LK}^Z & Aa_L^A S_{LZ}^A & \lambda\left(Ma_L^M + Za_L^Z\right) \\ 0 & 1 & \varepsilon S_{KL}^M & 0 & S_{KK}^M & 0 & 0 & 0 \\ 0 & 0 & 1+\varepsilon S_{KL}^Z & 0 & 0 & S_{KK}^Z & 0 & 0 \end{vmatrix},$$

Therefore,

$$|J|_1 = -d_1 \ldots d_8 \Delta.$$

Under the condition of a stable system, there must be $|J|_1 > 0$, and then $\Delta < 0$.

Appendix 2

Using Cramer's rule to solve the square matrix in Eq. (6.11), we get

$$\begin{aligned} \Delta_A = {} & \lambda(1+\lambda)\varepsilon\theta_{LA}\theta_{LM}S_{LK}^M S_{KK}^Z Ma_L^M + \left[\lambda\theta_{KM}S_{LL}^A Aa_L^A - \lambda\theta_{KM}(1+\lambda)\left(Ma_L^M + Za_L^Z\right)\right]\left(\varepsilon S_{KK}^Z - \theta_{ZA}\theta_{KZ}\right) \\ & - \lambda\theta_{LA}\theta_{KM}\left\{\left[BS_{KK}^Z - (1+\lambda)\left(1+\varepsilon S_{KL}^Z\right)S_{LK}^Z Za_L^Z\right] + Aa_L^A S_{LZ}^A\left(\varepsilon S_{KK}^Z - \theta_{KZ}\right)\right\} - \lambda(1+\lambda)\varepsilon\theta_{LA}S_{KK}^M S_{KK}^Z Ma_L^M, \end{aligned} \tag{6.21}$$

$$\Delta_M = \lambda\varepsilon\theta_{LA}Aa_L^A S_{KK}^Z S_{KK}^M < 0, \tag{6.22}$$

$$\Delta_Z = \lambda\theta_{LA}\theta_{KM}Aa_L^A S_{KK}^Z < 0, \tag{6.23}$$

$$\Delta_w = -\lambda\theta_{KM}\left(\varepsilon S_{KK}^Z - \theta_{KZ}\theta_{ZA}\right)Aa_L^A, \tag{6.24}$$

$$\Delta_{r_M} = -\lambda\varepsilon\theta_{LA}\theta_{LM}Aa_L^A S_{KK}^Z < 0, \tag{6.25}$$

$$\Delta_{r_Z} = -\lambda\left(1 + \varepsilon S_{KL}^Z\right)\theta_{LA}\theta_{KM}Aa_L^A, \tag{6.26}$$

$$\Delta_{P_Z} = \lambda\theta_{LA}\theta_{KM}\left(\varepsilon S_{KK}^Z - \theta_{KZ}\right)Aa_L^A, \tag{6.27}$$

$$\Delta_\lambda = (1+\lambda)\theta_{KM}\left(\varepsilon S_{KK}^Z - \theta_{KZ}\theta_{ZA}\right)Aa_L^A. \tag{6.28}$$

According to the Eqs. (6.22, 6.23, and 6.25), it is clear that the effects of the changes of the unit private mitigation expenditure on the output of the sector M and the sector Z and the capital interest rate of sector M. Whether the effects of the changes of the unit private mitigation expenditure on the output of the agricultural sector and the other variables are, however, ambiguous. And if inequality $\varepsilon S_{KK}^Z - \theta_{KZ}\theta_{ZA} < 0$ is hold, then the effects of the changes of the per unit private mitigation expenditure on the other variables (except the output of the agricultural sector A) will also be determined and the results are as follows:

$$\frac{\widehat{w}}{\widehat{\mu}} < 0, \frac{\widehat{\lambda}}{\widehat{\mu}} > 0, \frac{\widehat{r_Z}}{\widehat{\mu}} > 0, \frac{\widehat{P_Z}}{\widehat{\mu}} > 0, \frac{\widehat{A}}{\widehat{\mu}} = \frac{\Delta_A}{\Delta}.$$

Appendix 3

The determinant of square matrix in Eq. (6.12) is

$$\begin{aligned}\Omega = {} & \lambda(1+\lambda)\varepsilon\theta_{LA}Ma_L^M\left(Ma_K^M S_{KK}^M + Za_K^Z S_{KK}^Z\right)\\ & + \lambda(1+\lambda)\varepsilon\theta_{LA}Ma_K^M\left(Ma_L^M S_{LL}^M + Za_L^Z S_{LL}^Z\right)\\ & - \lambda(1+\lambda)\varepsilon\theta_{LA}Ma_K^M\left(Ma_L^M + Za_L^Z\right)(\theta_{KM} - \theta_{KZ})\\ & + \lambda(1+\lambda)\theta_{KM}\theta_{LA}\left(Ma_K^M Za_L^Z - Ma_L^M Za_K^Z\right)\\ & + \lambda\varepsilon\theta_{LA}(\theta_{KM}\theta_{LZ} - \theta_{LM}\theta_{KZ})Ma_K^M Aa_L^A S_{LZ}^A\\ & - \lambda(1+\lambda)\varepsilon\left(Ma_L^M + Za_L^Z\right)Ma_K^M\theta_{ZA}(\theta_{LM}\theta_{KZ} - \theta_{LZ}\theta_{KM})\\ & + \lambda\varepsilon\theta_{LA}Aa_L^A Ma_K^M\left(1 - S_{LZ}^A\right)(\theta_{KM}\theta_{LZ} - \theta_{LM}\theta_{KZ}) - \lambda\varepsilon\theta_{KM}\theta_{LA}Ma_K^M Aa_L^A\\ & + \lambda\varepsilon\theta_{KM}\theta_{LA}Ma_K^M Aa_L^A S_{LL}^A\end{aligned}$$

Since the sign of Ω cannot be directly determined, we will use dynamic adjustment to decide its sign, and the dynamic adjustment process of the model is as follows:

$$\dot{A} = d_1\left(1 - ha_L^A w - P_Z a_Z^A\right), \tag{6.29}$$

$$\dot{M} = d_2\left(P_M - ha_L^M \overline{w} - ra_K^M\right), \tag{6.30}$$

$$\dot{Z} = d_3\left(P_Z - ha_L^Z \overline{w} - ra_K^Z\right), \tag{6.31}$$

$$\dot{w} = d_4\left(\left(Ma_L^M + Za_L^Z\right)(1+\lambda) + Aa_L^A - hL\right), \tag{6.32}$$

$$\dot{r} = d_5\left(Ma_K^M + Za_K^Z - K\right), \tag{6.33}$$

$$\dot{P} = d_7\left(P_Z Z - \frac{\mu(1-h)}{h} Aa_L^A\right), \tag{6.34}$$

$$\dot{\lambda} = d_8\left(\overline{w} - (1+\lambda)w\right). \tag{6.35}$$

The determinant of the Jacobian matrix of Eqs. (6.29–6.35) is:

$$|J|_2 = d_1 \ldots d_7 \begin{vmatrix} 0 & 0 & -\varepsilon\theta_{LA} & -\theta_{LA} & 0 & -\theta_{ZA} & 0 \\ 0 & 0 & -\varepsilon\theta_{LM} & 0 & -\theta_{KM} & 0 & 0 \\ 0 & 0 & -\varepsilon\theta_{LZ} & 0 & -\theta_{KZ} & 1 & 0 \\ -1 & 0 & 1-\varepsilon S_{LL}^A + \frac{\varepsilon}{1-h} & -S_{LL}^A & 0 & 1-S_{LZ}^A & 0 \\ 0 & 0 & 0 & 1+\lambda & 0 & 0 & \lambda \\ Aa_L^A & (1+\lambda)Ma_L^M & B & Aa_L^A S_{LL}^A & C & Aa_L^A S_{LZ}^A & \lambda\left(Ma_L^M + Za_L^Z\right) \\ 0 & Ma_K^M & F & 0 & G & 0 & 0 \end{vmatrix},$$

Therefore,

$$|J|_2 = -d_1 \ldots d_7 \Omega.$$

Under the condition of a stable system, there must be $|J|_2 < 0$, and thus $\Omega > 0$.

Appendix 4

Using Cramer's rule to solve the square matrix in Eq. (6.12), we yield

$$\begin{aligned} \Omega_A = {} & \lambda(1+\lambda)\theta_{LA}\theta_{KM}\left(Ma_L^M Za_K^Z - Ma_K^M Za_L^Z\right) \\ & - \lambda(1+\lambda)\varepsilon\theta_{LA}\left(Ma_K^M S_{KK}^M + Za_K^Z S_{KK}^Z\right)Ma_L^M \\ & - \lambda(1+\lambda)\varepsilon\theta_{LA}\left(Ma_L^M S_{LL}^M + Za_L^Z S_{LL}^Z\right)Ma_K^M \\ & - \lambda\varepsilon Ma_K^M Aa_L^A S_{LL}^A(\theta_{LM}\theta_{KZ} - \theta_{LZ}\theta_{KM}) + \lambda\varepsilon\theta_{KM}\theta_{LA}Ma_K^M Aa_L^A \\ & + \lambda(1+\lambda)\varepsilon\theta_{ZA}\left(Ma_L^M + Za_L^Z\right)Ma_K^M(\theta_{LM}\theta_{KZ} - \theta_{LZ}\theta_{KM}), \end{aligned} \tag{6.36}$$

$$\Omega_M = \lambda\theta_{LA}Aa_L^A\left[\varepsilon S_{KK}^M Ma_K^M - \left(\varepsilon S_{KK}^Z + \theta_{KM}\right)Za_K^Z\right], \tag{6.37}$$

$$\Omega_Z = \lambda\theta_{LA}\theta_{KM}Aa_L^A Ma_K^M > 0, \tag{6.38}$$

$$\Omega_w = \lambda\varepsilon[\theta_{ZA}(\theta_{LM}\theta_{KZ} - \theta_{KM}\theta_{LZ}) - \theta_{LA}\theta_{KM}]Aa_L^A Ma_K^M, \tag{6.39}$$

$$\Omega_r = -\lambda\varepsilon\theta_{LM}\theta_{LA}Aa_L^A Ma_K^M > 0, \tag{6.40}$$

$$\Omega_{P_Z} = -\lambda\varepsilon\theta_{LA}(\theta_{LM}\theta_{KZ} - \theta_{KM}\theta_{LZ})Aa_L^A Ma_K^M, \tag{6.41}$$

$$\Omega_\lambda = -(1+\lambda)\varepsilon\{\theta_{ZA}(\theta_{LM}\theta_{KZ} - \theta_{KM}\theta_{LZ}) - \theta_{LA}\theta_{KM}\}Aa_L^A Ma_K^M. \tag{6.42}$$

From the Eqs. (6.38–6.40), it is clear that the changes of the unit private mitigation expenditure μ 1 makes the output of the sector Z and the capital interest rate r change in the same and opposed directions. We will get $\theta_{LM}\theta_{KZ}$-$\theta_{KM}\theta_{LZ} = 0$ through Assumption 1, and then the effects of the changes of the unit private mitigation expenditure on the other endogenous variables (except the output of the sector M) will be determined and the results are as follows:

$$\frac{\widehat{A}}{\widehat{\mu}} < 0, \frac{\widehat{\lambda}}{\widehat{\mu}} < 0, \frac{\widehat{Z}}{\widehat{\mu}} > 0, \frac{\widehat{w}}{\widehat{\mu}} > 0, \frac{\widehat{P}_Z}{\widehat{\mu}} = 0,$$

$$\frac{\widehat{M}}{\widehat{\mu}} = \frac{\Omega_M}{\Omega} = \frac{\lambda\theta_{LA}Aa_L^A\left[\varepsilon S_{KK}^M Ma_K^M - \left(\varepsilon S_{KK}^Z + \theta_{KM}\right)Za_K^Z\right]}{\Omega}.$$

Appendix 5

Differentiating the national income eq. $Y = h^2wL + rK - \mu(1 - h)L$, we can yield

$$\begin{aligned} Y\widehat{Y} &= \left(2h^2\varepsilon wL + \mu\varepsilon hL\right)\widehat{Z} + h^2wL\widehat{w} + rK\widehat{r} \\ \Rightarrow \frac{\widehat{Y}}{\widehat{\mu}} &= \frac{1}{Y\widehat{\mu}}\left\{\left(2h^2\varepsilon wL + \mu\varepsilon hL\right)\widehat{Z} + h^2wL\widehat{w} + rK\widehat{r}\right\}. \end{aligned} \tag{6.43}$$

And according to the Eqs. (6.38–6.40), the following equation will be obtained:

$$\frac{\widehat{Y}}{\widehat{\mu}} = \frac{\lambda\varepsilon Aa_L^A Ma_K^M}{\widehat{\mu}}\left\{\left[\left(2h^2w + \mu h\right)\theta_{LA}\theta_{KM} - h^2w\theta_{LA}\theta_{KM}\right]L - \theta_{LM}\theta_{LA}rK\right\}.$$

References

Bartik TJ (1988) Evaluating the benefits of non-marginal reductions in pollution using information on defensive expenditures. J Environ Econ Manag 15(1):111–127. https://doi.org/10.1016/0095-0696(88)90032-0

Baumgärtner S, Drupp MA, Meya JN, Munz JM, Quaas MF (2017) Income inequality and willingness to pay for environmental public goods. J Environ Econ Manag 85:35–61. https://doi.org/10.1016/j.jeem.2017.04.005

Chao CC, Kerkvliet JR, Yu ESH (2000) Environmental preservation, sectoral unemployment, and trade in resources. Rev Dev Econ 4(1):39–50. https://doi.org/10.1111/1467-9361.00077

Chao CC, Laffargue JP, Sgro PM (2012) Environmental control, wage inequality and national welfare in a tourism economy. Int Rev Econ Financ 22(1):201–207. https://doi.org/10.1016/j.iref.2011.10.013

Chiroleu-Assouline M, Chirouleu-Assouline M, Fodha M (2011) Environmental tax and the distribution of income among heterogeneous workers. Ann Econ Stat 103/104:71–92. https://doi.org/10.2307/41615494

Copeland B, Taylor M (1999) Trade, spatial separation, and the environment. J Int Econ 47:137–168. https://doi.org/10.1016/S0022-1996(98)00020-8

Courant PN, Porter RC (1981) Averting expenditure and the cost of pollution. J Environ Econ Manag 8(4):321–329. https://doi.org/10.1016/0095-0696(81)90044-9

Harris JR, Todaro MP (1970) Migration, unemployment and development: a two-sector analysis. Am Econ Rev 60(1):126–142. https://www.jstor.org/stable/1807860

Hotte L, Winer SL (2008) The demands for environmental regulation and for trade in the presence of private mitigation. In: SSRN Working Papers, 0810E. https://doi.org/10.2139/ssrn.1319677

Hotte L, Winer SL (2012) Environmental regulation and trade openness in the presence of private mitigation. J Dev Econ 97(1):46–57. https://doi.org/10.1016/j.jdeveco.2011.01.004

Kondoh K, Yabuuchi S (2012) Unemployment, environmental policy, and international migration. J Int Trade Econ Dev 21(5):677–690. https://doi.org/10.1080/09638199.2010.535613

Li X, Wu Y (2018) Environment and economy in the modern agricultural development. Asia-Pac J Account Econ 25(1–2):163–176. https://doi.org/10.1080/16081625.2016.1246191

Martínez Y, Albiac J (2004) Agricultural pollution control under Spanish and European environmental policies. Water Resour Res 40(10):W10501.1–W10501.12. https://doi.org/10.1029/2004WR003102

McKitrick R, Collinge RA (2002) The existence and uniqueness of optimal pollution policy in the presence of victim defense measures. J Environ Econ Manag 44(1):106–122. https://doi.org/10.1006/jeem.2001.1200

Shibata H, Winrich JS (1983) Control of pollution when the offended defend themselves. Economica 50(200):425–437. https://doi.org/10.2307/2554304

Sun B, Zhang L, Yang L, Zhang F, Norse D, Zhu Z (2012) Agricultural non-point source pollution in China: causes and mitigation measures. Ambio 41(4):370–379. https://doi.org/10.1007/s13280-012-0249-6

Taheripour F, Khanna M, Nelson CH (2008) Welfare impacts of alternative public policies for agricultural pollution control in an open economy: a general equilibrium framework. Am J Agric Econ 90(3):701–718. https://doi.org/10.1111/j.1467-8276.2008.01139.x

Tawada M, Sun S (2010) Urban pollution, unemployment and national welfare in a dualistic economy. Rev Dev Econ 14:311–322. https://doi.org/10.1111/j.1467-9361.2010.00554.x

Chapter 7
Agricultural Producer Service Subsidies and Agricultural Pollution: An Approach Based on Endogenous Agricultural Pollution

Abstract Agricultural producer services are indispensable link in promoting agricultural modernization in developing countries, while agricultural pollution has become the largest source of pollution in many developing countries. Given that agricultural pollution is different from the industrial pollution for its endogenous characteristic, we linked agricultural pollution with labors' human capital level and propose an endogenous model that reflecting agricultural pollution path, which is different from the traditional path. We studied the effects of government price subsidy, interest subsidy, and wage subsidy to agricultural producer service on agricultural pollution and other economic indicators by constructing a four-sector general-equilibrium model including agricultural producer service. And we found that the rise of price subsidy for the agricultural producer service and the wage subsidy of the agricultural producer service sector would increase the output of agricultural sector and reduce the output of agricultural producer service under certain conditions, but aggravate agricultural pollution; at the same time, the rise of interest subsidy of the agricultural producer service sector would decrease the output of agricultural sector, enhance the output of agricultural producer service conditionally, and decrease the agricultural pollution. Preconditions of the three subsidies to improve national welfare have been obtained.

Keywords Agricultural producer service · Agricultural pollution · Agricultural subsidies · Endogenous path

7.1 Introduction

Agricultural producer services refer to a series of services that integrate modern production factors such as science information technology, capital equipment, and talents into agricultural production to improve agricultural production efficiency. The development of agricultural producer service could have impact on the agricultural production mode, factor input structure, and rural labor transfer. Therefore, the rise of agricultural producer service may break the original production structure and then affect the agricultural ecological environment. In view of the important role of

X. Li, Y. Wu, *Research on Characteristic Issues in Current Developing Economies*, New Frontiers in Regional Science: Asian Perspectives 80, https://doi.org/10.1007/978-981-97-7284-1_7

agricultural producer service in agricultural development, many developing countries have taken the development of agricultural producer service as an important measure to promote agricultural modernization. Taking China as an example, in 2017, the Ministry of Agriculture, the National Development and Reform Commission, and the Ministry of Finance of the People's Republic of China jointly issued "the guiding opinions on accelerating the development of agricultural producer service," which proposed a vigorous promotion of the development of agricultural producer service, thus encouraging more farmers into the development track of modern agriculture and comprehensively promoting the construction of modern agriculture.[1] It can be predicted that agricultural producer service will be valued and receive more and more policy support in developing countries, such as the government's subsidy policy for agricultural producer services.

On the other hand, for a long time, petrochemical factors such as pesticides and chemical fertilizers have become indispensable input factors for agricultural production. However, the excessive use of such factors which can generate agricultural pollution (hereinafter referred to as "agricultural pollution factors") has led to increasingly serious agricultural pollution problems. At present, agricultural pollution in many developing countries has surpassed industrial pollution to become the largest pollution source. Taking China's water pollution as an example, according to the data of the second national census of pollution sources issued by China in 2020, the industrial source emissions of China's main water pollutants chemical oxygen demand (COD), ammonia nitrogen (AN), total nitrogen (TN), and total phosphorus (TP) were 909,600 tons, 44,500 tons, 155,700 tons, and 7900 tons, respectively, in 2017; and the agricultural source emissions of the above four pollutants are 10.671, three million tons of COD, 216,200 tons of AN, 1,414,900 tons of TN, and 212,000 tons of TP. It can be seen that the emission of water pollutants from agricultural sources is far greater than that from industrial sources in China.[2] The serious agricultural pollution has gradually become a constraint for the further development of agriculture in many developing countries.

As for the economic theoretical research on environmental pollution, Copeland and Taylor (1999) proposed an external transmission mechanism of industrial pollution affecting agricultural production, that is, pollutants such as wastewater, gas, and residue produced in the process of industrial production would destroy natural environment through air, flow of water, and other media, and then affect agricultural production, which is highly dependent on natural environmental conditions (hereafter referred to as C-T path). After that, many scholars have studied the

---

[1]Ministry of Agriculture, Development and Reform Commission and Ministry of Finance of the People's Republic of China: "Guiding Opinions on Accelerating the Development of Agricultural Productive Services," August 16, 2017. http://www.gov.cn/gongbao/content/2018/content_5271797.htm.

[2]Ministry of Ecology and Environment of the People's Republic of China, National Bureau of Statistics of the People's Republic of China, Ministry of Agriculture and Rural Affairs of the People's Republic of China: "Second National Pollution Source Census Bulletin," June 8, 2020. http://www.gov.cn/xinwen/2020-06/10/content_5518391.htm.

impacts of industrial pollution on economy under the C-T path. For instance, Daitoh (2003) discussed the sufficient conditions for environmental policy to promote welfare reform in Harris Todaro economy. Beladi and Chao (2006) studied the effects of pollution tax on dual developing economies with independent emission reduction departments. Tawada and Sun (2010) studied the impacts of industrial pollution on unemployment rate and national welfare under the background of urban-rural dual economy. Cole et al. (2011) investigated the relationship between economic growth and industrial pollution emissions. Kondoh and Yabuuchi (2012) studied the effects of carbon emission tax on employment, minimum wage, and national welfare in the context of industrial pollution. Li and Wu (2018) studied the impacts of policies to promote modern agriculture on the environment and economy under the framework of a three-sector general-equilibrium model with industrial pollution externalities. Wu and Li (2021) investigated the effects that international factor movements have on the environment in developing country under agricultural dualism.

The above literatures are related to the industrial pollution problem under the C-T framework, which is the mainstream perspective of current research on environmental issues. However, at present, there is little economic theoretical research on agricultural pollution. Taheripour et al. (2008) used the general-equilibrium method to evaluate the welfare impact of alternative policies to reduce agricultural nitrogen pollution in an open economy. However, this research did not reflect the characteristics of agricultural pollution path. Therefore, they fail to grasp the general law of agricultural pollution in the market economy. Because the path of agricultural pollution is different from that of industrial pollution, their nature and scope of influence are different. Agricultural pollution factors such as pesticides and chemical fertilizers will remain in agricultural products and directly damaging workers' health through channels such food, and affecting the effectiveness of labor factors in the production process, therefore the impact path of agricultural pollution on economic production is endogenous. And because agricultural products are people's necessities, the above damages will not only affect the health of agricultural workers, but also the health of workers in other industries in the economy, which shows that the endogenous impact path of agricultural pollution on the production process is universal. Thus, under the realistic background that the agricultural pollution has become the largest pollution source, it is urgent and necessary to carry out theoretical research from the perspective of agricultural pollution path. Based on the characteristics of agricultural pollution, this chapter will link agricultural pollution with labors' human capital level and propose an endogenous model that reflecting agricultural pollution path which is different from C-T path.

On the other hand, with regard to the economic effects of the development of producer service, urban industrial producer service mainly include the following: van Marrewijk et al. (1997) analyzed the general equilibrium relationships among producer services trade, economies of scale, and factor market in combination with factor abundance theory and monopoly competition theory. Liu et al. (2017) empirically tested the chain connection and transmission path between various elements in the coupling process of producer services agglomeration and manufacturing. Xi et al.

(2015) empirically studied the mode selection of China's Urban Producer Services under the guidance of industrial efficiency improvement. Li and Jia (2021) studied the impact of the privatization of mixed enterprises on the economy in an economy including producer services.

Li and Fu (2020) involved agricultural producer services, they analyzed the effects of migrant workers' remittances on the economy and environment under the background of agricultural producer service, and made a preliminary discussion on the path of agricultural pollution, but they did not consider the relationship between agricultural producer service and agricultural pollution into the research framework. Although there is few research on the relationship between the development of agricultural producer service and agricultural pollution in the existing literature, we believe that such research is necessary. This is because the development of agricultural producer service is an economic activity involving "hidden pollution," that is, agricultural producer services have nothing to do with agricultural pollution in the surface, but can form the following relationship chain with agricultural pollution by changing agricultural production process, production structure, and factor input structure:

Developing agricultural producer service → changing agricultural production process and factor input structure → adjusting the use of pollution factors → affecting agricultural pollution.

To sum up, considering the impact of the development of agricultural producer service on the environment under the condition of agricultural pollution path is a perspective that is closer to the economic reality of developing countries. The research conducted under this perspective will also be more in line with the economic reality of developing countries, and the research conclusions will also be more practical and feasible, which can provide a theoretical basis for the relevant economic policy practice of developing countries and also provide a new perspective and reference for the research on agricultural pollution. The research motivation of this chapter is studding the impact of the development of agricultural production services on agricultural pollution, clarifying its market mechanism, and enriching the research in this field.

Considering the difference between the agricultural pollution path and that of industrial pollution, this chapter proposed an endogenous model that reflecting agricultural pollution path and then investigating the effects of price subsidy, interest subsidy, and wage subsidy aimed at promoting the development of agricultural producer service on agricultural pollution, etc. The main contribution of this chapter is to investigate the effects of various government subsidies of agricultural producer service on agricultural pollution by using economic theoretical research methods from the perspective of agricultural pollution endogenous path. We found that the price subsidy and the wage subsidy for the agricultural producer service sector would aggravate the agricultural pollution, but the interest subsidy of the agricultural producer service sector would decrease agricultural pollution. This research conclusion was obtained for the first time in theoretical research, which shows the advantages of interest subsidy for agricultural producer services in environmental protection.

The rest of this chapter is structured as follows: We construct a three-sector general-equilibrium model framework including agricultural producer service in Sect. 7.2. In Sect. 7.3, we study the effects of agricultural producer service price subsidy, interest subsidy, and wage subsidy on agricultural pollution and other economic variables, and analyze the impact mechanism based on the model framework of Sect. 7.2. In the Sect. 7.4, we analyze the effects of three subsidies on national welfare. Finally, conclusion and policy recommendations of this chapter are in Sect. 7.5.

7.2 Model

In this section, we construct a small open agricultural dual economy including four sectors: agricultural sector (sector A), agricultural producer service sector (sector X), agricultural pollution factor production sector (sector Z), and manufacturing sector (sector M). Among them, the agricultural sector uses labor L_A, agricultural producer service X, and agricultural pollution factor Z to produce exportable agricultural products. Agricultural producer service sector uses labor L_X and capital K_X to provide intermediate inputs to the agricultural sector; agricultural pollution factor production sector inputs labor L_Z and capital K_Z to produce the intermediate factor for the agricultural sector, where both agricultural producer service and agricultural pollution factor are no-traded goods. The manufacturing sector uses labor L_M and capital K_M to produce manufacturing products that can be imported. We assume that the endowments of labor and capital are exogenous, labor can move among the above four sectors, and capital flow freely among the manufacturing sector, agricultural pollution factor production sector, and agricultural producer service sector. At the same time, we also assume that all product markets are completely competitive, and the prices of manufacturing products P_M and agricultural products are determined by the world market, therefore they are exogenous, the prices of agricultural producer service P_X and agricultural pollution factor P_Z are determined by the supply-demand relationship between agricultural producer service sector, agricultural pollution factor production sector, and agricultural sector. In addition, we standardize the price of agricultural products to 1, hence the prices of other products and factors are relative to that those of agricultural product.

However, the path of agricultural pollution is different from that of industrial pollution. Pollution factors such as pesticides and fertilizers will remain in crops and directly affect human health through food, hence agricultural pollution tends to directly destroy labors' health capital. Obviously, the study of agricultural pollution with such a path is beyond the reach of C-T path. Based on the characteristics of agricultural pollution, Li et al. (2020) treated the agricultural pollution path endogenously and proposed a model that can reflect the agricultural pollution path which is completely different from the C-T path. Therefore, based on the research of Li et al. (2020), we internalize the impact of agricultural pollution on economy.

In this chapter, we define h as the labor force health coefficient under the comprehensive influence of agricultural producer service and agricultural pollution factors. The specific form is as follows:

$$h = Z^{\varepsilon} X^{\rho}, \quad -1 < \varepsilon \leq 0, \quad 0 \leq \rho < 1,$$

where, the parameters ε and ρ are the influence coefficients which reflect the effects of agricultural pollution factors and agricultural producer service sector on labors' health capital. Due to agricultural producer services are more scientific in technical agricultural production links. For example, the use of pesticides and fertilizers is more scientific, which can reduce the excessive use of petrochemical elements, improve the use efficiency of pesticides and fertilizers and other elements, and reduce the harmful residue rate of pesticides and fertilizers. In the case of a given input of pollution factors, the increase of input of agricultural producer services in agricultural production will reduce the damage of petrochemical factors to human capital, so for the given variables Z, h is the increasing function of variable X.

Therefore, the production functions of the four sectors of the economy are as follows:

$$A = \alpha_1^{\alpha_1} \alpha_2^{\alpha_2} (1 - \alpha_1 - \alpha_2)^{1-\alpha_1-\alpha_2} (hL_A)^{\alpha_1} Z^{\alpha_2} X^{1-\alpha_1-\alpha_2},$$

$$M = \beta^{\beta} (1 - \beta)^{1-\beta} (hL_M)^{\beta} K_M^{1-\beta},$$

$$Z = \gamma^{\gamma} (1 - \gamma)^{1-\gamma} (hL_Z)^{\gamma} K_Z^{1-\gamma},$$

$$X = \sigma^{\sigma} (1 - \sigma)^{1-\sigma} (hL_X)^{\sigma} K_X^{1-\sigma}.$$

Among them, $\alpha_i (i = 1, 2)$, and parameters β, γ, and σ represent the output elasticity of corresponding input factors, respectively.

Under the conditions of perfect market competition, according to the zero-profit conditions of the four sectors above, we can yield to the following equations:

$$Z^{-\varepsilon\alpha_1} X^{-\rho\alpha_1} w^{\alpha_1} P_Z^{\alpha_2} P_X^{1-\alpha_1-\alpha_2} = 1, \tag{7.1}$$

$$Z^{-\varepsilon\beta} X^{-\rho\beta} \overline{w}^{\beta} r^{1-\beta} = P_M, \tag{7.2}$$

$$Z^{-\varepsilon\gamma} X^{-\rho\gamma} \overline{w}^{\gamma} r^{1-\gamma} = P_Z, \tag{7.3}$$

$$Z^{-\varepsilon\sigma} X^{-\rho\sigma} \overline{w}^{\sigma} r^{1-\sigma} = P_X. \tag{7.4}$$

In the above four equations, variables w and $\overline{w}$ represent the nominal wage levels of agricultural sector, agricultural producer service sector, agricultural pollution factors, and manufacturing sector, respectively, and the wage w of agricultural sector is elastic, while the wage of agricultural producer service sector and manufacturing sector, $\overline{w}$, are exogenous due to institutional factors such as the minimum wage law, thus w/h and $\overline{w}/h$ are the actual wage levels of the above four sectors; the variable r is the capital interest of the sector X, sector Z, and sector M.

According to the research of Harris and Todaro (1970), the distribution mechanism of urban and rural labor force is

$$\overline{w} = (1 + \lambda)w, \tag{7.5}$$

where, $\lambda = \frac{L_U}{L_M + L_X + L_Z}$ represents the ratio of unemployment to employment in urban areas, which is defined as urban unemployment rate in this chapter.

We define variables L and K as labor and capital endowments in the economy, respectively. Since agricultural producer services are intermediate inputs in the agricultural sector, the market-clearing conditions of production factors such as labor, capital, agricultural producer service, and the agricultural pollution factors are

$$\alpha_2 A = P_Z Z, \tag{7.6}$$

$$(1 - \alpha_1 - \alpha_2)A = P_X X, \tag{7.7}$$

$$(1 - \beta)P_M M + (1 - \gamma)P_Z Z + (1 - \sigma)P_X X = rK, \tag{7.8}$$

$$\frac{\alpha_1 A}{w} + (1 + \lambda)\frac{1}{\overline{w}}(\beta P_M M + \gamma P_Z Z + \sigma P_X X) = L. \tag{7.9}$$

So far, the model has been built. Eqs. (7.1)–(7.9) describe the economic behavior of market players in the economy. And the model includes nine endogenous variables A, X, Z, M, w, r, P_X, P_Z, λ and four exogenous variables $P_M, \overline{w}, L, K$.

7.3 Comparative Static Analysis

For our analysis, we make the following assumption:

Assumption 1 *The per capita capital of the sector M is greater than that of the sector Z, while the per capital of the sector Z is greater than that of the sector X, that is,* $\beta < \gamma < \sigma$.

7.3.1 The Economic and Environmental Effects of Price Subsidy for Agricultural Producer Service

We first analyze the economic and environmental effects of government price subsidy for the purchase of agricultural productive services by the agricultural sector. Assuming that the government's price subsidy rate for the agricultural sector to purchase agricultural producer services is $\theta_P(0 \le \theta_P < 1)$, then the zero-profit condition Eq. (7.1) of the agricultural sector changes into the following form:

$$Z^{-\varepsilon\alpha_1}X^{-\rho\alpha_1}w^{\alpha_1}P_Z^{\alpha_2}P_X^{1-\alpha_1-\alpha_2}(1-\theta_P)^{1-\alpha_1-\alpha_2}=1. \tag{7.1*}$$

In order to ensure the balance of budget revenue and expenditure, the government collects income tax on national income, so the condition of government budget balance is

$$\theta_P P_X X = \theta_{1I}(A + P_M M). \tag{7.10}$$

Eqs. (7.1*), (7.2)–(7.10) constitute a complete economic system with agricultural producer service price subsidy policy. By differentiating Eqs. (7.1*), (7.2), (7.5), and (7.6), we can obtain the following relationships:

$$\widehat{w} = \varepsilon\widehat{Z} + \rho\widehat{X} - \frac{\alpha_2}{\alpha_1}\widehat{P}_Z - \frac{(1-\alpha_1-\alpha_2)}{\alpha_1}\widehat{P}_X + \frac{(1-\alpha_1-\alpha_2)}{\alpha_1}\frac{\theta_P}{1-\theta_P}\widehat{\theta}_P, \tag{7.11}$$

$$\widehat{r} = \varepsilon\frac{\beta}{(1-\beta)}\widehat{Z} + \rho\frac{\beta}{(1-\beta)}\widehat{X}, \tag{7.12}$$

$$\widehat{\lambda} = -\frac{(1+\lambda)}{\lambda}\widehat{w}, \tag{7.13}$$

$$\widehat{A} = \widehat{Z} + \widehat{P}_Z. \tag{7.14}$$

Differentiating Eqs. (7.1*), (7.3), (7.4), (7.7), (7.8), and (7.9), and substituting the above four equations into the six total differential equations, we can obtain the following matrix equation (Please see Appendix 1 for the detailed process):

$$\begin{pmatrix} 0 & \varepsilon\frac{\beta-\gamma}{(1-\beta)} & \rho\frac{\beta-\gamma}{(1-\beta)} & -1 & 0 \\ 0 & \varepsilon\frac{\beta-\sigma}{(1-\beta)} & \rho\frac{\beta-\sigma}{(1-\beta)} & 0 & -1 \\ 0 & \left(1+\varepsilon\frac{\beta-\gamma}{(1-\beta)}\right) & -\left(1-\rho\frac{\beta-\gamma}{(1-\beta)}\right) & 0 & -1 \\ (1-\beta)P_M M & C_1 & C_2 & (1-\gamma)P_Z Z & (1-\sigma)PX \\ (1+\lambda)\frac{1}{\overline{W}}\beta P_M M & C_3 & C_4 & C_5 & C_6 \end{pmatrix} \begin{pmatrix} \widehat{M} \\ \widehat{Z} \\ \widehat{X} \\ \widehat{P}_Z \\ \widehat{P}_X \end{pmatrix} = \begin{pmatrix} 0 \\ 0 \\ 0 \\ 0 \\ C_7 \end{pmatrix}\widehat{\theta}_P. \tag{7.15}$$

where

$$C_1 = \left((1-\gamma)P_Z Z - \varepsilon \frac{\beta}{(1-\beta)} [(1-\beta)P_M M + (1-\gamma)P_Z Z + (1-\sigma)P_X X] \right) > 0,$$

$$C_2 = \left((1-\sigma)PX - \rho \frac{\beta}{(1-\beta)} [(1-\beta)P_M M + (1-\gamma)P_Z Z + (1-\sigma)P_X X] \right),$$

$$C_3 = \left[\left(1 + \varepsilon \frac{\beta-\gamma}{(1-\beta)} \right) \frac{\alpha_1 A}{w} + (1+\lambda)\frac{1}{\overline{\overline{w}}}\gamma P_Z Z - \varepsilon \left(\frac{\alpha_1 A}{w} + (1+\lambda)\frac{1}{\overline{\overline{w}}}\beta P_M M \right.\right.$$
$$\left.\left. + (1+\lambda)\frac{1}{\overline{\overline{w}}}\gamma P_Z Z + (1+\lambda)\frac{1}{\overline{\overline{w}}}\sigma P_X X \right) \right]$$
$$> 0,$$

$$C_4 = \left[\rho \frac{\beta-\gamma}{(1-\beta)} \frac{\alpha_1 A}{w} + (1+\lambda)\frac{1}{\overline{\overline{w}}}\sigma P_X X - \rho \left(\frac{\alpha_1 A}{w} + (1+\lambda)\frac{1}{\overline{\overline{w}}}\beta P_M M \right.\right.$$
$$\left.\left. + (1+\lambda)\frac{1}{\overline{\overline{w}}}\gamma P_Z Z + (1+\lambda)\frac{1}{\overline{\overline{w}}}\sigma P_X X \right) \right],$$

$$C_5 = \left[(1+\lambda)\frac{1}{\overline{\overline{w}}}\gamma P_Z Z + \frac{\alpha_2}{\alpha_1} \left(\frac{\alpha_1 A}{w} + (1+\lambda)\frac{1}{\overline{\overline{w}}}\beta P_M M + (1+\lambda)\frac{1}{\overline{\overline{w}}}\gamma P_Z Z \right.\right.$$
$$\left.\left. + (1+\lambda)\frac{1}{\overline{\overline{w}}}\sigma P_X X \right) \right]$$
$$> 0,$$

$$C_6 = \left[(1+\lambda)\frac{1}{\overline{\overline{w}}}\sigma P_X X + \frac{(1-\alpha_1-\alpha_2)}{\alpha_1} \left(\frac{\alpha_1 A}{w} + (1+\lambda)\frac{1}{\overline{\overline{w}}}\beta P_M M \right.\right.$$
$$\left.\left. + (1+\lambda)\frac{1}{\overline{\overline{w}}}\gamma P_Z Z + (1+\lambda)\frac{1}{\overline{\overline{w}}}\sigma P_X X \right) \right]$$
$$> 0,$$

$$C_7 = \frac{(1-\alpha_1-\alpha_2)}{\alpha_1}\frac{\theta_P}{1-\theta_P} \times \left(\frac{\alpha_1 A}{w} + (1+\lambda)\frac{1}{\overline{w}}\beta P_M M + (1+\lambda)\frac{1}{\overline{w}}\gamma P_Z Z + (1+\lambda)\frac{1}{\overline{w}}\sigma P_X X\right).$$

Define the symbol Δ_1 as the determinant value of the coefficient matrix of Eq. (7.15), thus we can get

$$\Delta_1 = P_M M \left\{ \begin{array}{l} \left(1+\rho\frac{\beta-\sigma}{(1-\beta)}+\varepsilon\frac{\beta-\gamma}{(1-\beta)}\right)\left[(1+\lambda)\frac{1}{\overline{w}}P_X X(\beta-\sigma)+(1+\lambda)\frac{1}{\overline{w}}P_Z Z(\beta-\gamma)-(1-\beta)\frac{\alpha_1 A}{w}\right] \\ +(1-\beta)\left[1-\frac{\beta-\gamma}{(1-\beta)}\frac{\alpha_2}{\alpha_1}-\frac{\beta-\sigma}{(1-\beta)}\frac{(1-\alpha_1-\alpha_2)}{\alpha_1}\right](\varepsilon+\rho)\left(\begin{array}{l}\frac{\alpha_1 A}{w}+(1+\lambda)\frac{1}{\overline{w}}\beta P_M M \\ \quad +(1+\lambda)\frac{1}{\overline{w}}\gamma P_Z Z+(1+\lambda)\frac{1}{\overline{w}}\sigma P_X X\end{array}\right) \\ -\frac{\beta}{(1-\beta)}\beta(\varepsilon+\rho)(1+\lambda)\frac{1}{\overline{w}}[(1-\beta)P_M M+(1-\gamma)P_Z Z+(1-\sigma)P_X X] \end{array} \right\}. \quad (7.16)$$

According to Eq. (7.16), if $\varepsilon+\rho<0$ and the absolute values of parameters ε and ρ are small enough, there is $\Delta_1<0$. Using Cramer's rule to solve Eq. (7.15), we can obtain the effects of agricultural producer service price subsidy on economy and agricultural pollution etc. Specific results are shown in Table 7.1 (please see Appendix 1 for detailed process).

Based on the results in Table 7.1, we can obtain the first proposition of this chapter:

Proposition 1 *The price subsidy of agricultural producer service can improve the output level of agricultural sector and reduce the output of manufacturing sector. At the same time, the price subsidy of agricultural producer service will also decrease the use of agricultural producer service, increase the input of pollution factors in the agricultural sector, and then aggravate agricultural pollution.*

The results of Proposition 1 and Table 7.1 show that the government's price subsidy for the use of agricultural producer service in the agricultural sector will aggravate agricultural pollution and improve the output level of the agricultural sector. The specific economic mechanisms are as follows: The government subsidizes the price of service factor X in the sector in order to promote the development of agricultural producer service. Intuitively, this will make the agricultural department increase its investment in service factor X. However, the theoretical analysis

Table 7.1 The effects of price subsidy on economy and agricultural pollution

	$\widehat{A}$	$\widehat{M}$	$\widehat{Z}$	$\widehat{X}$	$\widehat{r}$	$\widehat{w}$	$\widehat{P_Z}$	$\widehat{P_X}$	$\widehat{\lambda}$
$\widehat{\theta_P}$	+	–	+	–	–	\	+	+	\

Note: The symbols "+" and "–", respectively, indicate that the price subsidy of agricultural producer services has a positive or negative impact on relevant variables, and "\" means that the effects of the price subsidy of agricultural producer services on relevant variables are uncertain and calculation results of this chapter show that the demand for agricultural producer service factor X in the agricultural sector will decrease, which may be due to the high expectation of the market for the price subsidy of service factor X, this can lead to a situation that the supply of service factor X is in short supply, which makes the equilibrium price P_X of service factor rise, and its rise range is greater than the benefit given to the agricultural sector by the service price subsidy of agricultural producers, which makes the actual investment of the agricultural sector in agricultural producer service × decline. Thus, the agricultural sector will replace service factor X with pollution factor Z, and the market demand for pollution factor Z will increase, which in turn will cause the equilibrium price P_Z of pollution factor to rise. On the other hand, the promotion effect of increasing agricultural pollution factor Z on agricultural sector a is greater than the negative impact of the decrease of service factor X on a, which makes a rise. There is a factor of capital increase in the rise of Z, and the capital comes from the sector M and the sector X, so the output of the sector M decreases.

7.3.2 *The Economic and Environmental Effects of Interest Subsidy*

Since the development of agricultural producer service is an important condition for promoting agricultural modernization, developing countries have the incentives to subsidize agricultural producer service to support their development, so as to promote the development of agricultural modernization. Assuming that the government subsidizes the interest of agricultural producer service, and the subsidy rate is $\theta_r(0 \leq \theta_r < 1)$, the zero-profit conditions Eq. (7.4) of agricultural producer service, the Eq. (7.8), and the budget balance condition of the government change into the following forms, respectively:

$$Z^{-\varepsilon\sigma}X^{-\rho\sigma}\overline{w}^{\sigma}(1-\theta_r)^{(1-\sigma)}r^{(1-\sigma)} = P_X, \tag{7.4*}$$

$$(1-\beta)\frac{P_M M}{r} + (1-\gamma)\frac{P_Z Z}{r} + (1-\sigma)\frac{P_X X}{1-\theta_r} = K, \tag{7.8*}$$

$$\theta_r(1-\sigma)PX = \theta_{2l}(A + P_M M). \tag{7.17}$$

Equations (7.1)–(7.3), (7.4*), (7.5)–(7.9), and (7.17) constitute a complete economic system containing capital interest subsidy policy for agricultural producer service. By differentiating Eq. (7.1), we can obtain the following relationship:

$$\widehat{w} = \varepsilon\widehat{Z} + \rho\widehat{X} - \frac{\alpha_2}{\alpha_1}\widehat{P}_Z - \frac{(1-\alpha_1-\alpha_2)}{\alpha_1}\widehat{P}_X. \tag{7.18}$$

Differentiating Eqs. (7.2), (7.3), (7.4*), and (7.5)–(7.9), and substituting Eqs. (7.12)–(7.14) and (7.18) into the total differential equations of the other six equations and sort them out to get the Eq. (7.19) (please see Appendix 2 for the detailed process):

$$\begin{pmatrix} 0 & \varepsilon\frac{\beta-\gamma}{(1-\beta)} & \rho\frac{\beta-\gamma}{(1-\beta)} & -1 & 0 \\ 0 & \varepsilon\frac{\beta-\sigma}{(1-\beta)} & \rho\frac{\beta-\sigma}{(1-\beta)} & 0 & -1 \\ 0 & \left(1+\varepsilon\frac{\beta-\gamma}{(1-\beta)}\right) & -\left(1-\rho\frac{\beta-\gamma}{(1-\beta)}\right) & 0 & -1 \\ (1-\beta)P_M M & C_{1*} & C_{2*} & (1-\gamma)P_Z Z & (1-\sigma)P_X X \\ (1+\lambda)\frac{1}{\bar{\bar{w}}}\beta P_M M & C_3 & C_4 & C_5 & C_6 \end{pmatrix} \begin{pmatrix} \widehat{M} \\ \widehat{Z} \\ \widehat{X} \\ \widehat{P}_Z \\ \widehat{P}_X \end{pmatrix} = \begin{pmatrix} 0 \\ (1-\sigma)\frac{\theta_r}{1-\theta_r} \\ 0 \\ -\frac{\theta_r}{1-\theta_r}(1-\sigma)\frac{PX}{(1-\theta_r)} \\ 0 \end{pmatrix} \widehat{\theta}_P. \tag{7.19}$$

where

$$C_{1*} = \left((1-\gamma)P_Z Z - \varepsilon\frac{\beta}{(1-\beta)}\left[(1-\beta)P_M M + (1-\gamma)P_Z Z + (1-\sigma)\frac{P_X X}{(1-\theta_r)}\right]\right) > 0,$$

$$C_{2*} = \left((1-\sigma)P_X X - \rho\frac{\beta}{(1-\beta)}\left[(1-\beta)P_M M + (1-\gamma)P_Z Z + (1-\sigma)\frac{P_X X}{(1-\theta_r)}\right]\right).$$

The determinant of the coefficient matrix of Eq. (7.19) is defined as Δ_2, thus

$$\Delta_2 = P_M M \left\{ \begin{array}{l} \left(1+\varepsilon\frac{\beta-\gamma}{(1-\beta)}+\rho\frac{\beta-\sigma}{(1-\beta)}\right)(1+\lambda)\frac{1}{\bar{\bar{w}}}P_X X\left(\frac{\beta(1-\sigma)}{(1-\theta_r)}-(1-\beta)\sigma\right) \\ +\left(1+\varepsilon\frac{\beta-\gamma}{(1-\beta)}+\rho\frac{\beta-\sigma}{(1-\beta)}\right)(1+\lambda)\frac{1}{\bar{\bar{w}}}P_Z Z(\beta-\gamma)-\left(1+\varepsilon\frac{Z}{1+Z}\frac{\beta-\gamma}{(1-\beta)}+\rho\frac{\beta-\sigma}{(1-\beta)}\right)(1-\beta)\frac{\alpha_1 A}{w} \\ +(1-\beta)\left(1-\frac{\beta-\gamma}{(1-\beta)}\frac{\alpha_2}{\alpha_1}-\frac{\beta-\sigma}{(1-\beta)}\frac{(1-\alpha_1-\alpha_2)}{\alpha_1}\right)(\varepsilon+\rho)\left(\begin{array}{l}\frac{\alpha_1 A}{w}+(1+\lambda)\frac{1}{\bar{\bar{w}}}\beta P_M M \\ \quad +(1+\lambda)\frac{1}{\bar{\bar{w}}}\gamma P_Z Z+(1+\lambda)\frac{1}{\bar{\bar{w}}}\sigma P_X X\end{array}\right) \\ -\frac{\beta}{(1-\beta)}\beta(\varepsilon+\rho)(1+\lambda)\frac{1}{\bar{\bar{w}}}\left((1-\beta)P_M M+(1-\gamma)P_Z Z+(1-\sigma)\frac{P_X X}{(1-\theta_r)}\right) \end{array} \right\}.$$

Table 7.2 The effects of the interest subsidies on economic and agricultural pollution

	$\widehat{A}$	$\widehat{M}$	$\widehat{Z}$	$\widehat{X}$	$\widehat{r}$	$\widehat{w}$	$\widehat{P_Z}$	$\widehat{P_X}$	$\widehat{\lambda}$
$\widehat{\theta_r}$	–	+	–	+	+	\	–	–	\

Note: The symbols "+" and "–", respectively, indicate that the interest subsidy of agricultural producer services has a positive or negative impact on relevant variables, and "\" means that the effects of the interest subsidy of agricultural producer services on relevant variables are uncertain

If the interest subsidy rate is high enough, that is, $1 - \theta_r$ is small enough, we can get $\Delta_2 > 0$. Using Cramer's rule to solve the Eq. (7.19), we can get the effects of capital interest subsidy in agricultural producer service on agricultural pollution and relevant economic variables. The specific results are shown in Table 7.2 (please see Appendix 2 for the detailed process).

Based on the results in Table 7.2, we can get the second proposition of this chapter:

Proposition 2 *The interest subsidy of agricultural producer service sector can reduce the output level of agricultural sector and improve that of manufacturing sector. At the same time, the interest subsidy of the agricultural producer service sector will also increase the use of agricultural producer service, decrease the use of pollution factors in the agricultural sector, and then reduce agricultural pollution.*

From the above results, it can be found that the capital interest subsidy for agricultural producer service will not only promote the development of agricultural producer service, but also reduce agricultural pollution and improve the level of agricultural green development. And the specific economic mechanism is as follows: The interest subsidy for the sector *X* reduces the unit cost of capital used by the sector *X*. Therefore, the sector *X* employs more capital. In order to employ more capital, the sector *X* will attract capital by increasing the interest rate, thus increasing *r*. The output of sector *X* increased. The rise of *r* makes the capital outflow, and output of sector *Z* decline. Because the interest subsidy rate is large enough, the increase of *X* is large enough, its market supply exceeds the demand, P_Z decreases, and P_X also decreases. Due to the capital outflow from the sector *M*, the sector *M* increases labor employment to reduce the negative impact of capital outflow. On the other hand, due to the decline of output in the sector *Z*, some labor will be released and flow to the sector *M*. Therefore, there is a possibility that the output increase caused by the increasing employment labor in the sector *M* is greater than the output decrease caused by capital outflow. In sector *A*, due to the decline of Z, the rise of X is not enough to offset the negative impact caused by the decline of agricultural pollution factors *Z*, so the output of the sector *A* decreases, and as *Z* decreases, *h(z)* increases.

7.3.3 The Economic and Environmental Effects of Wage Subsidy

Next, we will analyze the economic and agricultural pollution effects of government wage subsidies for agricultural producer service. We assume that the government's wage subsidy rate for agricultural producer service is $\theta_w(0 \le \theta_w < 1)$, then the zero-profit condition Eq. (7.4) of agricultural producer service, the Eq. (7.9), and the budget balance condition of the government are changed into the following forms, respectively:

$$Z^{-\varepsilon\sigma}X^{-\rho\sigma}\overline{w}^{\sigma}(1-\theta_w)^{\sigma}r^{(1-\sigma)} = P_X, \tag{7.4 * *}$$

$$\frac{\alpha_1 A}{w} + (1+\lambda)\frac{1}{\overline{w}}\left(\beta P_M M + \gamma P_Z Z + \sigma\frac{P_X X}{(1-\theta_w)}\right) = L, \tag{7.9*}$$

$$\theta_w \sigma P_X X = \theta_{3l}(A + P_M M). \tag{7.20}$$

Equations (7.1)–(7.3), (7.4**), (7.5)–(7.8), and (7.9*) constitute a complete economic system with wage subsidies in agricultural producer service.

Differentiating Eqs. (7.3), (7.4**), (7.7), (7.8), (7.9*), and (7.20), and substituting Eqs. (7.12)–(7.14) and (7.18) into the total differential equations of the above six equations and sort them out to obtain Eq. (7.21) (please see Appendix 3 for the detailed process):

$$\begin{pmatrix} 0 & \varepsilon\frac{\beta-\gamma}{(1-\beta)} & \rho\frac{\beta-\gamma}{(1-\beta)} & -1 & 0 \\ 0 & \varepsilon\frac{\beta-\sigma}{(1-\beta)} & \rho\frac{\beta-\sigma}{(1-\beta)} & 0 & -1 \\ 0 & \left(1+\varepsilon\frac{\beta-\gamma}{(1-\beta)}\right) & -\left(1-\rho\frac{\beta-\gamma}{(1-\beta)}\right) & 0 & -1 \\ (1-\beta)P_M M & C_1 & C_2 & (1-\gamma)P_Z Z & (1-\sigma)P_X X \\ (1+\lambda)\frac{1}{\overline{w}}\beta P_M M & C_{3*} & C_{4*} & C_{5*} & C_{6*} \end{pmatrix} \begin{pmatrix} \widehat{M} \\ \widehat{Z} \\ \widehat{X} \\ \widehat{P}_Z \\ \widehat{P}_X \end{pmatrix} = \begin{pmatrix} 0 \\ \frac{\theta_w}{1-\theta_w}\sigma \\ 0 \\ -\frac{\theta_w}{1-\theta_w}(1+\lambda)\frac{1}{\overline{w}}\sigma\frac{P_X X}{(1-\theta_w)} \\ 0 \end{pmatrix}\widehat{\theta}_w. \tag{7.21}$$

where,

$$C_{3*} = \left[\left(1+\varepsilon\frac{\beta-\gamma}{(1-\beta)}\right)\frac{\alpha_1 A}{w} + (1+\lambda)\frac{1}{\overline{\overline{w}}}\gamma P_Z Z - \varepsilon\left(\frac{\alpha_1 A}{w} + (1+\lambda)\frac{1}{\overline{\overline{w}}}\beta P_M M\right.\right.$$

$$\left.\left. + (1+\lambda)\frac{1}{\overline{\overline{w}}}\gamma P_Z Z + (1+\lambda)\frac{1}{\overline{\overline{w}}}\sigma\frac{P_X X}{(1-\theta_w)}\right)\right]$$

$$> 0,$$

$$C_{4*} = \left[\rho\frac{\beta-\gamma}{(1-\beta)}\frac{\alpha_1 A}{w} + (1+\lambda)\frac{1}{\overline{\overline{w}}}\sigma\frac{P_X X}{(1-\theta_w)} - \rho\left(\frac{\alpha_1 A}{w} + (1+\lambda)\frac{1}{\overline{\overline{w}}}\beta P_M M\right.\right.$$

$$\left.\left. + (1+\lambda)\frac{1}{\overline{\overline{w}}}\gamma P_Z Z + (1+\lambda)\frac{1}{\overline{\overline{w}}}\sigma\frac{P_X X}{(1-\theta_w)}\right)\right],$$

$$C_{5*} = \left[(1+\lambda)\frac{1}{\overline{\overline{w}}}\gamma P_Z Z + \frac{\alpha_2}{\alpha_1}\left(\frac{\alpha_1 A}{w} + (1+\lambda)\frac{1}{\overline{\overline{w}}}\beta P_M M + (1+\lambda)\frac{1}{\overline{\overline{w}}}\gamma P_Z Z\right.\right.$$

$$\left.\left. + (1+\lambda)\frac{1}{\overline{\overline{w}}}\sigma\frac{P_X X}{(1-\theta_w)}\right)\right]$$

$$> 0,$$

$$C_{6*} = \left[(1+\lambda)\frac{1}{\overline{\overline{w}}}\sigma\frac{P_X X}{(1-\theta_w)} + \frac{(1-\alpha_1-\alpha_2)}{\alpha_1}\left(\frac{\alpha_1 A}{w} + (1+\lambda)\frac{1}{\overline{\overline{w}}}\beta P_M M\right.\right.$$

$$\left.\left. + (1+\lambda)\frac{1}{\overline{\overline{w}}}\gamma P_Z Z + (1+\lambda)\frac{1}{\overline{\overline{w}}}\sigma\frac{P_X X}{(1-\theta_w)}\right)\right]$$

$$> 0.$$

Define the symbol Δ_3 as the determinant value of the coefficient matrix of Eq. (7.21), then we have

$$\Delta_3 = P_M M \left\{ \begin{array}{l} \left(1+\varepsilon\frac{\beta-\gamma}{(1-\beta)}+\rho\frac{\beta-\sigma}{(1-\beta)}\right)(1+\lambda)\frac{1}{\overline{w}}P_X X\left(\beta(1-\sigma)-\frac{(1-\beta)\sigma}{(1-\theta_w)}\right) \\ +\left(1+\varepsilon\frac{\beta-\gamma}{(1-\beta)}+\rho\frac{\beta-\sigma}{(1-\beta)}\right)(1+\lambda)\frac{1}{\overline{w}}(\beta-\gamma)P_Z Z-\left(1+\varepsilon\frac{Z}{1+Z}\frac{\beta-\gamma}{(1-\beta)}+\rho\frac{\beta-\sigma}{(1-\beta)}\right)(1-\beta)\frac{\alpha_1 A}{w} \\ +(1-\beta)(\varepsilon+\rho)\left(1-\frac{\beta-\gamma}{(1-\beta)}\frac{\alpha_2}{\alpha_1}-\frac{\beta-\sigma}{(1-\beta)}\frac{(1-\alpha_1-\alpha_2)}{\alpha_1}\right) \\ \left(\frac{\alpha_1 A}{w}+(1+\lambda)\frac{1}{\overline{w}}\beta P_M M+(1+\lambda)\frac{1}{\overline{w}}\gamma P_Z Z+(1+\lambda)\frac{1}{\overline{w}}\sigma\frac{P_X X}{(1-\theta_w)}\right) \\ -(\varepsilon+\rho)\frac{\beta}{(1-\beta)}\beta(1+\lambda)\frac{1}{\overline{w}}[(1-\beta)P_M M+(1-\gamma)P_Z Z+(1-\sigma)P_X X] \end{array} \right\}. \tag{7.22}$$

According to Eq. (7.22), if $\varepsilon+\rho<0$ and the absolute values of parameters ε and ρ are small enough, we have $\Delta_3<0$. Using Cramer's rule to solve Eq. (7.21), we can yield the effects of agricultural producer service wage subsidy on economy and agricultural pollution, etc., and the specific results are shown in Table 7.3 (please see Appendix 3 for the detailed process).

Based on the results in Table 7.3, we can obtain the third proposition of this chapter:

Proposition 3 *Under certain conditions, the government's wage subsidy to department x will reduce the input of service factor X in the agricultural sector and increase the input of pollution factor Z, so as to aggravate agricultural pollution and finally improve the output level of the agricultural sector.*

From the above analysis results, it can be found that the wage subsidy for agricultural producer service sector will not increase the agricultural sector's use of service factor X, but will increase the agricultural sector's use of agricultural pollution factor Z, thereby aggravating agricultural pollution. Specific economic mechanism is as follows: The purpose of the government's wage subsidy for the sector X is to reduce the use cost of labor factors in sector X and promote the development of the sector X. However, our calculation result is that the output of department x decreases. The reason is that the wage subsidy for the sector X reduces the unit labor employment cost of department X and increases the labor employment of the sector X, resulting in the transfer of rural labor to cities. In order to cope with the outflow of agricultural labor force, the agricultural department can only use the factor Z and factor X to replace the outflow of labor. At the same time, in order to prevent the excessive outflow of agricultural labor force, the agricultural department will use factor Z instead of factor X to replace the agricultural labor force, resulting in the increase of pollution factor Z investment and the decrease of service factor

Table 7.3 The effects of the wage subsidy on economic and agricultural pollution

	$\widehat{A}$	$\widehat{M}$	$\widehat{Z}$	$\widehat{X}$	$\widehat{r}$	$\widehat{w}$	$\widehat{P_Z}$	$\widehat{P_X}$	$\widehat{\lambda}$
$\widehat{\theta_w}$	+	\	+	−	−	\	+	\	\

Note: The symbols "+" and "−", respectively, indicate that the wage subsidy of agricultural producer services has a positive or negative impact on relevant variables, and "\" means that the effects of the wage subsidy of agricultural producer services on relevant variables are uncertain

X investment in the agricultural sector. When the promotion effect of increasing factor Z on agricultural production is more than the side effects of labor outflow and the decreasing factor X input, agricultural output A increases.

7.4 National Welfare Analysis

Based on the previous analysis, we now turn our attention to the analysis of the national welfare effect of the three types of subsidy policies for agricultural producer service. We first assume that the social welfare function is in the form of Cobb-Douglas, that is, $U = D_A^{\rho} D_M^{1-\rho}, 0 < \rho < 1$, where D_A and D_M, respectively, represent the economic demand for agricultural products and manufacturing products. The budget constraint is $I = A + P_M M + tP_M^*(D_M - M)$, where t, D_M, and P_M^* represent tariff rate, domestic demand for manufactured goods, and world market price of manufactured products, respectively, and $P_M = (1+t)P_M^*$, for the convenience of research, we assume that the country forwards all the tariff income to the people, and the people use it to buy imported manufactured products. And we assume that the minimum national expenditure function is $e(1, P_M, U) = D_A + P_M D_M$, when the market is cleared, the following formula is hold

$$e(1, P_M, U) = D_A + P_M D_M = A + P_M M + tP_M^*(D_M - M). \tag{7.23}$$

Differentiating Eq. (7.23) and we can yield

$$\frac{\widehat{U}}{\widehat{\theta}_i} = \frac{1}{e_U U}\left(A\frac{\widehat{A}}{\widehat{\theta}_i} + P_M^* M\frac{\widehat{M}}{\widehat{\theta}_i} + tP_M^* D_M \frac{\widehat{D}_M}{\widehat{\theta}_i}\right) \tag{7.24}$$

where, e_U represents the partial derivative of the minimum expenditure function e to utility U, generally, $e_U > 0$. Assuming that the domestic production proportion of manufacturing product M is $\delta(0 < \delta \leq 1)$, the import proportion is $1 - \delta$, that is, $M = \delta D_M$. From this equation, we can get

$$\frac{\widehat{D}_M}{\widehat{\theta}_i} = \frac{\widehat{M}}{\widehat{\theta}_i}. \tag{7.25}$$

Substitute Eq. (7.25) into Eq. (7.24), and sorting the following equation can be obtained:

$$\frac{\widehat{U}}{\widehat{\theta}_i} = \frac{1}{e_U U}\left(A\frac{\widehat{A}}{\widehat{\theta}_i} + \left(1 + \frac{t}{\delta}\right)P_M^* M\frac{\widehat{M}}{\widehat{\theta}_i}\right). \tag{7.26}$$

It can be found from Eq. (7.26) that the effects of the three subsidies of agricultural producer service on the national welfare level depends on the effects of relevant subsidies on the outputs of the agricultural sector and the manufacturing sector. Next, the national welfare effects of three subsidies for agricultural producer service are analyzed according to Eq. (7.26).

Substituting Eqs. (7.14), (7.31)–(7.33), (7.36)–(7.38), (7.41)–(7.43) in the Appendix 3 into Eq. (7.26), respectively, and according to the relevant assumptions above, we can get

$$\frac{\widehat{U}}{\widehat{\theta}_P} = \frac{1}{e_U U}\frac{P_M M \frac{(1-\alpha_1-\alpha_2)}{\alpha_1}\frac{\theta_P}{1-\theta_P}}{\Delta_1}\left\{\left(1+\frac{t}{\delta}\right)[(1-\sigma)P_X X + (1-\gamma)P_Z Z] - (1-\beta)A\right\} \times \left(1+\varepsilon\frac{\beta-\gamma}{1-\beta}+\rho\frac{\beta-\sigma}{1-\beta}\right)\left(\frac{\alpha_1 A}{w} + (1+\lambda)\frac{1}{\overline{\overline{w}}}\beta P_M M + (1+\lambda)\frac{1}{\overline{\overline{w}}}\gamma P_Z Z + (1+\lambda)\frac{1}{\overline{\overline{w}}}\sigma P_X X\right), \tag{7.27}$$

$$\frac{\widehat{U}}{\theta_r} = \frac{1-\sigma}{e_U U}\frac{\theta_r}{1-\theta_r}\frac{P_M^* M}{\Delta_1}\sigma\frac{P_X X}{1-\theta_r}(Q_1 - Q_2), \tag{7.28}$$

$$\frac{\widehat{U}}{\theta_w} = \frac{1}{e_U U}\frac{\theta_w}{1-\theta_w}\frac{\sigma P_M M}{\Delta_3}(Q_3 + Q_4). \tag{7.29}$$

where

$$Q_1 = \left(1+\frac{t}{\delta}\right) \times \left\{\begin{aligned}&\left(1+\rho\frac{\beta-\sigma}{1-\beta}+\varepsilon\frac{\beta-\gamma}{1-\beta}\right)\frac{\alpha_1 A}{w}\\ &+\left(1-\rho\frac{\sigma-\gamma}{1-\beta}\right)(1+\lambda)\frac{1}{\overline{\overline{w}}}\gamma P_Z Z + \left(1+\varepsilon\frac{\sigma-\gamma}{1-\beta}\right)(1+\lambda)\frac{1}{\overline{\overline{w}}}\sigma P_X X\end{aligned}\right\},$$

$$Q_2 = (1+\lambda)\frac{1}{\overline{\overline{w}}}\beta\left(1+\varepsilon\frac{\beta-\gamma}{1-\beta}+\rho\frac{\beta-\sigma}{1-\beta}\right)A,$$

$$Q_3 = \left(1-\rho\frac{\sigma-\gamma}{1-\beta}\right)A\left[\begin{aligned}&(1+\lambda)\frac{1}{\overline{\overline{w}}}P_X X\left(\beta(1-\sigma)+\frac{(1-\beta)(1-\sigma)}{1-\theta_w}\right)\\ &-\frac{(1-\alpha_1-\alpha_2)}{\alpha_1}(1-\beta)\left(\frac{\alpha_1 A}{w}+(1+\lambda)\frac{1}{\overline{\overline{w}}}\beta P_M M+(1+\lambda)\frac{1}{\overline{\overline{w}}}\gamma P_Z Z+(1+\lambda)\frac{1}{\overline{\overline{w}}}\sigma\frac{P_X X}{1-\theta_w}\right)\end{aligned}\right],$$

$$Q_4 = \left(1 + \frac{t}{\delta}\right)\left\{\begin{array}{l} \left[\left(1 + \varepsilon\frac{\sigma-\gamma}{1-\beta}\right)(1-\sigma)P_X X + \left(1 - \rho\frac{\sigma-\gamma}{1-\beta}\right)(1-\gamma)P_Z Z\right] \\ \left[(1+\lambda)\frac{1}{\overline{w}}\sigma P_X X + \frac{(1-\alpha_1-\alpha_2)}{\alpha_1}\left(\begin{array}{l}\frac{\alpha_1 A}{w} + (1+\lambda)\frac{1}{\overline{w}}\beta P_M M \\ +(1+\lambda)\frac{1}{\overline{w}}\gamma P_Z Z + (1+\lambda)\frac{1}{\overline{w}}\sigma\frac{P_X X}{1-\theta_w}\end{array}\right)\right] \\ -(1+\lambda)\frac{1}{\overline{w}}\frac{P_X X}{1-\theta_w}\left(1 + \rho\frac{\beta-\sigma}{1-\beta} + \varepsilon\frac{\beta-\gamma}{1-\beta}\right)(1-\gamma)P_Z Z \\ -(1-\sigma)P_X X\left\{\begin{array}{l}\left(1 + \rho\frac{\beta-\sigma}{1-\beta} + \varepsilon\frac{\beta-\gamma}{1-\beta}\right)\frac{\alpha_1 A}{w} + \left(1 + \varepsilon\frac{\sigma-\gamma}{1-\beta}\right)(1+\lambda)\frac{1}{\overline{w}}\sigma P_X X \\ \quad + \left(1 + \rho\frac{\beta-\sigma}{1-\beta} + \varepsilon\frac{\beta-\gamma}{1-\beta}\right)(1+\lambda)\frac{1}{\overline{w}}\gamma P_Z Z\end{array}\right\}\end{array}\right\}.$$

From Eqs. (7.27)–(7.29), it can be seen that the effects of three subsidies for agricultural producer service on national welfare cannot be directly determined. If the absolute values of parameters ε and ρ are small enough, we can infer the effects of three subsidies for agricultural producer service on national welfare. According to the Eq. (7.27), combinig with Assumption 1, the effect of the rise of interest subsidies in the sector X on national welfare depends on the tariff rate imposed by the government on imported manufactured goods. The specific effects are as follows:

- If $t = t^* = \delta\frac{(1-\beta)A - (1-\sigma)P_X X - (1-\gamma)P_Z Z}{(1-\sigma)P_X X + (1-\gamma)P_Z Z}$, then $\widehat{U}/\theta_P = 0$, that means the change in the agricultural producer service price subsidy has no influence on national welfare.
- If $t > t^*$, then $\widehat{U}/\theta_P < 0$, that means the increase of the agricultural producer service price subsidy will decrease the national welfare.
- If $t < t^*$, then $\widehat{U}/\theta_P > 0$, that means the increase of the agricultural producer service price subsidy will enhance the national welfare.

According to the Eq. (7.28), if $\sigma < \frac{(1-\alpha_1-\alpha_2)}{(1-2\alpha_1-\alpha_2)+(1+\lambda)\beta}$ is hold, then $\widehat{U}/\theta_r > 0$, that means the increase of interest subsidies in the sector X will improve the national welfare. And according to the Eq. (7.29), the effect of change of wage subsidy in the sector X on national welfare is uncertain.

From the above analysis, we get the following proposition.

Proposition 4

- *The effect of price subsidy of agricultural producer services on national welfare depends on the import tariff rate of manufacturing products. If $t > t^*$, the rise of price subsidy rate of agricultural producer services will reduce national welfare; if $t = t^*$, the change of price subsidy rate of agricultural producer services will not affect the level of national welfare; and if $t < t^*$, the increase in the price* *subsidy rate of agricultural producer services will promote the improvement of national welfare.*

- *If* $\sigma < \frac{(1-\alpha_1-\alpha_2)}{(1-2\alpha_1-\alpha_2)+(1+\lambda)\beta}$, *the rise of interest subsidies for agricultural producer services will improve the level of national welfare.*

7.5 Conclusion

Agricultural productive services are the main means of promoting agricultural modernization in developing countries. Under the existing technical conditions, agricultural pollution is a common and unavoidable problem in the process of agricultural modernization in developing countries. It is an important issue to deal with the relationship between agricultural productive services and agricultural pollution to realize agricultural modernization and agricultural sustainable development.

At present, the academic community is still lack of research on the relationship between the development of agricultural producer service and agricultural pollution. However, we believe that it is necessary to study the relationship between the development of agricultural producer service and agricultural pollution, because the subsidies of agricultural producer service, which seems not directly related to agricultural pollution, are closely related to agricultural pollution in essence. By constructing a four-sector general-equilibrium model including agricultural producer service, this chapter revealed the endogenous characteristics of agricultural pollution and studied the effects of price subsidy, interest subsidy, and wage subsidy for agricultural producer service on agricultural pollution and other economic variables for the first time. The major conclusions of this chapter are the following conclusions:

- The rise of the price subsidy for the agricultural producer service and the wage subsidy of the agricultural producer service sector will increase the output of agricultural sector, but aggravate agricultural pollution.
- The rise of interest subsidy in the agricultural producer service sector will decrease the output of agricultural sector and decrease agricultural pollution under certain conditions.
- The effect of price subsidies for agricultural producer services on national welfare depends on the tariff rate of manufacturing products. Under certain conditions, the rise of interest subsidies in agricultural producer services will improve the level of national welfare. These provide certain reference for the policy decision-making and choice of government departments.

All these provide a theoretical basis for the policy design of governments in developing countries. In addition, this chapter only studies the impact of the promotion policy of agricultural productive services on agricultural pollution, but does not involve the impact of economic factor growth on the development of agricultural productive services and agricultural pollution. We will analyze and clarify it in the follow-up study.

Competing Interests No potential conflict of interest was reported by the authors.

Appendix

Appendix 1

Using Cramer's law to solve Eq. (7.15) yields the following:

$$\Delta_{1X} = -(1-\beta)P_M M \frac{(1-\alpha_1-\alpha_2)}{\alpha_1}\frac{\theta_P}{1-\theta_P} \times \begin{pmatrix} \frac{\alpha_1 A}{w} + (1+\lambda)\frac{1}{w}\beta P_M M \\ +(1+\lambda)\frac{1}{w}\gamma P_Z Z + (1+\lambda)\frac{1}{w}\sigma P_X X \end{pmatrix}\left(1+\varepsilon\frac{\sigma-\gamma}{(1-\beta)}\right), \tag{7.30}$$

$$\Delta_{1Z} = -(1-\beta)P_M M \frac{(1-\alpha_1-\alpha_2)}{\alpha_1}\frac{\theta_P}{1-\theta_P} \times \begin{pmatrix} \frac{\alpha_1 A}{w} + (1+\lambda)\frac{1}{w}\beta P_M M \\ +(1+\lambda)\frac{1}{w}\gamma P_Z Z + (1+\lambda)\frac{1}{w}\sigma P_X X \end{pmatrix}\left(1-\rho\frac{\sigma-\gamma}{(1-\beta)}\right), \tag{7.31}$$

$$\Delta_{1M} = \frac{(1-\alpha_1-\alpha_2)}{\alpha_1}\frac{\theta_P}{1-\theta_P}\begin{pmatrix} \frac{\alpha_1 A}{w} + (1+\lambda)\frac{1}{w}\beta P_M M \\ +(1+\lambda)\frac{1}{w}\gamma P_Z Z + (1+\lambda)\frac{1}{w}\sigma P_X X \end{pmatrix} \times \left\{ \begin{array}{l} \left(1+\varepsilon\frac{\beta-\gamma}{(1-\beta)}+\rho\frac{\beta-\sigma}{(1-\beta)}\right)(1-\sigma)P_X X \\ +\left(1+\varepsilon\frac{\beta-\gamma}{(1-\beta)}+\rho\frac{\beta-\sigma}{(1-\beta)}\right)(1-\gamma)P_Z Z \\ -(\varepsilon+\rho)\frac{\beta}{(1-\beta)}[(1-\beta)P_M M + (1-\gamma)P_Z Z + (1-\sigma)P_X X] \end{array} \right\}, \tag{7.32}$$

$$\Delta_{1P_Z} = -(1-\beta)P_M M \frac{(1-\alpha_1-\alpha_2)}{\alpha_1}\frac{\theta_P}{1-\theta_P} \times \begin{pmatrix} \frac{\alpha_1 A}{w} + (1+\lambda)\frac{1}{w}\beta P_M M \\ +(1+\lambda)\frac{1}{w}\gamma P_Z Z + (1+\lambda)\frac{1}{w}\sigma P_X X \end{pmatrix}(\varepsilon+\rho)\frac{\beta-\gamma}{(1-\beta)}, \tag{7.33}$$

$$\Delta_{1P_X} = -(1-\beta)P_M M\frac{(1-\alpha_1-\alpha_2)}{\alpha_1}\frac{\theta_P}{1-\theta_P} \times \begin{pmatrix} \frac{\alpha_1 A}{w} + (1+\lambda)\frac{1}{\overline{w}}\beta P_M M \\ +(1+\lambda)\frac{1}{\overline{w}}\gamma P_Z Z + (1+\lambda)\frac{1}{\overline{w}}\sigma P_X X \end{pmatrix} (\varepsilon+\rho)\frac{\beta-\sigma}{(1-\beta)}. \tag{7.34}$$

The symbols of the above five equations cannot be determined directly, but if the absolute values of parameters ε and ρ are small enough, and then $\varepsilon + \rho < 0$ and $1+\varepsilon\frac{\sigma-\gamma}{1-\beta}<0$ are hold, the symbols can be determined as follows:$\Delta_{1Z}<0, \Delta_{1X}>0, \Delta_{1M}>0, \Delta_{1P_Z}<0, \Delta_{1P_X}<0$.. Thus, we can yield the effects of the change in agricultural producer service price subsidy on the above five variables. And then substituting the results of Eqs. (7.30)–(7.34) into Eqs. (7.11)–(7.15) of the text, we can obtain the effects of agricultural producer service price subsidy on relevant variables, and then obtain the impact of the change of agricultural producer service price subsidy rate on each variable.

Appendix 2

Using Cramer's law to solve Eq. (7.19) yields the following:

$$\Delta_{2X} = -\frac{\theta_r}{1-\theta_r} \times (1-\sigma)P_M M \left\{ \begin{array}{l} \sigma\frac{P_X X}{(1-\theta_r)}(1+\lambda)\frac{1}{\overline{w}}\beta \\ +(1-\beta)\left[(1+\lambda)\frac{1}{\overline{w}}\sigma P_X X + \frac{(1-\alpha_1-\alpha_2)}{\alpha_1}\begin{pmatrix} \frac{\alpha_1 A}{w} + (1+\lambda)\frac{1}{\overline{w}}\beta P_M M \\ +(1+\lambda)\frac{1}{\overline{w}}\gamma P_Z Z + (1+\lambda)\frac{1}{\overline{w}}\sigma P_X X \end{pmatrix}\right] \end{array} \right\} \times \left(1+\varepsilon\frac{\sigma-\gamma}{(1-\beta)}\right), \tag{7.35}$$

$$\Delta_{2Z} = -\frac{\theta_r}{1-\theta_r} \times (1-\sigma)P_M M \left\{ \begin{array}{l} \sigma\frac{P_X X}{(1-\theta_r)}(1+\lambda)\frac{1}{\overline{w}}\beta \\ +(1-\beta)\left[(1+\lambda)\frac{1}{\overline{w}}\sigma P_X X + \frac{(1-\alpha_1-\alpha_2)}{\alpha_1}\begin{pmatrix} \frac{\alpha_1 A}{w} + (1+\lambda)\frac{1}{\overline{w}}\beta P_M M \\ +(1+\lambda)\frac{1}{\overline{w}}\gamma P_Z Z + (1+\lambda)\frac{1}{\overline{w}}\sigma P_X X \end{pmatrix}\right] \end{array} \right\} \times \left(1-\rho\frac{\sigma-\gamma}{(1-\beta)}\right), \tag{7.36}$$

$$
\Delta_{2M} = \frac{\theta_r}{1-\theta_r}
\times \left\{
\begin{array}{l}
\left[(1+\lambda)\frac{1}{w}\sigma P_X X + \frac{(1-\alpha_1-\alpha_2)}{\alpha_1} \left(\begin{array}{l} \frac{\alpha_1 A}{w} + (1+\lambda)\frac{1}{w}\beta P_M M \\ +(1+\lambda)\frac{1}{w}\gamma P_Z Z + (1+\lambda)\frac{1}{w}\sigma P X \end{array} \right) \right] (\varepsilon+\rho)\frac{\beta-\sigma}{(1-\beta)}(1-\sigma)\frac{P_X X}{(1-\theta_r)} \\
+ \left[(1+\lambda)\frac{1}{w}\gamma P_Z Z + \frac{\alpha_2}{\alpha_1} \left(\begin{array}{l} \frac{\alpha_1 A}{w} + (1+\lambda)\frac{1}{w}\beta P_M M \\ +(1+\lambda)\frac{1}{w}\gamma P_Z Z + (1+\lambda)\frac{1}{w}\sigma P_X X \end{array} \right) \right] (\varepsilon+\rho)\frac{\beta-\gamma}{(1-\beta)}\sigma(1-\sigma)\frac{P_X X}{(1-\theta_r)} \\
+\sigma(1-\sigma)\frac{P_X X}{(1-\theta_r)} \left\{ \begin{array}{l} \left(1+\rho\frac{\beta-\sigma}{(1-\beta)}+\varepsilon\frac{\beta-\gamma}{(1-\beta)}\right)\frac{\alpha_1 A}{w} + \left(1-\rho\frac{\sigma-\gamma}{(1-\beta)}\right)(1+\lambda)\frac{1}{w}\gamma P_Z Z + \left(1+\varepsilon\frac{\sigma-\gamma}{(1-\beta)}\right)(1+\lambda)\frac{1}{w}\sigma P_X X \\ -(\varepsilon+\rho)\left(\frac{\alpha_1 A}{w} + (1+\lambda)\frac{1}{w}\beta P_M M + (1+\lambda)\frac{1}{w}\gamma P_Z Z + (1+\lambda)\frac{1}{w}\sigma P_X X\right) \end{array} \right\} \\
+(1-\sigma) \left[\begin{array}{l} (1+\lambda)\frac{1}{w}\sigma P_X X \\ + \frac{(1-\alpha_1-\alpha_2)}{\alpha_1} \left(\begin{array}{l} \frac{\alpha_1 A}{w} + (1+\lambda)\frac{1}{w}\beta P_M M \\ +(1+\lambda)\frac{1}{w}\gamma P_Z Z + (1+\lambda)\frac{1}{w}\sigma P_X X \end{array} \right) \end{array} \right] \left\{ \begin{array}{l} \left(1+\varepsilon\frac{\sigma-\gamma}{(1-\beta)}\right)(1-\sigma)\frac{P_X X}{(1-\theta_r)} + \left(\varepsilon\frac{\beta-\gamma}{(1-\beta)}+\rho\frac{\beta-\sigma}{(1-\beta)}\right)(1-\gamma)P_Z Z \\ -(\varepsilon+\rho)\frac{\beta}{(1-\beta)}\left[(1-\beta)P_M M + (1-\gamma)P_Z Z + (1-\sigma)\frac{P_X X}{(1-\theta_r)}\right] \end{array} \right\}
\end{array}
\right\}, \tag{7.37}
$$

$$
\Delta_{2P_Z} = -\frac{\theta_r}{1-\theta_r}(1-\sigma)P_M M(\varepsilon+\rho)\frac{\beta-\gamma}{(1-\beta)} \left(\begin{array}{l} \sigma\frac{P_X X}{(1-\theta_r)}(1+\lambda)\frac{1}{w}\beta \\ +(1-\beta)\left[(1+\lambda)\frac{1}{w}\sigma P_X X + \frac{(1-\alpha_1-\alpha_2)}{\alpha_1} \left(\begin{array}{l} \frac{\alpha_1 A}{w} + (1+\lambda)\frac{1}{w}\beta P_M M \\ +(1+\lambda)\frac{1}{w}\gamma P_Z Z + (1+\lambda)\frac{1}{w}\sigma P_X X \end{array} \right) \right] \end{array} \right), \tag{7.38}
$$

$$
\begin{aligned}
\Delta_{2P_X} &= \frac{\theta_r}{1-\theta_r} \\
&\times (1-\sigma)P_M M \left\{
\begin{aligned}
&\left(1+\rho\frac{\beta-\sigma}{(1-\beta)}+\varepsilon\frac{\beta-\gamma}{(1-\beta)}\right)(1-\beta)\frac{\alpha_1 A}{w} - \left(1+\rho\frac{\beta-\sigma}{(1-\beta)}+\varepsilon\frac{\beta-\gamma}{(1-\beta)}\right)(1+\lambda)\frac{1}{\overline{w}}P_Z Z(\beta-\gamma) \\
&-\left(1-\frac{\beta-\gamma}{(1-\beta)}\frac{\alpha_2}{\alpha_1}\right)(\varepsilon+\rho)(1-\beta)\left(\frac{\alpha_1 A}{w}+(1+\lambda)\frac{1}{\overline{w}}\beta P_M M+(1+\lambda)\frac{1}{\overline{w}}\gamma P_Z Z+(1+\lambda)\frac{1}{\overline{w}}\sigma P_X X\right) \\
&+(\varepsilon+\rho)\frac{\beta}{(1-\beta)}\beta\left[\begin{aligned}&(1+\lambda)\frac{1}{\overline{w}}(1-\beta)P_M M \\ &+(1+\lambda)\frac{1}{\overline{w}}(1-\gamma)P_Z Z+(1+\lambda)\frac{1}{\overline{w}}(1-\sigma)\frac{P_X X}{(1-\theta_r)}\end{aligned}\right] \\
&-\left(1+\varepsilon\frac{\sigma-\gamma}{(1-\beta)}\right)(1+\lambda)\frac{1}{\overline{w}}P_X X\left(\frac{\beta(1-\sigma)}{(1-\theta_r)}-(1-\beta)\sigma\right) \\
&-(\varepsilon+\rho)\frac{\beta-\sigma}{(1-\beta)}(1+\lambda)\frac{1}{\overline{w}}\beta\frac{P_X X}{(1-\theta_r)}
\end{aligned}
\right\}.
\end{aligned}
\tag{7.39}
$$

The symbols of the above five equations cannot be determined directly, but if the absolute values of parameters ε and ρ are small enough and $\varepsilon + \rho < 0$ is hold, we can get $\Delta_{2Z} < 0, \Delta_{2P_Z} < 0$. Furthermore, if $1 + \varepsilon\frac{\sigma-\gamma}{1-\beta} < 0$ is hold too, we can obtain $\Delta_{2X} > 0$. And if the interest subsidy rate is large enough, then we have $\Delta_{2M} > 0, \Delta_{2P_X} < 0$. Thus, we can yield the effects of the change in agricultural producer service price subsidy rate on the above five variables. By substituting the results of Eqs. (7.35)–(7.39) into Eqs. (7.12)–(7.15) and (7.18) of the text, the effects of agricultural producer service price subsidy on relevant variables can be yield, the effects of the change of interest subsidy rate in agricultural producer service sector on each variable can then be obtained.

Appendix 3

Using Cramer's law to solve Eq. (7.19) yields the following:

$$\Delta_{3X} = \frac{\theta_w}{1-\theta_w}\sigma P_M M\left(1 + \varepsilon\frac{\sigma-\gamma}{(1-\beta)}\right) \times \left\{ \begin{array}{l} (1+\lambda)\frac{1}{\overline{w}}P_X X\left[\beta(1-\sigma) + \frac{(1-\beta)(1-\sigma)}{(1-\theta_w)}\right] \\ -\frac{(1-\alpha_1-\alpha_2)}{\alpha_1}(1-\beta)\left(\begin{array}{l} \frac{\alpha_1 A}{w} + (1+\lambda)\frac{1}{\overline{w}}\beta P_M M \\ +(1+\lambda)\frac{1}{\overline{w}}\gamma P_Z Z + (1+\lambda)\frac{1}{\overline{w}}\sigma\frac{P_X X}{(1-\theta_w)} \end{array}\right) \end{array} \right\}, \tag{7.40}$$

$$\Delta_{3Z} = \frac{\theta_w}{1-\theta_w}\sigma P_M M\left(1 - \rho\frac{\sigma-\gamma}{(1-\beta)}\right) \times \left[\begin{array}{l} (1+\lambda)\frac{1}{\overline{w}}P_X X\left(\beta(1-\sigma) + \frac{(1-\beta)(1-\sigma)}{(1-\theta_w)}\right) \\ -\frac{(1-\alpha_1-\alpha_2)}{\alpha_1}(1-\beta)\left(\begin{array}{l} \frac{\alpha_1 A}{w} + (1+\lambda)\frac{1}{\overline{w}}\beta P_M M \\ +(1+\lambda)\frac{1}{\overline{w}}\gamma P_Z Z + (1+\lambda)\frac{1}{\overline{w}}\sigma\frac{P_X X}{(1-\theta_w)} \end{array}\right) \end{array} \right], \tag{7.41}$$

$$\Delta_{3M}=\frac{\theta_w}{1-\theta_w}\sigma\left\{\begin{array}{l}\left[\begin{array}{l}\left(1+\varepsilon\frac{\sigma-\gamma}{(1-\beta)}\right)(1-\sigma)P_XX+\left(1-\rho\frac{\sigma-\gamma}{(1-\beta)}\right)(1-\gamma)P_ZZ\\-(\varepsilon+\rho)\frac{\beta}{(1-\beta)}[(1-\beta)P_MM+(1-\gamma)P_ZZ+(1-\sigma)P_XX]\end{array}\right]\left[(1+\lambda)\frac{1}{\overline{w}}\sigma P_XX+\frac{(1-\alpha_1-\alpha_2)}{\alpha_1}\left(\begin{array}{l}\frac{\alpha_1A}{w}+(1+\lambda)\frac{1}{\overline{w}}\beta P_MM\\+(1+\lambda)\frac{1}{\overline{w}}\gamma P_ZZ+(1+\lambda)\frac{1}{\overline{w}}\sigma\frac{P_XX}{(1-\theta_w)}\end{array}\right)\right]\\+(\varepsilon+\rho)\left[\frac{\beta-\gamma}{(1-\beta)}(1+\lambda)\frac{1}{\overline{w}}\sigma P_XX+\frac{\beta-\gamma}{(1-\beta)}\frac{(1-\alpha_1-\alpha_2)}{\alpha_1}\left(\frac{\alpha_1A}{w}+(1+\lambda)\frac{1}{\overline{w}}\beta P_MM+(1+\lambda)\frac{1}{\overline{w}}\gamma P_ZZ+(1+\lambda)\frac{1}{\overline{w}}\sigma\frac{P_XX}{(1-\theta_w)}\right)\right](1-\gamma)P_ZZ\\-(1+\lambda)\frac{1}{\overline{w}}\frac{P_XX}{(1-\theta_w)}\left\{\begin{array}{l}\left[(\varepsilon+\rho)\frac{\beta-\sigma}{(1-\beta)}+\left(1+\varepsilon\frac{\sigma-\gamma}{(1-\beta)}\right)\right](1-\sigma)P_XX\\+\left(1+\rho\frac{\beta-\sigma}{(1-\beta)}+\varepsilon\frac{\beta-\gamma}{(1-\beta)}\right)(1-\gamma)P_ZZ-(\varepsilon+\rho)\frac{\beta}{(1-\beta)}[(1-\beta)P_MM+(1-\gamma)P_ZZ+(1-\sigma)P_XX]\end{array}\right\}\\-(1-\sigma)P_XX\left\{\begin{array}{l}\left(1+\rho\frac{\beta-\sigma}{(1-\beta)}+\varepsilon\frac{\beta-\gamma}{(1-\beta)}\right)\frac{\alpha_1A}{w}+\left(1+\varepsilon\frac{\sigma-\gamma}{(1-\beta)}\right)(1+\lambda)\frac{1}{\overline{w}}\sigma P_XX+\left(1+\rho\frac{\beta-\sigma}{(1-\beta)}+\varepsilon\frac{\beta-\gamma}{(1-\beta)}\right)(1+\lambda)\frac{1}{\overline{w}}\gamma P_ZZ\\-(\varepsilon+\rho)\left(1-\frac{\beta-\gamma}{(1-\beta)}\frac{\alpha_2}{\alpha_1}\right)\left(\frac{\alpha_1A}{w}+(1+\lambda)\frac{1}{\overline{w}}\beta P_MM+(1+\lambda)\frac{1}{\overline{w}}\gamma P_ZZ+(1+\lambda)\frac{1}{\overline{w}}\sigma\frac{P_XX}{(1-\theta_w)}\right)\end{array}\right\}\end{array}\right\}, \tag{7.42}$$

$$\Delta_{3P_Z}=\frac{\theta_w}{1-\theta_w}\sigma P_MM(\varepsilon+\rho)\frac{\beta-\gamma}{(1-\beta)}\left[\begin{array}{l}(1+\lambda)\frac{1}{\overline{w}}P_XX(\beta-\sigma)-(1+\lambda)\frac{1}{\overline{w}}\beta(1+\lambda)\frac{1}{\overline{w}}\frac{P_XX}{(1-\theta_w)}\\-\frac{(1-\alpha_1-\alpha_2)}{\alpha_1}(1-\beta)\left(\begin{array}{l}\frac{\alpha_1A}{w}+(1+\lambda)\frac{1}{\overline{w}}\beta P_MM\\+(1+\lambda)\frac{1}{\overline{w}}\gamma P_ZZ+(1+\lambda)\frac{1}{\overline{w}}\sigma\frac{P_XX}{(1-\theta_w)}\end{array}\right)\end{array}\right], \tag{7.43}$$

$$
\Delta_{3P_X} = \frac{\theta_w}{1-\theta_w}\sigma P_M M \left\{
\begin{array}{l}
\left[(\varepsilon+\rho)\frac{\beta-\sigma}{(1-\beta)}(1-\beta) - \left(1+\varepsilon\frac{\sigma-\gamma}{(1-\beta)}\right)\left(\frac{\beta(1-\sigma)}{(1-\theta_w)} - (1-\beta)\sigma\right)\right](1+\lambda)\frac{1}{\bar{w}}P_X X \\
+\left(1+\rho\frac{\beta-\sigma}{(1-\beta)}+\varepsilon\frac{\beta-\gamma}{(1-\beta)}\right)(1-\beta)\frac{\alpha_1 A}{w} - \left(1-\rho\frac{\sigma-\gamma}{(1-\beta)}\right)(\beta-\gamma)(1+\lambda)\frac{1}{\bar{w}}P_Z Z - (\rho+\varepsilon)\frac{\beta-\gamma}{(1-\beta)}\beta(1-\gamma)(1+\lambda)\frac{1}{\bar{w}}P_Z Z \\
+(\varepsilon+\rho)\left[
\begin{array}{l}
\frac{\beta}{(1-\beta)}\left[(1+\lambda)\frac{1}{\bar{w}}\beta(1-\beta)P_M M + (1+\lambda)\frac{1}{\bar{w}}\beta(1-\gamma)P_Z Z + (1+\lambda)\frac{1}{\bar{w}}\beta(1-\sigma)P_X X\right] \\
+(1+\lambda)\frac{1}{\bar{w}}\gamma P_Z Z(\beta-\gamma) - \left((1-\beta)-\frac{\alpha_2}{\alpha_1}(\beta-\gamma)\right)\left(\frac{\alpha_1 A}{w} + (1+\lambda)\frac{1}{\bar{w}}\beta P_M M + (1+\lambda)\frac{1}{\bar{w}}\gamma P_Z Z + (1+\lambda)\frac{1}{\bar{w}}\sigma\frac{P_X X}{(1-\theta_w)}\right)
\end{array}
\right]
\end{array}
\right\}. \tag{7.44}
$$

According to the above five equations, if the absolute values of parameters ε and ρ are small enough to reaches $\varepsilon + \rho < 0$, then we can $\Delta_{3Z} < 0$, $\Delta_{3P_Z} < 0$. Furthermore, if the inequality $1 + \varepsilon \frac{\sigma - \gamma}{1 - \beta} < 0$ is hold too, we can obtain $\Delta_{3X} > 0$. But the symbols of Δ_{3M}, Δ_{3P_X} are uncertain. Thus, we can yield the effects of the change in agricultural producer service price subsidy on the variables of X, Z, and P_Z. And then substituting the results of Eqs. (7.40)–(7.44) into Eqs. (7.12)–(7.15) and (7.18) of the text can yield the effects of agricultural producer service price subsidy on relevant variables, and then obtain the effects of the change of interest subsidy in agricultural producer service sector on each variable.

References

Beladi H, Chao CC (2006) Environmental policy, comparative advantage, and welfare for a developing economy. Environ Dev Econ 11(5):559–568. https://doi.org/10.1017/S1355770X06003123

Cole MA, Elliott RJ, Zhang J (2011) Growth, foreign direct investment, and the environment: evidence from Chinese cities. J Reg Sci 51(1):121–138. https://doi.org/10.1111/j.1467-9787.2010.00674.x

Copeland B, Taylor M (1999) Trade, spatial separation, and the environment. J Int Econ 47:137–168. https://doi.org/10.1016/S0022-1996(98)00020-8

Daitoh I (2003) Environmental protection and urban unemployment: environmental policy reform in a polluted dualistic economy. Rev Dev Econ 7(3):496–509. https://doi.org/10.1111/1467-9361.00205

Harris JR, Todaro MP (1970) Migration, unemployment and development: a two-sector analysis. Am Econ Rev 60(1):126–142. https://www.jstor.org/stable/1807860

Kondoh K, Yabuuchi S (2012) Unemployment, environmental policy, and international migration. J Int Trade Econ Dev 21(5):677–690. https://doi.org/10.1080/09638199.2010.535613

Li X, Fu H (2020) Migrant remittance, agricultural producer service, and environmental pollution. Asia-Pac J Account Econ 29(5):1267–1282. https://doi.org/10.1080/16081625.2020.1808797

Li X, Jia T (2021) Partial privatization, producer services and unemployment in developing countries. Rev Dev Econ 26(1):423–441. https://doi.org/10.1111/rode.12814

Li X, Wu Y (2018) Environment and economy in the modern agricultural development. Asia-Pac J Account Econ 25(1–2):163–176. https://doi.org/10.1080/16081625.2016.1246191

Li X, Fu H, Wu Y (2020) Pollution mitigation, unemployment rate and wage inequality in the presence of agricultural pollution. China Econ Rev 61:101425. https://doi.org/10.1016/j.chieco.2020.101425

Liu Y, Xia JC, Li Y (2017) Producer services agglomeration and manufacturing upgrading. China Ind Econ 7:24–42. (in Chinese)

Taheripour F, Khanna M, Nelson CH (2008) Welfare impacts of alternative public policies for agricultural pollution control in an open economy: a general equilibrium framework. Am J Agric Econ 90(3):701–718. https://doi.org/10.1111/j.1467-8276.2008.01139.x

Tawada M, Sun S (2010) Urban pollution, unemployment and national welfare in a dualistic economy. Rev Dev Econ 14:311–322. https://doi.org/10.1111/j.1467-9361.2010.00554.x

van Marrewijk C, Stibora J, de Vaa A, Viaene JM (1997) Producer services, comparative advantage, and international trade patterns. J Int Econ 42:195–220. https://doi.org/10.1016/S0022-1996(96)01472-9

Wu Y, Li X (2021) International factor mobility and environment in a dual agricultural economy. Ann Reg Sci 66:75–89. https://doi.org/10.1007/s00168-020-01010-5

Xi QM, Chen X, Li GP (2015) Study on the pattern selection of Chinese urban producer services: oriented by the improvement of industrial efficiency. China Ind Econ 2:18–30. (in Chinese)

Part III
Producer Services Issues

Chapter 8
Partial Privatization, Producer Services, and Unemployment in Developing Countries

Abstract Existing literature argues that privatization tends to lower the output of the mixed-ownership firms in the manufacturing. Nevertheless, since manufacturing has closely linked to producer services recently, by incorporating producer services into the analysis, this paper investigates the impacts of partial privatization of the mixed-ownership firm in the manufacturing sector on output, unemployment, and social welfare in developing countries in a three-sector general equilibrium model. The main conclusion is that partial privatization would lower unemployment, and raise output conditionally if the profit of producer service firms is zero in the long run. Besides, the welfare impacts of partial privatization in the short and long run are considered. Compared with the existing literature, this paper provides a new perspective and derives some new results.

Keywords Partial privatization · Mixed ownership · Producer service · Unemployment · Welfare

8.1 Introduction

Privatization of mixed-ownership firms (partially state-owned) is an important issue in developing countries. Literature has discussed the conflicts between the dual objectives of the mixed-ownership firms under the game theory approach, that is, pursuing profits and maintaining employments (Chen 2017; Kim et al. 2019; Li and Xu 2002; Liu et al. 2006; Wang and Chiou 2015).

Mixed duopoly and oligopoly games have been established in studies on privatization, in which mixed-ownership firms compete with one or more private firms (Anderson et al. 1997; Matsumura and Kanda 2005; Matsumura and Matsushima 2004). Literature shows that privatization can reduce the output of the mixed-ownership firm and improve its productivity (Matsumura and Okamura 2015; Wang and Chen 2010; White 1996). In recent studies, Xu et al. (2017) and Lee et al. (2018) have analyzed the problem of privatization and liberalization in developing countries in a multistage game, both arguing that the timing of privatization is essential to the social welfare. Further, these theoretical results are also

X. Li, Y. Wu, *Research on Characteristic Issues in Current Developing Economies*, New Frontiers in Regional Science: Asian Perspectives 80,
https://doi.org/10.1007/978-981-97-7284-1_8

supported by empirical literature. For example, studies in India, China, and Turkey have documented output contraction and efficiency improvement that stem from changes in the objectives of mixed-ownership firms and in market structure during privatization (Bai et al. 2009; Chen et al. 2008; Gupta 2005; Jiang et al. 2013; Okten and Arin 2006).

But the game theory approach cannot evaluate the impacts of privatization on unemployment explicitly because factor market is not considered in these models. Therefore, the general-equilibrium model has been applied to investigate the effects of privatization on output, unemployment, and social welfare in a developing economy. The main findings under general equilibrium are contrast with the current analysis under partial equilibrium. For example, Chisari et al. (1999) established a computational general-equilibrium model to evaluate the effects of privatization. They found that privatization improved macroeconomic gains in Argentina, while it was not a major contributor to the rising unemployment. Beladi and Chao (2006) established a two-sector model for a developing country. In their model, partial privatization worsens unemployment in the short-run, capital-immobile case, while lowers unemployment in the long-run, capital-mobile case. Further, some literature discussed distributional effects of privatization. For example, Ghosh and Sen (2012) argued that privatization can raise the return to capital and lower the return to labor. Chao et al. (2016) found that partial privatization would narrow wage inequality between urban and rural labors and lower social welfare if the profit of mixed-ownership firms is not zero in the short run.

Although literature has discussed the impacts of privatization on the labor market, few analyses on the problem of partial privatization considers the usage of producer services in the manufacturing. Nevertheless, manufacturing process and producer services often exist simultaneously in practice. Recently, the linkage between producer services and manufacturing has been discussed frequently (Francois 1990; Rivera-Batiz and Rivera-Batiz 1990). The producer service sector can provide services to the manufacturing sector in forms of advertising, transportation, communication networks, legal supports, financial service, and so on. Both the manufacturing sector and the producer service sector account for large proportions in modern economies, even in developing countries, for example, India and China. The share of stated-owned enterprises (SOEs) has been declining over the past two decades (from over 40% in 2001 to less than 30% in 2018) compared to the entire national economy in China.[1] Meanwhile, China has been establishing huge transportation networks and power systems to support the production of the manufacturing sector. The producer service sector has been playing a growing role in job creation. Besides, the output of the mixed-ownership firms has been increasing.

[1] We estimated privatization degree of China from two sources: (i) the 2019 China Statistical Yearbook published by National Bureau of Statistics of China, see http://www.stats.gov.cn/english/Statisticaldata/AnnualData/ (ii) reports from SASAC (State-Owned Assets Supervision and Administration Commission of the State Council) of China, see http://en.sasac.gov.cn/

Therefore, this paper attempts to address the following questions: what impacts partial privatization of the mixed-ownership firms in the manufacturing sector would have on output, unemployment, and social welfare if the linkage between the producer service sector and the manufacturing sector is considered?

We evaluate the impacts of partial privatization by establishing a three-sector general-equilibrium model. These three sectors are the producer service sector, the manufacturing sector (with a partially privatized mixed-ownership firm), and the agricultural sector. We classify the analyses into short- and long run:

- In the short run, the profit of producer service firms may not be zero, and the number of producer service firms is exogenous.
- In the long run, profit of producer service firms is zero, and the number of producer service firms is endogenous.

Among all researches related to this field, we are the first group to find that partial privatization would raise the output of the mixed-ownership firms, lower unemployment, and raise social welfare in the long-run, capital-mobile case.

Our model generates favorable impacts of partial privatization, which differs from previous literature. Existing studies applying the mixed-oligopoly partial equilibrium model (Lee et al. 2018; Matsumura 1998; Matsumura and Kanda 2005; Xu et al. 2017) argued that privatization would lower the output of mixed-ownership firms. Besides, previous general-equilibrium literature (Beladi and Chao 2006; Chao et al. 2016; Chao and Yu 1994) discussed the impact of privatization on unemployment in an urban-rural two-sector model. They also found output decline of the mixed-ownership firms due to privatization. In contrast, in addition to discussing the impact of partial privatization on unemployment, we found that partial privatization may raise the output of the mixed-ownership firm. Our model differs from them in that we focus on the producer service sector. Therefore, our model's setup is different from previous studies:

- We establish a three-sector general equilibrium model and focus on the role of producer services in manufacturing, while former literature established a two-sector model.
- We classify short- and long run in terms of entry or exit (and hence zero profit) of producer service firms. While Beladi and Chao (2006) classified the model according to capital-immobile or capital-mobile condition, Chao et al. (2016) considered the short- and long run in terms of entry or exit of state-owned firms in manufacturing. Choosing this perspective enables us to gain a deeper understanding of the role of the producer service sector in the process of privatization, extending the horizon of the problem of privatization.

The rest of this paper is organized as follows. Section 8.2 provides a three-sector general-equilibrium model for a developing economy, in which varieties of producer service are treated as an intermediate input for a mixed-ownership firm in manufacturing. Section 8.3 discusses the short-run impacts of partial privatization on output and unemployment, and classifies the model into capital-immobile case and capital-mobile case. Moreover, Sect. 8.4 evaluates the long-run, capital-mobile effects of partial privatization. In addition, Sect. 8.5 provides further discussions of the impact of partial privatization on social welfare. At last, concluding remarks are mentioned in Sect. 8.6.

8.2 The Model

Consider a developing economy that includes the producer service sector, the manufacturing sector, and the agricultural sector. Producer service works as an intermediate input for producing manufacturing good (see Anwar 2010; Rivera-Batiz and Rivera-Batiz 1990; Van Marrewijk et al. 1997; Zhang 2012). Producer service, denoted by x, is produced by n private-owned service firms under monopolistic competition. The manufacturing good, denoted by Y, is produced by a monopolistic mixed-ownership (partially stated-owned) firm, while the agricultural good, denoted by Z, is produced by competitive rural firms.

Choose agricultural good Z as the numeraire. On the demand side of the economy, for analytical traceability, the quasi-linear utility function of a representative consumer is $U(Y, Z) = v(Y) + Z$.[2] The budget constraint is $I = p_Y Y + Z$, where p_Y is the relative price of manufacturing good Y. Utility maximization subject to the budget constraint yields the inverse demand for manufacturing good: $p_Y(Y) = v'(Y)$.

On the supply side of the economy, we first consider the producer service sector. Each producer service firm is assumed to specialize in the production of a single variety of service. Following Dixit and Stiglitz (1977), each service firm acts in a Cournot-Nash fashion. Thus, following a symmetric way, the price p and output of a single producer service good x are identical.

Each producer service is produced by the labor and capital with cost function $C = f^x(\overline{w}, r_X) + m^x(\overline{w}, r_X)x$, where f^x and m^x are the fixed cost and unit variable cost, respectively; $\overline{w}$ is the minimum wage in the urban area; r_X is the interest rate in producer service sector. By Shephard's lemma, demands for the labor and capital in this sector are, respectively, $n\left(f_w^x + m_w^x x\right)$ and $n\left(f_r^x + m_r^x x\right)$.

Besides, varieties of producer services are organized in the CES type as the input of producing good Y is given by $X \equiv \left(\sum_{i=1}^{n} x_i^\sigma\right)^{\frac{1}{\sigma}} = n^{\frac{1}{\sigma}}x$ and $p_X \equiv \frac{npx}{X}$,

where X represents the combination of services in the CES type, σ is a parameter in the range (0,1) representing constant elasticity of substitution among services, and p_X is the "price" of X.

Now for the profit maximization problem of producer service firms, each producer service firm chooses an output x to maximize its profit, and the first-order condition is $p(\varepsilon - 1)/\varepsilon = m^x(\overline{w}, r_X)$, where ε is the price elasticity of demand of x.

[2] The focus of this chapter is to incorporate the linkage between the producer service sector and the manufacturing sector. Therefore, consumer or final-expenditure services is not considered.

Note that the price elasticity parameter ε can be derived as $\varepsilon = 1/(1-\sigma)$. Therefore, the first order condition can be rewritten as

$$\sigma p = m^x(\overline{w}, r_X) \tag{8.1}$$

Parameter σ reveals the markup of the producer service firm.

Besides, we assume manufacturing good Y is generated by a mixed-ownership firm using the labor, capital, and producer services X with cost function $C^Y = f^Y(\overline{w}, r_Y, p_X) + m^Y(\overline{w}, r_Y, p_X)Y$. f^Y and m^Y are, respectively, fixed cost and unit variable cost; r_Y is the interest rate in sector Y. By Shephard's lemma, demands for the labor, capital, and producer service of the mixed-ownership firm are $f_w^Y + m_w^Y Y, f_r^Y + m_r^Y Y$, and $f_p^Y + m_p^Y Y$, respectively. Since the extent of the producer service market is determined by the demand from the mixed-ownership firm in the manufacturing sector, the market clearing condition for producer services is

$$f_p^Y + m_p^Y Y = X. \tag{8.2}$$

The mixed-ownership firm cares not only profit, but also social welfare. The profit of the mixed-ownership firm is $\pi^Y = p_Y Y - C^Y$. In addition, welfare that the mixed-ownership firm concerns include profits of the mixed-ownership firm and producer service firms, and consumer surplus from consuming good Y, that is, the welfare function is $W = \pi^Y + n\pi^x + CS$, where CS denotes consumers' surplus. The objective of the mixed-ownership firm is $k\pi^Y + (1-k)W$, where k represents the degree of private ownership and $k \in [0, 1]$. The mixed-ownership firm chooses an output Y to maximize the objective, and the first-order condition is:

$$(p_Y + p'_Y Y) + (1-k)(1-\sigma)p_X m_p^Y - (1-k)p'_Y Y = m^Y(\overline{w}, r_Y, p_X).. \tag{8.3}$$

The RHS of Eq. (8.3) is the marginal cost of the mixed-ownership firm mentioned before. The first term of LHS of Eq. (8.3) is the marginal revenue of producing one more unit of manufacturing good. Besides, the second term of the LHS refers to the increase in the profit of the producer service firms. In addition, the third term of the LHS can be explained as the increase in consumer surplus.

For the rural area, we assume the production of agricultural good Z requires the labor and capital under the constant-returns-to-scale technology. The corresponding unit cost function is $g(w, r_Z)$, where w represents wage in the rural area and r_Z is the interest rate in sector Z. By Shephard's lemma, the derived demands for the labor and capital in sector Z are $g_w Z$ and $g_r Z$, respectively. Besides, the first-order condition of the profit maximization of agricultural sector is

$$1 = g(w, r_Z). \tag{8.4}$$

For the labor market, according to Harris and Todaro (1970), the higher urban wage induces workers to migrate from the rural to urban area. We define L_u the unemployment in the urban areas, define $L_Y + L_X$ and L_Z the employment in the urban and rural area, respectively. A rural worker will continue to migrate to the city if the expected wage he can get in the city is higher than that in the rural area. By defining unemployment ratio by $\mu = L_u/(L_Y + L_X)$, labor migration condition is

$$\overline{w} = (1 + \mu)w. \tag{8.5}$$

Besides, the market clearing condition for labor is

$$(1 + \mu)\left[f_w^y + m_w^y Y + n\left(f_w^x + m_w^x x\right)\right] + g_w Z = \overline{L}, \tag{8.6}$$

where $\overline{L}$ represents the total labor endowment in the economy.

In addition, considering capital market segmentation stems from the urban-rural dualism structure in developing countries, the capital would be immobile among sectors. In this case, market clearing conditions for the capital are

$$n\left(f_r^x + m_r^x x\right) = \overline{K}_X, \tag{8.7}$$

$$f_r^y + m_r^y Y = \overline{K}_Y, \tag{8.8}$$

$$g_r Z = \overline{K}_Z, \tag{8.9}$$

where $\overline{K}_X$, $\overline{K}_Y$, and $\overline{K}_Z$ are capital endowments in sectors *X*, *Y*, and *Z*, respectively. Nevertheless, the economic development and growth of these countries calls for eliminating capital market fragmentation. When capital moves freely among three sectors, the market-clearing condition for the capital can be rewritten as

$$f_r^y + m_r^y Y + n\left(f_r^x + m_r^x x\right) + g_r Z = \overline{K}. \tag{8.10}$$

Finally, we consider time horizon and classify the model in the short- and long run. The number of producer service firms is exogenous in the short run, and hence the economic profit may not be zero. While in the long run, free entry or the exit of producer service firms guarantees zero unexploited profit. In the long run we have

$$px = f^x + m^x x. \tag{8.11}$$

We use this setup to describe the structure of a developing country and investigate the short- and long-run impacts of partial privatization on output, unemployment, and welfare. First, Eqs. (1)–(9) consist of the short-run, capital-immobile model. The endogenous variables are r_Y, r_X, r_Z, p, x, Y, Z, w, and μ. In addition, the exogenous variables in the model include a policy variable on privatization k, the fixed wage rate $\overline{w}$, and four production factor endowment variables $\overline{K}_Y$, $\overline{K}_X$, $\overline{K}_Z$, and $\overline{L}$. Second, Eqs. (8.1)–(8.6) and (8.10) consist of the short-run, capital-mobile model. In this case, there is no urban-rural capital market segmentation in developing countries and variables r_Y, r_X, and r_Z are replaced by equalized interest rate r, yet the entry or exit of producer service firms is not allowed in the short run.[3] Third, Eqs. (8.1)–(8.6), (8.10), and (8.11) consist of the long-run, capital-mobile model. The settings of endogenous and exogenous variables are similar.

8.3 Short-Run Effects

In this section, we evaluate the short-run effects of partial privatization.

8.3.1 Capital-Immobile Case

We first consider the capital-immobile case. Let a "^" over a variable denote its percentage change. We apply Eqs. (8.1)–(8.9) to evaluate the effects of privatization.

First, by totally differentiating Eq. (8.2), we have

$$s_{XK}^{Y}\widehat{r}_{Y} + s_{XX}^{Y}\widehat{p}_{X} + \lambda_{XY}^{m}\widehat{Y} = \widehat{x} + 1/\sigma\widehat{n}, \tag{8.12}$$

where $s_{ij}^{Y} = \varepsilon_{ijY}^{f}\theta_{jY}^{f}\lambda_{iY}^{f} + \varepsilon_{ijY}^{m}\theta_{jY}^{m}\lambda_{iY}^{m}$ is the substitution effect in demand for ith production factor. Following Jones (1965), we define ε_{ijY}^{f} as the elasticity of factor substitution between ith and jth factors in the fixed cost of good Y, that is, $\varepsilon_{XKY}^{f} = f^{Y}f_{pr}^{Y}/\left(f_{p}^{Y}f_{r}^{Y}\right)$. Besides, λ_{jY}^{f} and λ_{jY}^{m} are the allocation shares of the jth production factor in the fixed and variable cost of sector Y.

Moreover, by totally differentiating Eq. (8.3), we can obtain the change in mixed-ownership firm's output as

$$\begin{aligned} -(1+k+ke^{y})\widehat{Y} = {} & \varepsilon^{Y}b^{Y}\left[1-(1-k)(1-\sigma)\theta_{XY}^{m}\right]\left(\theta_{KY}^{m}\widehat{r}_{Y} + \theta_{XY}^{m}\widehat{p}_{X}\right) \\ & + \left(1+\varepsilon^{Y}b^{Y}(1-\sigma)\theta_{XY}^{m}\right)k\widehat{k}, \end{aligned} \tag{8.13}$$

where $e^{y} = p_{Y}''Y/p_{Y}'$ measures the curvature of the demand function, $\varepsilon^{y} = -p_{Y}/\left(Yp_{Y}'\right)$ is the price elasticity of demand for good Y, $\theta_{KY}^{m} = m_{r}^{Y}r^{Y}/m^{Y}$ represents the variable cost share of the capital in producing good Y, and $b^{y} = m^{Y}/p_{Y}$ is the ratio of the marginal cost to price. From Eq. (8.13) for a given capital cost r_{Y} and producer service price p_{X}, output of good Y decreases in face of increased degree of privatization.

In addition, by totally differentiating Eqs. (8.1) and (8.4), we have

[3] For similar settings, please see Anwar (2010) and Zhang (2012).

$$\widehat{p} = \theta^m_{KX}\widehat{r}_X, \tag{8.14}$$

$$\theta^g_{LZ}\widehat{w} + \theta^g_{KZ}\widehat{r}_Z = 0. \tag{8.15}$$

Equation (8.14) shows the relationship between the price of a single producer service and that of the capital input in the producer service sector, where θ^m_{KX} represents the variable cost share of capital in producing good x. Capital cost and producer service price move in the same direction due to input-output relationship. In addition, Eq. (8.15) demonstrates the relationship between the wage and the interest rate in the agricultural sector, in which θ^g_{LZ} and θ^g_{KZ} are the variable cost share of labor and capital in producing good Z, respectively.

Moreover, by totally differentiating Eq. (8.5), we have

$$(1 + \mu)\widehat{w} + \mu\widehat{\mu} = 0, \tag{8.16}$$

which means that the wage rate in the rural area and unemployment in the urban area moves in opposite directions.

In addition, from market clearing conditions for the capital and labor, we can obtain the overall changes in outputs x, Y, and Z, which will lead to further repercussions on production factor prices and unemployment. By totally differentiating Eqs. (8.6)–(8.9), we have

$$(1 + \mu)\left(\lambda^m_{LX}\widehat{x} + \lambda^m_{LY}\widehat{Y} + s^X_{LK}\widehat{r}_X + s^Y_{LK}\widehat{r}_Y + s^Y_{LX}\widehat{p}_X\right) + \lambda^g_{LZ}\widehat{Z} + s^Z_{LK}\widehat{r}_Z + s^Z_{LL}\widehat{w}$$
$$+ (1 - \lambda^g_{LZ})\mu\widehat{\mu} = 0, \tag{8.17}$$

$$\lambda^m_{KX}\widehat{x} = -s^X_{KK}\widehat{r}_X, \tag{8.18}$$

$$\lambda^m_{KY}\widehat{Y} = -s^Y_{KK}\widehat{r}_Y - s^Y_{KX}\widehat{p}_X, \tag{8.19}$$

$$\lambda^g_{KZ}\widehat{Z} = -s^Z_{KK}\widehat{r}_Z - s^Z_{KL}\widehat{w}. \tag{8.20}$$

Equations (8.12)–(8.20) fully describe the capital-immobile model. From these we can solve the differential system of Eq. (8.30) shown in Appendix 1 and obtain the effects of the increased degree of privatization of the mixed-ownership firm on the output, returns of production factors, and unemployment. Results are summarized in Table 8.1.

Table 8.1 The effects of partial privatization in the short-run, capital-immobile case

	$\widehat{Y}$	$\widehat{x}$	$\widehat{Z}$	$\widehat{r}_Y$	$\widehat{r}_X$	$\widehat{r}_Z$	$\widehat{p}$	$\widehat{w}$	$\widehat{\mu}$
$\widehat{k}$	–	–	+	–	–	+	–	–	+

Note: "+" and "–" denote directions of the comparative statics of the rise of the degree of privatization

Proposition 1 *In the short-run and, capital-immobile case, partial privatization of the mixed-ownership firm lowers outputs of the manufacturing sector and the producer service sector, raises outputs of the agricultural sector, and aggravates the unemployment rate.*

The proof of Proposition 1 is shown in Appendix 1. The mixed-ownership firm will focus more on profit during the increase in private ownership. The change of objective of the mixed-ownership firm will contribute to reduce its demand for labor input and hence lower the output of the manufacturing good. Part of those dismissed labors migrate from the urban to rural area and become agricultural workers, lowering the competitive wage rate in the agricultural sector. Besides, the other part may fall into the category of the unemployed in the urban area, which aggravates the unemployment rate.

8.3.2 Capital-Mobile Case

In the capital-mobile case, interest rates of three sectors are equalized. Totally differentiating Eq. (8.10) yields

$$\lambda_{KX}^{m}\widehat{x} + \lambda_{KY}^{m}\widehat{Y} + \lambda_{KZ}^{g}\widehat{Z} = -s_{KX}^{Y}\widehat{p} - \left(s_{KK}^{X} + s_{KK}^{Y} + s_{KK}^{Z}\right)\widehat{r} - s_{KL}^{Z}\widehat{w} \tag{8.21}$$

Equations (8.12)–(8.17) and (8.21) fully describe the short-run, capital-mobile case. We can again solve the differential system of Eq. (8.31) shown in Appendix 2 and gain the impacts of increased privatization of the mixed-ownership firm on the output and unemployment rate. Results are summarized in Table 8.2.

Proposition 2 *In the short-run, capital-mobile case, partial privatization lowers the output of the mixed-ownership firm in the manufacturing sector, raises outputs of the producer service sector and the agricultural sector, and lowers the unemployment rate.*

Proposition 2 differs from Proposition 1 by generating a favorable impact of partial privatization on unemployment. The proof of Proposition 2 is shown in Appendix 2. In contrast to the capital-immobile case, partial privatization of the mixed-ownership firm in the capital-mobile case may encourage labor and capital to migrate from the manufacturing sector toward the producer service sector and the agricultural sector. As the output of producer service sector expands, the mixed-ownership firm can substitute producer services for labor and capital, which improves production efficiency of the manufacturing sector. Besides, partial

Table 8.2 The effects of partial privatization in the short-run, capital-mobile case

	$\widehat{Y}$	$\widehat{x}$	$\widehat{Z}$	$\widehat{p}$	$\widehat{r}$	$\widehat{w}$	$\widehat{\mu}$
$\widehat{k}$	−	+	+	−	−	+	−

privatization lowers unemployment since the producer service sector can absorb the unemployed labors.

Previous literature of analyzing the general-equilibrium impacts of partial privatization in the dual economy (Beladi and Chao 2006; Chao et al. 2016) has also found that partial privatization may lower unemployment in the capital-mobile case. The fall in unemployment in these studies can be explained as the agricultural sector absorbing the migration of labors from the manufacturing sector in the capital-mobile case. Although this argument may shed some insights into the labor transfer in partial privatization, it is not easy to find a corresponding case in the real economy, especially when the initial urban-rural wage gap is large enough. Nevertheless, in an urban-rural dual economy, Harris-Todaro model is the main mechanism explaining the transfer of labor. Our conclusion of Proposition 2 differs from previous studies in that we propose an alternative explanation for the decline in unemployment. That is, the producer service sector may absorb the unemployed labors in the manufacturing sector in the capital-mobile case. Such an explanation would be more objective.

8.4 Long-Run Effects

In this section, we evaluate the long-run effects of partial privatization in the long-run, capital-mobile case.

Combining Eq. (8.1) with (8.11), we have $(1-\sigma)px=f^x$. By totally differentiating this equation and we may have

$$\widehat{p}+\widehat{x}-\theta^f_{KX}\widehat{r}=0. \tag{8.22}$$

Besides, the total differentiation of Eqs. (8.2), (8.6), and (8.10) now yields

$$s^Y_{XK}\widehat{r}+s^Y_{XX}\widehat{p}=\widehat{x}+\left(\frac{1}{\sigma}+\frac{1-\sigma}{\sigma}s^Y_{XX}\right)\widehat{n}-\lambda^m_{XY}\widehat{Y} \tag{8.23}$$

$$\begin{aligned}\lambda^m_{LX}\widehat{x}+\lambda^m_{LY}\widehat{Y}+\lambda^g_{LZ}\widehat{Z}= & -s^Y_{LX}\widehat{p}-\left(s^X_{LK}+s^Y_{LK}+s^Z_{LK}\right)\widehat{r}-s^Z_{LL}\widehat{w}-\left(1-\lambda^g_{LZ}\right)\\ & \times\frac{\mu}{1+\mu}\widehat{\mu}-\left(\lambda_{LX}-\frac{1-\sigma}{\sigma}s^Y_{LX}\right)\widehat{n}\end{aligned} \tag{8.24}$$

$$\begin{aligned}\lambda^m_{KX}\widehat{x}+\lambda^m_{KY}\widehat{Y}+\lambda^g_{KZ}\widehat{Z}= & -s^Y_{KX}\widehat{p}-\left(s^X_{KK}+s^Y_{KK}+s^Z_{KK}\right)\widehat{r}-s^Y_{KL}\widehat{w}\\ & -\left(\lambda_{KX}-\frac{1-\sigma}{\sigma}s^Y_{KX}\right)\widehat{n}\end{aligned} \tag{8.25}$$

Equations (8.13)–(8.16) and (8.22)–(8.25) fully describe the differentiation system of the long-run, capital-mobile model. We can solve the comparative statics using Eq. (8.32) in Appendix 3. Table 8.3 summarizes the long-run impacts of partial privatization of the mixed-ownership firm.

Table 8.3 The effects of partial privatization in the long-run, capital-mobile case

	$\widehat{Y}$	$\widehat{x}$	$\widehat{n}$	$\widehat{Z}$	$\widehat{p}$	$\widehat{r}$	$\widehat{w}$	$\widehat{\mu}$
$\widehat{k}$	[+]	−	[+]	[−]	−	−	+	−

Note: "[+]" and "[−]" refer to the situation that the signs of comparative statics are true under some mathematical conditions, see Appendix 3

Proposition 3 *In the long-run, capital-mobile case, partial privatization lowers the unemployment rate and contributes to the specialization of producer service firms and the increasing output of the mixed-ownership firm conditionally.*

Proof of Proposition 3 is shown in Appendix 3. Partial privatization of the mixed-ownership firm lowers the interest rate and hence lowers the fixed cost of producer service firms. Contrasting to the short-run, capital-mobile case, in the long run, the decrease in the fixed cost lowers the entry barrier in the producer service sector, thus may encourage the entry of new producer service firms. As a result, the variety of producer services would rise.

Considerable literature applying mixed oligopoly model such as Matsumura (1998), Xu et al. (2017), and Lee et al. (2018) argued that partial privatization lowers the output of the mixed-ownership firms. Our result in Proposition 3 differs from previous studies' arguments in that the entry of producer service firms in the long run in our model generates positive impacts on output and unemployment. The producer service sector can absorb the unemployed labors in the urban area. Besides, the specialization of the producer service sector is favorable to raise the output of the mixed-ownership firm in the manufacturing sector.

8.5 Welfare Analyses

In this section, we evaluate the impact of partial privatization on social welfare. The national income of the economy is $I = \overline{w}(L_X + L_Y) + wL_Z + r_Y\overline{K}_Y + r_X\overline{K}_X + r_Z\overline{K}_Z + n\pi_X + \pi_Y$. That is, the income is composed of factor income and profits from the urban firms in the producer service sector and the manufacturing sector. When capital is mobile among three sectors, we have $I = \overline{w}(L_X + L_Y) + wL_Z + r\overline{K} + n\pi_X + \pi_Y$.

Besides, the social welfare of the economy is expressed by the indirect utility of the consumer:

$$U = I - P_Y Y + v(Y). \tag{8.26}$$

The short-run welfare effect of partial privatization can be derived by totally differentiating Eq. (8.26):

$$\frac{\mathrm{d}U}{\mathrm{d}k} = \left(p_Y - m^Y\right)\frac{\mathrm{d}Y}{\mathrm{d}k} + n(p - m^x)\frac{\mathrm{d}x}{\mathrm{d}k} - w(L_Y + L_X)\frac{\mathrm{d}\mu}{\mathrm{d}k}. \tag{8.27}$$

That is, the welfare effect of privatization is determined by the changes in the manufacturing output, producer service output, and unemployment.

- In the short-run, capital-immobile case, according to Proposition 1, partial privatization worsens unemployment and lowers outputs of the producer service sector and the manufacturing sector. These unfavorable effects together lower the social welfare. That is, we have $\mathrm{d}U/\mathrm{d}k < 0$. Besides, we also have $\mathrm{d}^2U/\mathrm{d}k^2 > 0$ (see Appendix 4).
- In the short-run, capital-mobile case, according to Proposition 2, there are two controversial effects of partial privatization on the welfare. Although partial privatization lowers the output of the manufacturing firm ($\widehat{Y}/\widehat{k} < 0$), the output of the producer services rises ($\widehat{x}/\widehat{k} > 0$), and the unemployment ratio falls ($\widehat{\mu}/\widehat{k} < 0$). Therefore, partial privatization would raise social welfare if the latter two effects dominate. Besides, the optimal degree of partial privatization in the capital-mobile case, denoted by k^0, can be obtained by setting $\mathrm{d}U/\mathrm{d}k = 0$ in Eq. (8.27). In this case, we have

$$\frac{\mathrm{d}U}{\mathrm{d}k} = \left(k - k^0\right)\left[-p_Y'Y + (1 - \sigma)p_X m_p^Y\right]\frac{\mathrm{d}Y}{\mathrm{d}k}. \tag{8.28}$$

Social welfare is maximized when $k = k^0$. Besides, $\mathrm{d}U/\mathrm{d}k > 0$ when $k < k^0$, whereas $\mathrm{d}U/\mathrm{d}k < 0$ when $k > k^0$. In addition, we have $\mathrm{d}^2U/\mathrm{d}k^2 < 0$ (see Appendix 4).

- In the long-run, capital-mobile case, by totally differentiating Eq. (8.26), we have

$$\frac{\mathrm{d}U}{\mathrm{d}k} = \left(p_Y - m^Y\right)\frac{\mathrm{d}Y}{\mathrm{d}k} - w(L_Y + L_X)\frac{\mathrm{d}\mu}{\mathrm{d}k} + (p - m^x)\left(n\frac{\mathrm{d}x}{\mathrm{d}k} + x\frac{\mathrm{d}n}{\mathrm{d}k}\right). \tag{8.29}$$

According to Proposition 3, we have $\widehat{Y}/\widehat{k} > 0, \widehat{\mu}/\widehat{k} < 0, \widehat{x}/\widehat{k} < 0$, and $\widehat{n}/\widehat{k} > 0$. We may conclude $\mathrm{d}U/\mathrm{d}k > 0$ if $\mathrm{d}x/\mathrm{d}k + \mathrm{d}n/\mathrm{d}k > 0$. Besides, we have $\mathrm{d}^2U/\mathrm{d}k^2 < 0$ (see Appendix 4).

In addition, the welfare impact of partial privatization is an important basis for decision-making on whether the government of developing countries should implement privatization policy. Figure 8.1 summarizes the impacts of partial privatization on social welfare in the short- and long run. U in the vertical axis in Fig. 8.1 represents the indirect utility of the representative consumer, and k in the horizontal axis shows the degree of partial privatization of the mixed-ownership firm. Partial privatization would lower welfare ($\mathrm{d}U/\mathrm{d}k < 0$) in the short-run, capital-immobile case, shown in panel *a* of Fig. 8.1. Therefore, privatization policy might not be encouraged in this case. Besides, the impact of privatization on social welfare displays an inverted U curve in the short-run and capital-mobile case, shown in

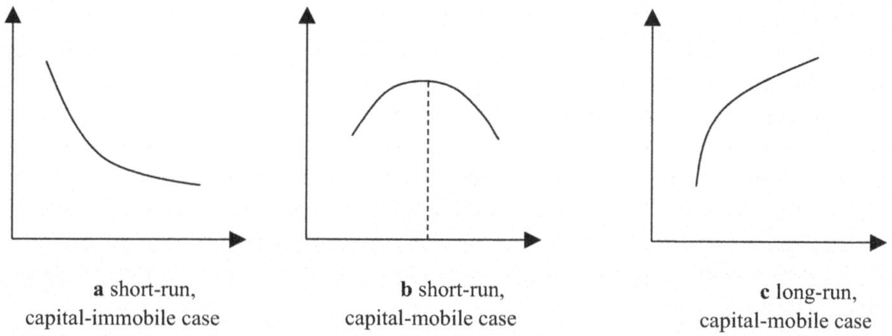

Fig. 8.1 The impact of privatization on social welfare

panel *b*. In this case, the optimal privatization degree k^0 is derived by letting $dU/dk = 0$. Therefore, the privatization policy should be supported if the initial privatization degree is smaller than k^0. Otherwise, one would oppose the privatization policy if initial privatization degree is larger than k^0. In addition, partial privatization would raise social welfare in the long-run, capital-mobile case, shown in panel *c*. Therefore, the government should increasingly deepen privatization and enlarge the proportion of private ownership in the mixed economy in the long run. Nevertheless, according to the concavity of social welfare U on privatization degree k in the long-run, capital-mobile case, the marginal effect of partial privatization on the promotion of social welfare is diminishing. Therefore, attention should be paid to the effectiveness of privatization policy.

8.6 Concluding Remarks

The producer service sector is rarely involved in theoretical literature in the problem of partial privatization. We combine the analyses of partial privatization of the manufacturing sector with producer services because producer services are closely linked to manufacturing in today's industrial conditions. Only by considering the producer service sector can our model reflect the actual situation of the current economic activities more objectively. Since this paper considers the producer service sector, which can absorb the unemployed in the mixed-ownership firm during partial privatization, our model has derived new conclusions about the impacts of partial privatization on the output and social welfare. This is the marginal contribution of this paper to the current literature.

We have found that: in the short-run, capital-mobile case, partial privatization would lower the unemployment rate; and in the long-run, capital-mobile case, partial privatization can lower the unemployment rate, lead to the specialization in producer service sector and increase the output of the mixed-ownership firm in the manufacturing sector conditionally.

We have evaluated the welfare impact of partial privatization in Sect. 8.5 and discussed when and how the governments in developing countries should implement privatization policy. Besides, we have provided some suggested policies to ease the negative impacts of partial privatization on the labor market and social welfare. On the one hand, the producer service sector can serve as the policy tool to offset the negative short-run impacts of partial privatization on unemployment and on social welfare. On the other, policy-makers in developing countries should take special care of capital market integration in the dual economy and the entry of producer service firms in the long run, which are crucial to determine the impacts of partial privatization.

Several topics on the impacts of partial privatization on the labor market can be further discussed considering the producer service sector. For example, the impact of partial privatization on wage inequality between skilled and unskilled workers has not been considered in this paper. Besides, one can analyze how complementary policies such as financial or fiscal policies for the development of the producer service sector in developing countries can offset the negative impacts of privatization on output, unemployment, and social welfare.

Competing Interests

Funding This work was supported by the Humanities and Social Sciences of the Ministry of Education, China, Project No. 17JJD630002.

Disclosure Statement No potential conflict of interest was reported by the authors.

Appendix

Appendix 1

Appendix 1 proves Proposition 1. In the short-run, capital-immobile case, we obtain the differential system (8.30) from Eqs. (8.12)–(8.20):

$$\begin{bmatrix} A & 0 & 0 & -B\theta_{XY}^m & -B\theta_{KY}^m & 0 & 0 & 0 & 0 \\ 0 & 0 & 0 & 1 & 0 & -\theta_{KX}^m & 0 & 0 & 0 \\ 0 & 0 & 0 & 0 & 0 & 0 & -\theta_{KZ}^g & -\theta_{LZ}^g & 0 \\ \lambda_{XY}^m & -1 & 0 & s_{XX}^Y & s_{XK}^Y & 0 & 0 & 0 & 0 \\ \lambda_{KY}^m & 0 & 0 & s_{KX}^Y & s_{KK}^Y & 0 & 0 & 0 & 0 \\ 0 & \lambda_{KX}^m & 0 & 0 & 0 & s_{KK}^X & 0 & 0 & 0 \\ 0 & 0 & \lambda_{KZ}^g & 0 & 0 & 0 & s_{KK}^Z & s_{KL}^Z & 0 \\ (1+\mu)\lambda_{LY}^m & (1+\mu)\lambda_{LX}^m & \lambda_{LZ}^g & (1+\mu)s_{LX}^Y & (1+\mu)s_{LK}^Y & (1+\mu)s_{LK}^X & s_{LK}^Z & s_{LL}^Z & (1-\lambda_{LZ}^g)\mu \\ 0 & 0 & 0 & 0 & 0 & 0 & 0 & -(1+\mu) & -\mu \end{bmatrix} \begin{bmatrix} \widehat{Y} \\ \widehat{x} \\ \widehat{Z} \\ \widehat{p} \\ \widehat{r}_Y \\ \widehat{r}_X \\ \widehat{r}_Z \\ \widehat{w} \\ \widehat{\mu} \end{bmatrix} = \begin{bmatrix} C \\ 0 \\ 0 \\ 0 \\ 0 \\ 0 \\ 0 \\ 0 \\ 0 \end{bmatrix} \widehat{k} \tag{8.30}$$

where $A = -(1 + k + ke^y) < 0, B = \left[1 - (1-k)(1-\sigma)\theta_{XY}^m\right]\varepsilon^Y b^Y > 0$, $C = \left[1 + \varepsilon^Y b^Y (1-\sigma)\theta_{XY}^m\right]k > 0$.

Define Δ the determinant of the coefficient matrix in system (8.30). One can confirm the sign of Δ cannot be determined directly. We then apply Marshall dynamic adjustment to decide its sign.

Stability

Let a "dot" over a variable denote its time derivative. Define the dynamic adjustment process as follows:

$$\dot{Y} = d_1\left[(p_Y + kp'_Y Y) + (1-k)(1-\sigma)p_X m_p^y - m^y\right],$$

$$\dot{x} = d_2(p - m^x/\sigma),$$

$$\dot{Z} = d_3(1 - g(w, r)),$$

$$\dot{p} = d_4\left(f_p^y + m_p^y Y - X\right),$$

$$\dot{r}_X = d_5\left(n\left(f_r^x + m_r^x x\right) - \overline{K}_X\right),$$

$$\dot{r}_Y = d_6\left(f_r^y + m_r^y Y - \overline{K}_Y\right),$$

$$\dot{r}_Z = d_7\left(g_r Z - \overline{K}_Z\right),$$

$$\dot{w} = d_8\left[(1+\mu)\left(f_w^y + m_w^y Y + nf_w^x + nm_w^x x_i\right) + g_w^z Z - \overline{L}\right],$$

$$\dot{\mu} = d_9(\overline{w} - (1+\mu)w),$$

where $d_i (i = 1, \ldots, 9)$ is the positive parameter measuring the speed of adjustment. We derive the Jacobian matrix of the dynamic adjustment process. The determinant of the Jacobian, denoted by $|J_1|$, is given by

$$|J_1| = d_1 \ldots d_9 \frac{-p'_Y \sigma n^{\frac{1}{\sigma}} \overline{K}_X \overline{K}_Y \overline{K}_Z \overline{L}}{r_x r_y r_z Z w \mu (1+\mu)} \Delta,$$

A necessary condition for stability is $|J_1| < 0$. We then conclude $\Delta < 0$.

Comparative Statics

We apply Cramer's rule to solve the square matrix in Eq. (8.30).

$$\widehat{Y}/\widehat{k} = -C\mu\left[\theta_{KX}^m \lambda_{KX}^m \left(s_{XX}^Y s_{KK}^Y - s_{KX}^Y s_{XK}^Y\right) + s_{KK}^X s_{KK}^Y\right]\Delta_Y/\Delta < 0,$$

where

$$\Delta_Y = \lambda^g_{KZ} s^Z_{LL} \theta^g_{KZ} - \lambda^g_{LZ} s^Z_{KL} \theta^g_{KZ} - \lambda^g_{KZ}(1+\mu)(1-\lambda^g_{LZ})\theta^g_{KZ} - \left(\lambda^g_{KZ} s^Z_{LK} - \lambda^g_{LZ} s^Z_{KK}\right)\theta^g_{LZ} < 0.$$

$$\widehat{x}/\widehat{k} = C\mu s^X_{KK}\left(\lambda^m_{XY} s^Y_{KK} - \lambda^m_{KY} s^Y_{XK}\right)\Delta_X/\Delta < 0,$$

where

$$\Delta_X = \left(\lambda^g_{KZ} s^Z_{LK} - \lambda^g_{LZ} s^Z_{KK}\right)\theta^g_{LZ} - \left[\lambda^g_{KZ} s^Z_{LL} - \lambda^g_{LZ} s^Z_{KL} - \lambda^g_{KZ}(1+\mu)(1-\lambda^g_{LZ})\right]\theta^g_{KZ} > 0.$$

$$\widehat{Z}/\widehat{k} = C\mu(1+\mu)\left(s^Z_{KK}\theta^g_{LZ} - s^Z_{KL}\theta^g_{KZ}\right)\Delta_Z/\Delta > 0,$$

where

$$\begin{aligned}\Delta_Z = {} & \left[\lambda^m_{XY}\left(s^Y_{KX} s^Y_{LK} - s^Y_{LX} s^Y_{KK}\right) - \lambda^m_{KY}\left(s^Y_{XX} s^Y_{LK} - s^Y_{LX} s^Y_{XK}\right) + \lambda^m_{LY}\left(s^Y_{XX} s^Y_{KK} - s^Y_{KX} s^Y_{XK}\right)\right]\lambda^m_{KX}\theta^m_{KX} \\ & - \left(\lambda^m_{KY} s^Y_{LK} - \lambda^m_{LY} s^Y_{KK}\right)s^X_{KK} - \left(\lambda^m_{XY} s^Y_{KK} - \lambda^m_{KY} s^Y_{XK}\right)\left(\lambda^m_{KX} s^X_{LK} - \lambda^m_{LX} s^X_{KK}\right) > 0.\end{aligned}$$

$$\widehat{p}/\widehat{k} = -C\mu\theta^m_{KX}\lambda^m_{KY}\left(\lambda^m_{XY} s^Y_{KK} - \lambda^m_{KY} s^Y_{XK}\right)\Delta_p/\Delta < 0,$$

where

$$\Delta_p = \theta^g_{LZ}\left(\lambda^g_{KZ} s^Z_{LK} - \lambda^g_{LZ} s^Z_{KK}\right) - \theta^g_{KZ}\left[\lambda^g_{KZ} s^Z_{LL} - \lambda^g_{LZ} s^Z_{KL} - \lambda^g_{KZ}(1+\mu)(1-\lambda^g_{LZ})\right] > 0.$$

$$\widehat{r}_X/\widehat{k} = \left(\widehat{p}/\widehat{k}\right)/\theta^m_{KX} < 0,$$

$$\widehat{r}_Y/\widehat{k} = C\mu\Delta_p\Delta_{RY}/\Delta < 0.$$

where

$$\Delta_{RY} = \theta^m_{KX}\lambda^m_{KX}\left(\lambda^m_{XY} s^Y_{KX} - \lambda^m_{KY} s^Y_{XX}\right) - s^X_{KK}\lambda^m_{KY} > 0.$$

$$\widehat{w}/\widehat{k} = C\mu(1+\mu)\theta^g_{KZ}\lambda^g_{KZ}\Delta_Z/\Delta < 0,$$

$$\widehat{r}_Z/\widehat{k} = (-\theta^g_{LZ}/\theta^g_{KZ})\widehat{w}/\widehat{k} > 0,$$

$$\widehat{\mu}/\widehat{k} = (-\mu/1+\mu)\widehat{w}/\widehat{k} > 0.$$

Appendix 2

Appendix 2 proves Proposition 2. The differential system of the short-run, capital-mobile case can be derived as system (8.31):

$$
\begin{bmatrix}
A & 0 & 0 & -B\theta^m_{XY} & -B\theta^m_{KY} & 0 & 0 \\
0 & 0 & 0 & 1 & -\theta^m_{KX} & 0 & 0 \\
0 & 0 & 0 & 0 & -\theta^g_{KZ} & -\theta^g_{LZ} & 0 \\
\lambda^m_{XY} & -1 & 0 & s^Y_{XX} & s^Y_{XK} & 0 & 0 \\
\lambda^m_{KY} & \lambda^m_{KX} & \lambda^g_{KZ} & s^Y_{KX} & s^X_{KK} + s^Y_{KK} + s^Z_{KK} & s^Z_{KL} & 0 \\
(1+\mu)\lambda^m_{LY} & (1+\mu)\lambda^m_{LX} & \lambda^g_{LZ} & (1+\mu)s^Y_{LX} & (1+\mu)\left(s^X_{LK} + s^Y_{LK}\right) + s^Z_{LK} & s^Z_{LL} & (1-\lambda^g_{LZ})\mu \\
0 & 0 & 0 & 0 & 0 & -(1+\mu) & -\mu
\end{bmatrix}
\begin{bmatrix} \widehat{Y} \\ \widehat{x} \\ \widehat{Z} \\ \widehat{p} \\ \widehat{r} \\ \widehat{w} \\ \widehat{\mu} \end{bmatrix}
=
\begin{bmatrix} C \\ 0 \\ 0 \\ 0 \\ 0 \\ 0 \\ 0 \end{bmatrix} \widehat{k} \tag{8.31}
$$

The sign of determinant of coefficient matrix in system (8.31), denoted by Ω, cannot be determined directly.

Stability

The Marshall dynamic adjustment is given by

$$\dot{Y} = d_1\left[(p_Y + kp'_Y Y) + (1-k)(1-\sigma)p_X m_p^y - m^y\right],$$

$$\dot{x} = d_2(p - m^x/\sigma),$$

$$\dot{Z} = d_3(1 - g(w,r)),$$

$$\dot{p} = d_4\left(f_p^y + m_p^y Y - X\right),$$

$$\dot{r} = d_5\left[n\left(f_r^x + m_r^x x\right) + f_r^y + m_r^y Y + g_r Z - \overline{K}\right],$$

$$\dot{w} = d_6\left[(1+\mu)\left(f_w^y + m_w^y Y + nf_w^x + nm_w^x x\right) + g_w Z - \overline{L}\right],$$

$$\dot{\mu} = d_7[\overline{w} - (1+\mu)w].$$

The Jacobian matrix of the dynamic adjustment process in system (8.31) is given by

$$|J_2| = d_1 \ldots d_7 \frac{-p'_Y \sigma n^{\frac{1}{\sigma}} \overline{KL}}{Zrw\mu(1+\mu)} \Omega.$$

A necessary condition for stability is $|J_2| < 0$. We then conclude $\Omega < 0$.

Comparative Statics

In a dual economy, capital intensity of the urban area is larger than that of the rural area. Therefore, we have $\Lambda_{XZ} \equiv \lambda_{KX}^m \lambda_{LZ}^g - (1+\mu)\lambda_{LX}^m \lambda_{KZ}^g > 0$ and$\Lambda_{YZ} \equiv \lambda_{KY}^m \lambda_{LZ}^g - (1+\mu)\lambda_{LY}^m \lambda_{KZ}^g > 0$.

$$\widehat{r}/\widehat{k} = C\mu\theta_{LZ}^g\left(\lambda_{XY}^m \Lambda_{XZ} + \Lambda_{YZ}\right)/\Omega < 0,$$

$$\widehat{p}/\widehat{k} = \theta_{KX}^m \widehat{r}/\widehat{k} < 0,$$

$$\widehat{w}/\widehat{k} = -C\mu\theta_{KZ}^g\left(\lambda_{XY}^m \Lambda_{XZ} + \Lambda_{YZ}\right)/\Omega > 0,$$

$\widehat{\mu}/\widehat{k} < 0$, since $\widehat{\mu}/\widehat{k} = (-\mu/1+\mu)\widehat{w}/\widehat{k}$.

Besides, a necessary condition to determine the impacts of partial privatization on the outputs of three sectors is $s_{XK}^{Y} + s_{XX}^{Y}\theta_{KX}^{m} < 0$. That is, cross-price elasticity of substitution s_{XK}^{Y} is outweighed by own-price elasticity s_{XX}^{Y}.

$$\widehat{x}/\widehat{k} = C\mu\Omega_X/\Omega > 0,$$

where

$$\Omega_X = \Lambda_{YZ}\left(s_{XK}^{Y} + \theta_{KX}^{m} s_{XX}^{Y}\right)\theta_{LZ}^{g} + \lambda_{XY}^{m}\Delta_p + \lambda_{XY}^{m}\theta_{KX}^{m}\theta_{LZ}^{g}\left[(1+\mu)\lambda_{KZ}^{g} s_{LX}^{Y} - \lambda_{LZ}^{g} s_{KX}^{Y}\right]$$
$$+\lambda_{XY}^{m}\theta_{LZ}^{g}\left[(1+\mu)\lambda_{KZ}^{g}\left(s_{LK}^{X} + s_{LK}^{Y}\right) - \lambda_{LZ}^{g}\left(s_{KK}^{X} + s_{KK}^{Y}\right)\right] < 0.$$

$$\widehat{Y}/\widehat{k} = -C\mu\Omega_Y/\Omega < 0,$$

where

$$\Omega_Y = \Lambda_{XZ}\left(s_{XK}^{Y} + \theta_{KX}^{m} s_{XX}^{Y}\right)\theta_{LZ}^{g} - \Delta_p - \theta_{KX}^{m}\theta_{LZ}^{g}\left[(1+\mu)\lambda_{KZ}^{g} s_{LX}^{Y} - \lambda_{LZ}^{g} s_{KX}^{Y}\right]$$
$$-\theta_{LZ}^{g}\left[(1+\mu)\lambda_{KZ}^{g}\left(s_{LK}^{X} + s_{LK}^{Y}\right) - \lambda_{LZ}^{g}\left(s_{KK}^{X} + s_{KK}^{Y}\right)\right] < 0.$$

$$\widehat{Z}/\widehat{k} = -C\mu(1+\mu)\Omega_Z/\Omega > 0,$$

where

$$\Omega_Z = \theta_{LZ}^{g}\left(\lambda_{KY}^{m}\lambda_{LX}^{m} - \lambda_{LY}^{m}\lambda_{KX}^{m}\right)\left(s_{XK}^{Y} + \theta_{LZ}^{g}\theta_{KX}^{m} s_{XX}^{Y}\right)$$
$$-\theta_{LZ}^{g}\left(\lambda_{XY}^{m}\lambda_{LX}^{m} + \lambda_{LY}^{m}\right)\left(s_{KK}^{X} + s_{KK}^{Y} + s_{KK}^{Z} + \theta_{KX}^{m} s_{KX}^{Y}\right)$$
$$+\theta_{LZ}^{g}\left(\lambda_{XY}^{m}\lambda_{KX}^{m} + \lambda_{KY}^{m}\right)\left[s_{LK}^{X} + s_{LK}^{Y} - \theta_{KX}^{m} s_{LX}^{Y} + s_{LK}^{Z}/(1+\mu)\right] > 0.$$

Appendix 3

Appendix 3 proves Proposition 3. The differential system of the long-run, capital-mobile case can be derived as

$$\begin{bmatrix} A & 0 & 0 & -B\theta_{XY}^{m} & -B\theta_{KY}^{m} & 0 & 0 & -B\theta_{XY}^{m}(1-1/\sigma) \\ 0 & 0 & 0 & 1 & -\theta_{KX}^{m} & 0 & 0 & 0 \\ 0 & 0 & 0 & 0 & -\theta_{KZ}^{g} & -\theta_{LZ}^{g} & 0 & 0 \\ \lambda_{XY}^{m} & -1 & 0 & s_{XX}^{Y} & s_{XK}^{Y} & 0 & 0 & D \\ \lambda_{KY}^{m} & \lambda_{KX}^{m} & \lambda_{KZ}^{g} & s_{KX}^{Y} & s_{KK}^{X}+s_{KK}^{Y}+s_{KK}^{Z} & s_{KL}^{Z} & 0 & E \\ (1+\mu)\lambda_{LY}^{m} & (1+\mu)\lambda_{LX}^{m} & \lambda_{LZ}^{g} & (1+\mu)s_{LX}^{Y} & (1+\mu)\left(s_{LK}^{X}+s_{LK}^{Y}\right)+s_{LK}^{Z} & s_{LL}^{Z} & (1-\lambda_{LZ}^{g})\mu & F \\ 0 & 0 & 0 & 0 & 0 & -(1+\mu) & -\mu & 0 \\ 0 & 1 & 0 & 1 & -\theta_{KX}^{f} & 0 & 0 & 0 \end{bmatrix} \begin{bmatrix} \widehat{Y} \\ \widehat{x} \\ \widehat{Z} \\ \widehat{p} \\ \widehat{r} \\ \widehat{w} \\ \widehat{\mu} \\ \widehat{n} \end{bmatrix} = \begin{bmatrix} C \\ 0 \\ 0 \\ 0 \\ 0 \\ 0 \\ 0 \\ 0 \end{bmatrix} \widehat{k} \quad (8.32)$$

where $D = -\left(\frac{1}{\sigma}+\frac{1-\sigma}{\sigma}s_{XX}^{Y}\right) < 0$, $E = \lambda_{LX} - \frac{1-\sigma}{\sigma}s_{LX}^{Y}$, and $F = \lambda_{KX} - \frac{1-\sigma}{\sigma}s_{KX}^{Y}$. We may have $E > 0$ and $F > 0$ if σ is relatively large. While we may have $E < 0$ and $F < 0$ if σ is relatively small.

The sign of the determinant of coefficient matrix in system (8.32), denoted byΨ, cannot be determined directly.

Stability

The Marshall dynamic adjustment is given by

$$\dot{Y} = d_1\left[\left(p_Y + kp'_Y Y\right) + (1-k)(1-\sigma)p_X m_p^y - m^y\right],$$

$$\dot{x} = d_2(p - m^x/\sigma),$$

$$\dot{Z} = d_3(1 - g(w, r)),$$

$$\dot{p} = d_4\left(f_p^y + m_p^y Y - X\right),$$

$$\dot{r} = d_5\left[n(f_r^x + m_r^x x) + f_r^y + m_r^y Y + g_r Z - \overline{K}\right],$$

$$\dot{w} = d_6\left[(1+\mu)\left(f_w^y + m_w^y Y + nf_w^x + nm_w^x x\right) + g_w Z - \overline{L}\right],$$

$$\dot{\mu} = d_7[\overline{w} - (1+\mu)w],$$

$$\dot{n} = d_8(px - f^x - m^x x).$$

The Jacobian matrix of the dynamic adjustment process in system (8.32) is given by

$$|J_3| = d_1 \dots d_8 \frac{-p'_Y \sigma n^{\frac{1}{\sigma}-1} \overline{KL}}{Zrw\mu(1+\mu)} \Psi.$$

A necessary condition for stability is $|J_3| > 0$. We then conclude $\Psi > 0$.

Comparative Statics

By applying Cramer's rule, we have
$\widehat{r}/\widehat{k} = (C\mu\theta_{LZ}^g/\Psi)\left[\lambda_{XY}^m(\lambda_{KZ}^g F - \lambda_{LZ}^g E) + D\left(\lambda_{KY}^m \lambda_{LZ}^g - (1+\mu)\lambda_{LY}^m \lambda_{KZ}^g\right)\right] < 0.$
Besides, given $\widehat{r}/\widehat{k} < 0$, we obtain $\widehat{p}/\widehat{k} < 0$, $\widehat{w}/\widehat{k} > 0$, and $\widehat{\mu}/\widehat{k} < 0$.

$$\widehat{x}/\widehat{k} = (C\mu\theta_{LZ}^g/\Psi)\left(\theta_{KX}^f - \theta_{KX}^m\right) \times \left[\lambda_{XY}^m(\lambda_{KZ}^g F - \lambda_{LZ}^g E) + D\left(\lambda_{KY}^m \lambda_{LZ}^g - (1+\mu)\lambda_{LY}^m \lambda_{KZ}^g\right)\right] < 0.$$

$$\begin{aligned}\widehat{n}/\widehat{k} = {} & (C\mu\theta_{LZ}^g/\Psi)\cdot\left\{\Lambda_{XZ}\lambda_{XY}^m\left(\theta_{KX}^f - \theta_{KX}^m\right) - \Lambda_{YZ}\left[s_{XK}^Y + \theta_{KX}^m s_{XX}^Y - \left(\theta_{KX}^f - \theta_{KX}^m\right)\right]\right\} \\ & + (C\mu\theta_{LZ}^g/\Psi)\cdot\lambda_{XY}^m\lambda_{KZ}^g\left[s_{LL}^Z - s_{LK}^Z - (1+\mu)(1 - \lambda_{LZ}^g + s_{LK}^X + \theta_{KX}^m s_{LX}^Y + s_{LK}^Y)\right] \\ & + (C\mu\theta_{LZ}^g/\Psi)\cdot\lambda_{XY}^m\lambda_{LZ}^g\left(s_{KK}^X + s_{KK}^Y + \theta_{KX}^m s_{KX}^Y + s_{KK}^Z - s_{KL}^Z\right).\end{aligned}$$

The first term of $\widehat{n}/\widehat{k}$ is positive, while the second and third terms are negative. Therefore, $\widehat{n}/\widehat{k} > 0$ if the first term is larger than the other two terms.

Moreover,

$$\widehat{Y}/\widehat{k} = -(\mu C/\Psi)\Psi_Y = -(\mu C/\Psi)\left[D\theta_{KZ}^{g}\Psi_Y^1 + \theta_{LZ}^{g}(\lambda_{KZ}^{g}F - \lambda_{LZ}^{g}E)\Psi_Y^2 + D\theta_{LZ}^{g}\Psi_Y^3\right],$$

where

$$\begin{gathered}
\Psi_Y^1 = \lambda_{KZ}^{g}\left[s_{LL}^{Z} - (1+\mu)(1-\lambda_{LZ}^{g})\right] - \lambda_{LZ}^{g}s_{KL}^{Z} < 0, \\
\Psi_Y^2 = \left(s_{XK}^{Y} + \theta_{KX}^{m}s_{XX}^{Y}\right) - \left(\theta_{KX}^{f} - \theta_{KX}^{m}\right) < 0, \\
\Psi_Y^3 = \left(\theta_{KX}^{f} - \theta_{KX}^{m}\right)\Lambda_{XZ} - \theta_{KX}^{m}\left[\lambda_{KZ}^{g}(1+\mu)s_{LX}^{Y} - \lambda_{LZ}^{g}s_{KX}^{Y}\right] \\
-\left(\lambda_{KZ}^{g}s_{LK}^{Z} - \lambda_{LZ}^{g}s_{KK}^{Z}\right) - \left[\lambda_{KZ}^{g}(1+\mu)\left(s_{LK}^{X} + s_{LK}^{Y}\right) - \lambda_{LZ}^{g}\left(s_{KK}^{X} + s_{KK}^{Y}\right)\right] > 0.
\end{gathered}$$

The first two terms of Ψ_Y are positive and the last term is negative. We can have$\Psi_Y < 0$ (and $\widehat{Y}/\widehat{k} > 0$) if $\frac{\lambda_{KZ}^{g}F - \lambda_{LZ}^{g}E}{D} < \frac{\theta_{LZ}^{g}|\Psi_Y^3| - \theta_{KZ}^{g}|\Psi_Y^1|}{\theta_{LZ}^{g}|\Psi_Y^2|}$.

Appendix 4

First, in the short-run, capital-immobile case, according to Eq. (8.27) we can obtain

$$\frac{\mathrm{d}^2U}{\mathrm{d}k^2} = \left(-\frac{1}{\Delta}\frac{\mathrm{d}\Delta}{\mathrm{d}k}\right)\left[\left(p_Y - m^Y\right)\frac{\mathrm{d}Y}{\mathrm{d}k} - w(L_Y + L_X)\frac{\mathrm{d}\mu}{\mathrm{d}k} + n(p - m^x)\frac{\mathrm{d}x}{\mathrm{d}k}\right] > 0.$$

Second, in the short-run, capital-mobile case, recall that according to Eq. (8.3) we have $p_Y - m^Y = -kp'_YY - (1-k)p_Xm_p^Y$. By substituting this equation into Eq. (8.27), we can confirm Eq. (8.28). Besides, we can solve for k^0 from Eq. (8.28):

$$k^0 = \frac{p_Y - m^Y - p_Xm_p^Y}{-p'_YY + p_Xm_p^Y} = \frac{1 - b^Y + b^Y\theta_{XY}^{m}}{1/\varepsilon^Y + b^Y\theta_{XY}^{m}}.$$

In addition, from Eq. (8.29) we have

$$\frac{\mathrm{d}^2U}{\mathrm{d}k^2} = \left[-p'_YY + (1-\sigma)p_Xm_p^Y\right]\frac{\mathrm{d}Y}{\mathrm{d}k} < 0.$$

At last, in the long-run, capital-mobile case, according to Eq. (8.29) we can obtain

$$\frac{\mathrm{d}^2U}{\mathrm{d}k^2}=\left(-\frac{1}{\Psi}\frac{\mathrm{d}\Psi}{\mathrm{d}k}\right)$$
$$\times\left[\left(p_Y-m^Y\right)\frac{\mathrm{d}Y}{\mathrm{d}k}-w(L_Y+L_X)\frac{\mathrm{d}\mu}{\mathrm{d}k}+n(p-m^x)\frac{\mathrm{d}x}{\mathrm{d}k}+x(p-m^x)\frac{\mathrm{d}n}{\mathrm{d}k}\right]<0.$$

References

Anderson SP, De Palma A, Thisse JF (1997) Privatization and efficiency in a differentiated industry. Eur Econ Rev 41(9):1635–1654

Anwar S (2010) Wage inequality, increased competition, and trade liberalization: short run vs long run. Rev Int Econ 18(3):574–581

Bai CE, Lu J, Tao Z (2009) How does privatization work in China? J Comp Econ 37(3):453–470

Beladi H, Chao CC (2006) Mixed-ownership, unemployment, and welfare for a developing economy. Rev Dev Econ 10(4):604–611

Chao CC, Yu ES (1994) Foreign capital inflows and welfare in an economy with imperfect competition. J Dev Econ 45(1):141–154

Chao CC, Nabin M, Nguyen X, Sgro PM (2016) Wage inequality and welfare in developing countries: privatization and reforms in the short and long run. Int Rev Econ Financ 42:474–483

Chen TL (2017) Privatization and efficiency: a mixed oligopoly approach. J Econ 120(3):251–268

Chen G, Firth M, Xin Y, Xu L (2008) Control transfers, privatization, and corporate performance: efficiency gains in China's listed companies. J Financ Quant Anal 43:161–190

Chisari O, Estache A, Romero C (1999) Winners and losers from the privatization and regulation of utilities: lessons from a general equilibrium model of Argentina. World Bank Econ Rev 13(2): 357–378

Dixit AK, Stiglitz JE (1977) Monopolistic competition and optimum product diversity. Am Econ Rev 67(3):297–308

Francois JF (1990) Producer services, scale, and the division of labor. Oxf Econ Pap 42(4):715–729

Ghosh A, Sen P (2012) Privatization in a small open economy with imperfect competition. J Publ Econ Theory 14(3):441–471

Gupta N (2005) Partial privatization and firm performance. J Financ 60(2):987–1015

Harris JR, Todaro MP (1970) Migration, unemployment and development: a two-sector analysis. Am Econ Rev 60(1):126–142

Jiang C, Yao S, Feng G (2013) Bank ownership, privatization, and performance: evidence from a transition country. J Bank Financ 37(9):3364–3372

Jones RW (1965) The structure of simple general equilibrium models. J Polit Econ 73(6):557–572

Kim SL, Lee SH, Matsumura T (2019) Corporate social responsibility and privatization policy in a mixed oligopoly. J Econ 128(1):67–89

Lee SH, Matsumura T, Sato S (2018) An analysis of entry-then-privatization model: welfare and policy implications. J Econ 123(1):71–88

Li W, Xu LC (2002) The political economy of privatization and competition: cross-country evidence from the telecommunications sector. J Comp Econ 30(3):439–462

Liu GS, Sun P, Woo WT (2006) The political economy of Chinese-style privatization: motives and constraints. World Dev 34(12):2016–2033

Matsumura T (1998) Partial privatization in mixed duopoly. J Public Econ 70(3):473–483

Matsumura T, Kanda O (2005) Mixed oligopoly at free entry markets. J Econ 84(1):27–48

Matsumura T, Matsushima N (2004) Endogenous cost differentials between public and private enterprises: a mixed duopoly approach. Economica 71(284):671–688

Matsumura T, Okamura M (2015) Competition and privatization policies revisited: the payoff interdependence approach. J Econ 116(2):137–150

Okten C, Arin KP (2006) The effects of privatization on efficiency: how does privatization work? World Dev 34(9):1537–1556

Rivera-Batiz FL, Rivera-Batiz LA (1990) The effects of direct foreign investment in the presence of increasing returns due to specialization. J Dev Econ 34(1–2):287–307. https://doi.org/10.1016/0304-3878(90)90086-Q

Van Marrewijk C, Stibora J, De Vaal A, Viaene JM (1997) Producer services, comparative advantage, and international trade patterns. J Int Econ 42(1–2):195–220

Wang LF, Chen TL (2010) Do cost efficiency gap and foreign competitors matter concerning optimal privatization policy at the free entry market? J Econ 100(1):33–49

Wang CC, Chiou JR (2015) An analysis of policy harmonization on privatization and trade liberalization. Int Rev Econ Financ 38:279–290

White MD (1996) Mixed oligopoly, privatization and subsidization. Econ Lett 53(2):189–195

Xu L, Lee SH, Matsumura T (2017) Ex-ante versus ex-post privatization policies with foreign penetration in free-entry mixed markets. Int Rev Econ Financ 50:1–7

Zhang J (2012) Inflow of labour, producer services and wage inequality. Econ Lett 117(3):600–603

Chapter 9
Capital Market Distortion, Agricultural Producer Service, and Wage Inequality in the Small-Scale Agriculture

Abstract Agriculture in developing countries operates on small-scale plots in general, which makes the direct utilization of durable capital equipment difficult. An intermediate sector is needed to facilitate the usage of capital. By accommodating the agricultural producer service sector, this chapter builds three-sector general equilibrium models and investigates the impact of mitigation of capital market distortion on wage inequality between skilled and unskilled labor. The chapter highlights the agricultural producer service sector and substitution between service and unskilled labor and arrives that mitigation of capital market distortion may widen wage inequality. The main conclusion is different from existing literature and provides new insights into this issue.

Keywords Capital market distortion · Agricultural producer service · Wage inequality · Small-scale agriculture

9.1 Introduction

Capital market distortion refers that long-run equilibrium is characterized by differentials between the value marginal products of capital in different sectors. Restuccia and Rogerson (2017) summarizes three general categories of potential sources of factor market misallocation: statutory provisions, discretionary provisions made by the government or other entities (such as banks), and market imperfections (examples include monopoly power, market frictions, and enforcement of property rights). Although capital market distortion exists in both developed and developing economies, weak market mechanism and pervasive interference by government make low-income countries face much severe capital market distortion. And the severe capital market distortion is manifested by various aspects: a higher interest rate in the rural area than in the urban area, credit plan and subsidized credit implemented by government, capital market dualism with two different credit markets (formal and informal credit market) (Chaudhuri and Gupta 2014), uniformly formulated credit rating system, and rigid banking regulations that lead to a higher cost of finance for

X. Li, Y. Wu, *Research on Characteristic Issues in Current Developing Economies*, New Frontiers in Regional Science: Asian Perspectives 80,
https://doi.org/10.1007/978-981-97-7284-1_9

emerging sectors, a much high cost of finance for agriculture-related enterprises (Lin and He 2020).

Recently, capital market distortion and wage inequality in developing countries are discussed by scholars from different perspectives. Mitigation of capital market distortion can be seen as financial development, and wage inequality can be viewed as one of the most significant parts of income distribution. Then one question arises: how does mitigation of capital market distortion affect wage inequality? Generally, mitigation of capital market distortion favors unskilled-intensive sectors and raises wage rate of unskilled labor and narrows down wage inequality. Pi and Chen (2016) employ the general- equilibrium approach to show mitigation rural-urban capital market distortion reduces skilled–unskilled wage inequality. Beladi et al. (2019) introduces oligopolistic competition in urban manufacturing and finds an increase in the capital market distortion widens wage inequality. Both Pi and Chen (2016) and Beladi et al. (2019) assume the agriculture in developing countries could employ capital directly. However, the existing literature neglects to consider the small-scale agriculture that prevails in developing countries.[1] The small-scale agriculture faces many difficulties in employing capital directly. On the one hand, farmers cannot afford to purchase relatively expensive modern inputs, such as agricultural machinery. On the other hand, their small-scale operations also make them unable to exploit economies of scale. Therefore, the development path of small-scale agriculture is far different with the development path of large-scale agriculture, and small-scale agriculture requires an intermediate sector to utilize capital indirectly.

Accommodating an intermediate sector is motivated by three concurrent events that occurred in China during the past two decades.[2] First, the well-known fact that massive rural labor flows into the urban region but agricultural output keeps growing. Second, the less well-known fact is that the growth rate of the price index of agricultural means of production is more sluggish than that of rural migrants' income.[3] Third, perhaps the least known fact is that the agricultural production structure has changed in the past few decades with the intermediate inputs becoming

[1] Sarah et al. (2016) offered a comprehensive summary on the size of farms worldwide. They showed that farms greater than 5 ha in size cover 27% of the farmland in low-income countries, while 97% in the high-income countries. The share of farmland controlled by larger farms is higher in countries with larger average incomes.

[2] The research utilizes a dual economy structure and considers this issue in the context of a developing economy. Though we take China as an example, the analysis of the research has implications for other developing countries. Two reasons support this argument. First, this phenomenon is prominent in China because of rapid economic growth and severe land fragmentation. Second, results shed light on other developing countries. Along with industrialization, many developing countries also face similar issues and develop some kind of agricultural producer service (mainly in machinery services form). For example, Bangladesh (Mottaleb et al. 2017), Myanmar (Belton et al. 2021), and Ethiopia (Ayele 2022).

[3] From 2009 to 2019, the average growth rate of migrants' income was 10.47%, while the price index was only 2.42%. Data for rural migrants' income comes from the Department of Household Surveys National Bureau of Statistics of China. The growth rate of the price index comes from the National Bureau of Statistics of China 2020.

increasingly important followed by a decrease of labor and land with the contribution of capital keeping at an extremely low level.[4] By using the National Fixed Points dataset of more than 20,000 households from 1995 to 2017, Wang et al. (2020) estimate that the contribution of capital is around 0.02 due to small-scale agriculture. We hold that three events are linked. When the growth of wage is greater than that of the price of intermediate inputs, agricultural production uses more intermediate inputs to substitute labor. This contributes to labor migration and the change of production structure. And if we ignore an intermediate sector, we could not explain the phenomenon that with the large-scale outflow of rural labor and extremely low capital elasticity, how small-scale agriculture utilizes increasing intermediate inputs to sustain high agricultural output. In practice, smallholders purchase agricultural producer service, through which speeds up the employment of nonagricultural inputs.[5]

Since the backwardness of agriculture has not been fundamentally improved and financial market is poorly developed, finance is one of the main constraints on the growth of agricultural producer service sector and many firms face financing difficulties and high funding costs (Huang and Yu 2010). On the one hand, agriculture in developing countries is still characterized by low productivity and high risk. Correspondingly, enterprises of agricultural service sector are exposed to covariant risks arising from agricultural production. On the other hand, the backward financial system that hinders the allocation of capital is manifested by various aspects. For instance, the credit rating system of financial institution is uniformly formulated. And due to newness of this sector, there is no credit rating system specifically aimed for the characteristics of agricultural producer service sector. Thus, many enterprises in the agricultural producer service sector are less likely to have optimal access to bank loans. This argument is backed by real economic data. In 2019, the China Economic Net published one report on financial constraints of new agricultural business entities. The report shows that 68.49% of enterprises face the shortage of funds. Due to financing difficulties, in general, enterprises are facing a higher borrowing cost than urban manufacturing firms correspondingly. Government of Jiangsu Province has published one article concerning the borrowing cost of new forms of agricultural business enterprises. The article has shown that financing fees were generally around 8%–9%, which was more than 30% higher than the

[4]Here, intermediate inputs refer to purchase inputs, like fertilizers, pesticides, and weedicides . The small-scale agriculture could purchase this intermediate inputs directly. Without rural labor migration, the utilization of such intermediate inputs could promote agricultural output. Capital refers to durable capital equipment, for example, tractors, harvesters, weed cutters, and pump sets for irrigation purpose.

[5]Specifically, firms in this sector, as the substitute for individual farmers' investment, provide services to smallholders. Thus, smallholders could use modern technology and inputs without paying the corresponding high sunk costs. Meanwhile, firms provide services to a large number of small plots and greatly lower their unit cost of operation.

benchmark interest rate.[6] Wang et al. (2018) has surveyed 131 new agricultural business entities and arrived the similar conclusion. To promote development of agricultural producer service sector, central and local government make efforts to reduce the borrowing cost. For central government, in May 2021, China's top financial regulators issued "Opinions Concerning Financial Support for the Development of New Forms of Agricultural Business Enterprises." The opinions aim to improve financial system that is adapted to the development of agricultural producer service sector. Meanwhile, through the implementation of financial incentives, local government coordinates with financial institutions to reduce interest rates.

There are many studies investigating the issue of the skilled-unskilled wage inequality from different aspects. Recently, scholars pay more attention to domestic factors to explain wage inequality. A variety of mechanisms are proposed to model the impact of a change in a domestic factor on the wage inequality, such as migrants' remittance (Li and Zhou 2013), privatization (Chao et al. 2016), capital market distortion (Pi and Chen 2016; Beladi et al. 2019), development of modern agriculture (Dong and Li 2019), skill formation (Zhang 2019), and appropriation activities (Yu and Chao 2021). Among the above-mentioned studies, Pi and Chen (2016) and Beladi et al. (2019) especially highlight the impact exerted by capital market distortion on the skilled-unskilled wage inequality. However, the impact generated by capital market distortion in the presence of agricultural producer service sector on the skilled-unskilled wage gap in developing countries is largely ignored. The existing literatures analyzing the relation between capital market distortion and skilled-unskilled wage gap leave small-scale agriculture aside and at the same time assume agriculture employs capital directly. In the real world, due to small-scale operation, farmers purchase service and utilize capital indirectly through service outsourcing approach (Zhang et al. 2017). The small-scale agriculture uses agricultural producer service in production. And at the same time, service could substitute rural unskilled labor and promote rural labor migration, leading to the reallocation of production factors among sectors. Since mitigation of capital market distortion and development of agricultural producer service affect labor allocation simultaneously, it is necessary for us to analyze how mitigation of capital market distortion in the presence of agricultural producer service sector impacts the wage inequality between skilled and unskilled labor.

The purpose of our study is to investigate the impacts of mitigation capital market distortion on wage inequality between skilled and unskilled labor. And we incorporate agricultural producer service sector that provides intermediate inputs to agriculture, and divide the development of this sector into the initial stage and the popularization stage. At the initial stage, when the elasticity of substitution between service and unskilled labor is relatively small, mitigation of capital market distortion narrows down the wage inequality. When the elasticity is relatively large, mitigation of capital market distortion expands (narrows down) the wage inequality if the ratio

[6] Available at http://nynct.jiangsu.gov.cn/art/2019/5/30/art_13274_8358419.html (accessed April 15, 2022) (in Chinese).

of the allocative share of capital in the agricultural service sector to the share in the manufacturing sector is relatively small (large). Then the robustness of the main results that mitigation of capital market distortion may worsen the wage gap is substantiated by the extended model that considers the feature of the popularization stage. In sum, this chapter highlights the agricultural producer service sector and substitution between service and unskilled labor and arrives that mitigation of capital market distortion may widen wage inequality. Our conclusions are different from those of the existing literature and provide new insights into this issue.

The studies most closely related to this chapter are Pi and Chen (2016) and Beladi et al. (2019). This chapter is very different from their works in the following respects. Firstly, the setups of the models are fundamentally different. The agricultural producer service sector is not incorporated in two papers. As we mentioned above, due to small-scale agriculture and outflow of rural labor, the production structure of agriculture has changed, and agricultural growth heavily depends on intermediate inputs. To facilitate the use of intermediate inputs, an intermediate sector is needed. Secondly, the chapter considers a different type of capital market distortion. Pi and Chen (2016) and Beladi et al. (2019) considered rural-urban capital distortion. And this chapter investigates the distortion within the urban region, which differs greatly from previous papers. Thirdly, as for the role of nonagricultural inputs, Pi and Chen (2016) and Beladi et al. (2019) assumed labor and capital are complementary. Under this assumption, mitigation of capital distortion unambiguously raises the wage of unskilled labor and reduces the wage of skilled labor and cuts down wage inequality. However, nonagricultural inputs usually substitute unskilled labor and promote rural labor migration. Taking into account substitution between service and labor will largely change the main results in Pi and Chen (2016) and Beladi et al. (2019), and we try to answer this question from a new perspective.

The rest of this chapter is organized as follows. Sections 9.2 and 9.3 conduct analysis with the initial case and the popularization case, respectively. Concluding remarks are made in Sect. 9.4.

9.2 Initial Stage of Agricultural Producer Service

Before the establishment of the theoretical model, we would like to classify the definition of the agricultural producer service sector in the model. Following Li and Fu (2022), agricultural producer service refers to integrating modern production elements such as scientific information technology, capital equipment, and talents into agricultural production by providing productive services and intermediate inputs for agriculture. Since rural region lags behind urban region under the framework of the dual economy, Li and Fu (2022) assumed the agricultural producer service sector lies in the urban region. One question appears: since production and consumption of service are taking place at the same time, how does rural agriculture utilize service from the urban sector. Ministry of Agriculture and Rural Affairs of China (2020) published a book (Typical Cases of National Agricultural Socialization

Services) to promote successful experiences. From this book, we could understand this question. Take the first case as an example (from Page 2 to 4). The firm established a four-tier service network of "Platform- Subsidiaries-Township Service Center-Service Advisor." The platform provides technical solutions, input supply, training support for the whole firm. Subsidiaries are located in counties or districts and provide services in their respective counties through the use of inputs and technical solutions provided by the platform. Township Service Centers act as grassroots platforms for the firm to serve customers. Service advisor is the "peripheral nerve" of the firm to implement the service. The platform provides training on interpretation of the contract, agricultural technology, operating procedures, and other aspects to the service advisor. The service advisor signs the service contract with the customer on behalf of the firm. From the production structure, though part of the operation locates in the rural region, the firm belongs to the urban region in essence and contracts with all employees.

In this section, we consider the initial stage of agricultural producer service sector with the following characteristics: (1) the sector provides services with little differentiation. In the beginning stage, services concentrate on several fields, such as harvesting service, plowing, and sowing service; (2) the sector employs capital and unskilled labor for production; (3) firms enter into this sector with little barriers, and we consider the market structure of service sector is competitive competition with the constant return to scale; (4) during agricultural production, there exists an imperfect substitution between service and unskilled labor.

9.2.1 The Model

Considering a small open economy that composes of three sectors: an urban manufacturing sector (sector M), an urban agricultural producer service sector (service sector or sector X), and a rural small-scale agricultural sector (sector A). Sector X is an upstream sector in the sense that it supplies intermediate inputs to agriculture. The manufacturing sector (sector M) uses skilled labor S_M, unskilled labor L_M, and capital K_M to produce good M. Sector X uses unskilled labor L_X and capital K_X to produce the producer service X. The production functions of sector M and X are[7] $M = S_M^{\beta} L_M^{\gamma} K_M^{1-\beta-\gamma}$, $X = L_X^{\rho} K_X^{1-\rho}$, β, γ, ρ are parameters that all belong to (0,1). Two functions satisfy Cobb-Douglas conditions (strictly quasi-concave and linearly homogeneous). The cost minimization conditions of sector M and X yield

$$\psi_M w_S^{\beta} \overline{w}^{\gamma} r_M^{1-\beta-\gamma} = p_M, \tag{9.1}$$

[7]To avoid complexity and make the model more tractable, we use explicit functions.

$$\psi_X \overline{w}^{\rho} r_X^{1-\rho} = p_X, \tag{9.2}$$

where $\psi_M = \beta^{-\beta}\gamma^{-\gamma}(1 - \beta - \gamma)^{\beta + \gamma - 1} > 0$ and $\psi_X = \rho^{-\rho}(1 - \rho)^{\rho - 1} > 0$. Set agricultural price as numeraire, p_M and p_X are the relative price of sector M and X, respectively. w_S is the wage of skilled labor. However, unskilled labor in the urban region faces the regulated wage rate $\overline{w}$ that is higher than the market-clearing wage rate, causing unemployment in the urban region. r_M and r_X are the interest rate of the capital utilized in sector M and X, respectively.

We consider capital market distortion expresses as a higher interest rate of capital in sector X than that in sector M, and $r_X > r_M$. Following Pi and Chen (2016) and Beladi et al. (2019), distortion in the capital market can be specified as

$$r_X = \alpha r_M, \alpha \geq 1. \tag{9.3}$$

The parameter α measures the degree of distortion in the capital market. The greater the α is, the larger the degree of distortion. And when $\alpha = 1$, no distortion exists in the capital market.

Next, we turn to the agricultural sector. This sector lies in rural region and uses unskilled labor L_A, services from sector X, and land T. Agricultural goods A are produced under perfect competition with constant returns to scale, $A = U_A^{\varphi} T^{1-\varphi}$, where $0 < \varphi < 1$. U_A is not just raw unskilled labor, but rather a CES aggregate of unskilled labor and services X, $U_A = \left[(1-\psi)L_A^{(\theta-1)/\theta} + \psi X^{(\theta-1)/\theta}\right]^{\theta/(\theta-1)}$, where ψ governs the weight of service and $\theta > 1$is the elasticity of substitution between unskilled labor and intermediate goods. Price of composite labor U_A is $W = \left[(1-\psi)^{\theta} w^{1-\theta} + \psi^{\theta} p_X^{1-\theta}\right]^{1/(1-\theta)}$, where w is the flexible wage rate of unskilled labor in the rural area. Cost minimization condition yields

$$\psi_A W^{\varphi} \tau^{1-\varphi} = 1, \tag{9.4}$$

where $\psi_A = \varphi^{-\varphi}(1 - \varphi)^{\varphi - 1} > 0$, τ is the land rent. By Shephard's lemma, demands for unskilled labor L_A, service X, and land T are $\varphi A W^{\theta - 1}(1 - \psi)^{\theta} w^{-\theta}$, $\varphi A W^{\theta - 1}\psi^{\theta} p_X^{-\theta}$, and $(1-\varphi)A/\tau$, respectively. By using the demand for X, we obtain the demand-supply equilibrium condition as

$$X = \varphi A W^{\theta-1} \psi^{\theta} p_X^{-\theta}. \tag{9.5}$$

Next, we turn to the factor market. Due to the shortage of skilled labor, we assume no unemployment in the skilled labor market. However, because of the higher rigid wage rate in the urban region, unskilled labor faces unemployment and migration. Regarding rural-urban unskilled labor migration, we follow the Harris-Todaro labor allocation mechanism (see Harris and Todaro 1970):

$$\overline{w} = (1 + \lambda)w, \tag{9.6}$$

where λ is the ratio of urban unemployment to urban employment (including sector M and X).

The market-clearing conditions of factors yield

$$\beta p_M M w_S^{-1} = S, \tag{9.7}$$

$$(1 + \lambda)\left(\gamma p_M M \overline{w}^{-1} + \rho p_X X \overline{w}^{-1}\right) + \varphi A W^{\theta - 1}(1 - \psi)^{\theta} w^{-\theta} = L, \tag{9.8}$$

$$(1 - \varphi)A\tau^{-1} = T, \tag{9.9}$$

$$(1 - \beta - \gamma)p_M M r_M^{-1} + (1 - \rho)p_X X r_X^{-1} = K, \tag{9.10}$$

where S, L, T, and K are the endowment of skilled labor, unskilled labor, land, and capital, respectively. So far, the establishment of model is completed. Equations (9.1) to (9.10) determine 10 endogenous variables, w_S, w, r_M, r_X, τ, p_X, X, M, A, and λ, the exogenous variable is α. Furthermore, from Eqs. (9.6) and (9.8), it is not hard to verify that the average wage rate of unskilled labor is w, which implies the average wage rate of unskilled labor is equal to that in the agricultural sector. Thus, we use the wage of skilled labor and the average wage of unskilled labor, as well as their change to investigate the effect of mitigation of capital market distortion on skilled-unskilled wage gap.[8]

9.2.2 Comparatively Analysis

Taking total differentiation to Eqs. (9.1)–(9.10), and writing in a matrix notation, we can obtain the following equation:

$$\begin{pmatrix} -\dfrac{\varphi\beta(1-\rho)\theta_{XA}}{1-\beta-\gamma} & \varphi\theta_{LA} & 1-\varphi \\ \dfrac{(1-\gamma)\lambda_{KM}+\beta\Omega_1}{1-\beta-\gamma} & \lambda_{KX}(\theta-1)\theta_{LA} & \lambda_{KX} \\ (1+\lambda)\lambda_{LM} - \dfrac{(1-\rho)\beta\Omega_3}{1-\beta-\gamma} & -1-\Omega_3 & \Omega_2 \end{pmatrix} \begin{pmatrix} \widehat{w_S} \\ \widehat{w} \\ \widehat{A} \end{pmatrix}$$
$$= \begin{pmatrix} -\varphi\theta_{XA}(1-\rho) \\ \Omega_1 \\ -(1-\rho)\Omega_3 \end{pmatrix} \widehat{\alpha}, \tag{9.11}$$

[8] Such methods can be referred to Pi and Chen (2016) and Beladi et al. (2019) and others.

where "∧" denotes the percentage change, λ_{ij} is the allocative share of factor i in the jth sector (e.g., $\lambda_{KM} = (1\text{-}\beta\text{-}\gamma)Mp_M/(r_M K)$). Define$\theta_{LA} = (1-\psi)^{\theta} w^{1-\theta}/W^{1-\theta}$, $\theta_{XA} = \psi^{\theta} p_X^{1-\theta}/W^{1-\theta}$, and we have $\theta_{XA} + \theta_{LA} = 1.\Omega_1 = \lambda_{KX}[(\theta-1)\theta_{LA}(1-\rho)+1] > 0, \Omega_2 = (1+\lambda)\lambda_{LX} + \lambda_{LA} > 0$, $\Omega_3 = \theta_{XA}\lambda_{LA}(\theta-1)(1-\rho) > 0$. In addition, since sector M uses advanced equipment in developing countries, it is realistic to suppose that, as compared with the other two sectors (sector X and A), sector M is more capital -intensive. In mathematical terms, this further implies that $\lambda_{KX}/\Omega_2 < \lambda_{KM}/(1+\lambda)\lambda_{LM}$.

Use Δ_1 to denote the value of the determinant of the coefficient matrix in (9.11),

$$\Delta_1 = -\frac{\varphi\beta(1-\rho)\lambda_{KX}}{1-\beta-\gamma}[\theta_{XA} + \Omega_3 + \Omega_2(\theta-1)\theta_{LA}] + \varphi(1+\lambda)\lambda_{LM}\lambda_{KX}\theta_{LA}$$

$$-\theta_{LA}\frac{(1-\gamma)\lambda_{KM} + \beta\lambda_{KX}}{1-\beta-\gamma}$$

$$[\Omega_2\varphi + (1-\varphi)\theta_{LA}(\theta-1)\lambda_{KX}] - (1-\varphi)(\theta-1)\theta_{LA}\lambda_{KX}\left[(1+\lambda)\lambda_{LM} + \frac{\beta(1-\rho)}{1-\beta-\gamma}\right]$$

$$< 0.$$

Next, we investigate the impacts of mitigation of capital market on wage rate of skilled and unskilled labor and the output of agricultural sector, which could be obtained by solving Eq. (9.11):

$$\frac{\widehat{w}_S}{\widehat{\alpha}} = -\frac{\lambda_{KX}\{\varphi(1-\rho)[(\theta-1)\theta_{LA}\Omega_2 + \Omega_3 + \theta_{XA}] + \varphi\theta_{LA}\Omega_2 + (1-\varphi)(1+\Omega_3) + (1-\rho)(1-\varphi)(\theta-1)\theta_{LA}]\}}{\Delta_1}$$

$$< 0$$

$$\frac{\widehat{w}}{\widehat{\alpha}} = \frac{\varphi\theta_{XA}(1-\rho)}{\Delta_1}\left[\frac{\lambda_{KM}(1-\gamma)\Omega_2}{1-\beta-\gamma} - \lambda_{KX}(1+\lambda)\lambda_{LM}\right] - \frac{(1-\varphi)}{\Delta_1}$$

$$\times\left\{\frac{(1-\rho)\Omega_3\lambda_{KM}(1-\gamma)}{1-\beta-\gamma} + \Omega_1(1+\lambda)\lambda_{LM}\right\}$$

and

$$\frac{\widehat{A}}{\widehat{\alpha}} = \frac{\varphi\theta_{LA}\lambda_{KX}(1+\lambda)\lambda_{LM}[1+(\theta-1)(1-\rho)]}{\Delta_1} + \frac{\varphi\lambda_{KM}(1-\gamma)(1-\rho)(\theta_{XA}+\Omega_3)}{1-\beta-\gamma} < 0$$

From the above results, the magnitude of $\widehat{w}_S/\widehat{\alpha}$ is determined by the allocative share of capital in sector X. When λ_{KX} is relatively small, an alleviation of capital market distortion has a small effect on the wage rate of skilled labor. The sign of $\widehat{w}/\widehat{\alpha}$ is ambiguous, the first term is negative while the second term is positive. According to the definition of Ω_1 and Ω_3, if θ is relatively small, $\widehat{w}/\widehat{\alpha}$ is determined by the first term, and $\widehat{w}/\widehat{\alpha} < 0$. When θ is relatively large, $\widehat{w}/\widehat{\alpha} > 0$. Suppose that θ^* solves

$\widehat{w}/\widehat{\alpha}=0$, if $\theta > \theta^*$, then $\widehat{w}/\widehat{\alpha}>0$; and if $1 < \theta < \theta^*$, then $\widehat{w}/\widehat{\alpha}<0$. Lemma 1 summarizes the main results discussed above.

Lemma 1 *(i) An alleviation of capital market distortion expands agricultural output and reduces the wage rate of skilled labor and (ii) its impact on the wage rate of unskilled labor is ambiguous. If the elasticity of substitution between service and unskilled labor is relatively large (small), mitigation of capital distortion reduces (increases) wage of unskilled labor.*

The economic intuition of Lemma 1 is as follows. Mitigation of capital market distortion attracts an inflow of capital into sector X. Given the price of M, the outflow of capital from sector M reduces the value of marginal product of skilled labor. Since the market is perfectly competitive, the wage of skilled labor reduces. An inflow of capital into sector X cuts down r_X and as a result the price of sector X falls and the output rises. Since services are used in agriculture, mitigation of capital market distortion contributes to raising agricultural output. For the wage of unskilled labor, on the one hand, more capital employed in the labor-intensive sector raises the demand for unskilled labor in the urban region. On the other hand, due to the substitution between service and unskilled labor in agricultural production, a decrease in p_X raises the demand for services in agriculture and encourages rural labor migration. If the elasticity of substitution between service and unskilled labor is relatively large, which implies that expansion of X substitutes relatively large amount of unskilled labor, making unskilled labor relatively surplus. As a consequence, wage of unskilled labor reduces. If the elasticity of substitution is relatively small, then the expansion of X substitutes relatively few amount of unskilled labor. In this case, raising demand for unskilled labor will be dominant, so the demand for unskilled labor rises, which leads to an increase in w.

Using above results, the effect of mitigation of capital market distortion on the wage gap can be expressed as.

$$\frac{\widehat{w}_S-\widehat{w}}{\widehat{\alpha}}=\frac{\lambda_{KM}(1-\gamma)(1-\rho)[(1-\varphi)\Omega_3-\varphi\theta_{XA}\Omega_2]}{(1-\beta-\gamma)\Delta_1}-\frac{\lambda_{KX}[(1-\varphi\rho\theta_{XA})\Omega_2+(1-\rho)(\theta-1)\theta_{LA}\Omega_2+(1-\rho\varphi)\Omega_3]}{\Delta_1}$$

If $\theta < 1+\varphi\Omega_2/[\lambda_{LA}(1-\varphi)(1-\rho)]$, $(\widehat{w}_S-\widehat{w})/\widehat{\alpha}>0$; If $\theta > 1+\varphi\Omega_2/[\lambda_{LA}(1-\varphi)(1-\rho)]$, define $\zeta_1=\frac{(1-\gamma)(1-\rho)[(1-\varphi)\Omega_3-\varphi\theta_{XA}\Omega_2]}{(1-\beta-\gamma)}>0$, and $\zeta_2=\Omega_2[(1-\varphi\rho\theta_{XA})+(1-\rho)(\theta-1)\theta_{LA}]+(1-\rho\varphi)\Omega_3>0$, and we have $\frac{\widehat{w_S-w}}{\widehat{\alpha}}=\frac{\lambda_{KM}\zeta_2}{\Delta_1}\left(\frac{\zeta_1}{\zeta_2}-\frac{\lambda_{KX}}{\lambda_{KM}}\right)$. Thus, if $\frac{\lambda_{KX}}{\lambda_{KM}}<\frac{\zeta_1}{\zeta_2}$, $\frac{\widehat{w_S-w}}{\widehat{\alpha}}<0$; if $\frac{\lambda_{KX}}{\lambda_{KM}}>\frac{\zeta_1}{\zeta_2}$, $\frac{\widehat{w_S-w}}{\widehat{\alpha}}>0$.

Proposition 1 summarizes how the wage gap will change after an improvement of capital market distortion.

Proposition 1 *Consider a small, open developing country with an agricultural producer service sector at the initial stage, (i) when the elasticity of substitution between service and unskilled labor is relatively small, mitigation of capital market distortion narrows down the wage inequality; (ii) when the elasticity is relatively large, mitigation of capital market distortion expands(narrows down) the wage inequality if the ratio of the allocative share of capital in the agricultural service sector to the share in the manufacturing sector is relatively small(large).*

According to Lemma 1, we show the economic mechanism behind Proposition 1. When the elasticity of substitution between service and unskilled labor is relatively small, mitigation of capital distortion raises wage of unskilled labor and falls wage of skilled labor, and narrows down the wage gap. When the elasticity is relatively large, an improvement of capital market distortion reduces both wage of skilled and unskilled labor, exerting an ambiguous impact on the wage gap.

On the one hand, if the ratio of the allocative share of capital in the agricultural service sector to the share in the manufacturing sector is relatively small, then mitigation of distortion will lead to a reallocation of capital between sector M and X in a small magnitude. In this case, the demand for skilled labor will decrease slightly, resulting in a less decrease in the wage of skilled labor. However, competition for employment of unskilled labor becomes fiercer because (1) a relatively small amount of capital flows into sector X, thus the raised demand for unskilled labor is limited; (2) θ is relatively large, and the substitution of service for unskilled labor will be relatively easy, then the demand for unskilled labor will fall greatly. Those aspects contribute to a more decrease of unskilled wage rate. Thus, wage inequality will expand.

On the other hand, if the ratio is relatively large, then mitigation of distortion affects the reallocation of capital greatly. Then, the demand for skilled labor will decrease severely, resulting in a more decrease in the wage of skilled labor. Its impact on unskilled wage rate is more complicated. A relatively large amount of capital flows into sector X raises its demand for unskilled labor, while a relatively large θ makes a relatively large substitution effect. Two conflicting effects bring relatively little fluctuation of demand for unskilled labor, so does its wage rate. In this case, wage inequality narrows down.

Proposition 1 obtains different results and provides new insights to this issue. Here, we focus on the case that mitigation of capital market distortion expands the wage inequality. Although the conclusion requires two conditions to be valid, these two conditions are easy to be satisfied in a real economy. At the initial stage, the allocative share of capital in this sector accounts a few percent of whole capital endowment. Thus, an improvement of capital market distortion exerts relatively little impact on wage of skilled labor. Meanwhile, generally, services that substitute labor significantly emerge in the market first, like agricultural machinery services. Thus, the elasticity of substitution is relatively large. When two conditions hold, mitigation of capital market distortion worsens wage inequality.

9.3 Popularization Stage of Agricultural Producer Service

With the development of industrialization, rural-urban migration persists and small-scale agriculture raises its demand for service that contributes to the popularization of agricultural service in agricultural production. As the agricultural service develops, this sector is increasingly technology or knowledge intensive, which makes economies of scale internal to the firms. In this section, we extend the basic theoretical model by considering the characteristics of popularization stage.

At this stage, (1) firms could provision differential services, which is the core feature. Different from the initial stage, firms could provide various services, for instance, agricultural material distribution, agricultural technology extension, agricultural information service, agricultural product quality and safety service, epidemic prevention and control service, and agricultural product marketing services. (2) The service sector utilizes not only unskilled labor and capital but also skilled labor. (3) Firms can enter this market by paying a fixed setup cost and the market structure of the service sector is monopolistic competition. (4) Service could perfectly substitute unskilled labor in agricultural production. At this stage, firms could offer whole course services to conduct all farming works. For instance, after purchasing land trust service, peasants do not need to engage in agricultural production at all.

9.3.1 The Model

The relationships between the production of sector M and A, capital market distortion, and unskilled labor migration mechanism are the same as before, shown as (9.1), (9.3), (9.6), and (9.9). Since firms need to pay a fixed cost to enter this sector, thus, the number of firms is finite, and assume sector X exists n firms. Firm i produces variety x_i and sold in a monopolistically competitive market under the increasing returns-to-scale technology. Assume θ amounts of capital are needed as the fixed input. And skilled labor and unskilled labor are the variable inputs, with the marginal cost given by $\overline{w}^{1-\phi}w_S^{\phi}$. Total cost faced by each service firm is $TC_i = \theta r_X + \overline{w}^{1-\phi}w_S^{\phi}x_i$. The presence of internal economies of scale implies that each firm specializes in the production of a single variety, and the number of firms equals the number of varieties.

The total output of sector X is assumed to be of the CES type and could perfect substitute unskilled labor in sector A, $X = \left[\sum_{i=1}^{n} x_i^{\frac{\sigma-1}{\sigma}}\right]^{\frac{\sigma}{\sigma-1}}$, where $\sigma > 1$ is a parameter and represents the elasticity of substitution among varieties. $P = \left[\sum_{i=1}^{n} p_{xi}^{1-\sigma}\right]^{\frac{1}{1-\sigma}}$ is the price index of X, p_{xi} is the price of variety i. Given X, the agricultural sector generates the demand for each variety $x_i = p_{xi}^{-\sigma} P^{\sigma} X$. Following the demand function and cost function of each variety, a firm sets the price to maximize its profit, which yields

$$p_{xi} = \frac{\sigma}{\sigma - 1} \overline{w}^{1-\phi} w_S^{\phi}. \tag{9.12}$$

Here, the pricing rule is independent of the variety index i. Since p_{xi}, rX, $\overline{w}$, and w_S are the same for all firms, each firm would also produce the same amount of output, and set $x_i = x_j = x$, $p_{xi} = p_{xj} = p_x$. Further, we have $P = p_x n^{1/(1-\sigma)}$, and $X = xn^{\sigma/(\sigma-1)}$. $\sigma > 1$, expansion of the number of varieties, n, reduces the price index P and raises X, even if each firm keeps its price and output constant. As the value of σ goes to infinite, the influence of n on P and X disappears. The reason is that X becomes the simple sum of the quantities of services and varieties become perfect substitutes for each other. On the other hand, as the value ofσdeclines toward 1, the importance of diversity becomes more significant.

Next, we turn to the agricultural sector. This sector uses unskilled labor L_A, services from sector X and land T. Service does routine farm work and are the perfect substitute for unskilled labor. Hence, define effective labor U_A used in agriculture as follows: $U_A = L_A + sX$, where s represents the substitution between unit service and unskilled labor, and a larger s implies unit service could substitute unskilled labor in a greater margin. The perfect substitution implies sector A employs the service only if the unit price of service is no larger than the unskilled wage rate w multiples s, and in equilibrium, we must have

$$p_x n^{1/(1-\sigma)} = sw. \tag{9.13}$$

The production function is the same as before. The cost minimization condition yields

$$\psi_A w^{\varphi} \tau^{1-\varphi} = 1. \tag{9.14}$$

The market-clearing conditions of the skilled labor, urban unskilled labor, and capital could be shown as follows:

$$\beta p_M M w_S^{-1} + nx\phi \overline{w}^{1-\phi} w_S^{\phi-1} = S. \tag{9.15}$$

$$(1+\lambda)\left[\gamma M p_M \overline{w}^{-1} + (1-\phi)\overline{w}^{-\phi} w_S^{\phi} xn\right] = L - L_A. \tag{9.16}$$

$$\varphi A w^{-1} = L_A + sX. \tag{9.17}$$

and

$$(1-\beta-\gamma) M p_M r_M^{-1} + \theta n = K. \tag{9.18}$$

The long-run equilibrium is characterized by free entry and exit of firms, which means total revenue $p_x x$ equals total cost TC and the zero profit of all firms in this sector. Using Eq. (9.14), the zero-profit condition occurs

$$\frac{x\overline{w}^{1-\phi}w_S^{\phi}}{\sigma-1}=\theta r_X. \tag{9.19}$$

Equation (9.19) determines the number of firms (i.e., n). Accordingly, the long-run equilibrium involves 12 Eqs. (9.1), (9.3), (9.6), (9.9), and (9.12) to (9.19) and 12 endogenous variables w, p_x, w_S, τ, λ, rX, rM, A, x, M, n, and L_A.

9.3.2 Comparative Analysis

Totally differentiating those equations, we can obtain the following matrix:

$$\begin{pmatrix} -1 & \phi & 0 & 0 & -\dfrac{1}{\sigma-1} \\ 0 & -(1-\phi\lambda_{SX}) & \lambda_{SM} & \lambda_{SX} & \lambda_{SX} \\ 0 & \dfrac{\beta\lambda_{KM}}{1-\beta-\gamma} & \lambda_{KM} & 0 & \lambda_{KX} \\ \dfrac{1}{\delta_2}+\dfrac{1+\delta_1}{1-\varphi} & -\dfrac{\phi\lambda_{LX}^U}{\delta_2} & -\dfrac{\lambda_{LM}^U}{\delta_2} & \delta_1-\dfrac{\lambda_{LX}^U}{\delta_2} & \dfrac{\sigma\delta_1}{\sigma-1}-\dfrac{\lambda_{LX}^U}{\delta_2} \\ 0 & \phi+\dfrac{\beta}{1-\beta-\gamma} & 0 & 1 & 0 \end{pmatrix}$$

$$\times\begin{pmatrix} \widehat{w} \\ \widehat{w_S} \\ \widehat{M} \\ \widehat{x} \\ \widehat{n} \end{pmatrix}=\begin{pmatrix} 0 \\ 0 \\ 0 \\ 0 \\ 1 \end{pmatrix}\widehat{\alpha}, \tag{9.20}$$

where $\delta_1 = sX/L_A$, $\delta_2 = L_A/(L - L_A)$, $\lambda_{LX}^U=(1-\phi)\overline{w}^{-\phi}w_S^{\phi}xn/\left[\gamma Mp_M\overline{w}^{-1}+(1-\phi)\overline{w}^{-\phi}w_S^{\phi}xn\right]$, represents the share of unskilled labor employment of sector X in the total employment of urban region, and $\lambda_{LM}^U=1-\lambda_{LX}^U$. And by calculation, we have $\delta_1>\lambda_{LX}^U/\delta_2$. In the popularization stage, two urban sectors utilize both skilled labor and capital. Since training skilled labor needs more time than the time needed for capital accumulation, it is easy to generate the situation that the capital per capita of skilled labor in the service sector is higher than that of manufacturing sector. Therefore, it is realistic to suppose that the service sector is more capital- intensive than skilled-labor intensive, as compared with sector M. In mathematical terms, this implies that $\lambda_{KM}\lambda_{SX}$-$\lambda_{SM}\lambda_{KX} < 0$. Denote the determinant of the coefficient matrix of (9.20) as Δ_2, and by calculation

$$\Delta_2 = -\left(\frac{\beta\lambda_{SM}}{1-\beta-\gamma} + \lambda_{KM}\right)\left(\delta_1 - \frac{\lambda_{LX}^U}{\delta_2}\right) - \left(\frac{\beta\lambda_{SX}}{1-\beta-\gamma} + \lambda_{KX}\right)\frac{\lambda_{LM}^U}{\delta_2}$$
$$+\left(\frac{1}{\delta_2} + \frac{1+\delta_1}{1-\varphi} - \delta_1\right)\left[\phi(\lambda_{SM}\lambda_{KX} - \lambda_{SX}\lambda_{KM}) + \frac{1}{\sigma-1}\frac{(1-\gamma)\lambda_{KM}}{1-\beta-\gamma}\right].$$

The sign of Δ_2 is undetermined by the direct calculation of the determinant. According to the dynamic adjustment process (see Appendix 1), the sign of Δ_2 is negative. Note that the presence of external economies raises to stability problem. If σ is relatively large, which implies external economies are relatively small, the sign of Δ_2 is unambiguously positive. The rest of this chapter assumes that the system is stable, which ensures $\Delta_2 < 0$. By solving (9.20)[9]

$$\frac{\widehat{w}}{\widehat{\alpha}} = \left(\delta_1 - \frac{\lambda_{LX}^U}{\delta_2}\right)$$
$$\times\left\{\frac{\phi(\lambda_{SX} - \lambda_{KX})}{\Delta_2} - \frac{\lambda_{KM}(1-\phi\lambda_{SX}) + \lambda_{SX}\lambda_{KM}\phi\sigma}{(\sigma-1)\Delta_2} - \frac{\lambda_{KM}\beta\lambda_{SM}}{(\sigma-1)\Delta_2(1-\beta-\gamma)}\right\}$$
$$-\left(\phi\lambda_{KX} + \frac{1}{\sigma-1}\frac{\beta\lambda_{SM}}{1-\beta-\gamma}\right)\frac{\lambda_{SX}\lambda_{LM}^U}{\delta_2\Delta_2} > 0$$

and

$$\frac{\widehat{w}_S}{\widehat{\alpha}} = \frac{\lambda_{SX}\lambda_{KM}}{\Delta_2(\sigma-1)}\left(\frac{1+\delta_1}{1-\varphi} - 1 + \frac{1}{\delta_2}\right) - \frac{\lambda_{KX}\lambda_{SM}}{\Delta_2}\left(\delta_1 - \frac{\lambda_{LX}^U}{\delta_2}\right) - \frac{\lambda_{SX}\lambda_{KX}\lambda_{LM}^U}{\delta_2\Delta_2}.$$

Different with Sect. 9.2, at the popularization stage, the sign of $\widehat{w}_S/\widehat{\alpha}$ is ambiguous, and the first term is negative while the second term and the third term are positive. If σ is relatively small, the sign of $\widehat{w}_S/\widehat{\alpha}$ is determined by the first term, and $\widehat{w}_S/\widehat{\alpha} < 0$. When σ is relatively large, $\widehat{w}_S/\widehat{\alpha} > 0$. Suppose that σ^* solves $\widehat{w}_S/\widehat{\alpha} = 0$, if$\sigma > \sigma^*$,then $\widehat{w}_S/\widehat{\alpha} > 0$; and if $1 < \sigma < \sigma^*$, then $\widehat{w}_S/\widehat{\alpha} < 0$. Lemma 2 summarizes the main results discussed above.

Lemma 2 *At the popularization stage, an alleviation of capital market distortion will decrease the wage rate of unskilled labor, while its impact on wage of skilled labor is ambiguous. If the elasticity of substitution among varieties is relatively large (small), mitigation of capital distortion reduces (increases) wage of skilled labor.*

An improvement of capital market distortion leads to the reallocation of capital between sector *M* and *X*, making the interest rate of sector *X* reduce and that in the

[9] Other results are shown in Appendix 2.

sector M rise. Faced with this situation, firms in sector X reduce its fixed cost and have positive profits. With free entry and exit of firms, mitigation of capital market distortion attracts new firms into this sector and enlarges the number of varieties. Expansion of the number of varieties generates external economies, which exerts different impacts on wage of skilled and unskilled labor.

At this stage, skilled labor can be employed in sector M and X. The outflow of capital results in a decrease in output of sector M that brings down the demand for skilled labor. Consequently, a decrease in α generates a skilled-wage-reducing effect, which is similar with the result in Sect. 9.2. However, total demand for skilled labor is also affected by the employment of skilled labor in the sector X.

On the one hand, if the elasticity of substitution among varieties is relatively small, then the substitution between varieties will be relatively hard, an increase in n has relatively large external economies. At this case, each firm also raises its output x, generating a skilled-wage-enhancing effect that dominates the skilled-wage-reducing effect. That is, the total demand for skilled labor ascends. Therefore, the wage of skilled labor raises.

On the other hand, if the elasticity of substitution among varieties is relatively large, then the substitution between varieties will be relatively easy. The enlargement of the number of varieties generates relatively small external economies. To restore the zero-profit condition, each firm cuts down its output. Thus, the demand for skilled labor in sector X increases slightly. As a consequence, the limited increase of the demand from sector X cannot effectively stop the decrease of the demand from sector M. The decrease of demand for skilled labor will be dominant, which leads to a decrease in the wage of skilled labor.

Even though the impact of mitigation capital market distortion on the wage rate of skilled labor is ambiguous, a decrease in α raises X and cuts down its price index P unambiguously. Due to the perfect substitution between service and unskilled labor in agricultural production, a decrease in P reduces the wage rate of unskilled labor.

Now, we investigate how capital market distortion exerts an impact on the skilled-unskilled wage inequality.

$$\frac{\widehat{w}_S-\widehat{w}}{\widehat{\alpha}}=\frac{\left\{\lambda_{SX}\left[\frac{\beta\lambda_{KM}}{1-\beta-\gamma}\frac{\lambda_{LM}^U}{\delta_2}+\lambda_{KM}\left(\frac{1}{\delta_2}+\frac{1+\delta_1}{1-\varphi}-\delta_1\right)\right]+\left(\delta_1-\frac{\lambda_{LX}^U}{\delta_2}\right)\left(\lambda_{KM}+\frac{\beta\lambda_{SM}\lambda_{KM}}{1-\beta-\gamma}\right)\right\}}{\Delta_2(\sigma-1)}$$
$$-\frac{\lambda_{KX}(1-\phi)\left[\lambda_{SM}\left(\delta_1-\frac{\lambda_{LX}^U}{\delta_2}\right)+\lambda_{SX}\frac{\lambda_{LM}^U}{\delta_2}\right]}{\Delta_2}$$

The first term is negative, while the second term is positive. Define $\zeta_3=\frac{\left\{\lambda_{SX}\left[\frac{\beta\lambda_{KM}}{1-\beta-\gamma}\frac{\lambda_{LM}^U}{\delta_2}+\lambda_{KM}\left(\frac{1}{\delta_2}+\frac{1+\delta_1}{1-\varphi}-\delta_1\right)\right]+\left(\delta_1-\frac{\lambda_{LX}^U}{\delta_2}\right)\left(\lambda_{KM}+\frac{\beta\lambda_{SM}\lambda_{KM}}{1-\beta-\gamma}\right)\right\}}{(\sigma-1)}>0$ and $\zeta_4=\lambda_{KX}(1-\phi)$

$\left[\lambda_{SM}\left(\delta_1 - \frac{\lambda_{LX}^U}{\delta_2}\right) + \lambda_{SX}\frac{\lambda_{LM}^U}{\delta_2}\right] > 0$, and we have $\frac{\widehat{w_S} - \widehat{w}}{\widehat{\alpha}} = \frac{1}{\Delta_2}\left(\frac{\zeta_3}{\sigma - 1} - \zeta_4\right)$. Thus, if $\sigma > \frac{\zeta_3}{\zeta_4} + 1$, $\frac{\widehat{w_S} - \widehat{w}}{\widehat{\alpha}} > 0$; if $\sigma < \frac{\zeta_3}{\zeta_4} + 1$, $\frac{\widehat{w_S} - \widehat{w}}{\widehat{\alpha}} < 0$.

Proposition 2 summarizes how the wage gap will change after an improvement of capital market distortion.

Proposition 2 *At the popularization stage, an alleviation of capital market distortion will widen (cut down) the wage inequality when the elasticity of substitution among varieties is relatively small(large).*

From Lemma 2, a decrease in α reduces wage of unskilled labor. And if the elasticity of substitution among varieties is relatively small, which implies the substitution between services is relatively hard, mitigation of capital distortion increases wage of skilled labor. At this case, wage inequality widens unambiguously. If the elasticity of substitution is relatively large, which implies the external economies are relatively small. Therefore, expansion of n has relatively little impacts on P and wage of unskilled labor. Consequently, wage of unskilled labor decreases slightly. Regarding skilled labor, the demand for skilled labor will fall greatly, so does the wage of skilled labor. In this case, the reduction of the wage of skilled labor will be dominant. Thus, the wage inequality will be narrowed down.

Proposition 2 confirms the main result that mitigation of capital market distortion may worsen wage inequality. We pay attention to the condition that worsens wage inequality, which requires the elasticity of substitution among varieties is relatively small. Considering that capital market distortion impedes the development of the service sector, if one service already exists in the market, a new entrant will make efforts to provide different services. Therefore, it is reasonable to assume that firms offer services with relatively little substitution and substitution among varieties is relatively small.

9.4 Conclusions

Small-scale agriculture faces difficulties in employing modern intermediate inputs directly. And agricultural producer service sector that acts as an intermediate sector could facilitate this process. By incorporating the service sector into the general equilibrium model, this chapter explores the impacts of mitigation of capital market distortion on the wage inequality. This chapter divides the development of service sector into initial stage and popularization stage. Two stages are divided based on four aspects: differential of services, employment of skilled labor, entry barriers, and substitution between service and labor. We find that at the initial stage, when the elasticity of substitution between service and unskilled labor is relatively small, mitigation of capital market distortion narrows down the wage inequality. When the elasticity is relatively large, mitigation of capital market distortion expands (narrows down) the wage inequality if the ratio of the allocative share of capital in the agricultural service sector to the share in the manufacturing sector is relatively small (large). Then the robustness of the main result is substantiated by the extended model that considers the feature of the popularization stage. In sum, this chapter highlights agricultural producer service sector and substitution between service and unskilled labor, and arrives that mitigation of capital market distortion may widen wage inequality. Our conclusions are different from those of the existing literature and provide new insights into this issue.

Here, we give some possible extensions for future research. Firstly, in this chapter, the manufacturing and service sector have no upstream and downstream linkages. When the service sector needs manufacturing output for production, we may draw different results. Secondly, migrants move from rural to urban regions, while remittances flow in the opposite way, thus we can assume parts of remittances are used to purchase service and investigate its impact on wage inequality in future studies. Thirdly, rural public infrastructure is crucial for the development of agricultural service. An improvement of rural infrastructure reduces the operation cost of service sector and promotes its development, which also affects wage inequality from different aspects.

Competing Interests

Funding This work was supported by Postdoctoral Science Foundation, China, Project No. 2020 M671414.

Disclosure Statement No potential conflict of interest was reported by the authors.

Appendix

Appendix 1. Dynamic Adjustment Process of Eq. (9.20)

The dynamic adjustment process is based on the principle of the excess demand function, and methodology and approach are the same as those in Beladi et al. (2008). After substitutions, the dynamic adjustment process for the system can be expressed as

$$\dot{M} = d_1\left(p_M - \psi_M w_S^{\beta} \overline{w}^{\gamma} r_M^{1-\beta-\gamma}\right) \tag{9.21}$$

$$\dot{x} = d_2\left(p_X - \frac{\sigma}{\sigma-1}\overline{w}^{1-\phi} w_S^{\phi}\right) = d_2\left(\frac{sw}{n^{1/(1-\sigma)}} - \frac{\sigma}{\sigma-1}\overline{w}^{1-\phi} w_S^{\phi}\right) \tag{9.22}$$

$$\dot{A} = d_3\left(1 - \psi_A w^{\varphi} \tau^{1-\varphi}\right) \tag{9.23}$$

$$\dot{w}_S = d_4\left(\beta p_M M w_S^{-1} + nx\phi\overline{w}^{1-\phi}w_S^{\phi-1} - S\right) \tag{9.24}$$

$$\dot{L}_A = d_5\left\{(L - L_A) - \frac{\overline{w}}{w}\left[\gamma M p_M \overline{w}^{-1} + (1-\phi)\overline{w}^{-\phi}w_S^{\phi}xn\right]\right\} \tag{9.25}$$

$$\dot{w} = d_6\left(\varphi A w^{-1} - L_A - sxn^{\sigma/(\sigma-1)}\right) \tag{9.26}$$

$$\dot{r}_M = d_7\left[(1-\beta-\gamma)p_M M r_M^{-1} + \theta n - K\right] \tag{9.27}$$

$$\dot{\tau} = d_8\left[(1-\varphi)A\tau^{-1} - T\right] \tag{9.28}$$

$$\dot{n} = d_9\left\{\frac{x\overline{w}^{1-\phi}w_S^{\phi}}{\sigma-1} - \theta r_M \alpha\right\} \tag{9.29}$$

where "." denotes differentiation with regard to time, and parameter *di* is strictly positive measuring the speed rate of adjustment. The determinant of the Jacobian matrix of Eqs. (9.21)–(9.29) is given by

$$H = \begin{pmatrix} 0 & 0 & 0 & -\beta & 0 & 0 & \beta+\gamma-1 & 0 & 0 \\ 0 & 0 & 0 & -\phi & 0 & 1 & 0 & 0 & 1/(\sigma-1) \\ 0 & 0 & 0 & 0 & 0 & -\varphi & 0 & \varphi-1 & 0 \\ \lambda_{SM} & \lambda_{SX} & 0 & -\lambda_{SM}-\lambda_{SX}(1-\phi) & 0 & 0 & 0 & 0 & \lambda_{SX} \\ -\lambda_{LM}^U & -\lambda_{LX}^U & 0 & -\phi\lambda_{LX}^U & -\delta_4 & 1 & 0 & 0 & -\lambda_{LX}^U \\ 0 & -\delta_3 & 1 & 0 & -1 & -1 & 0 & 0 & \delta_3\sigma/(1-\sigma) \\ \lambda_{KM} & 0 & 0 & 0 & 0 & 0 & -\lambda_{KM} & 0 & \lambda_{KX} \\ 0 & 1 & 0 & \phi & 0 & 0 & -1 & 0 & 0 \\ 0 & 0 & 1 & 0 & 0 & 0 & 0 & -1 & 0 \end{pmatrix}$$

The principal minors of the above coefficient matrix are as follows:

$$H_1 = H_2 \cdots = H_6 = 0$$

$$H_7 = -\varphi\phi(1-\beta-\gamma)\lambda_{KM}\delta_4\lambda_{SX} < 0$$

$$H_8 = (1-\varphi)(1-\gamma)\delta_4\lambda_{KM} > 0$$

$$H_9 = (1-\varphi)(1-\beta-\gamma)\delta_4\Delta_2$$

To ensure the stability of the model, the odd principal minors are required to be nonpositive and even principal minors are required to be nonnegative. That is, we need $\Delta 2 < 0$.

Appendix 2

Solving Eq. (9.20) yields

$$\frac{\widehat{M}}{\widehat{\alpha}}=-\frac{1}{\Delta_2}\left\{\lambda_{KX}\left(\delta_1-\frac{\lambda_{LX}^U}{\delta_2}\right)+\frac{\lambda_{SX}}{\sigma-1}\left(\frac{1}{\delta_2}+\frac{1+\delta_1}{1-\varphi}-\delta_1\right)\left(\phi\lambda_{KX}(\sigma-1)+\frac{\beta\lambda_{KM}}{1-\beta-\gamma}\right)\right\}>0$$

$$\frac{\widehat{x}}{\widehat{\alpha}}=\frac{1}{\Delta_2}\left\{\begin{array}{l}\frac{(\lambda_{SM}\lambda_{KX}-\lambda_{SX}\lambda_{KM})\sigma\phi}{\sigma-1}\left(\frac{1}{\delta_2}+\frac{1+\delta_1}{1-\varphi}-\delta_1\right)+\frac{\lambda_{LX}^U}{\delta_2}\left(\phi\lambda_{SX}\lambda_{KX}-\lambda_{KX}-\frac{\beta\lambda_{SX}\lambda_{KM}}{1-\beta-\gamma}\right)\\+\left(\phi\lambda_{KX}\lambda_{SM}-\lambda_{KM}-\frac{\beta\lambda_{SM}\lambda_{KM}}{1-\beta-\gamma}\right)\left[\frac{\delta_1\sigma}{\sigma-1}-\frac{\lambda_{LX}^U}{\delta_2}-\frac{1}{\sigma-1}\left(\frac{1}{\delta_2}+\frac{1+\delta_1}{1-\varphi}\right)\right]\end{array}\right\}$$

and

$$\frac{\widehat{n}}{\widehat{\alpha}}=\frac{1}{\Delta_2}\left\{\lambda_{SX}\left(\frac{\beta\lambda_{KM}}{1-\beta-\gamma}\frac{\lambda_{LM}^U}{\delta_2}+\frac{\lambda_{KM}\phi\lambda_{LM}^U}{\delta_4}+\frac{1+\delta_1}{1-\varphi}\phi\lambda_{KM}\right)\right.$$
$$\left.+\left(\delta_1-\frac{\lambda_{LX}^U}{\delta_2}\right)\left[(1-\phi\lambda_{SX})\lambda_{KM}+\frac{\beta\lambda_{KM}\lambda_{SM}}{1-\beta-\gamma}\right]\right\}$$
$$<0$$

Furthermore, we have $\frac{\widehat{X}}{\widehat{\alpha}}=\frac{\widehat{x}}{\widehat{\alpha}}+\frac{\sigma}{\sigma-1}\frac{\widehat{n}}{\widehat{\alpha}}<0$, and $\frac{\widehat{P}}{\widehat{\alpha}}=\frac{\widehat{p_x}}{\widehat{\alpha}}-\frac{1}{\sigma-1}\frac{\widehat{n}}{\widehat{\alpha}}=\phi\frac{\widehat{w_S}}{\widehat{\alpha}}-\frac{1}{\sigma-1}\frac{\widehat{n}}{\widehat{\alpha}}>0$.

References

Ayele S (2022) The resurgence of agricultural mechanisation in Ethiopia: rhetoric or real commitment? J Peasant Stud 49(1):137–157

Beladi H, Chaudhuri S, Yabuuchi S (2008) Can international factor mobility reduce wage rate inequality in a dual economy? Rev Int Econ 16(5):893–903

Beladi H, Chao CC, Ee MS (2019) Capital market distortion, firm entry and wage inequality. China Econ Rev 56(101312):101312

Belton B, Win MT, Zhang X, Filipski M (2021) The rapid rise of agricultural mechanization in Myanmar. Food Policy 101:102095

Chao CC, Nabin M, Nguyen X, Sgro PM (2016) Wage inequality and welfare in developing countries: privatization and reforms in the short and long run. Int Rev Econ Financ 42:474–483

Chaudhuri S, Gupta MR (2014) International factor mobility, informal interest rate and capital market imperfection: a general equilibrium analysis. Econ Model 37:184–192

Dong Z, Li X (2019) Rural dual economics, subsidy policy and the income inequality between skilled and unskilled workers. Asia Pac J Acc Econ 26(5):609–621

Harris JR, Todaro MP (1970) Migration, unemployment and development: a two-sector analysis. Am Econ Rev 60:126–142

Huang Z, Yu N (2010) New agricultural business entities: current situation, constraints and development ideas—an analysis of Zhejiang province as an example. Chin Rural Econ 10: 16–26. (In Chinese)

Li X, Fu H (2022) Migrant remittance, agricultural producer services, and environmental pollution. Asia Pac J Acc Econ 29(5):1267–1282

Li X, Zhou Y (2013) An economic analysis of remittance of unskilled migration on skilled-unskilled wage inequality in labor host region. Econ Model 33:428–432

Lin C, He L (2020) Targeted monetary policy and agriculture business loans. N Am J Econ Financ 54:101290

Ministry of Agriculture and Rural Affairs of China (2020) Typical cases of National Agricultural Socialization Services. China Agriculture Press(in Chinese), Beijing

Mottaleb KA, Rahut DB, Ali A, Gérard B, Erenstein O (2017) Enhancing smallholder access to agricultural machinery services: lessons from Bangladesh. J Dev Stud 53(9):1502–1517

Pi J, Chen X (2016) The impacts of capital market distortion on wage inequality, urban unemployment, and welfare in developing countries. Int Rev Econ Financ 42:103–115

Restuccia D, Rogerson R (2017) The causes and costs of misallocation. J Econ Perspect 31(3): 151–174

Sarah L, Jakob S, Terri R (2016) The number, size, and distribution of farms, smallholder farms, and family farms worldwide. World Dev 87:16–29

Wang J, Xiao Q, Li J (2018) Financing predicament and countermeasure of new agricultural proprietors. Agric Econ Quest 2:71–77. (In Chinese)

Wang L, Yang R, Wu B (2020) A study on total factor productivity of agricultural production of rural households in China. Manage World 12:77–90. (In Chinese)

Yu ESH, Chao CC (2021) Appropriation, firm dynamics, and wage inequality. Int J Econ Theory 17(1):118–129

Zhang P (2019) Skill formation, environmental pollution, and wage inequality. Ann Reg Sci 62: 405–424

Zhang X, Yang J, Thomas R (2017) Mechanization outsourcing clusters and division of labor in Chinese agriculture. China Econ Rev 43:184–195

Chapter 10
Migrant Remittance, Agricultural Producer Services, and Environmental Pollution

Abstract This chapter established a general equilibrium model to study the effects of the changes of remittance rate in the urban-rural migrants' income on environmental pollution. We found that, in the capital-specific case, the increase of urban-rural migrants' remittance rate will increase the total remittance of the migrant workers, increase the demand of agricultural sector for agricultural producer services, and decrease the environmental level, but it has no influence on the output level of the urban industrial sector; and in the mobile capital case, the increase of urban-rural migrants' remittance rate will increase the total remittance of the migrant workers, increase the demand of agricultural sector for agricultural producer services, decrease the output level of the urban industrial sector, and improve the environmental level.

Keywords Migrants' remittance · Agricultural producer services · Environmental pollution

10.1 Introduction

Urban-rural migrants'[1] remittances (hereinafter referred to as "RUMs' remittances") mainly refer to the behavior of cross-regional employment workers who subsidize their family using their income, which is widespread in developing countries with urban-rural dual economic characteristics. According to Stalker (2002), remittance in India, Philippines, and Mexico formed 2.6%, 8.9%, and 1.7% of their gross domestic products (GDP) in 1999, respectively. According to World Bank data, the total amount of global immigrant remittance in 2010 reached 325 billion dollars, most of which were from western developed countries to developing countries in Asia, Africa, and Latin America. As a typical dual economy and the largest developing country in the world, China has formed the largest scale of domestic urban-

[1] The urban-rural migration in this chapter refer in particular to the urban-rural migration which for the purpose of seeking employment in urban, not for the purpose of settling in urban, and the migrant workers in China is a typical representative of this kind of migration.

X. Li, Y. Wu, *Research on Characteristic Issues in Current Developing Economies*, New Frontiers in Regional Science: Asian Perspectives 80,
https://doi.org/10.1007/978-981-97-7284-1_10

rural labor transfer in human history since the reform and opening up in 1978, so the migrant remittance in China mainly comes from the domestic migrant workers.

Researches on migrant remittance have mainly focused on the effects of migrant remittance on urban-rural income inequality, economic development, and welfare of labor-exporting areas. Lundahl (1985) researched the impact of remittances from emigrants on real incomes for different groups in their country of origin in a two-by-two model with one traded and one nontraded good. It shows that emigration does not necessarily raise the real income of the emigrants themselves. Kirwan and Holden (1986) analyzed the welfare effect of emigration on a source country whose output consists in part of non-traded goods but where emigrants make remittances to the source country and the remittances are used solely for consumption. They found that the welfare effect of emigration is indeterminate but depends on the magnitude of remittances. In particular, the welfare will decrease where remittances merely maintain source country nominal income at its pre-emigration level. Where remittances are sufficiently large enough that can compensate for the emigration-induced disruption of internal trade in internationally non-traded goods. Quibria (1997) explored the welfare impact of emigration under a wide variety of circumstances. The author found that pure emigration can be beneficial to the non-emigrants in the source country, irrespective of the welfare criteria adopted, if accompanied by sufficient remittances. Djajic (1998) compared the welfare implications of remittance flows back to the source country when they are used to finance consumption and when they are used to finance capital accumulation. Ball et al. (2013) used a theoretical model and panel vector autoregression techniques to explore the role exchange rate regimes play in understanding the effect of remittances. The analysis considered yearly and quarterly data for seven Latin American countries and predicted that remittances temporarily increase inflation and generate an increase in the domestic money supply under a fixed regime, but temporarily decrease inflation and generate no change in the money supply under a flexible regime. Li and Wang (2015) investigated the impacts of an increase in remittances on wage, employment, and welfare level in the urban regions. They found that an increase in remittances will reduce the output of the informal sector and decrease urban residents' welfare in the capital-specific case, while it will increase the output of the informal sector and augment urban residents' welfare in the mobile capital case.

So far, there are many economic research papers focusing on environmental issues. For instance, Beladi and Frasca (1999) used a generalized Harris-Todaro model that incorporates an urban nonpolluting sector to examine the backward incidence of pollution control on some key variables of interest in an LDC. Chao et al. (2000) developed a general-equilibrium model to examine the optimal level of environmental preservation in terms of its costs and benefits for a closed as well as an open economy. Chaudhuri and Mukhopadhyay (2006) investigated the efficiency of imposing a pollution emission tax on the formal manufacturing sector in a three-sector general-equilibrium model that included pollution effects that arose from the informal sector.

However, there is few studies on the environmental effects of migrant remittance. At present, we only find one research literature by Li and Zhou (2015). They established a two-sector general-equilibrium model and investigated the short-run and long-run impacts of an increase in remittance of migrants on the environment. And they found that the increase of the migrant remittance will lead to environmental improvement in the short run, but will deteriorate the environment in the long term. The authors considered that the migrant remittance would influence on the production scale of urban sector and then exerts impact on the environment, but they did not consider the impact of remittances on agricultural producer services and environmental pollution. However, many developing countries with dual economic characteristics regard the agricultural development as an important way of economic development and the agricultural producer services sector is an indispensable sector for the development of agriculture. Agricultural producer services refer to integrating modern production elements such as scientific information technology, capital equipment, and talents into agricultural production by providing productive services and intermediate inputs for agriculture, so as to improve agricultural production efficiency, promote the supply and demand balance of agricultural products market, and enhance agricultural value. According to Reinert (1998), agricultural producer services include agricultural machinery operation, agricultural material distribution, agricultural technology extension, agricultural information services, agricultural product quality and safety services, epidemic prevention and control services, agricultural product marketing services, infrastructure management services, labor transfer services, and financial insurance services. The development of agricultural producer services will influence on agricultural production mode, factor input structure, industrial structure and scale, agricultural product production structure, farmers' management behavior, and agricultural labor transfer, which may break the original ecological balance and influence on the environment. Especially because of the development of agricultural producer services industry, the use of pesticides, fertilizers, and catalysts will be more convenient, and then has influence on environment. In addition, agricultural machinery operation, agricultural infrastructure construction, and so on will also influence on the environment.

On the other hand, migrant remittance injects funds into rural areas, which increases the demand for agricultural producer services in the agricultural sector, thus promoting the development of agricultural producer services. It has been estimated by Li and Zhou (2015) that the rural-urban migrant remittance in China was more than 1000 billion RMB (around US$160 billion) in 2012, while the fiscal expenditure on agriculture in 2012 was 1190.3 billion yuan.[2] With the continuous development of China's economy, the income of migrant workers is rising, and the number of remittances is also rising year by year. There is undoubtedly that the migrant remittance has increasingly become an important source of funding for agricultural development in rural areas.

[2] January 22, 2013, Ministry of Finance of the People's Republic of China: Financial Revenue and Expenditure in 2013, http://gks.mof.gov.cn/tongjishuju/201301/t20130122_729462.htm.

In order to explore the environmental effects of RUMs' remittances in the presence of agricultural producer services, we establish a three-sector general-equilibrium model which includes agricultural producer service sector to analyze the effect of the change in the proportion of remittance in the income of urban-rural migrant (hereinafter referred to as "the changes of RUMs' remittances rate") on environment both in the capital-specific case and the mobile capital case. We found that the conclusions drawn in this chapter were contrary to those of previous studies if considering the effects of agricultural producer services on the environment.

The rest of the chapter is organized as follows: We establish a basic model in Sect. 10.2. In Sect. 10.3, we analyze the effects of the changes of remittance rate on environmental pollution both in the capital-specific case and mobile capital case. In Sect. 10.4, we used relevant economic data from China in 2017 to calibrate the parameters of the model, and then we used the calibrated parameters to perform numerical simulations in order to examine whether the model constructed in this chapter correctly explains the impacts of the changes of RUMs' remittance rate on agricultural pollution and national welfare, etc. Lastly, we will state our conclusion in Sect. 10.5.

10.2 Model

We consider a small open developing economy with three sectors which are urban industrial sector, agricultural sector, and agricultural producer services sector. Among them, the industrial sector employs labor L_M and capital K_M to produce importable competing industrial product M; the agricultural sector uses labor L_A and agricultural producer services S to produce exportable agricultural product A; and the agricultural producer services sector uses labor and capital K_X to produce different service products x_i ($i = 1,2...n$) for agricultural production. We also assume that the agricultural producer services sector is a monopolistic competition sector, and the relationship between S and x_i satisfies the form of CES (see Markusen 1989, Reinert 1998):

$$S = \left[\sum_{i=1}^{n} (x_i)^{\delta} \right]^{\frac{1}{\delta}}, \quad 0 < \delta < 1, \tag{10.1}$$

where, S represents the standard quantity of differentiated producer services used by the agricultural sector. Besides the definition of Reinert (1998), the agricultural producer services in this chapter also include the industries of pesticide and fertilizer.

In addition, labor perfectly mobile among the three sectors, and capital also perfectly mobile between the urban industrial sector and the agricultural producer services sector in the mobile capital case. However, the production of the urban industrial sector and the agricultural producer services sector generate environmental pollution, which impose damage to the environment through mediums such as air, water, and land. The markets of industrial product and agricultural product are perfectly competitive, and the factor endowments are exogenously given.

The aggregate output of the agricultural productive service sector is

$$X = \sum_{i=1}^{n} x_i. \tag{10.2}$$

where, X represents the aggregate output of agricultural producer services sector; x_i represents the output of the agricultural producer services sector for the production of the ith ($i = 1,2\ldots n$) product.

In this chapter, we consider a symmetric equilibrium where all varieties, that are produced, are equally priced, so the following equations $x_i = x_j = x$, $\sum_{i=1}^{n} x_i = nx$ are hold. And according to the relationships among S, X, and x_i in Eqs. (10.1) and (10.2), we can induce $X = n^{-\frac{1-\delta}{\delta}} S$.

Denote E as the quality of environment after pollution; E^{ε} (where $0 < \varepsilon < 1$), represents the effect of environmental level on agricultural productivity. And the environment level in the economy is as follows:

$$E = \overline{E} - M^{\alpha} S^{\beta} \quad 0 < \alpha, \beta < 1. \tag{10.3}$$

where $\overline{E}$ is the environmental endowment when there is no pollution in the economy, which is regarded as given; parameters α, β express the environmental pollution effects of production in the urban industrial sector and agricultural producer services sector.

Under the condition that the markets of the urban industrial product and agricultural product are perfectly competitive, in the capital-specific case, the following conditions can be obtained by the zero-profit conditions:

$$\overline{w} a_L^M + r_M a_K^M = P_M, \tag{10.4}$$

$$w a_L^A + n^{-\frac{1-\delta}{\delta}} P a_S^A = E^{\varepsilon}. \tag{10.5}$$

Among them, a_i^j ($i = L, K, S$; $j = A, M, X$) is a function of factor price which represents the quantity of the i-th factor used in the j-th sector to produce one unit of output. P_M is the relative price of urban industrial sector to the price of agricultural products when we standardize the price of agricultural product to 1, P is the relative price of the agricultural producer services to the agricultural product; the capital price of urban industrial sector is r_M in the capital-specific case; w indicates the wage of agricultural sector which is flexible, and $\overline{w}$ indicates the wage of urban industrial sector and agricultural producer services sector, which is institutionally set.

Because we consider the symmetric-equilibrium of agricultural producer services industry, the cost function of the agricultural producer services sector is

$$c(\overline{w}, r_X, x) = xm(\overline{w}, r_X) + f(\overline{w}, r_X).$$

In the equation, $m(\overline{w}, r_X)$ and $f(\overline{w}, r_X)$ respectively represent the convertible cost and the fixed cost of the agricultural producer services sector, and the capital price of the agricultural producer services sector is r_X in the capital specific case.

We assume that the migrant workers remit a given proportion of their income θ $(0 < \theta < 1)$ to their hometown, and then k is defined as the total RUMs' remittances. Without losing generality and in order to simplify analysis, we also assume that all the workers employed in the urban industrial sector and the agricultural producer services sector are migrant worker and all remittance from the migrant workers is used to purchase agricultural producer services products. Thus, the following conditions are obtained:

$$k = \theta\overline{w}\left\{Ma_L^M + n[xm_L(\overline{w}, r_X) + f_L(\overline{w}, r_X)]\right\}, \tag{10.6}$$

$$n^{-\frac{1-\delta}{\delta}} PS = k. \tag{10.7}$$

Unlike the urban industrial sector and the agricultural sector, the agricultural producer services sector is a monopolistic competitive sector, and $1/(1 - \delta)$ is the price elasticity of demand for each variety products in agricultural producer services sector. The market entity produces according to the principle that the marginal revenue is equal to the marginal cost, that is, $MR = MC$, thus we can induce the following condition:

$$\delta P = m(\overline{w}, r_X). \tag{10.8}$$

We use L_U to represent the unemployment in the urban industrial sector and the agricultural producer services sector and use λ to denote the unemployment rate of labor in these two sectors, hence $\lambda = L_U/\left\{Ma_L^M + n[xm_L(\overline{w}, r_X) + f_L(\overline{w}, r_X)]\right\}$. Thus, the allocation mechanism can be shown as

$$\overline{w} = (1 + \lambda)w. \tag{10.9}$$

The labor endowments L in the economy is

$$E^{-\varepsilon}Aa_L^A + (1 + \lambda)\left\{Ma_L^M + n[xm_L(\overline{w}, r_X) + f_L(\overline{w}, r_X)]\right\} = L. \tag{10.10}$$

The capital market-clearing conditions in the capital-specific case are

$$Ma_K^M = K_M, \tag{10.11}$$

$$n[xm_K(\overline{w}, r_X) + f_K(\overline{w}, r_X)] = K_X. \tag{10.12}$$

In the mobile capital case, capital can perfectly mobile between the urban industrial sector and the agricultural producer services sector, so the equations $r_M = r_X = r$ are hold in equilibrium, therefore, Eqs. (10.4), (10.6), (10.8), and (10.10) can be rewritten as follows:

$$\overline{w}a_L^M + ra_K^M = P_M, \tag{10.4*}$$

$$k = \theta\overline{w}\{Ma_L^M + n[xm_L(\overline{w}, r) + f_L(\overline{w}, r)]\}, \tag{10.6*}$$

$$\delta P = m(\overline{w}, r), \tag{10.8*}$$

$$E^{-\varepsilon}Aa_L^A + (1+\lambda)\{Ma_L^M + n[xm_L(\overline{w}, r) + f_L(\overline{w}, r)]\} = L. \tag{10.10*}$$

In addition, we define K as the capital endowments in the economy, thus the capital market-clearing condition in the mobile capital case is

$$Ma_K^M + n[xm_K(\overline{w}, r) + f_K(\overline{w}, r)] = K. \tag{10.13}$$

Thus, our basic theoretical model has been established. Among them, Eqs. (10.3)–(10.12) describe the behaviors of economic entities in the capital-specific case, which has 10 endogenous variables M, A, S, k, r_M, r_X, w, E, P, and λ and nine exogenous variables $\overline{w}$, δ, ε, P_M, μ, K_M, K_X, L, and n; Eqs. (10.3), (10.4*), (10.5), (10.6*), (10.7), (10.8*), (10.9), (10.10*), and (10.13) describe the behaviors of economic entities in the mobile-specific case, which has nine endogenous variables M, A, S, k, r, w, E, P, and λ and eight exogenous variables $\overline{w}$, P_M, δ, ε, μ, K, L, and n.

10.3 Comparative Static Analysis

10.3.1 Capital-Specific Case

We can induce $\widehat{r}_M = 0$ by differentiating Eq. (10.4), and substituted this result into the total differential equation of Eq. (10.11) will obtain $\widehat{M} = 0$. Then, differentiating Eqs. (10.3), (10.5)–(10.10), (10.12) and substituted the above two results into the eight total differential equations will get the following matrix equation:

$$\begin{pmatrix} 0 & \beta\varepsilon E^{\varepsilon}M^{\alpha}S^{\beta} & wa_L^A & n^{-\frac{1-\delta}{\delta}}a_S^A\frac{r_X m_K}{\delta} & 0 \\ 0 & \theta\overline{w}n^{-\frac{1-\delta}{\delta}}Sm_L & 0 & \theta\overline{w}\left(n^{-\frac{1-\delta}{\delta}}Sm_L S_{LK}^m + nf_L S_{LK}^f\right) & -k \\ 0 & 1 & 0 & \frac{r_X m_K}{\delta P} & -1 \\ E^{-\varepsilon}Aa_L^A & D & B_1 & C & 0 \\ 0 & n^{-\frac{1-\delta}{\delta}}Sm_K & 0 & n^{-\frac{1-\delta}{\delta}}Sm_K S_{KK}^m + nf_K S_{KK}^f & 0 \end{pmatrix}$$
$$\times \begin{pmatrix} \widehat{A} \\ \widehat{S} \\ \widehat{w} \\ \widehat{r}_X \\ \widehat{k} \end{pmatrix} = \begin{pmatrix} 0 \\ -k \\ 0 \\ 0 \\ 0 \end{pmatrix}\widehat{\theta}, \tag{10.14}$$

where "$\wedge$" indicates the rate of change of the variables, $S_{ij}^t = \left(\partial a_i^t/\partial P_j\right)\left(P_j/a_i^t\right)$, ($t = M, A, m, f$; $i, j = L, K, S$), and $S_{ii}^t < 0$, if $i \neq j$, $S_{ij}^t > 0$ is hold, such as $S_{LL}^A = \left(\partial a_L^A/\partial w\right)\left(w/a_L^A\right) < 0$, $S_{LK}^M = \left(\partial a_L^M/\partial r_M\right)\left(r_M/a_L^M\right) > 0$, $S_{LK}^m = (\partial m_L/\partial r_X)(r_X/m_L) > 0$, $S_{KK}^f = (\partial f_K/\partial r_X)(r_X/f_K) < 0$; $B_1 = E^{-\varepsilon}Aa_L^A S_{LL}^A - (1+\lambda)\left(Ma_L^M + n^{-\frac{1-\delta}{\delta}}Sm_L + nf_L\right) < 0$, $C = (1+\lambda)\left(n^{-\frac{1-\delta}{\delta}}m_L S_{LK}^m + nf_L S_{LK}^f\right) + E^{-\varepsilon}Aa_L^A S_{LS}^A(r_X m_K/\delta P) > 0$, $D = (1+\lambda)n^{-\frac{1-\delta}{\delta}}Sm_L + \varepsilon E^{-(1+\varepsilon)}\beta M^{\alpha}S^{\beta}Aa_L^A > 0$. We define "$\Delta$" as the determinant of the coefficient matrix of Eq. (10.14) and because $S_{ii}^n < 0$ is hold, that if $i \neq j$ is hold, $S_{ij}^n > 0$ can be induced, the following inequality is also hold:

$$\Delta = \theta\overline{w}E^{-\varepsilon}wA\left(a_L^A\right)^2\left\{\begin{array}{l} nxm_K\left[nxm_L\left(S_{LL}^m + \frac{r_X m_K}{m}\right) + nf_L\left(S_{LL}^f + \frac{r_X m_K}{m}\right) + Ma_L^M\frac{r_X m_K}{m}\right] \\ -\left(Ma_L^M + nf_L\right)\left(nxm_K S_{KK}^m + nf_K S_{KK}^f\right) \end{array}\right\}.$$

From the equation, if $nxm_L\left(S_{LL}^m + \frac{r_X m_K}{m}\right) + nf_L\left(S_{LL}^f + \frac{r_X m_K}{m}\right) + Ma_L^M\frac{r_X m_K}{m} \geq 0$ then $\Delta > 0$. According to Cramer's rule, we can induce the effects of the change of RUMs' remittance rate θ on relevant variables

$$\frac{\widehat{A}}{\widehat{\theta}} = \frac{1}{\Delta}k\left\{\begin{array}{l} wa_L^A\left[D\left(nxm_K S_{KK}^m + nf_K S_{KK}^f\right) - nxm_K C\right] \\ -B_1\left[\varepsilon E^{\varepsilon}\beta M^{\alpha}S^{\beta}\left(nxm_K S_{KK}^m + nf_K S_{KK}^f\right) - n^{-\frac{(1-\delta)}{\delta}}nxa_S^A\frac{r_X m_K}{\delta}m_K\right] \end{array}\right\} < 0, \tag{10.15}$$

$$\frac{\widehat{w}}{\widehat{\theta}} = \frac{1}{\Delta}E^{-\varepsilon}Aa_L^A k\left[\beta\varepsilon E^{\varepsilon-1}M^{\alpha}S^{\beta}\left(nxm_K S_{KK}^m + nf_K S_{KK}^f\right) - n^{-\frac{(1-\delta)}{\delta}}nxa_S^A\frac{r_X(m_K)^2}{\delta}\right], \tag{10.16}$$

$$\frac{\widehat{S}}{\widehat{\theta}} = -\frac{1}{\Delta}E^{-\varepsilon}wA\left(a_L^A\right)^2 k\left(nxm_K S_{KK}^m + nf_K S_{KK}^f\right) > 0, \tag{10.17}$$

$$\frac{\widehat{r}_X}{\widehat{\theta}} = \frac{1}{\Delta}E^{-\varepsilon}wA\left(a_L^A\right)^2 knxm_K > 0, \tag{10.18}$$

$$\frac{\widehat{k}}{\widehat{\theta}} = -\frac{1}{\Delta}E^{-\varepsilon}A\left(a_L^A\right)^2 k\left[\left(nxm_K S_{KK}^m + nf_K S_{KK}^f\right) - nx\frac{r_X(m_K)^2}{\delta P}\right] > 0. \tag{10.19}$$

In view of Eqs. (10.15)–(10.19), it is clear that the effects of the changes of RUMs' remittance rate θ on the output of the agricultural sector and the agricultural producer services sector, the wage level in the agricultural sector, the total RUMs' remittances and the capital interest rate in the agricultural producer services sector. By combining Eqs. (10.16) and (10.17) with the total differential of Eqs. (10.3) and (10.9), respectively, we can get $\widehat{\lambda}/\widehat{\theta} > 0, \widehat{E}/\widehat{\theta} < 0$; because $\widehat{M} = 0$ and $\widehat{r}_M = 0$, we can induc e$\widehat{M}/\widehat{\theta} = 0$, $\widehat{r}_M/\widehat{\theta} = 0$.

In summary, in the capital-specific case, the effects of the change in RUMs' remittance rate of urban-rural migrant on various variables are shown in Table 10.1.

Table 10.1 shows that the increase of the remittance rate θ will enhance the total RUMs' remittance k, the demand of agricultural sector for agricultural producer services S, the urban unemployment rate λ, and reduce the environmental level. At the same time, the change of RUMs' remittance rate θ has no influence on the output M and the capital price r_M of the urban industrial sector. From these, the following propositions can be obtained:

Proposition 1 *In the capital-specific case, the increase in the RUMs' remittance rate θ will increase the demand of agricultural sector for agricultural producer services S, but has no effect on the output of the urban industrial sector M, thus decrease the environmental level of labor-exporting areas E.*

For the results of Table 10.1 and the conclusion of Proposition 1, we think that because capital cannot flow between the urban industrial sector and the agricultural producer services sector, the capital price r_M of urban industrial sector is only determined by the capital supply and demand situation of urban industrial sector, and the rigidity of urban industrial sector's wage determines that the labor

Table 10.1 Summary of calculation results in the capital-specific case

	$\widehat{M}$	$\widehat{A}$	$\widehat{S}$	$\widehat{w}$	$\widehat{r}_M$	$\widehat{r}_X$	$\widehat{E}$	$\widehat{\lambda}$	$\widehat{k}$
$\widehat{\theta}$	0	–	+	–	0	+	–	+	+

Note: Symbols "+" or "–" indicate that the change of the RUMs' remittance rate θ has the same or opposite effects on the corresponding variables, respectively, while "0" indicates that the change of the RUMs' remittance rate θ has no effect on the corresponding variables employment of urban industrial sector and the agricultural producer services sector remains unchanged, so the output level of urban industrial sector is not affected by the change of RUMs' remittance rate. Under the condition of constant employment in the urban industrial sector and the agricultural producer services sector, the increase of RUMs' remittance rate will inevitably increase the total RUMs' remittance that inflow into rural areas, thus enhancing the demand for agricultural producer services S in the agricultural sector and decreasing the environmental level E. The increase in the demand for agricultural producer services in the agricultural sector will make the agricultural producer services sector has the tendency to increase the input of factors and expand the supply of service products, thus increasing the demand for capital in the agricultural producer services sector. However, due to the non-mobility of capital sectors, the rising demand for capital elements in this condition will only lead to the higher capital price r_X in the agricultural producer services sector. In additional, the increased demand for agricultural producer services in the agricultural sector has replaced labor and put downward pressure on wages in the agricultural sector, which in turn has prompted the transfer of rural labor to cities, thus raising the urban unemployment rate.

10.3.2 Mobile Capital Case

At beginning, to simplify the analysis, we make the following assumption.

Assumption 1 *The inequality* $\frac{m_K}{m_L} - \frac{Ma_K^M}{Ma_L^M} \geq 0$ *is hold.*[3]

We can yield the equation $\widehat{r}=0$ by differentiating the Eq. (10.4*), and we also induce the equation $\widehat{P}=0$ by substituting equation $\widehat{r}=0$ into total differential equation of Eq. (10.8*). Differentiating Eqs. (10.3), (10.5), (10.6*), (10.7), (10.9), (10.10*), (10.13) and using the results $\widehat{r}=0$ and $\widehat{P}=0$, so the following matrix equation can be obtained:

$$\begin{pmatrix} 0 & \alpha M^\alpha S^\beta & \beta M^\alpha S^\beta & \frac{wa_L^A}{\varepsilon E^{\varepsilon-1}} & 0 \\ 0 & -\theta \overline{w} Ma_L^M & -\theta \overline{w} n^{-\frac{1-\delta}{\delta}} Sm_L & 0 & k \\ 0 & 0 & 1 & 0 & -1 \\ E^{-\varepsilon} Aa_L^A & (1+\lambda) Ma_L^M & (1+\lambda) n^{-\frac{1-\delta}{\delta}} Sm_L & B_2 & 0 \\ 0 & Ma_K^M & n^{-\frac{1-\delta}{\delta}} Sm_K & 0 & 0 \end{pmatrix} \begin{pmatrix} \widehat{A} \\ \widehat{M} \\ \widehat{S} \\ \widehat{w} \\ \widehat{k} \end{pmatrix} = \begin{pmatrix} 0 \\ k \\ 0 \\ 0 \\ 0 \end{pmatrix} \widehat{\theta}, \quad (10.20)$$

[3]This assumption has practical basis, for example, in China, the agricultural producer service industry is still a new industry, which started late but started at a high level. Many technologies intensive, knowledge-intensive, and capital-intensive enterprises have joined the industry, which has resulted in the phenomenon that the capital intensity is greater than that of the industrial sector.

where $B_2 = E^{-\varepsilon}Aa_L^A S_{LL}^A - (1+\lambda)\left(Ma_L^M + n^{-\frac{1-\delta}{\delta}}Sm_L + nf_L\right) - \frac{wa_L^A Aa_L^A}{E^{2\varepsilon}} < 0$. We define "Ω" as the determinant of the coefficient matrix of the Eq. (10.20), so the value of "Ω" is:

$$\Omega = \frac{wA\left(a_L^A\right)^2}{\varepsilon E^{2\varepsilon-1}}\left\{\theta\overline{w}Ma_L^M n^{-\frac{1-\delta}{\delta}}Sm_K - Ma_K^M\left(\theta\overline{w}n^{-\frac{1-\delta}{\delta}}Sm_L - k\right)\right\} > 0.$$

According to Cramer's rule, we can induce the effects of the change of RUMs' remittance rate θ on relevant variables.

$$\frac{\widehat{A}}{\widehat{\theta}} = \frac{1}{\Omega}k\left\{M^\alpha S^\beta B\beta n^{-\frac{1-\delta}{\delta}}Sm_K\left(\frac{Ma_K^M}{n^{-\frac{1-\delta}{\delta}}Sm_K} - \frac{\alpha}{\beta}\right)\right. \tag{10.21}$$

$$\left. + (1+\lambda)\frac{wa_L^A}{\varepsilon E^{\varepsilon-1}}Ma_L^M n^{-\frac{1-\delta}{\delta}}Sm_L\left(\frac{m_K}{m_L} - \frac{a_K^M}{a_L^M}\right)\right\},$$

$$\frac{\widehat{w}}{\widehat{\theta}} = -\frac{1}{\Omega}kAa_L^A M^\alpha S^\beta \beta n^{-\frac{1-\delta}{\delta}}Sm_K\left(\frac{Ma_K^M}{n^{-\frac{1-\delta}{\delta}}Sm_K} - \frac{\alpha}{\beta}\right), \tag{10.22}$$

$$\frac{\widehat{M}}{\widehat{\theta}} = -\frac{1}{\Omega}kAa_L^A\frac{wa_L^A}{\varepsilon E^{2\varepsilon-1}}n^{-\frac{1-\delta}{\delta}}Sm_K < 0, \tag{10.23}$$

$$\frac{\widehat{S}}{\widehat{\theta}} = \frac{1}{\Omega}kAa_L^A\frac{wa_L^A}{\varepsilon E^{2\varepsilon-1}}Ma_K^M > 0, \tag{10.24}$$

$$\frac{\widehat{k}}{\widehat{\theta}} = \frac{1}{\Omega}kAa_L^A Ma_K^M\frac{wa_L^A}{\varepsilon E^{2\varepsilon-1}} > 0. \tag{10.25}$$

In view of Eqs. (10.23)–(10.25), it is clear that the effects of the changes of RUMs' remittance rate θ on the output of the urban industrial sector and the agricultural producer services sector and the total RUMs' remittances. Whether the effects of the change of RUMs' remittance rate θ on the output of the agricultural sector and the wage level in the agricultural sector are, however, ambiguous. If $\left(\frac{Ma_K^M}{n^{-\frac{1-\delta}{\delta}}Sm_K} - \frac{\alpha}{\beta}\right) \leq 0$, and combined with Assumption 1, then we obtain $\widehat{A}/\widehat{\theta} > 0$, $\widehat{w}/\widehat{\theta} > 0$. By combining Eqs. (10.22) and (10.23) with the total differential of Eqs. (10.3) and (10.9), respectively, we can we can induce $\widehat{\lambda}/\widehat{\theta} > 0, \widehat{E}/\widehat{\theta} > 0$.

In summary, in the mobile capital case, the effects of the changes of RUMs' remittance rate θ on various variables are shown in Table 10.2.

Table 10.2 shows that the increase of RUMs' remittance rate θ will enhance the total RUMs' remittance k, the wage level of agricultural sector, the demand for agricultural producer services S in the agricultural sector, decrease the urban

Table 10.2 Summary of calculation results in the mobile capital case

	$\widehat{M}$	$\widehat{A}$	$\widehat{S}$	$\widehat{w}$	$\widehat{r}$	$\widehat{E}$	$\widehat{\lambda}$	$\widehat{k}$
$\widehat{\theta}$	–	+	+	+	0	+	–	+

Note: Symbols "+" or "–" indicate that the change of the RUMs' remittance rate θ has the same or opposite effects on the corresponding variables, respectively, while "0" indicates that the change of the RUMs' remittance rate θ has no effect on the corresponding variables

unemployment rate λ, the output level of urban industrial sector and improve the environmental level E. At the same time, the change of RUMs' remittance rate θ has no influence on the capital price r. From these conclusions, the following proposition can be obtained:

Proposition 2 *In the mobile capital case, if the capital intensity of the urban industrial sector is no more than that of the agricultural producer services sector, the increase of RUMs' remittance rate θ will increase the total RUMs' remittance k, enhance the demand of agricultural sector for agricultural producer services S, decrease the output level of the urban industrial sector M, and improve the environmental level E.*

Comparing Table 10.1, Proposition 1 and Table 10.2, Proposition 2, it is not difficult to find that the effects of the change of RUMs' remittance rate θ on the output of the urban industrial sector, the demand for agricultural producer services, and the environmental level are contrary both in the capital-specific case and in the mobile capital case. These results show that capital liquidity between sectors plays a very important role in the impact mechanism of the change of remittance rate on the environmental level and other related economic variables. Based on the above analysis, in the capital-specific case and in the mobile capital case, the effects of the change of remittance rate on the total RUMs' remittance k and the demand for agricultural producer services are consistent, but the effects of the change in the RUMs' remittance rate on the environmental level between the capital-specific case and the mobile capital case are opposite. This is because wage rigidity, the employment of urban industrial sector is not affected by the change of RUMs' remittance rate whether in the capital-specific case or in the mobile capital case. As a result, the scale and rate of RUMs' remittance in the same direction. With the increase of RUMs' remittance rate θ and the increase of the total RUMs' remittance k, sufficient funds are injected into the agricultural sector, which enhance the demand of agricultural sector for agricultural service products S. This increase in demand makes the agricultural producer services sector tend to expand the supply scale of products. In the capital-specific case, due to the special use of capital in sectors and rigid wage, the input of factors of the urban industrial sector as well as the output of the urban industrial sector unchanged, and the total RUMs' remittance k also increase with the increase of RUMs' remittance rate which will lead to the decline of environmental level. In the mobile capital case, due to the free flow of capital among sectors, the tendency of expansion of agricultural producer services sector will lead to the redistribution of capital between the agricultural producer services sector and the urban industrial sector, which results in the increase of capital input in agricultural producer services sector and the contraction of capital input in the urban industrial sector. Thus, the output of the urban industrial sector will decrease and the output of agricultural producer services sector increase. When the environmental improvement effect of the decline of the urban industrial sector output is greater than the effect of environmental deterioration of the increase of agricultural production service sector output, the environmental level will be improved.

The conclusions of Propositions 1 and 2 in this chapter are contrary to those of Li and Zhou (2015). That is mainly because our study took into account both the role of agricultural producer services and industrial production activities on the environment, while they only considered the impact of industrial production activities on the environment. Moreover, the mechanism of migrant remittance's influence on the urban industrial sector in this chapter is different from Li and Zhou (2015). These differences make the conclusions of ours different from those of previous studies.

10.3.3 National Welfare Analysis

We now turn our attention to the national welfare effect of the change of RUMs' remittance rate based on the analysis in the previous section. Because this chapter considers a small economy with dual economic characteristics, the price of agricultural and industrial products is exogenously given. According to the nature of indirect effect function $v(p, y)$, the effect level of representative consumers is only related to the income level, that is, the higher the income level, the higher the effect level. Hence, to investigate the effect of the change of RUMs' remittance rate on national welfare, we simply focus on the national income, which is denoted as $Y = P_M M + A$. Thus, we can get

$$\frac{\widehat{Y}}{\widehat{\theta}} = P_M \frac{\widehat{M}}{\widehat{\theta}} + \frac{\widehat{A}}{\widehat{\theta}}. \tag{10.26}$$

According to Eqs. (10.21) and (10.23), we can find that the national welfare effect of the change in the RUMs' remittance rate will be decided by the relative size of the effects of the change in the RUMs' remittance rate on the output of the sector A and M. If the effect of the change in the RUMs' remittance rate on the output of the sector A is large enough, then the increase of RUMs' remittance rate will increase national income and improve national welfare. Otherwise, the national welfare will be decreased.

10.4 Parameter Calibration, Estimation, and Numerical Simulation

10.4.1 Calibration and Estimation of Parameters

The above theoretical model analysis gives the influence direction of the change of RUMs' remittance rate on the demand of agricultural sector for agricultural producer services and the environmental pollution, etc. In this section we will investigate the numerical characteristics of the theoretical model about the effects of the change of RUMs' remittance rate on the relevant variables in the mobile capital case, therefore this section first calibrates the parameters of the model with the relevant macroeconomic data of China in 2017, then simulates the model based on the calibrated parameters, and finally conducts sensitivity analysis to test the robustness of the numerical simulation results.

We set up the production functions in the agricultural sector and the urban industrial sector and the cost function of the agricultural producer services sector are as follows:

$$A = E^{\varepsilon}(L_A)^{\gamma_1}\left(\sum_{i=1}^{n} x_i^{\delta}\right)^{\frac{1-\gamma_1}{\delta}},$$

$$M = (L_M)^{\gamma_2} K_M^{1-\gamma_2},$$

$$c(\overline{w}, r, x) = x\sqrt{\overline{w}r} + \left(\overline{w}L_f + rK_f\right),$$

where γ_1 and γ_2 are the respective output elasticities of labor in the agricultural sector and the urban industrial sector.

Based on three strata of industry in the China Statistical Yearbook (2017) issued by the National Bureau of Statistics of China, we take the primary industry as the rural agricultural sector, the agricultural producer services sector of this chapter are pesticide and fertilizer industry and agriculture, forestry, animal husbandry, and fishery service industry, and the remaining sectors in secondary and tertiary industries are regarded as the urban industry sector.

According to the data published on the official website of the National Bureau of statistics of the people's Republic of China,[4] in the primary industry, the value-added in 2017 was 6209.95 billion yuan, the number of employed persons was 209.44 million people, and the per capita disposable income of rural households was 13,432 yuan, which is defined as the labor wage of the rural agricultural sector. We can then calculate the output elasticity in the rural agricultural sector.

[4] http://data.stats.gov.cn/easyquery.htm?cn=C01.

Because the agricultural producer services sector defined in this chapter includes the pesticide and fertilizer industries in the China Industrial Statistical Yearbook, and the agriculture, forestry, animal husbandry, and fishery service industries. According to the data in Chinese Industry Statistical Yearbook (2018), we take the average number of workers in the pesticide and chemical fertilizer industry in 2017 as the employment number of the pesticide and chemical fertilizer industry, which are 0.679,4 and 0.161,six million, respectively. In addition, we regard the total employment of agriculture, forestry, animal husbandry, and fishery in cities and towns as the employment of agriculture, forestry, animal husbandry, and fishery services, because this model assumes that the wages of agricultural producer services sector are equal to those of urban manufacturing sector. And according to the data in 2017 published on the official website of the National Bureau of statistics of the people's Republic of China, the total employment of agriculture, forestry, animal husbandry, and fishery in cities in 2017 is 284.6. Thus, the total employment of agricultural producer services in this chapter is 368.7. At the same time, according to the Statistical Yearbook of China's Tertiary Industry (2018), the total output value of China's agriculture, forestry, animal husbandry, and fishery services in 2017 was 535.31 billion yuan. And according to the data in Chinese Industry Statistical Yearbook (2018), the total output value of the pesticide and chemical fertilizer industry are 886.15 billion yuan and 293.49 billion yuan.[5] Therefore, the total output value of the agricultural producer services sector is 1665.26 billion yuan.

And according to the data in 2017 published on the official website of the National Bureau of statistics of the people's Republic of China, the value-added of China's secondary and tertiary industries was 33,274.27 billion yuan and 42,591.21 billion yuan, respectively, and the number of employed labors in secondary and tertiary industries was 218.24 million and 348.72 million, respectively. This chapter takes the value-added of the secondary and tertiary industries and the number of employed labors minus the value-added and the number of employed labors of the agricultural producer services sector, respectively, as the basic data of the urban industrial sector, while the average employment wage of urban units in 2017 was 74,318 yuan, which is defined as the labor wage level of the urban industrial sector and the agricultural producer services sector, and then the factor output elasticity of factors in the urban industrial sector can be obtained.

As for the capital price, according to benchmark one-to-five-year lending rate announced by China's central bank in 2017, it could represent as 4.75%, the lower limit of the bank's loan interest rate is 0.9 times of the benchmark interest rate, and the maximum floating coefficient is 2.3 times of the loan benchmark interest rate. Here, the middle value of the floating coefficient is 1.6, which means the interest rate level of urban manufacturing and producer services sector is 7.6%. In addition, following the model set in the previous article, the price of sector *A*'s product is set to 1, and the relative price of sector *M* and sector *Z* product is compared with that of

[5] These two data are the total output value of chemical fertilizer and pesticide minus their respective export delivery value, because the agricultural producer services in this chapter are non-tradable.

Table 10.3 The calibration results of relevant parameters in the mobile capital case

Parameter	γ_1	γ_2	K_{MO}	K_{XO}	θ	ε
Calibration value	0.564,5	0.453,0	4,255,118.00	183,059.28	0.039,7	0.338,0

sector *A*'s product, respectively. According to Eq. (10.3), we assign $\overline{E}$ to M_O*X_O, M_O and X_O are the initial output of manufacturing industry and agricultural producer services industry, respectively, then we assume $\alpha + \beta = 1$.

Based on the above economic data, we first calibrated the parameters in the mobile capital case. The results are shown in Table 10.3.

In Table 10.3, K_{MO} and K_{XO} are the capital stock of manufacturing industry and agricultural producer services industry estimated by numerical simulation model, respectively. To satisfy the Assumption 1, that is, $\frac{Ma_K^M}{n^{\frac{1-\delta}{\delta}}Sm_K} < \frac{\alpha}{\beta}$, we assign 0.96 and 0.04 to α and β, respectively. According to definition of the coverage of agricultural producer services in Reinert (1998), we assign parameter $n = 10$. At the same time, because the agricultural producer services sector is a monopolistic competition sector, although there are differences among various service products x_i, they also have strong substitutability, we assign 0.9 to parameter δ.

10.4.2 Numerical Simulation

In this section, we will use the parameters which were calibrated based on the China's macroeconomic data in 2017 to conduct numerical simulation and investigate the numerical characteristics of the theoretical model about the effects of the change in the RUMs' remittance rate on the relevant variables in the mobile capital case.

The numerical simulation results of the model in the mobile capital case which is based on the relevant macroeconomic data of China in 2017 are shown in Fig. 10.1.

Figure 10.1a–e, respectively, reflect the effects of the change of RUMs' remittance rate on the output of each sector, the total RUMs' remittances, and the environmental level in the mobile capital case. The trend characteristics of each figure are consistent with the conclusion of Proposition 2 of this chapter, thus verifying the conclusion of this chapter. It can be seen from Fig. 10.1a, b, f that within the range (−1%, 3%) of the change of remittance rate, the negative effect of the change of RUMs' remittance rate on the output of sector *M* is greater than the positive impact on the output of sector *A*, and the national income shows a downward trend. Thus, the increase of RUMs' remittance rate would not always be positive effects.

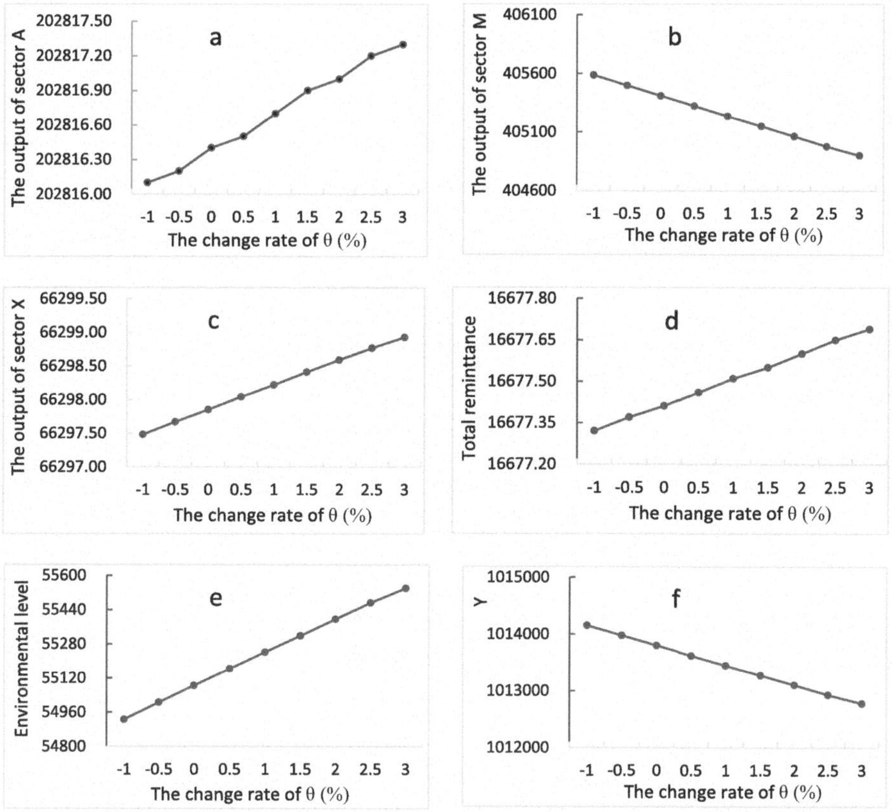

Fig. 10.1 The economic effects of the change of RUMs' remittance rate, where $\delta = 0.90$

10.4.3 Sensitivity Test

In this model, we assume that the sector A and the sector M are completely competitive, while the agricultural producer services sector is monopolistic competition. According to the substitutability of various products in the monopolistic competition market, we set the parameter δ reflecting the substitution elasticity of various services of agricultural producers to 0.9, so that the substitution elasticity of various services is about 10. In this part, we set δ as 0.95 and 0.80, respectively, to test whether different δ assignments will impact the conclusion of this chapter.

The numerical simulation results of the model in the mobile capital case which based on $\delta = 0.95$ and $\delta = 0.8$ are shown in Figs. 10.2 and 10.3, respectively.

From the numerical simulation results of Figs. 10.2 and 10.3, we can find that the different initial values of the parameters δ will not have a substantial influence on the conclusion and numerical characteristics of this chapter, which fully shows that the numerical simulation results and model conclusions of Proposition 2 is stable.

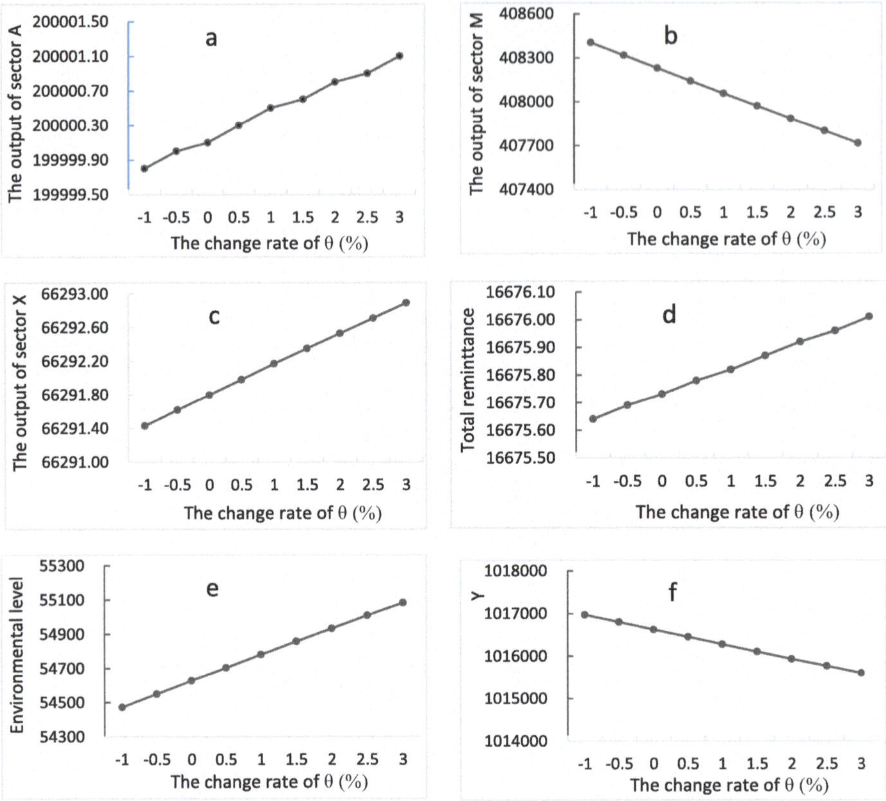

Fig. 10.2 The economic effects of the change of RUMs' remittance rate, where $\delta = 0.95$

10.5 Conclusion

This chapter explored the effect of the change of RUMs' remittance rate on environmental pollution in a general equilibrium framework which contains three sectors. One difference between this chapter and the existing studies is that we take into account the role of agricultural producer services in the environment pollution. We believe that the development of agricultural producer services sector will also have an influence on the environment, so we considered both the impacts of the urban industrial sector and the agricultural producer services sector on environment when we constructed the environmental model in this chapter. Such consideration is more consistent with the actual situations of developing countries. With the economic development of these countries, it can be predicted that of the agricultural producer services will play an increasingly role in agricultural production in these countries, and its influences on the economy and the environment will also increase. This viewpoint can also be verified by the conclusions of this chapter. We can draw the

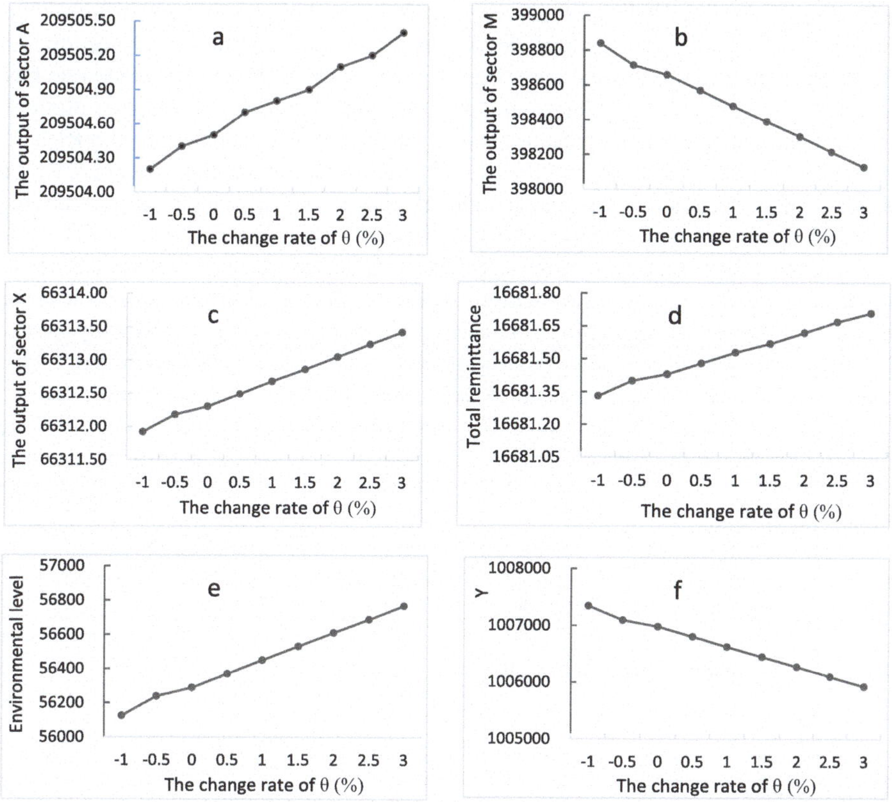

Fig. 10.3 The economic effects of the change of RUMs' remittances rate, where $\delta = 0.80$

following conclusions through the previous theoretical analysis: Firstly, in the capital specific case, the increase of remittance rate will increase the total RUMs' remittance, increase the demand of agricultural sector for agricultural producer services and decrease the level of environment, but it has no effect on the output level of urban industrial sector; Secondly, in the mobile capital case, the increase of remittance rate will increase the total amount of remittance, increase the demand of agricultural sector for agricultural producer services, reduce the output level of the urban industrial sector, and improve the environmental level. The two conclusions above are contrary to that of Li and Zhou (2015). We also investigated the numerical characteristics of the effects of the change of RUMs' remittance rate on the output of the agricultural sector, the output of the urban industrial sector, the total RUMs' remittances and the environmental level, etc., and the results of numerical simulation also verify the relevant conclusions of this chapter.

In view of the fact that the industry of agricultural producer services is indispensable industry in the agricultural development of developing countries, thus the conclusions of this chapter are closer to the economic reality of developing countries. Therefore, it has reference value for developing countries to formulate relevant policies for agricultural development and environmental protection. In addition, in the mobile capital case, the increase in the RUMs' remittance rate has a two-way positive effect of improving the environment and increasing the output of the agricultural sector. At the same time, if the effect of the change in the RUMs' remittance rate on the output of the sector A is large enough, then the increase of RUMs' remittance rate will increase national income and improve national welfare. Otherwise, the national welfare will be decreased.

In the theoretical analysis process of this chapter, we did not include the rural-urban migration costs into the theoretical model. The rural-urban migration costs include the time cost of looking for work, the transportation cost, and the psychological cost of leaving familiar environment to adapt to the new environment, etc. These rural-urban migration costs may have more or less impact on labor migration. Therefore, we can include the rural-urban migration cost into the theoretical model in the future research in order to explore the potential economic effects of these costs.

Competing Interests

Funding This work was supported by the Humanities and Social Sciences of the Ministry of Education, China, Project No. 17JJD630002.

Disclosure Statement No potential conflict of interest was reported by the authors.

References

Ball CP, Lopez C, Reyes J (2013) Remittance, inflation and exchange rate regimes in small open economies. World Econ 36(4):487–507. https://doi.org/10.1111/twec.12042

Beladi H, Frasca R (1999) Pollution control under an urban binding minimum wage. Ann Regional Sci 33:523–533. https://doi.org/10.1007/s001680050119

Chao CC, Kerkvliet JR, Yu ESH (2000) Environmental preservation, sectoral unemployment, and trade in resources. Rev Dev Econ 4(1):39–50. https://doi.org/10.1111/1467-9361.00077

Chaudhuri S, Mukhopadhyay U (2006) Pollution and informal sector: a theoretical analysis. J Econ Integr 21(2):363–378

Djajic S (1998) Emigration and welfare in an economy with foreign capital. J Dev Econ 56(2): 433–445. https://doi.org/10.1016/S0304-3878(98)00073-X

Kirwan F, Holden D (1986) Emigrants' remittances, non-traded goods and economic welfare in the source country. J Econ Stud 13(2):52–58. https://doi.org/10.1108/eb002623

Li X, Wang D (2015) The impacts of rural–urban migrants' remittances on the urban economy. Ann Regional Sci 54:591–603. https://doi.org/10.1007/s00168-015-0668-y

Li X, Zhou J (2015) Environmental effects of remittance of rural–urban migrant. Econ Model 47: 174–179. https://doi.org/10.1016/j.econmod.2015.02.023

Lundahl M (1985) International migration, remittances and real incomes: effects on the source country. Scand J Econ 87(4):647–657. https://doi.org/10.2307/3439977

Markusen JR (1989) Trade in producer services and in other specialized intermediate inputs. Am Econ Rev 79(1):85–95. https://www.jstor.org/stable/1804775

Quibria MG (1997) International migration, remittances and income distribution in the source country: a synthesis. Bull Econ Res 49(1):29–46. https://doi.org/10.1111/1467-8586.00025
Reinert KA (1998) Rural non-farm development: a trade theoretic view. J Int Trade Econ Dev 7(4): 425–437. https://doi.org/10.1080/09638199800000024
Stalker P (2002) Migration trends and migration policy in Europe. Int Migr 40(5):151–179. https://doi.org/10.1111/1468-2435.00215

Part IV
Development Issues

Chapter 11
Research on Effects of Integration of Primary, Secondary, and Tertiary Industries in Rural Areas of Developing Countries: An Approach of Rural Capital Subsidies

Abstract We set up a four-sector general-equilibrium model and a rural industrial integration indicator to investigate impacts of capital subsidies given to capital-using sectors in rural industrial chain on rural industrial integration and social welfare. Our findings are as follows: Rural capital subsidies can enhance rural industrial integration (but need to satisfy certain conditions in the short run) and reduce economic gap between urban and rural areas. In numerical simulation part, we discover that capital subsidy for rural secondary industry has a more favorable impact on rural industrial integration, social welfare, and narrowing urban-rural economic gap than rural tertiary capital subsidy.

Keywords Rural capital subsidy · General-equilibrium analysis · Rural industrial integration · Urban-rural economic gap · Social welfare

11.1 Introduction

The integration of primary, secondary, and tertiary industries (hereinafter referred to as "rural industrial integration") considered in this article refers to the forward integration of agriculture into rural secondary and tertiary industries in rural areas.[1] Its significance stems from the possibility that farmers may boost their income by gaining value-added revenue from processing and distribution of agricultural product and the potential for a thriving rural economy (Imamura 1996; Jiang 2015). In this regard, rural secondary industry is the "agro-processing industry," which refers to the on-site processing of agricultural product; rural tertiary industry is the "rural service industry" that rely on the distinctive natural and social resources of rural areas to attract tourists and trade activities from urban and other areas to promote marketing of agricultural product (e.g., rural tourism, rural science education, and other consumer services). For instance, Chinese city of Baoding produces

[1] Refer to the 'Sixth Industrialization Strategy' of Japan, which promotes using locally produced agricultural product as raw material for processing and selling to prevent the value of agricultural product from spilling over through manufacturing and marketing links (Yamashita 2015).

X. Li, Y. Wu, *Research on Characteristic Issues in Current Developing Economies*, New Frontiers in Regional Science: Asian Perspectives 80,
https://doi.org/10.1007/978-981-97-7284-1_11

large quantities of corn, based on this, rural enterprises in this region have developed agro-processing industries that produce corn-related goods like instant corn flour and corn juice, as well as related tourism services like corn eco-farms and picking gardens, thereby incorporating agriculture into rural secondary and tertiary industries (Meng 2020).

The ultimate goal of rural industrial integration strategy is to boost rural income by promoting the combined growth of agriculture and higher-productivity rural industries (Cui 2010). From experiences of Japan and South Korea in the past 20 years, rural industrial integration policy is conducive to expand farmers' revenue sources (Jiang 2015). In recent years, rural industrial integration has grown in significance as a method for developing countries to boost rural economy. According to a 2015 Chinese government proposal,[2] policy supports for rural industrial integration is essential to increase rural income and rural competitiveness. Farmers, however, might not have the same perspective on rural industrial integration. For example, Hjalager (1996) revealed that farmers tend to place a higher priority on the development of agriculture than on rural industrial integration in Europe. Additionally, the experience of Japan demonstrates that rural entities' progress in fostering rural industrial integration is sluggish due to restrictions in resource, capability, and marketing channel (Jiang 2015). Because of this, designing a method that motivates farmers to take part in rural industrial integration is crucial. The introduction of e-commerce (Galloway et al. 2011; Turland and Slade 2020), financial services (Lu and Jiang 2016), and subsidies (Han 2019) has been evaluated as having favorable effects on enhancing the participation rate and quality of rural industrial integration. The research mentioned above, however, mostly relied on empirical methods to assess the policy impact of rural industrial integration. Due to the growing importance of rural industrial integration for rural growth in developing nations, it is vital to define its role and function in the economic structure, which necessitates the study of rural industrial integration from a theoretical perspective.

For rather a long period of time, developing countries have formed a dual capital structure in which urban and rural capital are separated.[3] Because rural industries operate in small production units, their attractiveness to urban capital is constrained by high costs of input-output price, technology, infrastructure, and industrial structure (Sinn 1992; Taylor 1996; Abbott and Vita 2003). Considering that labor input alone is not enough to achieve value appreciation of rural products and to increase farmers' income, certain scale of capital accumulation and capital investment are required. Yet, this is difficult for the small-peasant economy to finance (Wu and Li 2021). If capital subsidy policy and rural industry integration were taken into account jointly, that is, the capital subsidy is entitled to stimulating market activities related to rural industrial integration, farmers' enthusiasm to participate in rural

[2] http://www.moa.gov.cn/ztzl/yhwj2015/zywj/201502/t20150202_4378754.htm.

[3] In theoretical studies, the phase where capital is sector-specific is often designated as the short run, where capital is mobile between sectors is typically designated as the long run (see Corden and Findlay 1975; Gupta 1995; Rapanos 2007; Choi and Yu 2010; Li and Zhou 2015).

industrial integration would inevitably increase, which would enhance the development momentum of rural industrial integration. Subsidy policy, however, may potentially have some undetermined implications: agricultural sector would likely to get less assistance if subsidies were skewed toward the integration of rural sectors. Therefore, it is unclear which of the two consequences mentioned above would be more important in increasing farmer's revenue. This is mostly due to the dearth of studies linking rural industrial integration with rural subsidies policies.

In addition, studies on rural industrial integration have generally concentrated on the policy implications of integrating agriculture with rural secondary industry (Garrett et al. 2013; VanWey et al. 2013), or integrating agriculture with rural tertiary industry (Fleischer and Felsenstein 2000). Researches on the policy effects of the simultaneous integration of agriculture and rural secondary industry and agriculture and rural tertiary industry remain scarce. However, simultaneous integration is typical in the actual economy; thus, study on this subject should not be disregarded within the context of rural industrial integration.

This article aims to explain the economic impact of capital subsidies for rural secondary and tertiary industries to promote rural industrial integration. Our primary findings by building a four-sector general-equilibrium model are that rural capital subsidies would encourage rural industrial integration (under certain conditions in the short run) and narrow economic gap between urban and rural areas. Our numerical simulation results demonstrate that rural capital subsidies can increase agricultural production in the long run, and that rural secondary capital subsidies have a more positive impact on social welfare, urban-rural economic gap, and rural integration than rural tertiary capital subsidy. Such conclusions are obtained for the first time in related fields.

The remainder of this paper is structured as follows: in Sect. 11.2, we establish a general-equilibrium model with four sectors that includes rural capital subsidies. The economic effects of rural capital subsidies on associated endogenous variables are covered in Sect. 11.3. The analysis is expanded to a numerical simulation in Sect. 11.4. The paper's conclusion is given in Sect. 11.5.

11.2 Model

We consider a small open economy consists of four sectors (agriculture sector, rural secondary industry, rural tertiary industry, and urban sector). Agriculture sector (sector 1) uses labor to produce agricultural product that can be exported, rural secondary industry (sector 2) and rural tertiary industry (sector 3) both use labor, capital, and agricultural product for production. Product of rural secondary industry is supplied domestically for rural and urban consumers; rural tertiary industry provides services only to urban consumer. Urban sector (sector 4) uses labor and capital to produce importable product. Production functions of each sector are

$$X_1 = F^1(L_1),$$
$$X_2 = F^2(L_2, X_{12}, K_2),$$
$$X_3 = F^3(L_3, X_{13}, K_3),$$
$$X_4 = F^4(L_4, K_4).$$

Among them, $X_j(j = 1,2,3,4)$ represents the output of sector j, $L_j(j = 1,2,3,4)$ denotes the amount of labor employed by sector j; $K_j(j = 2,3,4)$ represents the amount of capital used by rural secondary industry, rural tertiary industry, and urban sector; the production function $F^j(j = 1,2,3,4)$ is assumed to satisfy first-order homogeneity and quasi-concave; X_{12} and X_{13} represent the input of agricultural product in rural secondary and tertiary industries. Set agricultural product as *Numeraire*, therefore $P_j(j = 2,3,4)$ represents the product price of sector j relative to agricultural product.

Since the rural industrial integration investigated in this research seeks to incorporate low-value-added agricultural product as a fundamental component in the value chain of rural secondary and tertiary industries; from the input-output perspective, we use a weighted average of the distributive share of agricultural product in rural secondary and tertiary industries [$\theta_{X2} = X_{12}/(P_2X_2)$ and $\theta_{X3} = X_{13}/(P_3X_3)$], namely, I, as an indicator to assess the level of rural industrial integration,[4] the weight is the proportion of the output value of two industries:

$$I = \frac{P_2X_2}{P_2X_2 + P_3X_3}\theta_{X_2} + \frac{P_3X_3}{P_2X_2 + P_3X_3}\theta_{X_3}.$$

Therefore, we have

$$I = \frac{X_{12} + X_{13}}{P_2X_2 + P_3X_3}.$$

A greater I indicates a higher level of rural industrial integration, which means that rural secondary and tertiary industries depend more on agricultural product as an intermediate input.

Our goal is to analyze the economic effects of granting capital subsidies to rural secondary industry and rural tertiary industry, respectively. Let the capital subsidies for rural secondary and tertiary industries as τ_2 and τ_3, and make $\tau_i = 0$ $(i = 2,3)$ at the initial stage. The following equations hold in a market with perfect competition where each of the four sectors maximizes its profit:

[4]To measure industrial integration, academics primarily use input-output method, technology coefficient (such as the Herfindahl index and Patent coefficient), and econometric method (such as Stochastic frontier, VAR model, and spatial measurement model). The input-output approach, among others, is more appropriate to measure the rural industrial integration designed in this paper because it depicts how intermediate inputs and outcomes are interdependent across industries.

$$wa_{L1}=1, \tag{11.1}$$

$$wa_{L2}+a_{X2}+r(1-\tau_2)a_{K2}=P_2, \tag{11.2}$$

$$wa_{L3}+a_{X3}+r(1-\tau_3)a_{K3}=P_3, \tag{11.3}$$

$$\overline{w}a_{L4}+r_4a_{K4}=P_4, \tag{11.4}$$

there, $a_{ij}(i = L, K, X_1; j = 1, 2, 3, 4)$ represents the amount of factor i required to produce a unit product in sector j, it is a function of factor prices, for example, $a_{L2}[w, P_1, r(1 - \tau_2)]$; w and $\overline{w}$ denote labor wages in rural sectors and urban sector, w is flexible, while $\overline{w}$ is constant due to the rigidity of wage in urban sector, and generally we have $\overline{w} > w$; r and r_4 represent interest rate of rural sectors and urban sectors, respectively.

Labor shifts from the rural to the urban sector, with L_U indicating the number of unemployed in urban sector and $\lambda = L_U/L_4$ indicating the urban unemployment rate. When labor transfer approaches equilibrium, the wage for rural labor equals the expected wage in the urban sector (Harris and Todaro 1970):

$$w=\frac{L_4}{L_4+L_U}\overline{w}\Leftrightarrow w(1+\lambda)=\overline{w}. \tag{11.5}$$

Now turn our attention to the demand side, we consider that the economy consists of two types of consumers (urban and rural consumers). Let the utility function of urban consumer be $U_U=D_{1U}^{\alpha}D_{2U}^{\delta}D_{3U}^{\gamma}D_{4U}^{1-\alpha-\delta-\gamma}$, where D_{1U}, D_{2U}, D_{3U}, D_{4U} denote the demand of urban consumer for three rural products and urban product, respectively. Parameters α, δ, γ, $1 - \alpha - \delta - \gamma$ denote the consumption ratio of urban consumer for those four products to its income ($0 < \alpha, \delta, \gamma < 1$). The budget constraint for urban consumer is $Y_U=\overline{w}L_4 + r_4K_4$.[5] By solving utility maximization, the indirect utility function for urban consumer can be obtained: $V_U(1, P_2, P_3, P_4, Y_U) = \alpha^{\alpha}\delta^{\delta}\eta^{\eta}(1 - \alpha - \delta - \eta)^{(1-\alpha-\delta-\eta)}P_2^{-\delta}P_3^{-\eta}P_4^{-(1-\alpha-\delta-\eta)}Y_U$. Likewise, the utility function of rural consumer is $U_R=D_{1R}^{\phi}D_{2R}^{\varphi}D_{4R}^{1-\phi-\varphi}$, where D_{1R}, D_{2R}, $D_{4R}D_{4R}$ denote the rural consumer's demand for products of agriculture, rural secondary industry, and urban sector, respectively, and parameters ϕ, φ, $1 - \phi - \varphi$ denote the consumption share of rural consumer for corresponding products ($0 < \phi, \varphi < 1$). The budget constraint for rural consumer is $Y_R=w\left[\overline{L}-(1+\lambda)L_4\right]+rK_R$, thus the indirect utility function can be solved as $V_R(1, P_2, P_4, Y_R) = \phi^{\phi}\varphi^{\varphi}(1 - \phi - \varphi)^{(1-\phi-\varphi)}P_2^{-\varphi}P_4^{-(1-\phi-\varphi)}Y_R$. From this, demand for products of rural secondary and tertiary industries can be obtained, they are $D_2=D_{2U}+D_{2R}=\frac{\delta Y_U}{P_2}+\frac{\varphi Y_R}{P_2}$, $D_3=\frac{\eta Y_U}{P_3}$. Hence, market clearing conditions for those two products are

[5]To highlight the targets of our investigation, we assume that the source of subsidies is the general tax revenue that does not cause economic distortions. Therefore, we do not take the source of subsidies into consideration when analyzing consumer income.

$$X_2 = D_{2U} + D_{2R}, \tag{11.6}$$

$$X_3 = D_3. \tag{11.7}$$

Let $\overline{L}$ be the labor endowment. The full employment condition for labor can be demonstrated as

$$a_{L1}X_1 + a_{L2}X_2 + a_{L3}X_3 + a_{L4}X_4(1+\lambda) = \overline{L}. \tag{11.8}$$

While capital does not move between urban and rural sectors in the short run, full employment conditions for capital are

$$a_{K2}X_2 + a_{K3}X_3 = K_R, \tag{11.9}$$

$$a_{K4}X_4 = K_U. \tag{11.10}$$

Here, K_R and K_U represent the endowment of rural-specific capital and urban-specific capital. In the long run, capital is perfectly mobile between rural and urban sectors, therefore full employment condition for capital becomes

$$a_{K2}X_2 + a_{K3}X_3 + a_{K4}X_4 = K_R + K_U = \overline{K}, \tag{11.11}$$

where $\overline{K}$ denotes the economy's capital endowment. At this point, capital equilibrium is reached. There is $r = r_4$.

To this end, our general-equilibrium model has been established. In the short run, 10 endogenous variables (w, r, r_4, λ, P_2, P_3, X_1, X_2X_2, X_3X_3, and X_4X_4) can be determined from Eqs. (11.1)—(11.11). $\overline{w}$, P_1, P_4, $\overline{L}$, K_R, K_U are exogenous variables. Long-run model consists of Eqs. (11.1)–(11.8) and (11.11), which determines 9 endogenous variables: w, r, λ, P_2, P_3, X_1, X_2X_2, X_3X_3, and X_4X_4; exogenous variables are $\overline{w}$, P_1, P_4, $\overline{L}$, and $\overline{K}$.

11.3 Analysis

11.3.1 Short-Run Case

By totally differentiating Eqs. (11.1) and (11.5), we can get $\widehat{w} = 0$, then $\widehat{\lambda} = 0\widehat{\lambda} = 0$. And $\widehat{X}_4 = 0$, $\widehat{X}_3 = -\widehat{P}_3$ by totally differentiating Eqs. (11.7) and (11.10). Here, '^' represents the percentage change of a variable (e.g., $\widehat{w} = dw/w$).

Utilizing Eqs. (11.2), (11.3), and substituting the above results into the differential outcomes of Eqs. (11.6), (11.8), and (11.9), we have

$$\begin{pmatrix} \lambda_{L1} & \lambda_{L2} & \lambda_{L2}S_{LK}^{2} + \lambda_{L3}\theta_{K3} + \lambda_{L3}S_{LK}^{3} \\ 0 & \alpha_{K2} & \alpha_{K2}S_{KK}^{2} + \alpha_{K3}\theta_{K3} + \alpha_{K3}S_{KK}^{3} \\ \beta_{L1}^{R} & \beta_{L2}^{R} + \beta_{K2}^{R} - \dfrac{1}{\Omega_R^2} & D \end{pmatrix} \begin{pmatrix} \widehat{X}_1 \\ \widehat{X}_2 \\ \widehat{r} \end{pmatrix}$$

$$= \begin{pmatrix} \lambda_{L2}S_{LK}^{2} \\ \alpha_{K2}S_{KK}^{2} \\ E \end{pmatrix} \tau_2\widehat{\tau}_2 + \begin{pmatrix} \lambda_{L3}\theta_{K3} + \lambda_{L3}S_{LK}^{3} \\ \alpha_{K3}\theta_{K3} + \alpha_{K3}S_{KK}^{3} \\ F \end{pmatrix} \tau_3\widehat{\tau}_3, \quad (11.12)$$

where, $\theta_{ij}(i = L, K, X_1; j = 1, 2, 3, 4)$ represents the distributive share of factor i in sector$j$ (e.g., $\theta_{K2} = ra_{K2}/p_2$); $\lambda_{ij}(i = L, K, X_1; j = 1, 2, 3, 4)$ represents the proportion of factor i employed in sector j; $S_{ih}^{j}(i, h = L, K, X_1; j = 1, 2, 3, 4)$ represents partial elasticity of substitution between factors i and h in sector j (e.g., $S_{LK}^{1} = \frac{\partial a_{L1}}{\partial r}\frac{r}{a_{L1}}$), and there are $S_{ih}^{j} > 0(i \neq h)$ and $S_{ih}^{j} < 0(i = h)$; $\alpha_{Kj} = K_j/K_R(j = 2, 3)$ records the ratio of the amount of capital input to the total amount of rural capital in sector j; $\beta_f^R(f = L_1, L_2, L_3, K_2, K_3)$ indicates the ratio of factor f's income to total rural income (e.g., $\beta_{L1}^{R} = wL_1/Y_R$); $\Omega_R^2 = D_R^2/X_2$ indicates rural consumption share of rural secondary product:

$$D = \beta_{L2}^{R}S_{LK}^{2} + \beta_{L3}^{R}S_{LK}^{3} + \beta_{K2}^{R}\left(1 + S_{KK}^{2}\right) + \beta_{K3}^{R}\left(1 + S_{KK}^{3}\right) + \theta_{K3}\left(\beta_{L3}^{R} + \beta_{K3}^{R}\right) - \frac{\theta_{K2}}{\Omega_R^2},$$

$$E = \beta_{L2}^{R}S_{LK}^{2} + \beta_{K2}^{R}S_{KK}^{2} - \frac{\theta_{K2}}{\Omega_R^2},$$

$$F = \beta_{L3}^{R}S_{LK}^{3} + \beta_{K3}^{R}S_{KK}^{3} + \theta_{K3}\left(\beta_{L3}^{R} + \beta_{K3}^{R}\right).$$

To obtain analyzable results, we make the following assumption:

Assumption

$$\text{Assumption}: \quad \theta_{K3} < \left|S_{KK}^{3}\right|.$$

This indicates that capital's partial elasticity of self-substitution in rural tertiary industry is relatively large, while this sector employs small capital mostly and capital normally contributes little to product price.

Defining the determinant of the coefficient in Eq. (11.2) as Δ_1, we get

$$\Delta_1 = \lambda_{L1}\left[\frac{\theta_{K3}}{\Omega_R^2}(\alpha_{K3} - \alpha_{K2}) + \alpha_{K2}\beta_K^R + \frac{1}{\Omega_R^2}\left(\alpha_{K3}S_{KK}^{3} + \alpha_{K2}S_{KK}^{2}\right)\right],$$

Table 11.1 The impact of short-run rural capital subsidies

	$\widehat{X}_1$	$\widehat{X}_2$	$\widehat{X}_3$	$\widehat{X}_4$	$\widehat{w}$	$\widehat{\lambda}$	$\widehat{r}$	$\widehat{P}_2$	$\widehat{P}_3$	$\widehat{K}_2$	$\widehat{K}_3$	$\widehat{L}_2$	$\widehat{L}_3$	$\widehat{I}$
$\widehat{\tau}_2$	\	+	−	0	0	0	+	−	+	+	−	+	$^{(+)}1$	$^{(+)}2$
$\widehat{\tau}_3$	\	\	+	0	0	0	+	+	−	−	+	\	\	$^{(+)}3$

Note: Symbols "+", "−", and "0" indicate that the change in capital subsidies $\tau_i (i = 2, 3)$ have the same, opposite, or no effect on the corresponding endogenous variables, respectively; while "\" indicates that the change of τ_i have ambiguous impacts on endogenous variables; "(+)" means that the change of τ_i make the endogenous variables change in the same direction under specific conditions. "1": $\theta_{K3} < S_{LK}^3$; "2": $\theta_{K3} < \frac{1}{1-\varsigma}\left[\upsilon S_{X_1K}^2 + S_{X_1K}^3(1-\upsilon)\right]$; "3": $\theta_{K2} < \frac{1}{\varsigma} \times \left[\upsilon S_{X_1K}^2 + S_{X_1K}^3(1-\upsilon)\right]$

where $\beta_K^R = \beta_{K2}^R + \beta_{K3}^R$. In developing countries, urban consumption share of rural secondary product is generally large, when Ω_R^2 is sufficiently small to reach: $\Omega_R^2 < \frac{-\left[\alpha_{K3}\left(\theta_{K3}+S_{KK}^3\right)+\left(S_{KK}^2-\theta_{K3}\right)\alpha_{K2}\right]}{\alpha_{K2}\beta_K^R}$,[6] we have $\Delta_1 < 0$.

Solving Eq. (11.2) by Cramer's rule, we can get Table 11.1 (see Appendix 2 for detailed calculation):

From Table 11.1, we can summarize:

Proposition 1 *In the short run, rural capital subsidies would not have an impact on urban production or the unemployment rate, but they would raise the rural interest rate, and promote rural industrial integration conditionally.*

In the short run, mechanism for rural capital subsidies to affect the rural industrial integration is factor substitution. From Fig. 11.1 (here, take τ_2 as an example, situations in τ_3 can be analyzed in the same way), we can see that as τ_2 increases, the rural secondary industry's actual cost of capital input would decrease and its demand for capital would increase from K_2^* to K_2^{**}. The quantity of capital accessible to rural tertiary industry would go from K_3^* to K_3^{**} as rural capital is constrained in the short run. As shown in Table 11.1, the direction of change for K_3 and r is opposite; as a result, the rural interest rate would rise from r^* to r^{**}. At this point, the share of agricultural input rises as a result of a drop in the relative cost to capital; and since rural industries use small capital mostly and generally the contribution of capital to product price is less, rising interest rates have little impact on product prices: when θ_{K3} is sufficiently small to reach $\theta_{K3} < \frac{1}{1-\varsigma}\left[\upsilon S_{X_1K}^2 + S_{X_1K}^3(1-\upsilon)\right]$ [where $\upsilon = X_{12}/(X_{12} + X_{13})$, $\varsigma = \frac{P_2X_2}{P_2X_2+P_3X_3}$], the distributive share of agricultural product in the output value of rural secondary and tertiary industries would increase, thus promoting rural industrial integration.[7]

---

[6]We obtain $0.24 = \Omega_R^2 < \frac{-\left[\alpha_{K3}\left(\theta_{K3}+S_{KK}^3\right)+\alpha_{K2}\left(S_{KK}^2-\theta_{K3}\right)\right]}{\alpha_{K2}\beta_K^R} = 5.08$ by using China's macroeconomic data in 2018. Thus, this assumption may be established in developing countries with characteristics of China's economic development.

[7]The condition for $\widehat{I}/\tau_3\widehat{\tau}_3 > 0$ in the short run is $\theta_{K2} < \frac{1}{\varsigma}\left[\upsilon S_{X_1K}^2 + S_{X_1K}^3(1-\upsilon)\right]$.

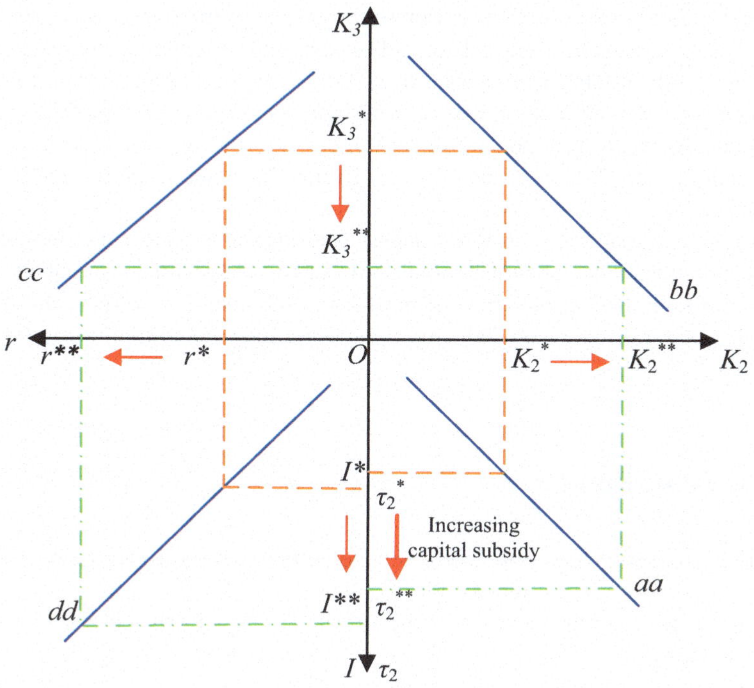

Fig. 11.1 The impact of short-run rural capital subsidies on rural industrial integration

Additionally, we found some intriguing conclusions. As τ_2 increase, on the one hand, production of rural secondary industry would rise, thus increasing demand for agricultural product and encouraging the output of X_1. But on the other hand, since we assume agricultural sector only uses labor for production, even though wages in rural sectors are comparable, agricultural sector would, however, have less developed production environments and working conditions than the other two rural industries. As a result, growing rural secondary and tertiary industries would draw workers away from agricultural sector, hence there are $\widehat{L_2}/\tau_2\widehat{\tau}_2 > 0$ and $\widehat{L_3}/\tau_2\widehat{\tau}_2(\geq)0$.[8] Due to a loss of labor,[9] production in agricultural sector would decline. The impacts of τ_2 on X_1 are thus ambiguous, which dependent upon the two opposing effects mentioned above.

Skuras et al. (2003) discovered that there is a negative correlation between the amount of capital subsidies given to small- and medium-sized firms in rural Greece and the rate of job growth there. Research by Li and Shen (2012) found that capital subsidies for modern agriculture can encourage the migration of labor from

---

[8]More labor can be used to replace capital when the substitution elasticity of capital for labor in the rural tertiary industry is large enough to reach $S_{LK}^3 > \theta_{K3}$; when $S_{LK}^3 = \theta_{K3}$, there is $\widehat{L_3}/\tau_2\widehat{\tau}_2 = 0$.

[9]Our field study revealed that the shortage of labor in agricultural sector in developing countries has become a widespread social phenomenon.

traditional agriculture to modern agriculture. Similar to the results of Li and Shen (2012), we discover that capital subsidies for rural secondary industry would encourage a shift of labor from agricultural sector to agricultural-extension industry in the short run. The utilization rate of rural labor would rise by internalizing labor that would otherwise flow outside of rural areas. In other words, capital subsidies may encourage the shift of labor from agricultural to nonagricultural industries in rural region.

Besides, the impact of τ_3 on X_2 is unclear. Although an increase in τ_3 would result in a rise in capital cost of rural secondary industry and a fall in output, it is also possible, through the income effect of rural tertiary industry, to increase the demand for product of rural secondary industry, which promotes the output of rural secondary industry.

11.3.2 Long-Run Case

In the long run, capital can flow freely between urban and rural sectors. At this time, Eqs. (11.9) and (11.10) are replaced by (11.11).

Using the differential results of Eqs. (11.2), (11.3), (11.6), (11.7), (11.8), and (11.11), we have

$$\begin{pmatrix} \lambda_{L1} & \lambda_{L2} & \lambda_{L3} & (1+\lambda)\lambda_{L4} \\ 0 & \lambda_{K2} & \lambda_{K3} & \lambda_{K4} \\ \Omega_R^2\beta_{L1}^R & \Omega_R^2\beta_{L2}^R + \Omega_R^2\beta_{K2}^R - 1 & \Omega_R^2\beta_{L3}^R + \Omega_R^2\beta_{K3}^R & 1-\Omega_R^2 \\ 0 & 0 & -1 & 1 \end{pmatrix} \begin{pmatrix} \widehat{X}_1 \\ \widehat{X}_2 \\ \widehat{X}_3 \\ \widehat{X}_4 \end{pmatrix}$$
$$= \begin{pmatrix} \lambda_{L2}S_{LK}^2 \\ \lambda_{K2}S_{KK}^2 \\ \Omega_R^2\beta_{L2}^R S_{LK}^2 + \Omega_R^2\beta_{K2}^R S_{KK}^2 - \theta_{K2} \\ 0 \end{pmatrix} \tau_2\widehat{\tau}_2 + \begin{pmatrix} \lambda_{L3}S_{LK}^3 \\ \lambda_{K3}S_{KK}^3 \\ \Omega_R^2\beta_{L3}^R S_{LK}^3 + \Omega_R^2\beta_{K3}^R S_{KK}^3 \\ -\theta_{K3} \end{pmatrix} \tau_3\widehat{\tau}_3. \tag{11.13}$$

Defining the determinant of the coefficient in Eq. (11.13) as Δ_2, we could get:

$$\Delta_2 = \Omega_R^2\beta_{L1}^R(\Lambda_{24}+\Lambda_{23}) - \left(\beta_{K2}^R\Omega_R^2 + \beta_{K3}^R\Omega_R^2 - 1\right)\lambda_{L1}(\lambda_{K3}+\lambda_{K4})$$
$$+ \lambda_{L1}\lambda_{K2}\left[\left(1-\Omega_R^2\right) + \Omega_R^2\left(\beta_{L3}^R + \beta_{K3}^R\right)\right].$$

In developing countries, urban sector and rural tertiary industry are generally more capital-intensive compared with rural secondary industry, therefore we have

Table 11.2 The impact of long-run rural capital subsidies

	$\widehat{X}_1$	$\widehat{X}_2$	$\widehat{X}_3$	$\widehat{X}_4$	$\widehat{w}$	$\widehat{\lambda}$	$\widehat{P}_2$	$\widehat{P}_3$	$\widehat{K}_2$	$\widehat{K}_3$	$\widehat{K}_4$	$\widehat{L}_2$	$\widehat{L}_3$	$\widehat{L}_4$	$\widehat{I}$
$\widehat{\tau}_2$	\	+	−	−	0	0	−	0	+	−	−	+	−	−	+
$\widehat{\tau}_3$	\	\	$(+)^4$	−	0	0	0	−	\	+	−	\	\	−	+

Note: The meanings of symbols are the same as those in Table 11.1. "4": $\left(1-\Omega_R^2\right) > \frac{\lambda_{K3}\left|S_{KK}^3\right|}{\lambda_{K2}\theta_{K3}}$

$\Lambda_{24} = \lambda_{L2}\lambda_{K4} - \lambda_{L4}\lambda_{K2} > 0$ and $\Lambda_{23} = \lambda_{L2}\lambda_{K3} - \lambda_{L3}\lambda_{K2} > 0$. Hence, $\Delta_2 > 0$. Solving Eq. (11.13) by Cramer's rule, we can get Table 11.2:

Summarizing results in Table 11.2, we can obtain:

Proposition 2 *In the long run, rural capital subsidies would improve the integration of rural industries, at the same time:*

- *As rural secondary subsidy increases, the output of rural secondary industry increases, rural tertiary and urban outputs decline.*
- *As rural tertiary subsidy increases, output of rural tertiary industry increases conditionally, output of urban sector decreases.*

In the long run, when capital subsidy is provided to rural secondary industry, output of this sector increases as its actual cost of capital input decreases while the overall interest rate remains unchanged. And because the prices of all input factors stay the same, the amount of inputs increases proportionally, the price of the product decreases. Unlike the short run where increase in τ_3 can promotes the output of this sector directly, in the long run, when τ_3 is provided, only when $\left(1-\Omega_R^2\right) > \frac{\lambda_{K3}\left|S_{KK}^3\right|}{\lambda_{K2}\theta_{K3}}$ is satisfied, can output of rural tertiary industry be promoted. From the differential result of Eq. (11.7): $\widehat{X}_3 = \widehat{X}_4 - \widehat{P}_3$, we can find that at this time, urban output declines, results in a lower urban demand for rural tertiary product; only when the capital subsidy causes a decline in P_3 that is substantial enough to offset or even outweigh the aforementioned falling demand, will the urban demand for rural tertiary product rebound, ultimately promoting the production of rural tertiary.

It is worth noting that, just as in the short run, a change in τ_i would not have an impact on the unemployment rate, but the mechanism of its effect is slightly different. In the long run, an increase in τ_i reduces production and labor demand L_4 in the urban sector as urban capital flows to the subsidy-receiving sector, whereas increases labor demand in rural sector and leads to a reduction in L_U. When L_4 and L_U fall in the same proportion, the unemployment rate λ is unaffected.

Through calculations, in the long run, τ_i would not affect interest rate. As capital subsidy increases, actual capital cost of rural subsidy-receiving industry decreases, which results in lower product prices, meaning that the distributive share of agricultural product in the output value of rural secondary and tertiary industries would increase, therefore integration rate of rural industries rises.

11.3.3 Comparison of Two Types of Capital Subsidies on Rural Industrial Integration

Through the above analysis, we found that in the short- and long run, effects of τ_i on I are both positive. To compare the effects of the two types of rural capital subsidies on rural industrial integration, that is, $\tau_2\widehat{\tau}_2 = \tau_3\widehat{\tau}_3$, we have (see Appendix 1 for detailed calculation):

$$\frac{\widehat{I}}{\tau\widehat{\tau}} = \frac{\widehat{I}}{\tau_2\widehat{\tau}_2} - \frac{\widehat{I}}{\tau_3\widehat{\tau}_3} = \frac{P_2X_2\theta_{K_2} - P_3X_3\theta_{K_3}}{P_2X_2 + P_3X_3}.$$

When $\frac{P_2X_2}{P_3X_3} > (<)\frac{\theta_{K3}}{\theta_{K2}} \Leftrightarrow K_2 > (<)K_3$ is met, we have: $\frac{\widehat{I}}{\tau\widehat{\tau}} > (<)0$. That is to say, in the integration process of rural industries in developing countries, the quantity of capital input in capital-using sectors determines how much of an impact capital subsidy have on rural industrial integration. At the same change rate, rural capital subsidies would have a greater impact on rural industrial integration in sector that uses more rural capital.

11.3.4 Welfare Analysis

In the analysis of social welfare, we use a Cobb-Douglas function of indirect utility for urban and rural consumers to reflect the overall welfare level of society V, namely

$$V = (V_U)^{\psi}(V_R)^{1-\psi},$$

where $\psi(0 < \psi < 1)$ indicates the welfare weight of urban consumer to overall social welfare. By totally differentiating above formula, we can obtain (see Appendix 4 for detailed calculation):

$$\frac{\widehat{V}}{\tau_i\widehat{\tau}_i} = \psi\frac{\widehat{Y}_U}{\tau_i\widehat{\tau}_i} + (1-\psi)\frac{\widehat{Y}_R}{\tau_i\widehat{\tau}_i} - \varphi\frac{\widehat{P}_2}{\tau_i\widehat{\tau}_i} - \varphi\eta\frac{\widehat{P}_3}{\tau_i\widehat{\tau}_i}, \tag{11.14}$$

there, $\widehat{Y}_U = \beta_L^U\widehat{L}_4 + \beta_K^U\widehat{K}_4$, $\widehat{Y}_R = -\frac{w(1+\lambda)L_4}{Y_R}\widehat{L}_4 - \frac{rK_4}{Y_R}\widehat{K}_4 + \beta_K^R\widehat{r}$, $\beta_L^U = \frac{\overline{w}L_4}{Y_U}$, and $\beta_K^U = \frac{r_4K_4}{Y_U}$. From Eq. (11.14), we could find that the impact of rural capital subsidies on social welfare is influenced by a combination of income impact on rural and urban consumers $(\psi\frac{\widehat{Y}_U}{\tau_i\widehat{\tau}_i} + (1-\psi)\frac{\widehat{Y}_R}{\tau_i\widehat{\tau}_i})$ and price effect on rural secondary and tertiary products $(-\varphi\frac{\widehat{P}_2}{\tau_i\widehat{\tau}_i} - \varphi\eta\frac{\widehat{P}_3}{\tau_i\widehat{\tau}_i})$. If consumer income increases, the income impact is positive and if product prices decline, the price effect will be positive, which

Table 11.3 Impact of rural capital subsidies on urban and rural incomes

	Short run		Long run	
	$\widehat{\tau_2}$	$\widehat{\tau_3}$	$\widehat{\tau_2}$	$\widehat{\tau_3}$
$\widehat{Y_U}$	0	0	–	–
$\widehat{Y_R}$	+	+	+	+

Note: The meanings of symbols are the same as those in Table 11.1

suggests that customers can purchase comparably less expensive goods with higher factor income, thereby increasing social welfare.

Firstly, we analyze the impact of rural capital subsidies on urban and rural incomes by only considering the first two items on the LHS of Eq. (11.14). According to results in Tables 11.1 and 11.2, we can get:

It can be seen from Table 11.3 that rural capital subsidies can increase rural income while keeping urban income unchanged in the short run and declining in the long run. As a result, we can draw the conclusion that rural capital subsidies are helpful in maintaining the value-added part of the rural industrial chain in rural areas, which results in a decreasing gap in gross regional income between urban and rural areas (hereinafter referred to as urban-rural economic gap).

After considering the price impact of rural capital subsidies, it is found that the two types of subsidies have different effects on those variables both in the short- and long run. As a result, the impact of rural capital subsidies on social welfare is ambiguous. To obtain $\frac{\widehat{V}}{\widehat{\tau_i}\tau_i} > 0$, the share of capital cost per unit of rural output need to be large enough to reach $\frac{rK_R}{Y_R} > \frac{\varphi}{1-\psi}(\theta_{K2} + \eta\theta_{K3})$ in the short run and for the long-run, the urban-rural output ratio need to be greater than the urban-rural welfare weighting ratio to reach: $\frac{Y_U}{Y_R} > \frac{\psi}{1-\psi}$. From this, we can get:

Proposition 3 *Whether in the short- or long run, rural capital subsidies can increase rural income and reduce urban-rural economic gap.*

Existing researches on urban-rural income gap mainly focus on the wage inequality between urban and rural labors (Yabuuchi and Chaudhuri 2007; Chaudhuri and Banerjee 2007; Gupta and Dutta 2010; Gupta and Dutta 2011; Li and Zhou 2013; Chao et al. 2010, 2012, 2016; Li et al. 2020). In comparison, our study analyzes this topic from a perspective of urban-rural gross regional incomes. From Proposition 3, we can see that in the process of encouraging rural industrial integration, rural capital subsidies enable the value-added income of the rural industrial chain remains in the rural areas. This will allow farmers to share more of the value-added benefits of the rural industrial chain, which will increase farmers' income and, in turn, help to narrow the urban-rural economic gap in developing countries.

11.4 Numerical Analysis

In this section, we calibrate the model's parameters using China's macroeconomic data. Then, we perform numerical simulations and analyze the numerical properties of our model to quantify the impacts of rural capital subsidies on the economy of developing countries.

11.4.1 Parameter Calibration

Based on our assumptions, production functions for the four sectors are set as:

$$X_1 = \mu L_1, X_2 = L_2^{\alpha_1} K_2^{\alpha_2} X_{12}^{1-\alpha_1-\alpha_2}, X_3 = L_3^{\beta_1} K_3^{\beta_2} X_{13}^{1-\beta_1-\beta_2}, X_4 = L_4^{\gamma} K_4^{1-\gamma},$$

where μ represents labor efficiency of agricultural sector, α_1, α_2, β_1, β_2, and γ are output elasticity of the corresponding factors, respectively.

We separated the 153 sectors of China's Input-Output Table 2018 into agricultural sector, rural secondary industry, rural tertiary industry, and urban sectors based on the characteristics of four sectors. Macroeconomic statistics from the China Statistical Yearbook 2019 are used to calibrate the values of the parameters, which are displayed in Table 11.4 (Appendix 5 contains more information on the calibration process).

Table 11.4 Parameter calibration

Parameter	Description	Calibration value
μ	Labor efficiency of agricultural sector	3.647
α_1	Labor output elasticity of rural secondary industry	0.180
α_2	Capital output elasticity of rural secondary industry	0.273
β_1	Labor output elasticity of rural tertiary industry	0.325
β_2	Capital output elasticity of rural tertiary industry	0.491
γ	Labor output elasticity of urban sector	0.518
α	Urban consumption share of agricultural product in urban income	0.013
δ	Urban consumption share of rural secondary industry product in urban income	0.082
η	Urban consumption share of rural tertiary industry product in urban income	0.005
ϕ	Rural consumption share of agricultural product in rural income	0.047
φ	Rural consumption share of rural secondary industry product in rural income	0.191
ψ	Weight of urban welfare to total social welfare	0.596

Source: Authors' own calculation based on China's Input-Output Table 2018 and China's Statistical Yearbook 2019

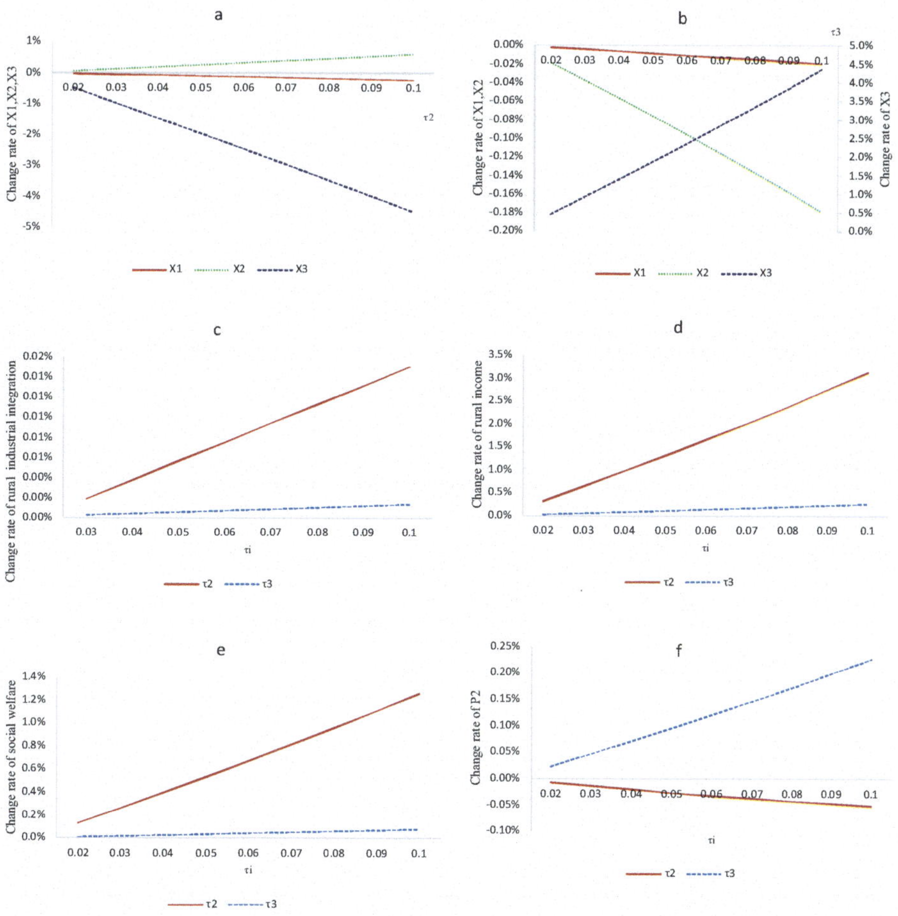

Fig. 11.2 The numerical simulation results of rural capital subsidies in the short run. Note: Rural capital subsidies have no impact on urban output and urban income in the short run

11.4.2 Numerical Simulation

According to calibrated parameters obtained above, we now increase the exogenous policy variables—capital subsidy rates from 0.01 to 0.10[10] for numerical simulation.

Short-Run Situation

Figure 11.2a, b show that in the short run, as τ_i increases, agricultural output decreases; additionally, as shown in Fig. 11.2c, d, τ_2 has a more positive effect

---

[10]We use the growth rate of endogenous variable relative to its base value when $\tau_i(i = 2, 3) = 0.01$.

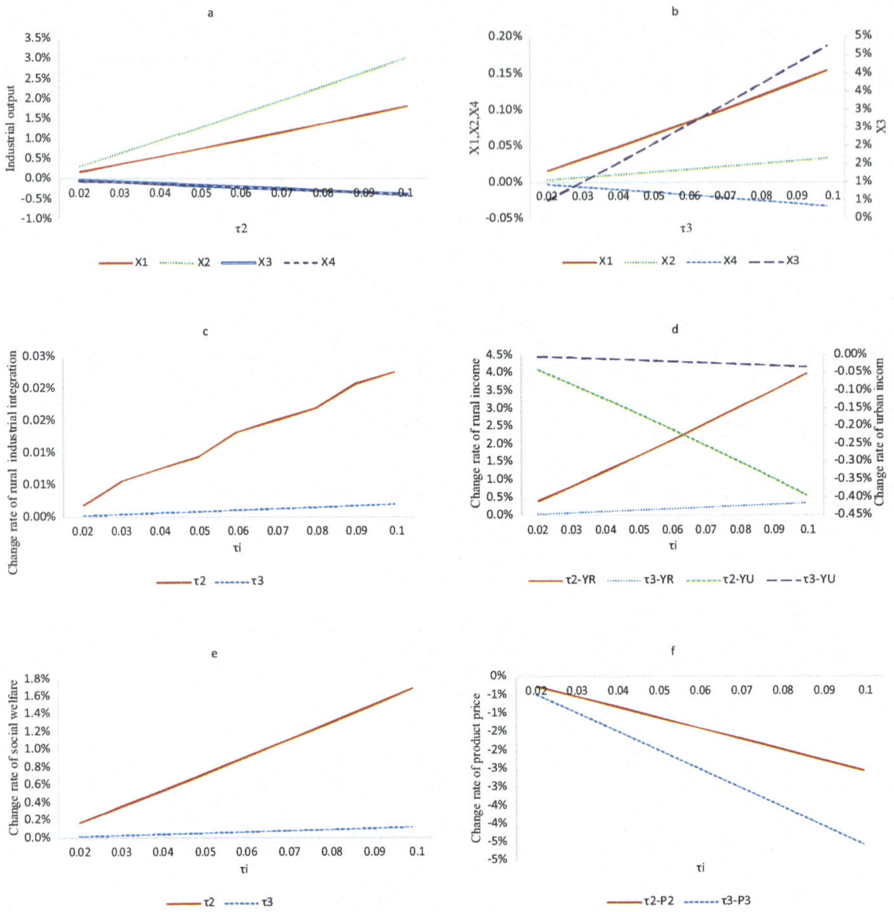

Fig. 11.3 The numerical simulation results of rural capital subsidies in the long run

than τ_3 on rural industrial integration and rural income. Furthermore, the negative impact of the price effect [which is shown in Fig. 11.2f] is lower in comparison to the income effect, and as a result, as it illustrated in Fig. 11.2e, capital subsidies promote social welfare.

Long-Run Situation

In the long run, as shown in Fig. 11.3a, b, capital subsidies can promote the output of agricultural sector. Figure 11.3c, d show that τ_2 has a greater effect than τ_3 in boosting rural industrial integration and narrowing rural-urban income gap. Impacts of rural capital subsidies on social welfare are shown in Fig. 11.3e: As τ_i increase, price effect of capital subsidies [see Fig. 11.3f] is positive, while the negative impact of income effect is smaller comparatively. As a result, social welfare improves, and the contribution of τ_2 to social welfare is greater than that of τ_3.

Combining results from the above theoretical analysis and numerical simulation, we get:

Proposition 4 *In economies with Chinese characteristics, rural capital subsidies would promote the agricultural output in the long run. Additionally, effects of rural secondary industrial capital subsidy on enhancing rural industrial integration, reducing urban-rural economic gap and promoting social welfare are greater than those of capital subsidy for rural tertiary industry.*

11.5 Conclusion

This paper divides the rural sector of developing countries into agricultural sector, rural secondary industry, rural tertiary industry, and establishes a four-sector general-equilibrium model while taking into account the fact that capital markets of urban and rural sectors in developing countries are separated. We explore the impact of rural capital subsidies on the economies of developing countries in the process of promoting rural industrial integration. In the numerical simulation part, we calibrate parameters of theoretical model based on Chinese macroeconomic data and conduct numerical simulation of subsidy shocks to quantify the economic effects of rural capital subsidies. We found that rural capital subsidies can promote rural industrial integration (under certain conditions in the short run), narrow urban-rural economic gap and improve social welfare; in an economy with Chinese characteristics, the economic effect of capital subsidy to rural secondary industry is better than that of capital subsidy to rural tertiary industry.

The following are the key distinctions between this paper and the existing researches: (1) For the first time in related field, we take into consideration the simultaneous integration of agriculture and rural secondary industry and agriculture and rural tertiary industry; (2) Our study focuses on the economic implications of capital subsidy for different industries within rural sector, thus revealing one of the goals of this paper, which is to provide a theoretical foundation for the application of precisely targeted subsidy to encourage the integration of rural industries.

With regard to agricultural subsidies, there typically include salary subsidy and price subsidy, also, horizontal integration of three rural industries can also be a topic within the context of rural industrial integration. They have not all been covered in this paper due to space restrictions; nevertheless, we will explore them individually in our future research.

Competing Interests

Disclosure Statement No potential conflict of interest was reported by the authors.

Appendix

Appendix 1

Totally differentiating $I = \frac{X_{12}+X_{13}}{P_2X_2+P_3X_3}$, there is

$$\widehat{I} = -\varsigma\widehat{X}_2 - \varsigma\widehat{P}_2 + (\varsigma-1)\widehat{X}_3 + (\varsigma-1)\widehat{P}_3 + \upsilon\widehat{X}_{12} + (1-\upsilon)\widehat{X}_{13},$$

where $\varsigma = \frac{P_2X_2}{P_2X_2+P_3X_3}$, $\upsilon = \frac{X_{12}}{X_{12}+X_{13}}$, $0 < \varsigma < 1, 0 < \upsilon < 1$.

The effect of rural capital subsidies for rural secondary and tertiary industries on rural industrial integration can be obtained as:

$$\begin{aligned}\frac{\widehat{I}}{\tau_2\widehat{\tau}_2} &= \frac{\widehat{X}_2}{\tau_2\widehat{\tau}_2}(\upsilon-\varsigma) + \frac{\widehat{X}_3}{\tau_2\widehat{\tau}_2}(\varsigma-\upsilon) + \frac{\widehat{r}}{\tau_2\widehat{\tau}_2} \\ &\times \left[\varsigma(\theta_{K3}-\theta_{K2}) - \theta_{K3} + \upsilon\left(S^2_{X_1K} - S^3_{X_1K}\right) + S^3_{X_1K}\right] + \varsigma\theta_{K2},\end{aligned}$$

$$\begin{aligned}\frac{\widehat{I}}{\tau_3\widehat{\tau}_3} &= \frac{\widehat{X}_2}{\tau_3\widehat{\tau}_3}(\upsilon-\varsigma) + \frac{\widehat{X}_3}{\tau_3\widehat{\tau}_3}(\varsigma-\upsilon) + \frac{\widehat{r}}{\tau_3\widehat{\tau}_3} \\ &\times \left[\varsigma(\theta_{K3}-\theta_{K2}) - \theta_{K3} + \upsilon\left(S^2_{X_1K} - S^3_{X_1K}\right) + S^3_{X_1K}\right] + (1-\varsigma)\theta_{K3}.\end{aligned}$$

We explore a particular situation where the distributive share of agricultural product in rural secondary and tertiary industries are equal in order to generate results that can be analyzed; thus, we have $\theta_{X2} = \theta_{X3} \Rightarrow \varsigma = \upsilon$.

Appendix 2. Short-Run Static Analysis

Solving Eq. (11.2) by Cramer's rule, we get:

$$\frac{\widehat{X}_1}{\tau_2\widehat{\tau}_2} = \frac{1}{\Delta_1}\left\{\beta^R_{L2}S^2_{LK}\lambda_{L2}\alpha_{K3}\theta_{K3} - \beta^R_{K2}S^2_{KK}\lambda_{L3}\alpha_{K2}\left(\theta_{K3} + S^3_{LK}\right)\right.$$
$$+ \frac{\theta_{K2}}{\Omega^2_R}\left(\lambda_{L3}\alpha_{K2} - \lambda_{L2}\alpha_{K3}\right)\left(\theta_{K3} + S^3_{LK}\right)$$
$$+ \left(\beta^R_{K2} + \beta^R_{K3} - \frac{1}{\Omega^2_R}\right)\left[\lambda_{L3}\alpha_{K2}S^2_{KK}\left(\theta_{K3} + S^3_{LK}\right) - S^2_{LK}\lambda_{L2}\alpha_{K3}\theta_{K3}\right]$$
$$+ \left(\beta^R_{K2}S^2_{LK} - \beta^R_{L3}S^3_{LK}S^2_{KK}\right)\lambda_{L2}\alpha_{K2} - \left(\beta^R_{K2} + \beta^R_{K3}\right)\lambda_{L2}\alpha_{K2}S^2_{KK}$$
$$\left. + \left(\beta^R_{K3}S^2_{LK} - \theta_{K3}\beta^R_{L3}S^2_{KK} + \theta_{K3}\beta^R_{K3}S^2_{LK}\right)\lambda_{L2}\alpha_{K2} + \frac{1}{\Omega^2_R}\lambda_{L2}S^2_{LK}\alpha_{K3}S^3_{KK}\right\},$$

$$\frac{\widehat{X}_2}{\tau_2\widehat{\tau}_2} = \frac{1}{\Delta_1}\left[\frac{\theta_{K2}}{\Omega^2_R}\lambda_{L1}\alpha_{K3}\left(S^3_{KK} + \theta_{K3}\right) + \left(\beta^R_{K2} + \beta^R_{K3}\right)\lambda_{L1}\alpha_{K2}S^2_{KK}\right](>0)$$
$$\times\left(if : \left|S^3_{KK}\right| \geq \theta_{K3}\right),$$

$$\frac{\widehat{r}}{\tau_2\widehat{\tau}_2} = \frac{\lambda_{L1}\alpha_{K2}}{\Delta_1}\frac{S^2_{KK} - \theta_{K2}}{\Omega^2_R} > 0.$$

$$\frac{\widehat{X}_1}{\tau_3\widehat{\tau}_3} = \frac{1}{\Delta_1}\left[\left(\lambda_{L3}\alpha_{K2}S^3_{LK} - \lambda_{L2}\alpha_{K3}S^3_{KK}\right)\left(\beta^R_{K2} + \beta^R_{K3}\right)\right.$$
$$+ S^2_{KK}\lambda_{L2}\alpha_{K2}\beta^R_{L3}\left(S^3_{LK} + \theta_{K3}\right) - \theta_{K3}\beta^R_{K3}S^2_{LK}\lambda_{L2}\alpha_{K2}$$
$$- \left(\beta^R_{K2} + \beta^R_{K3} - \frac{1}{\Omega^2_R}\right)\left(\theta_{K3}\lambda_{L3}\alpha_{K2}S^2_{KK} + \lambda_{L3}\alpha_{K2}S^3_{LK}S^2_{KK}\right.$$
$$\left. + S^2_{LK}\lambda_{L2}\alpha_{K3}\theta_{K3}\right) + \lambda_{L3}\alpha_{K2}\left(S^3_{LK} + \theta_{K3}\right)\left(\beta^R_{K2}S^2_{KK} - \frac{\theta_{K2}}{\Omega^2_R}\right)$$
$$\left. - \lambda_{L2}\alpha_{K3}S^3_{KK}\left(\beta^R_{K2} + \beta^R_{K3}\right) - \lambda_{L2}\alpha_{K3}\theta_{K3}\beta^R_{L2}S^2_{LK}\right],$$

$$\frac{\widehat{X}_2}{\tau_3\widehat{\tau}_3} = \frac{1}{\Delta_1}\left[\left(\beta_{K2}^R\lambda_{L1}\alpha_{K3} + \beta_{K3}^R\lambda_{L1}\alpha_{K3}\right)\left(\theta_{K3} + S_{KK}^3\right) - \frac{\theta_{K2}}{\Omega_R^2}\lambda_{L1}\alpha_{K3}\theta_{K3}\right.$$
$$\left. - \alpha_{K3}\left(\beta_{L1}^R\theta_{K3}\lambda_{L3}S_{LK}^3 + \frac{\theta_{K2}}{\Omega_R^2}\lambda_{L1}S_{KK}^3\right)\right],$$

$$\frac{\widehat{r}}{\tau_3\widehat{\tau}_3} = \frac{1}{\Delta_1}\frac{\lambda_{L1}\alpha_{K3}}{\Omega_R^2}\left(S_{KK}^3 + \theta_{K3}\right)(\geq 0) \quad \left(\text{if} : \left|S_{KK}^3\right| \geq \theta_{K3}\right).$$

The impact of τ_i on production factors and rural industrial integration in the short run (Here take τ_2 as an example, τ_3 case can be analyzed in the same way)

$$\frac{\widehat{K}_2}{\tau_2\widehat{\tau}_2} = S_{KK}^2\left(\frac{\widehat{r}}{\tau_2\widehat{\tau}_2} - 1\right) + \frac{\widehat{X}_2}{\tau_2\widehat{\tau}_2} > 0,$$

$$\frac{\widehat{K}_3}{\tau_2\widehat{\tau}_2} = S_{KK}^3\frac{\widehat{r}}{\tau_2\widehat{\tau}_2} + \frac{\widehat{X}_3}{\tau_2\widehat{\tau}_2} < 0,$$

$$\frac{\widehat{L}_2}{\tau_2\widehat{\tau}_2} = S_{LK}^2\left(\frac{\widehat{r}}{\tau_2\widehat{\tau}_2} - 1\right) + \frac{\widehat{X}_2}{\tau_2\widehat{\tau}_2} > 0,$$

$$\frac{\widehat{L}_3}{\tau_2\widehat{\tau}_2} = S_{LK}^3\frac{\widehat{r}}{\tau_2\widehat{\tau}_2} + \frac{\widehat{X}_3}{\tau_2\widehat{\tau}_2}(>0)\left(if : \theta_{K3} < S_{LK}^3\right).$$

$$\frac{\widehat{K}_4}{\tau_2\widehat{\tau}_2} = S_{KK}^4\frac{\widehat{r}_4}{\tau_2\widehat{\tau}_2} + \frac{\widehat{X}_4}{\tau_2\widehat{\tau}_2} = 0.$$

$$\frac{\widehat{I}}{\tau_2\widehat{\tau}_2} = \frac{\widehat{r}}{\tau_2\widehat{\tau}_2}\left[\varsigma(\theta_{K3} - \theta_{K2}) - \theta_{K3} + \upsilon\left(S_{X_1K}^2 - S_{X_1K}^3\right) + S_{X_1K}^3\right]$$
$$+ \varsigma\theta_{K2}(>0) \quad \left(\text{if} : \theta_{K3} < \frac{1}{1-\varsigma}\left[\upsilon S_{X_1K}^2 + S_{X_1K}^3(1-\upsilon)\right]\right).$$

Note: Rural secondary sector is still emerging in developing countries, and its labor share is often lower than that of the rural primary sector, that is, $\lambda_{L1} > \lambda_{L2}$; and when Ω_R^2 is small enough to reach $\Omega_R^2 < (\theta_{K3} - \theta_{K2})/\beta_K^R$, there is $\left(\frac{\widehat{r}}{\tau_2\widehat{\tau}_2} - 1\right) < 0$. We obtain $0.27 = \lambda_{L1} > \lambda_{L2} = 0.06$ and $0.24 = \Omega_R^2 < (\theta_{K3} - \theta_{K2})/\beta_K^R = 0.92$ by using China's 2018 macroeconomic data.

Appendix 3. Long-Run Static Analysis

Solving Eq. (11.13) by Cramer's rule can get:[11]

$$\begin{aligned}\frac{\widehat{X}_1}{\tau_2\widehat{\tau}_2} = \frac{1}{\Delta_2}\Big\{ &(\beta^R_{L3}+\beta^R_{K3})\Omega^2_R\lambda_{L2}\lambda_{K2}(S^2_{LK}-S^2_{KK}) \\ &+(\Lambda_{24}+\Lambda_{23})(\Omega^2_R\beta^R_{L2}S^2_{LK}+\Omega^2_R\beta^R_{K2}S^2_{KK}-\theta_{K2}) \\ &-(\beta^R_{K2}\Omega^2_R+\beta^R_{K3}\Omega^2_R-1)\left[\lambda_{L2}(\lambda_{K4}+\lambda_{K3})S^2_{LK}-(\lambda_{L3}+\lambda_{L4})\lambda_{K2}S^2_{KK}\right] \\ &+(1-\Omega^2_R)\lambda_{L2}\lambda_{K2}(S^2_{LK}-S^2_{KK})\Big\},\end{aligned}$$

$$\begin{aligned}&\frac{\widehat{X}_2}{\tau_2\widehat{\tau}_2} \\ &=\frac{1}{\Delta_2}\Big\{\theta_{K2}\lambda_{L1}(\lambda_{K3}+\lambda_{K4})-\Omega^2_R S^2_{KK}\beta^R_{L1}\lambda_{K2}\lambda_{L4}(1+\lambda)+\lambda_{L1}S^2_{KK}\left[\lambda_{K2}(1-\Omega^2_R)-\Omega^2_R\beta^R_{K2}\lambda_{K4}\right]\Big\}>0,\end{aligned}$$

$$\frac{\widehat{X}_3}{\tau_2\widehat{\tau}_2} = \frac{1}{\Delta_2}\{\beta^R_{L1}\Omega^2_R\lambda_{L2}\lambda_{K2}S^2_{KK}-\lambda_{L1}\lambda_{K2}[(\beta^R_{K3}\Omega^2_R-1)S^2_{KK}+\theta_{K2}]\}<0,$$

$$\frac{\widehat{X}_4}{\tau_2\widehat{\tau}_2} = \frac{1}{\Delta_2}\{\beta^R_{L1}\Omega^2_R\lambda_{L2}\lambda_{K2}S^2_{KK}-\lambda_{L1}\lambda_{K2}[(\beta^R_{K3}\Omega^2_R-1)S^2_{KK}+\theta_{K2}]\}<0.$$

$$\begin{aligned}\frac{\widehat{X}_1}{\tau_3\widehat{\tau}_3}=\frac{1}{\Delta_2}\{&(\beta^R_{L3}+\beta^R_{K3})\Omega^2_R(-\theta_{K3}\Lambda_{24}+\lambda_{L3}\lambda_{K2}S^3_{LK}-\lambda_{L3}\lambda_{K3}S^3_{KK}) \\ &+(1-\Omega^2_R)(-\theta_{K3}\Lambda_{23}-\lambda_{L3}\lambda_{K2}S^3_{LK}+\lambda_{L2}\lambda_{K3}S^3_{KK})-(\beta^R_{K2}\Omega^2_R+\beta^R_{K3}\Omega^2_R-1) \\ &\left[-\theta_{K3}\Lambda_{24}+\lambda_{L3}(\lambda_{K4}+\lambda_{K3})S^3_{LK}-(\lambda_{L3}+\lambda_{L2})\lambda_{K3}S^3_{KK}\right]+\Omega^2_R(\beta^R_{L3}S^3_{LK}+\beta^R_{K3}S^3_{KK}) \\ &(\Lambda_{23}+\Lambda_{24}),\end{aligned}$$

$$\begin{aligned}\frac{\widehat{X}_2}{\tau_3\widehat{\tau}_3} = \frac{1}{\Delta_2}\{&\theta_{K3}\beta^R_{L1}\Omega^2_R(\lambda_{L4}\lambda_{K3}-\lambda_{L3}\lambda_{K4})+S^3_{KK}\beta^R_{L1}\Omega^2_R(\lambda_{L3}\lambda_{K4}S^3_{LK}-\lambda_{L4}\lambda_{K3}) \\ &+S^3_{KK}\lambda_{L1}\left[(1-\Omega^2_R)\lambda_{K3}-\beta^R_{K3}\Omega^2_R\lambda_{K4}\right]+\lambda_{L1}\theta_{K3}(\Omega^2_R\beta^R_{L3}\lambda_{K4}-\Omega^2_U\lambda_{K3}) \\ &+\Omega^2_R\lambda_{L1}\lambda_{K4}(\beta^R_{K3}\theta_{K3}-\beta^R_{L3}S^3_{LK})\},\end{aligned}$$

[11] In developing countries, the urban-rural capital ratio is sufficiently large and $\frac{\lambda_{K4}}{\lambda_{K2}} > \frac{1-\Omega^2_R}{\beta^R_{K2}\Omega^2_R}$ can be met; our 2018 data satisfy this assumption.

$$\frac{\widehat{X}_3}{\tau_3\widehat{\tau}_3} = \frac{1}{\Delta_2}\Big\{\beta_{L1}^{R}\Omega_R^2\theta_{K3}\Lambda_{24} - \left(\beta_{K2}^{R}\Omega_R^2 + \beta_{K3}^{R}\Omega_R^2 - 1\right)\lambda_{L1}\lambda_{K4}\theta_{K3}$$

$$+ \lambda_{L1}\left[\left(1-\Omega_R^2\right)\lambda_{K2}\theta_{K3} + \lambda_{K3}S_{KK}^3\right]\Big\}(>0)\left(\text{if} : \left(1-\Omega_R^2\right) > \frac{\lambda_{K3}\left|S_{KK}^3\right|}{\lambda_{K2}\theta_{K3}}\right),$$

$$\frac{\hat{X}_4}{\tau_3\hat{\tau}_3} = \frac{1}{\Delta_2}\left[\beta_{L1}^{R}\Omega_R^2\left(\lambda_{L2}\lambda_{K3}S_{KK}^3 - \theta_{K3}\Lambda_{23}\right) - \left(\beta_{K2}^{R}\Omega_R^2 + \beta_{K3}^{R}\Omega_R^2 - 1\right)\lambda_{L1}\lambda_{K3}\left(S_{KK}^3 - \theta_{K3}\right)\right.$$

$$\left. - \left(\beta_{L3}^{R} + \beta_{K3}^{R}\right)\Omega_R^2\lambda_{L1}\lambda_{K2}\theta_{K3} + \beta_{K3}^{R}S_{KK}^3\Omega_R^2\lambda_{L1}\lambda_{K2}\right)\Big](<0)\left(if\left|S_{KK}^3\right| > \theta_{K3}\right).$$

Similar to the short run, impact of two capital subsidies on factor inputs and rural industrial integration in the long run can be analyzed, which is omitted here.

Appendix 4. Social Welfare

By our setting of social welfare: $V = (V_U)^{\psi}(V_R)^{1-\psi}$, we have

$$V = \left[\left(\frac{\alpha Y_U}{P_1}\right)^{\alpha}\left(\frac{\delta Y_U}{P_2}\right)^{\delta}\left(\frac{\eta Y_U}{P_3}\right)^{\eta}\left(\frac{(1-\alpha-\delta-\eta)Y_U}{P_4}\right)^{1-\alpha-\delta-\eta}\right]^{\psi}$$

$$*\left[\left(\frac{\phi Y_R}{P_1}\right)^{\phi}\left(\frac{\varphi Y_R}{P_2}\right)^{\varphi}\left(\frac{(1-\phi-\varphi)Y_R}{P_4}\right)^{1-\phi-\varphi}\right]^{1-\psi} \Rightarrow V{P_1}^{\alpha+\phi}{P_2}^{\delta+\varphi}P_3^{\eta}{P_4}^{1-\alpha-\delta-\eta+1-\phi-\varphi}$$

$$= \left[\alpha^{\alpha}\delta^{\delta}\eta^{\eta}(1-\alpha-\delta-\eta)^{1-\alpha-\delta-\eta}Y_U{P_1}^{\phi}{P_2}^{\varphi}{P_4}^{1-\phi-\varphi}\right]^{\psi*}$$

$$\left[\phi^{\phi}\varphi^{\phi}(1-\phi-\varphi)^{(1-\phi-\varphi)}Y_R{P_1}^{\alpha}{P_2}^{\delta}P_3^{\eta}{P_4}^{1-\alpha-\delta-\eta}\right]^{1-\psi}.$$

Here, $Y_R = w\left[\overline{L} - (1+\lambda)L_4\right] + rK_R$. By total differentiating of the above equation, we can obtain:

$$\widehat{V} = \psi\widehat{Y}_U + (1-\psi)\widehat{Y}_R - \varphi\widehat{P}_2 - \psi\eta\widehat{P}_3.$$

Appendix 5. Detailed Process of Parameter Calibration

Based on characteristics of different sectors, we divide the 153 sectors of China's Input-Output Table 2018 into four sectors as follows:

Industry	Subdivided industry
Agricultural sector	Agricultural products, forest products, livestock products, fishery products
Rural secondary industry	Grain mill products; processed feed products; processed vegetable oil products; sugar and sugar products; slaughter and processed meat products; processed aquatic products; vegetables, fruits, nuts, and other processed agricultural and side-line food products; dairy products; condiments; fermented products; alcohol and liquor; refined tea; tobacco products; cotton, chemical fiber textiles products; wool textiles and dying products; hemp, silk, and silk textiles and processed products; knitting or crocheting products, textiles products; textiles and apparel; leather, fur, feathers, and their products; wood processing and wood, bamboo, rattan, palm, and grass products
Rural tertiary industry	Rural service products, rural accommodation industry[a]
Urban sector	The rest of above sectors

[a]We allocated 7.2% of the output value of "accommodation industry" in the Input-Output 2018 table to rural accommodation industry (considering the share of China's rural GDP was 7.2% in 2018)

In 2018, labor compensation in China's agricultural sector was 6542.492 billion yuan (this part of added-value is equal to the output value of agricultural sector according to its production function), based on Eq.(11.1) and related factor prices,[12] we obtain: $\mu = w = 3.647$ and L_1=179,393,797.800. The added value of China's rural secondary sector was 3964.346 billion yuan, of which 1579.121 billion yuan went to labor compensation, resulting in a capital compensation of 2385.225 billion yuan; this sector used intermediate input (agricultural product) worth 4787.379 billion yuan, thus the total output value of rural secondary industry (added value + value of intermediate input) was 8751.725 billion yuan; from this, we can calculate: $\alpha_1 = 0.180, \alpha_2 = 0.273$, L_2=43,299,164.220, K_2= 2,293,486,140. The added-value of China's rural tertiary sector was 312.375 billion yuan, and the labor remuneration was 124.335 billion yuan, therefore, capital compensation was 188.040 billion yuan; this sector used 70.756 billion yuan of agricultural product as intermediate input, which gives the total output value of the rural tertiary sector: 383.131 billion yuan; it can be calculated that $\beta_1 = 0.325$, $\beta_2 = 0.491$, L_3=3,409,247.835, K_3=180,807,816.100. Total output value of China's urban sector was 81,386.504 billion yuan and labor remuneration was 39,236.722 billion yuan, thus capital compensation was 42,149.782 billion yuan, This gives $\gamma = 0.518$,

[12]According to the China Statistical Yearbook 2019, we obtained that the average wage for urban and rural workers were, respectively, 87,881 and 36,470 yuan (in software simulation, we unified the unit to ten-thousand yuan); and referred to Li and Wu (2020), interest rate of China in urban sector: $r_4 = 6.9\%$ and rural sectors: $r = 10.35\%$.

$L_4 = 446{,}705{,}021.100$, $K_4 = 61{,}086{,}640{,}687$. At this point, we have obtained the production functions for the four sectors. According to the China Statistical Yearbook 2019, the number of urban registered unemployed in China was 9,740,000 in 2018, which according to the definition of unemployment rate in this paper gives: $\lambda = 0.022$.

About the demand side, based on urban and rural consumption share of products,[13] balance of payments, import-export balance, and market clearing conditions, we can get: agricultural products was consumed by urban consumer worth of 1052.305 billion yuan while rural consumers spent 514.300 billion yuan on them; rural secondary products was consumed 6682.941 billion yuan by urban consumer and 2068.784 billion yuan by rural consumer; rural tertiary products was consumed by urban consumer worth of 383.131 billion yuan; and urban products was consumed 73268.127 billion yuan by urban consumer and 8236.129 billion yuan by rural consumer. We use a social accounting matrix to describe the flow of relationships between the supply and demand for different products, see Table 11.5.

In the part of social welfare, we estimate the weight of welfare share of urban and rural residents using the population percentage of urban and rural inhabitants. In China Statistical Yearbook 2019, we get the proportion of China's urban population in 2018 is 0.596, so $\psi = 0.596$.

[13] Products of agricultural sector was consumed by urban and rural consumers in the ratio of 0.672: 0.328, and the ratio for rural secondary industry product is 0.764:0.236, as measured by the 2018 China Input-Output Table.

Table 11.5 Social accounting matrix (billion Yuan) (authors' own calculation)

		Commodities				Factors		Households		ROW	Total
		Agriculture	Rural secondary	Rural tertiary	Urban Sector	Labor	Capital	Urban consumer	Rural consumer	Export	Total demand
Commodities	Agriculture		4787.379	70.756				1052.305	514.300	117.752	6542.492
	Rural secondary							6682.941	2068.784		8751.725
	Rural tertiary							383.131			383.131
	Urban sector							73,268.127	8236.129		81,504.256
Factors	Labor	6542.492	1579.121	124.335	39,236.722						47,482.670
	Capital		2385.225	188.040	42,149.782						44,723.047
Households	Urban consumer					39,236.722	42,149.782				81,386.504
	Rural consumer					8245.948	2573.265				10,819.213
ROW	Import				117.752						117.752
Total	Total supply	6542.492	8751.725	383.131	81,504.256	47,482.670	44,723.047	81,386.504	10,819.213	117.752	

References

Abbott AJ, Vita GD (2003) Another piece in the Feldstein—Horioka puzzle. Scott J Polit Econ 50(1):69–89

Chao CC, Laffargue JP, Sgro PM (2010) Foreign aid, wage inequality, and welfare for a small open economy with tourism. Rev Int Econ 18(3):454–464

Chao CC, Laffargue JP, Sgro PM (2012) Environmental control, wage inequality and national welfare in a tourism economy. Int Rev Econ Financ 22(1):201–207

Chao CC, Nabin M, Nguyen X, Sgro PM (2016) Wage inequality and welfare in developing countries: privatization and reforms in the short and long run. Int Rev Econ Financ 42:474–483

Chaudhuri S, Banerjee D (2007) Economic liberalization, capital mobility and informal wage in a small open economy: a theoretical analysis. Econ Model 24(6):924–940

Choi JY, Yu ES (2010) Imperfect capital mobility: a general approach to the two-sector Harris Todaro model. Rev Int Econ 18(1):81–94

Corden WM, Findlay R (1975) Urban unemployment, intersectoral capital mobility and development policy. Economica 42(165):59–78

Cui Z (2010) The six industrialization of Japanese agriculture and its enlightenment. Agric Dev 12: 6–8

Fleischer A, Felsenstein D (2000) Support for rural tourism: does it make a difference? Ann Tour Res 27(4):1007–1024

Galloway L, Sanders J, Deakins D (2011) Rural small firms' use of the internet: from global to local. J Rural Stud 27(3):254–262

Garrett RD, Lambin EF, Naylor RL (2013) Land institutions and supply chain configurations as determinants of soybean planted area and yields in Brazil. Land Use Policy 31:385–396

Gupta MR (1995) Tax on foreign capital income and wage subsidy to the urban sector in the Harris-Todaro model. J Dev Econ 47(2):469–479

Gupta MR, Dutta PB (2010) Skilled–unskilled wage inequality: a general equilibrium analysis. Res Econ 64(4):247–263

Gupta MR, Dutta PB (2011) Skilled–unskilled wage inequality and unemployment: a general equilibrium analysis. Econ Model 28(4):1977–1983

Han J (2019) Prioritizing agricultural, rural development and implementing the rural revitalization strategy. China Agric Econ Rev 12:14

Harris JR, Todaro MP (1970) Migration, unemployment and development: a two-sector analysis. Am Econ Rev:126–142

Hjalager AM (1996) Agricultural diversification into tourism: evidence of a European Community development programme. Tour Manag 17(2):103–111

Imamura N (1996) The creation of the sixth industry as the 21st century agricultural flower-shaped industry. Mon Reg Prod 89:1

Jiang C (2015) 'The sixth-industrialization for agriculture' in Japan and promoting the industrial integration-development among rural first industry, second industry, and the third industry in China. Agric Econ Manag 03:5–10

Li X, Shen Q (2012) A study on urban private capital and the transfer of labour in the modern agriculture sector. J Econ Policy Reform 15(2):135–152

Li X, Zhou Y (2013) An economic analysis of remittance of unskilled migration on skilled–unskilled wage inequality in labour host region. Econ Model 33:428–432

Li X, Zhou J (2015) Environmental effects of remittance of rural–urban migrant. Econ Model 47: 174–179

Li X, Wu Y (2020) Environmental effects of international factors movement under the rural vitalization strategy. J Audit Econ 35(01):100–110. (in Chinese)

Li X, Fu H, Wu Y (2020) Pollution mitigation, unemployment rate and wage inequality in the presence of agricultural pollution. China Econ Rev 61:101425

Lu Q, Jiang C (2016) Analysis and thinking on promoting the integrated development of primary, secondary and tertiary industries in rural areas—based on the investigation of Yichang City, Hubei Province. Jianghuai Tribune 1:12–16

Meng Y (2020) Research on the development path of integration of three Industries of Fresh Corn Industry in Hebei Province. Mod Food 20:75–87. https://doi.org/10.16736/j.cnki.cn41-1434/ts.2020.20.021

Rapanos VT (2007) Environmental taxation in a dualistic economy. Environ Dev Econ 12(1):73–89

Sinn S (1992) Saving-investment correlations and capital mobility: on the evidence from annual data. Econ J 102(414):1162–1170

Skuras D, Dimara E, Stathopoulou S (2003) Capital subsidies and job creation in rural areas: a Greek case study. Int J Manpow 24:947

Taylor AM (1996) International capital mobility in history: the saving-investment relationship. In: NBER working Paper 5743

Turland M, Slade P (2020) Farmers' willingness to participate in a big data platform. Agribusiness 36(1):20–36

VanWey LK, Spera S, de Sa R, Mahr D, Mustard JF (2013) Socioeconomic development and agricultural intensification in Mato Grosso. Philos Trans R Soc B Biol Sci 368(1619):20120168

Wu Y, Li X (2021) International factor mobility and environment in a dual agricultural economy. Ann Reg Sci 66(1):75–89

Yabuuchi S, Chaudhuri S (2007) International migration of labour and skilled–unskilled wage inequality in a developing economy. Econ Model 24(1):128–137

Yamashita H (2015) Japanese legislation and policies on increasing agricultural and rural incomes (in Japanese). In: Materials for the 19th China-Japan civil and commercial law seminar

Chapter 12
Industrial Upgrading: Rural-Urban Migrant's Training Costs and Heterogeneous Labor Migration

Abstract This article uses H-T model to analyze economic effects of training costs and heterogeneous labor migration from the prospect of short and long terms. We build a general-equilibrium model with three sectors and apply comparatively static methods in discussing economic effects of decreasing training cost for migrants when developing countries are going through industrial upgrading. The main conclusions are a decrease in training costs reduces rural employment in the short run; there is a threshold in the long term: when rural wage is lower than this value, reducing training cost could increase rural employment, while decrease industrial employment with lower unemployment.

Keywords Industrial upgrading · Labor migration · Training costs · Heterogeneous labor

12.1 Introduction

Adjusting and upgrading industrial structure refers to transformation of low-capital, low-tech industries into high-capital, high-tech ones, which is one of the most important stuffs many developing countries, especially emerging economies, are working on recently. In China, for instance, it has been major target for Chinese government since 2013: eliminating poor production problems, adjusting industrial structure, and transforming enterprises from labor-intensive to tech- and capital-intensive ones.[1] Many firms are engaged in this process, which made Chinese labor market change a lot either. Firms are searching for workers with higher human capital. This demand for skilled workers exceeds supply, meanwhile it becomes more difficult for traditional unskilled workers to find a job for the same reason. Moreover, there is a huge gap of human-capital level between main labor force–migrants and urban workers. Take China as an example. The length of education per

[1] *Report on the Work of the Government*, the Twelfth National People's Congress on March 5, 2013, please refer to http://www.gov.cn/2013lh/content_2356704.htm.

X. Li, Y. Wu, *Research on Characteristic Issues in Current Developing Economies*,
New Frontiers in Regional Science: Asian Perspectives 80,
https://doi.org/10.1007/978-981-97-7284-1_12

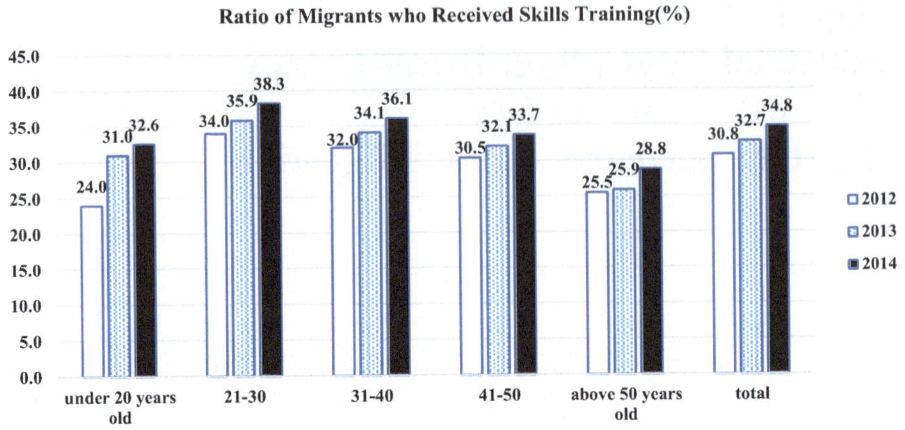

Fig. 12.1 Ratio of migrants with skill training among different age groups (2012–2014) (National Monitoring Survey of Migrant Workers 2012–2014) (National Bureau of Statistics of the People's Republic of China (http://www.stats.gov.cn/))

capita in the rural area was 2 years shorter than urban residents in 2010. There were about 75% of migrant workers whose education level was no more than junior high school and it does not change so much as 15 years ago (Li and Qian 2011). Some scholars calculated and concluded that the elasticity of education to domestic economic growth is 0.21 (Wang 2011). If the educating length for migrating rural labor can be improved by 1 year, national education length will rise to 10.32 years and output will increase about 1%. It is thus clear that improving human capital level for migrants is a fundamental step for industrial upgrading and economic development. In recent years, government are in charge in peasant-worker training. According to China's National Monitoring Surveys of Migrant Workers (2012–2014), the number of migrants with skill training within all the age groups is growing annually. It is shown in Fig. 12.1.

When upgraded enterprises set stricter hiring standards, lots of migrants would decide to grasp more skills in order to find a job with better income. Most of the training fee would be paid by government and individuals themselves. Li and Zhou (2013a) mentioned that both central and local governments in China spent large amount of money and resources on rural-labor training in recent years. Central government appropriated 157 million dollars in 2015 and 198 million dollars in 2016 just for migrant training.[2] In total, more than one million migrants professionally have been trained for various job positions. Even with this kind of scale, it remains difficult to guarantee billions of migrants or migrant-to-be to take skill training. Plenty of rural workers had to pay for their own education and improvement of human-capital level in order to meet higher hiring qualification. It might be due to (1) the huge gap between the training programs governments funded and their

[2]Data from the State Council of the People's Republic of China. Please refer to http://www.gov.cn/.

personal requirements and (2) insufficient financial resources from governments or some other reasons. Undoubtedly, lack of money for training might still be the major reason why some rural workers kept migrating to urban area without any skills or education. In other words, it remains to be a common phenomenon that many unskilled migrants are searching for jobs in big city nowadays. As a result, with industrial upgrading, rural-labor migration faces some novel changes: the case of homogeneous unskilled-labor migration turns into that of both skilled and unskilled workers migrating simultaneously. Training cost plays an important role in this new situation.

Previous theoretical studies on labor migration in dual economy were mainly based on the Harris-Todaro model (1970), which were merely used for homogeneous labor migration. Marjit and Kar (2005) were the first economists who took skilled and unskilled labor into consideration and investigated its impact on wage gap in the developing world as both skilled and unskilled workers emigrated. After that, some researchers just like Yabuuchi and Chaudhuri (2007), Chaudhuri and Banerjee (2010), Beladi et al. (2010), and Gupta and Dutta (2010) studied the economic effects of heterogeneous migration. However, those studies had two similarities:

- Most of them emphasized wage inequality (only Li and Zhou 2013b) and investigated the impact exerted by increasing remittance of unskilled migrants on skilled-unskilled wage inequality in labor-host region.
- They assumed that there existed skilled and unskilled labor already. That is, they rarely considered the training costs of unskilled labor.

In order to clarify the economic effects of skill training which is migrants' natural response to industrial upgrading, this paper focuses on training costs for unskilled labor. It uses Harris-Todaro model to find the economic effects of training costs and heterogeneous-labor migration in the short and long terms, respectively. There are three highlights in this paper:

- Discussion on heterogeneous-labor migration is based upon H-T model.
- We study training cost with heterogeneous-labor migration.
- Training cost indicates the cultivating process of skilled labor.

The main conclusions are decreasing training costs reduces rural employment in the short run; there is a threshold in the long term, when rural wage is lower than the value of threshold, decreasing cost will increase rural employment, and reduce industrial employment with lower urban unemployment.

The remaining parts are organized as follows: we establish a theoretical model in Sect. 12.2. Section 12.2 is theoretical analysis and conclusions are provided in Sect. 12.3.

12.2 Model

We consider a small open developing economy with three sectors, namely, urban high-tech sector with industrial upgrading (sector 1), urban traditional manufacture sector (sector 2), and rural agricultural sector (sector 3). Our model assumes that sector 1 has been established recently and is still growing in the process. The labor employed in sector 1 is skilled labor with high human-capital level. Three sectors use two producing factors: labor and capital. In order to perfect the model, we assume that

- Rural migrants move to urban region to search for jobs. They have to attend skill training before working in sector 1. However, it is not a sufficient condition: not all of trained workers can find a job in sector 1. Those who cannot will be hired by sector 2. Skilled workers do not have to worry about unemployment, since they are relatively scarce resources. Untrained migrants will work in sector 2 with the risk of unemployment. Capital sticks in separate sectors in the short term, but it moves freely in the long term.
- Wage in sector 2 is exogenous while it is elastic in both sector 1 and sector 3. In order to simplify analysis, we assume that the wage for trained labor is linear in skill level.
- Product market is perfectly competitive and all the factor endowments are exogenous.

12.2.1 Short-Run Model and Comparative Static Analysis

Model

Short run refers to particular capital stocked in different sectors. In the short term, production functions of three sectors are given by

$$X_1 = F^1\left(hL_1, \overline{K}_1\right), \tag{12.1}$$

$$X_2 = F^2\left(L_2, \overline{K}_2\right), \tag{12.2}$$

$$X_3 = F^3\left(L_3, \overline{K}_3\right). \tag{12.3}$$

Here, X_1, X_2, and X_3 refer to the productions of sector 1, sector 2, and sector 3, respectively. F^1, F^2, and F^3 are production functions marginally increasing with each factor and have strictly quasi-concave properties, subscripts to F^i denote the first or second derivative with respect to production factors indicated. L_1, L_2, and L_3 are the labor employed by each sector; $\overline{K}_i (i = 1, 2, 3)$ are the specific capital used in each sector. We normalize the efficiency of each unskilled labor. h represents the efficiency of each worker after training, h depends upon the per unit time cost of training a rural worker:

$$h = h(c),$$

where c is the per unit time cost of training per unit labor. The per unit time cost of training means that we divide the total training costs by corresponding total working hours in Sector 1 or sector 2. In accordance with the parameters established in Galor and Moav (2004), $h(\cdot)$ satisfies the conditions $h(0) = 1$, $h' > 0$, and $h'' < 0$.

With profit-maximization condition, we could obtain following equations:

$$p_1 h F_L^1(hL_1, \overline{K}_1) = h\overline{w}, \tag{12.4}$$

$$p_2 F_L^2(L_2, \overline{K}_2) = \overline{w}, \tag{12.5}$$

$$F_L^3(L_3, \overline{K}_3) = w, \tag{12.6}$$

where $\overline{w}$ is wage in sector 2 and larger than the per unit time of training cost c. Wage in sector 1 is $h\overline{w}$ and w is rural wage. We normalize the price of output of sector 3. $p_j (j = 1, 2)$ is the relative price in terms of agricultural product. In this paper, we assume that all the products are tradable and hence product prices are given internationally.

On the labor market, L^H, L_1, and L_2^H denote migrants who attend skill training, the number of trained workers in sector 1, and the number of trained workers in sector 2, separately. Let L^L and L_2^L be untrained migrants and the number of untrained workers in sector 2. Entire unemployment is L_U, and for most developing countries, $L^L > L^H$. Then

$$L^H = L_1 + L_2^H, \tag{12.7}$$

$$L^L = L_2^L + L_U, \tag{12.8}$$

$$L_2 = L_2^H + L_2^L. \tag{12.9}$$

Market-clearing condition for labor could be shown as follows:

$$L_1 + L_2 + L_3 + L_U = \overline{L}. \tag{12.10}$$

Allocating mechanisms of the trained labor and untrained labor are shown as

$$w + c = \frac{L_1}{L^H} h\overline{w} + \frac{L^H - L_1}{L^H} \overline{w}, \tag{12.11}$$

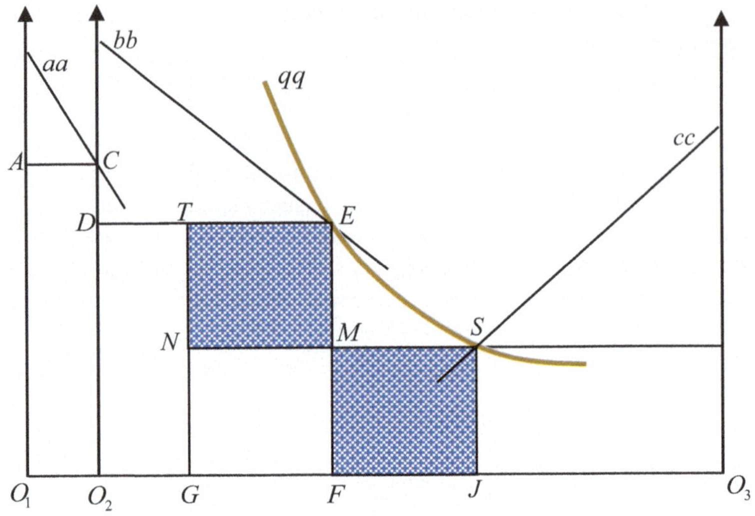

Fig. 12.2 Labor allocating mechanism

$$w = \frac{L_2 - (L^H - L_1)}{L^L}\overline{w}. \tag{12.12}$$

In Fig. 12.2, horizontal axis refers to labor endowment; the left vertical axis started from O_1 is wage in sector 1. The right vertical axis started from O_3 is wage in sector 3. Given levels of human capital in sector 1 and wage in sector 2, we set $O_1A = h\overline{w}$, and draw a line AC paralleling to horizontal axis through point A. It meets the line aa—marginal labor production in sector 1—at the point C. We draw a vertical axis (Sector 2's wage) through point C intersecting horizontal axis with point O_2 and have $O_1O_2 = L_1$. Assuming $O_2D = \overline{w}$, we draw a line DE paralleling to horizontal axis through point D and meeting the line bb—marginal labor production in sector 2—at the point E. Draw a line through point E vertical to line O_1O_3 and meet it at the point F. Then we have $O_2F = L_2$. Find a point G on the left vertical axis which satisfies $O_2G = L^H - L_1$. Draw a line through point G vertical to line O_1O_3 and intersecting lines DE at the point T. Finally, we draw a hyperbolic curve qq through point E, intersecting sector 3's marginal labor production line cc at point S. Draw a line through point S paralleling to line O_1O_3 and meet the right vertical axis at point I, which intersects lines FE at the point M, and lines TG at the point N, which has $O_3I = w_3$. We draw a line through point S vertical to line O_1O_3 and meet it at the point J. In other words, the hyperbolic curve qq indicates labor allocating mechanism of Eqs. (12.11) and (12.12), then we have $O_3J = L_3$ and $FJ = L_U$, and $S_{TEMN} = S_{MSJF}$.

Comparative Static Analysis

Totally differentiating Eqs. (12.4)–(12.12), we can get $\frac{\mathrm{d}L_1}{\mathrm{d}c} = -\frac{L_1}{c} S_{hc} < 0$, and $\frac{\mathrm{d}L_2}{\mathrm{d}c} = 0$, where $S_{hc} = \frac{\mathrm{d}h}{\mathrm{d}c}\frac{c}{h}$ is the elasticity of cost to efficiency. Therefore, we can have the following equation:

$$\begin{pmatrix} 0 & F_{LL}^3 & -1 \\ w + c - \overline{w} & 0 & L^H \\ \overline{w} - w & -w & L^L \end{pmatrix} \begin{pmatrix} \mathrm{d}L^H \\ \mathrm{d}L_3 \\ \mathrm{d}w \end{pmatrix} = \begin{pmatrix} 0 \\ A \\ B \end{pmatrix} \mathrm{d}c, \tag{12.13}$$

where $A = \frac{L_1 \overline{w} S_{hc} - cL^H}{c}$, $B = -\frac{\overline{w} L_1 S_{hc}}{c} < 0$. Let Δ_1 be the determinant of coefficient matrix, we have

$$\Delta_1 = F_{LL}^3 L^H (\overline{w} - w) - F_{LL}^3 L^L (w + c - \overline{w}) + w(w + c - \overline{w}).$$

To simplify calculation, we assume that.

Assumption 1 Per capita training cost for migrants satisfies $c > (\overline{w} - w)\left(1 + \frac{L^L}{L_3 + L^L}\right)$.

Assumption 2 The elasticity of cost to efficiency satisfies $S_{hc} > \frac{cL^H}{\overline{w} L_1}$.

According to Assumption 1, we have $\Delta_1 > 0$ (more details can be found in Appendix). Moreover, based on Cramer's rule and Assumption 2, solve Eq. (12.13) to obtain $\frac{\mathrm{d}w}{\mathrm{d}c} < 0$, $\frac{\mathrm{d}L_3}{\mathrm{d}c} > 0$, and $\frac{\mathrm{d}L^H}{\mathrm{d}c} > 0$. Summarize those results above in Table 12.1:

According to these results, we have Proposition 1:

Proposition 1 *Decreasing training cost does not affect labor usage in sector 2, while sector 1 will hire more workers in respond to lower training cost; with* Assumption 1 and 2, *migrants are unwilling to attend skill training when facing lower training cost; sector 3 hires fewer workers with increasing wage.*

In the short run, labor usage in sector 2 is only related to sectional wage, while unaffected by training cost which is essential for sector 1. In other words, different training cost does not affect its employment. However, it is not the whole story. With lower training cost, human capital decreases either. It has negative effects on the

Table 12.1 Calculating results

	$\mathrm{d}L_1$	$\mathrm{d}L_2$	$\mathrm{d}L_3$	$\mathrm{d}L_U$	$\mathrm{d}L^H$	$\mathrm{d}w$
dc	–	0	+	/	+	–

Note: '–' and '+' mean that the changes of exogenous variables in the vertical column will make the endogenous ones in the horizontal column change in the opposed and same directions, respectively; '/' means that we cannot determine the impact of exogenous variables in the vertical column on endogenous ones in the horizontal column

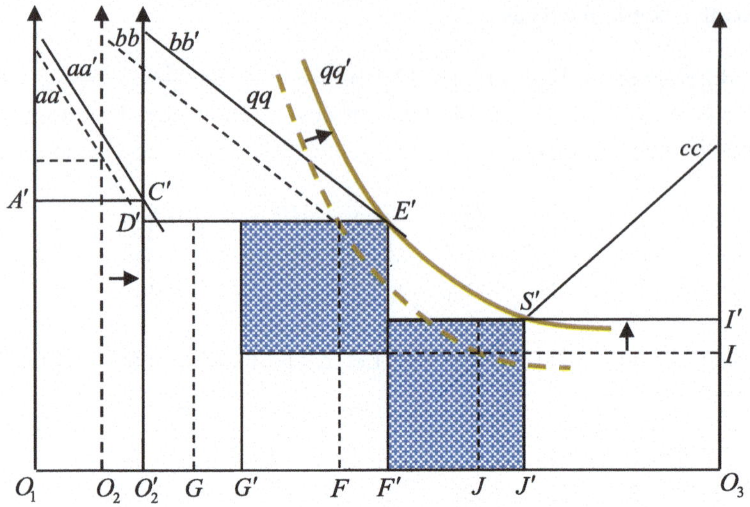

Fig. 12.3 Effects of decreasing training cost on labor market

working efficiency in sector 1. As a profit-maximizing firm, they would use more workers to offset this side effects. Moreover, it is riskier for rural labor to attend training, because some of them cannot find a position in sector 1, and then sector 2 turns out to be their final choice. Therefore, they treat sector 1's wage $h\overline{w}$ as an important signal: once it decreases, they will be more unlikely to learn additional skills. In order to meet the higher requirements in sector 1, it hires more workers. Combined with constant labor usage in sector 2, it results in more unskilled migrants entering in sector 2. Therefore, sector 3 hires fewer workers with increasing wage.

The effects of decreasing training cost on labor market are indicated in Fig. 12.3: the two lines aa and bb shift leftward to aa' and bb', respectively, decreasing training cost will move curve qq upward to curve qq', and intersect curve cc at the point S'. Then rural wage increases from O_3I to O_3I' and rural employment decreases from O_3J to O_3J'. Curve bb' meets line $D'E'$ at the point E'. Labor usage in sector 2 is constant, and $O_2F = O_2'F'$. Sector 1 hires O_1O_2' workers with new wage: O_1A'. Unemployment changes from FJ to $F'J'$.

12.2.2 Long-Term Model and Comparative Static Analysis

Long term means that each input adjusts without obstacles among three sectors. Sectional production functions turn into

$$X_1 = F^1(hL_1, K_1), \tag{12.14}$$

$$X_2 = F^2(L_2, K_2), \tag{12.15}$$

$$X_3 = F^3(L_3, K_3), \tag{12.16}$$

where F^1, F^2, and F^3 are production functions marginally increasing with each factor and have strictly quasi-concave properties. F^2 and F^3 are homogeneous of degree one. L_1, L_2, and L_3 are the labor employed by each sector. K_i (i = 1, 2, 3) refers to capital employed in each sector and they move freely in the long term.

The profit-maximization condition yields

$$p_1 h F_L^1(hL_1, K_1) = h\overline{w}, \tag{12.17}$$

$$p_1 F_K^1(hL_1, K_1) = r, \tag{12.18}$$

$$p_2 F_L^2(L_2, K_2) = \overline{w}, \tag{12.19}$$

$$p_2 F_K^2(L_2, K_2) = r, \tag{12.20}$$

$$F_L^3(L_3, K_3) = w, \tag{12.21}$$

$$F_K^3(L_3, K_3) = r, \tag{12.22}$$

where r is interest rate.

The market-clearing condition for capital could be shown as follows:

$$K_1 + K_2 + K_3 = K. \tag{12.23}$$

Equations (12.7)–(12.12) for labor market still hold. Therefore, we have established long-term model.

Entirely differentiating Eqs. (12.19) and (12.20) and using these relationships in the calculation of joint Eqs. (12.17) and (12.18), we have

$$\frac{dK_1}{dh} = 0, \quad \frac{dL_1}{dh} = -\frac{L_1}{h}, \quad \frac{dK_1}{dc} = 0, \quad \frac{dL_1}{dc} = -\frac{L_1}{h}\frac{dh}{dc} < 0.$$

Notice that

$$\frac{dX_1}{dc} = hF_L^1\frac{dL_1}{dc} + F_K^1\frac{dK_1}{dc} + h'L_1F_L^1 = 0.$$

In sum, we can conclude that: in the long term, decreasing training cost will not affect capital usage in sector 1, while it will increase labor usage in sector 1 and keep its production constant. Lower training cost will have negative effects on training quality; thus, it can reduce working efficiency for labor. As a result, it is necessary for sector 1 to increase labor employment without hurting production.

Next, we begin to analyze the effects of decreasing training cost on sector 2 and sector 3. Entirely differentiating Eqs. (12.7)–(12.12) and (12.19)–(12.23), we have

$$\begin{pmatrix} p_2F_{LL}^2 & 0 & 0 & p_2F_{LK}^2 & 0 & 0 & 0 \\ p_2F_{KL}^2 & 0 & 0 & p_2F_{KK}^2 & 0 & 0 & -1 \\ 0 & F_{LL}^3 & 0 & 0 & F_{LK}^3 & -1 & 0 \\ 0 & F_{KL}^3 & 0 & 0 & F_{KK}^3 & 0 & -1 \\ 0 & 0 & 0 & 1 & 1 & 0 & 0 \\ 0 & 0 & w+c-\overline{w} & 0 & 0 & L^H & 0 \\ \overline{w} & w & w-\overline{w} & 0 & 0 & -L^L & 0 \end{pmatrix} \begin{pmatrix} dL_2 \\ dL_3 \\ dL^H \\ dK_2 \\ dK_3 \\ dw \\ dr \end{pmatrix} = \begin{pmatrix} 0 \\ 0 \\ 0 \\ 0 \\ 0 \\ \dfrac{\overline{w}L_1S_{hc}}{c} - L^H \\ \dfrac{\overline{w}L_1S_{hc}}{c} \end{pmatrix} dc. \tag{12.24}$$

Denote the determinant of coefficient matrix of Eq. (12.24) as Δ_2, then we have

$$\Delta_2 = \frac{P_2F_{LK}^2F_{KL}^3}{k_3}(w+c-\overline{w})(k_3\overline{w}-k_2w),$$

where $k_i = K_i/L_i(i{=}2{,}3)$, which is the per capita capital in ith sector. In the following analysis, we need to clarify the symbol of $\overline{w}k_3 - wk_2$, which is equal to $(\overline{w}L_2/K_2) - (wL_3/K_3)$. Generally, it is common to have $\overline{w}k_3 - wk_2 > 0$, since many developing countries have less developed agriculture, and labor income per unit of capital in industrial sectors is usually higher than that in agriculture (i.e., $(\overline{w}L_2/K_2) - (wL_3/K_3) > 0$). However, it is also possible to have $\overline{w}k_3 - wk_2 < 0$ when they begin to modernize agriculture in developing countries. Therefore, we should consider these two cases separately when study further on our models.

- When $\overline{w}k_3 - wk_2 > 0$, we have $\Delta_2 > 0$. With Cramer's rule, we can solve Eq. (12.24):

$$\frac{dL_2}{dc} = \frac{P_2F_{LK}^2F_{LK}^3[\overline{w}L_1S_{hc} - (\overline{w}-w)L^H]}{\Delta_2},$$

Where, according to Assumption 2, we have

$$\frac{dL_2}{dc} > 0, \quad \frac{dL_3}{dc} = -\frac{k_2}{k_3}\frac{dL_2}{dc} < 0, \quad \frac{dK_2}{dc} = \frac{K_2}{L_2}\frac{dL_2}{dc} > 0, \quad \frac{dK_3}{dc} = \frac{K_3}{L_3}\frac{dL_3}{dc} < 0,$$

$$\frac{dX_2}{dc} = F_L^2\frac{dL_2}{dc} + F_K^2\frac{dK_2}{dc} > 0, \quad \frac{dX_3}{dc} = F_L^3\frac{dL_3}{dc} + F_K^2\frac{dK_3}{dc} < 0,$$

$$\frac{dL^H}{dc} = \frac{(\overline{w}L_1S_{hc} - cL^H)}{c(w + c - \overline{w})} > 0, \quad \frac{dw}{dc} = 0, \quad \frac{dr}{dc} = 0, \quad \frac{dL_U}{dc} = -\frac{dL_1}{dc} - \left(1 - \frac{k_2}{k_3}\right) \times \frac{dL_2}{dc} > 0.$$

- When $\overline{w}k_3 - wk_2 < 0$, we get $\Delta_2 < 0$. We use the Cramer's rule and Assumption 2 to solve Eq. (12.24) and get

$$\frac{dL_2}{dc} < 0, \quad \frac{dL_3}{dc} > 0, \quad \frac{dK_2}{dc} < 0, \quad \frac{dK_3}{dc} > 0, \quad \frac{dX_2}{dc} < 0, \quad \frac{dX_3}{dc} > 0, \quad \frac{dL^H}{dc} > 0, \quad \frac{dw}{dc} = 0, \quad \frac{dr}{dc} = 0.$$

We should notice that, similar with short-run case, lower training cost will decrease wage in sector 1. It is less attractive for migrants. Therefore, fewer migrants are willing to attend skill training. However, much different from short run, rural wage and interest rate are not affected by training cost in the long run. For rural wage, it is because per capita capital k_3 in rural sector does not change when capital moves freely in the long term. The latter result is due to constant per capita capital k_2 in industrial sector, which is the only factor that affect long-term interest rate. If we let $\lambda = k_3/k_2$, for rural wage w, there exists a threshold $\lambda\overline{w}$in the long term. Its value has large impacts on endogenous variants L_2, L_3, K_2, K_3, L_u, X_2, and X_3. Conclusively, we can have Table 12.2.

As a result, we could have the following proposition:

Proposition 2 *If rural wage $w < \lambda\overline{w}$ holds, decreasing training cost will reduce both labor and capital usages with lower production in sector 2; urban unemployment decreases; sector 3 will hire more labor and capital with higher production.*

Rural wage $w < \lambda\overline{w}$ means sector 3 is less developed. Migrants will care more about the risk associated with training cost. Therefore, they are more willing to work

Table 12.2 Calculations of Eq. (12.24)

	dL_2	dL_3	dK_2	dK_3	dL_U	dX_2	dX_3
dc $w < \lambda\overline{w}$	+	–	+	–	+	+	–
dc $w > \lambda\overline{w}$	–	+	–	+	/	–	+

Note: The meanings of the signs are the same as those in Table 12.1

in sector 3 without training requirements. On the other hand, sector 1 demands more labor and other inputs, which results in less labor and capital usages with less output in sector 2. When rural wage is higher than the value of threshold, that is, $w > \lambda\overline{w}$, different from Proposition 2, we can obtain Proposition 3:

Proposition 3 *If rural wage* $w > \lambda\overline{w}$*, decreasing training cost will increase labor and capital usages in sector 2 with more output; sector 3 will hire less labor and capital with less production.*

For sector 1 with industrial upgrading, no matter which process it is in at present, decreasing training cost will reduce its employment. Because lower cost will definitely result in decreasing effective productivity for labor associated with lower high-technic wage. Then it will demand more workers. However, comparing Propositions 1, 2, and 3, it is totally different between long terms and short terms when considering the economic effects of decreasing training costs on urban unemployment and rural economy.

12.3 Conclusion

It is the case for many developing countries that industrial upgrading is one of the most significant paths for economic development. Thus, migrant's training is an inevitable problem in this process. It is not only for theoretical purposes but also for essentially empirical researches to take sectoral migration of heterogeneous labor with industrial upgrading into consideration. This paper uses H-T migration model to analyze economic effects of training costs. It includes two kinds of labor migration: trained workers and untrained ones, which are rarely discussed in previous literature. We have two conclusions which are

- Decreasing training cost can reduce rural employment in the short term.
- There exists a threshold in the long term: when rural wage is lower than the value of threshold, decreasing training cost will increase rural labor usage, reduce industrial employment and unemployment rate.

Since its economic meaning is quite coherent and perspicuous, this threshold can be used as reference for relevant departments when work on policies in practical fields.

Competing Interests

Funding This work was supported by the Humanities and Social Sciences of the Ministry of Education, China, Project No. 17JJD630002 and the Strategy Consultation on the Double Leads in Jiangsu Province, China, Project No. 17SSL074.

Disclosure Statement No potential conflict of interest was reported by the authors.

Appendix

If $c > (\overline{w} - w)\left(1 + \frac{L^L}{L_1 + L^L}\right)$, considering the elasticity of labor wages S_{Lw}^3 in sector 3, generally $S_{Lw}^3 < 0$ and $\left|S_{Lw}^3\right| \leq 1$, so we have $1 + \frac{L^L}{L_3 + L^L} > \frac{1 - 2S_{Lw}^3 \frac{L^L}{L_3}}{1 - S_{Lw}^3 \frac{L^L}{L_3}} = \frac{w - 2F_{LL}^3 L^L}{w - F_{LL}^3 L^L}$. For most developing countries, the number of untrained workers is greater than trained workers, so $L^L > L^H$, and we have $\frac{w - 2F_{LL}^3 L^L}{w - F_{LL}^3 L^L} > \frac{w - F_{LL}^3 L^L - F_{LL}^3 L^H}{w - F_{LL}^3 L^L}$, Finally we get $\Delta_1 > 0$.

References

Beladi H, Chakrabarti A, Marjit S (2010) Skilled-unskilled wage inequality and urban unemployment. Econ Inq 48(4):997–1007

Chaudhuri S, Banerjee D (2010) Foreign capital inflow, skilled–unskilled wage inequality and unemployment of unskilled labour in a fair wage model. Econ Model 27(1):477–486

Galor O, Moav O (2004) From physical to human capital accumulation: inequality and the process of development. Rev Econ Stud 71(4):1001–1026. https://doi.org/10.1111/0034-6527.00312

Gupta MR, Dutta PB (2010) Skilled–unskilled wage inequality: a general equilibrium analysis. Res Econ 64(4):247–263

Harris JR, Todaro MP (1970) Migration, unemployment and development: a two-sector analysis. Am Econ Rev 60:126–142

Li X, Qian X (2011) Economic analysis on the urban-rural disparity in human capital in China. South Afr J Econ 79(2):146–160

Li X, Zhou Y (2013a) Development policies, transfer of pollution abatement technology and trans-boundary pollution. Econ Model 31:183–188

Li X, Zhou Y (2013b) An economic analysis of remittance of unskilled migration on skilled-unskilled wage inequality in labor host region. Econ Model 33:428–432

Marjit S, Kar S (2005) Emigration and wage inequality. Econ Lett 88:141–145

Wang L (2011) The contribution of vocational education to regional economic growth—an empirical analysis based on cross-province panel data. J Cent Univ Finance Econ 8:80–85. (in Chinese) https://kns.cnki.net/kcms2/article/abstract?v=eoCTaIZmBONvEzLPhUHMTnNEi0r9vpsIVGJ8IFk9NA01qgqZ-MXsVVg0Cs6ijX0dASqo1pvCrHhmT1u1QnHOTlL0lVT8ozgZWKf1eFB4uwlV157dn8eRwHrefRtJ5bqE&uniplatform=NZKPT&language=CHS

Yabuuchi S, Chaudhuri S (2007) International migration of labour and skilled–unskilled wage inequality in a developing economy. Econ Model 24(1):128–137

Chapter 13
Rural-Urban Migrants' Remittances and Wage Inequality: Evidence from China

Abstract There is a link between rural-urban remittances and wage inequality. However, the existing literature sheds little light on this topic. In this study, we establish a three-sector general-equilibrium model to investigate the effects of rural-urban migrants' remittances on wage inequality. Further, we use Chinese macroeconomic data to calibrate the parameters and conduct analysis with numerical simulation. We find that, when rural-urban migrants raise their remittance rate, wage inequality between skilled labor and the urban formal sector remains unchanged in the sector-specific capital case but narrows in the sector-mobile capital case. Moreover, in the sector-specific case, skilled and unskilled wage inequalities, w_{SY} and w_{SZ}, decrease at the same rate as the urban-rural wage inequalities, w_{XY} and w_{XZ}, respectively. In the mobile case, however, the former declines faster than the latter.

Keywords Endogenous remittance · Externality · Developing country · Rural-urban migration · Wage inequality

13.1 Introduction

"Rural-urban migrants' remittances" refers to the portion of income that rural-urban migrants earn in urban areas and transfer to rural areas in developing countries. To support their family still living in a rural area, rural-urban migrants either travel in person or entrust friends to physically carry part of their income to their family. In this study, all funds from rural-urban migrants transferred back to rural areas constitute their remittances. The rural-urban migrants' remittances are income transfers within one economy, which differentiates it from external or international remittances. There is a massive number of rural-urban migrants in developing countries. For example, in China, there were 281.71 million rural-urban migrants in 2016 according to National Bureau of Statistics of China (2017a). Along with economic development and people's increasing incomes, rural-urban migrants' remittances are increasing yearly. In the numerical simulation conducted in this study, the volume of rural-urban migrants' remittances within China in 2016 was estimated as being US$367,414 million, accounting for 3.3% of China's gross

X. Li, Y. Wu, *Research on Characteristic Issues in Current Developing Economies*, New Frontiers in Regional Science: Asian Perspectives 80,
https://doi.org/10.1007/978-981-97-7284-1_13

domestic product (GDP) and roughly twice the GDP of New Zealand in the same year. Thus, rural-urban migrants' remittances are significant for the development of rural areas in developing countries.

Recently, the literature on migrant remittances has become richer and more diverse. They mainly consider the economic impacts of remittances on rural income distribution, agricultural production, the development of the rural economy, and some macroeconomic elements, such as the current exchange rate. Such studies have included those by Lundahl (1985), Taylor and Wyatt (1996), Quibria (1997), Djajic (1998), Pradhan et al. (2008), and Ball et al. (2013), but they focus on international remittances. Li and Zhou (2013), Li and Wang (2015), and Li and Zhou (2015) investigate the rural-urban migrants' remittances, but Li and Zhou (2013) do not consider the rural sector, Li and Wang (2015) do not consider skilled labor, and Li and Zhou (2015) focus on the environment. In addition, Li and Wang (2015) treat the number of remittances as an exogenous variable. However, the remittance volume is determined for the whole economy, including the amount of labor migration, consumption, and rural income.

Moreover, researchers who studied wage inequality did not consider remittances. For example, Beladi et al. (2008) analyze the influence of the liquidity of international elements on wage inequality in a dual economy. Chaudhuri and Yabuuchi (2007) study the impact of the economic system on wage inequality and find that when the degree of economic liberalization is higher, the wage gap becomes greater. Wang (2019) investigates the impacts of environmental protection policies and a rise in the self-mitigation cost of skilled and unskilled labor on wage inequality. Some researchers demonstrate the impacts of technological innovation in developing countries on wage inequality, such as Kar and Beladi (2004), Moore and Ranjan (2005), Fang et al. (2008). Das (2002) and Chaudhuri and Banerjee (2010) research the impacts of foreign direct investment on wage inequality.

Few studies consider the effects of remittances on income distribution from both sides of migration—the labor-outsourcing and labor host regions. The above studies consider either the impacts of international remittances in the labor-outsourcing country (i.e., a developing country) or the impacts of rural-urban migrants' remittances from an urban area (labor host region). However, rural-urban migrants' remittances are greatly helpful in improving the production environment of rural areas and raising rural productivity (Rozelle et al. 1999). As a result, on one hand, they influence the income of rural areas, but on the other hand, they cause input factors to flow into rural areas, which in turn affects the urban economy and then influences the income of urban laborers, including skilled laborers. Therefore, the effect of rural-urban migrants' remittances on wage inequality is not clear.

To deal with this topic, the present study establishes a three-sector general-equilibrium model with the characteristics of a developing country. We consider two cases: one where capital was sector-specific and the other where capital was mobile between sectors. Then, the paper examines the effects of an increase in the rural-urban migrants' remittance rate on wage inequality. Finally, we use Chinese macroeconomic data to calibrate the parameters and conduct a numerical simulation.[1] The chapter is organized as follows. In Sect. 13.2, we set up the theoretical model. Sections 13.3 and 13.4 deal with the sector-specific capital case and the mobile capital case, respectively. In Sect. 13.5, we present analyses by numerical simulation, and we present a conclusion in Sect. 13.6.

13.2 Theoretical Model

Consider a small, open, developing country consisting of three sectors: an urban formal sector, an urban informal sector, and a rural sector, denoted by the indices X, Y, and Z, respectively. The economy uses labor and capital as production factors, and they do not move internationally. Labor is divided into skilled labor and unskilled labor. Because the rate of education is lower in rural areas than in urban areas in developing countries, the human-capital level of urban laborers is higher than that of rural laborers. Therefore, it should simply be assumed that the urban laborers are skilled but that rural laborers are unskilled. Rural-urban migrants can find jobs in sector X or sector Y as unskilled laborers. The urban informal sector depends only on those migrants who do not have jobs in sector Y.[2] Further, as mentioned, the rural-urban migrants' remittances will raise the production of sector Z.

Under the condition that the market is perfectly competitive, we could obtain the following:

$$p_X = a_{SX}w_S + a_{LX}\overline{w}_X + a_{KX}r_X, \tag{13.1}$$

$$p_Y = a_{LY}w_Y, \tag{13.2}$$

$$1 = \frac{a_{LZ}}{g(k)}w_Z + \frac{a_{KZ}}{g(k)}r_Z, \tag{13.3}$$

where a_{ij} ($i = S, L, K; j = X, Y, Z$) represents the factor i used in producing a unit product in sector j without considering rural-urban migrants' remittances k in the economy.[3] The function $g(k)$ expresses the positive externality generated by k on rural production, with the properties $g \geq 1$, $g' > 0$, and $g'' < 0$. r_X and r_Z are the interest rates of capital in sector X and sector Z, respectively. w_S is the wage rate of skilled labor used in sector X. Generally, the developing countries lack skilled laborers, so we assume that skilled laborers could be fully employed in sector X. Thus, w_S is flexible. $\overline{w}_X$ is the wage rate of unskilled labor in sector X, which is downwardly rigid due to some political and institutional considerations. w_Y and w_Z

[1] Because China has the largest population of rural-urban migrants in the world, conducting a numerical simulation of migrant remittances using China's data is regarded as representative of conditions in other countries.

[2] See, for example, Chatterjee and Turnovsky (2018), who discussed the informal sector in detail.

[3] Because the market is perfectly competitive, a_{L2} is constant.

are the wage rates in sector Y and sector Z, respectively, which are both flexible. Suppose that rural goods are exported and serve as *numeraire*, so that their price equals unity, while the urban formal goods are importable goods with a fixed world price, p_X; the urban informal goods are non-traded goods, and their price, p_Y, is determined endogenously in the domestic market.

It is supposed that goods and services produced by sector Y can only be provided to urban residents. Thus, the equilibrium condition of the urban informal market is shown as:

$$p_Y Y = \phi(p_X X + p_Y Y - k). \tag{13.4}$$

Here, ϕ $(0 < \phi < 1)$ is the proportion of their budget that people in urban areas spend on urban informal products and X and Y are the outputs in sector X and sector Y, respectively.

Skilled labor is fully employed, and unskilled labor moves freely between sectors. Thus, the market-clearing condition of skilled labor and unskilled labor could be shown as follows:

$$a_{SX}X = S, \tag{13.5}$$

$$a_{LX}X + a_{LY}Y + \frac{a_{LZ}}{g(k)}Z = L, \tag{13.6}$$

where Z is the output in sector Z and S and L represent the endowments of skilled labor and unskilled labor, respectively, in the entire economy.

According to Harris and Todaro (1970), rural labor moves to urban regions until the expected urban wage equals the actual rural wage. Thus, the unskilled labor allocation mechanism between sectors can be shown as follows:

$$\begin{aligned} &\frac{a_{LX}X}{a_{LX}X + a_{LY}Y}\overline{w}_X + \frac{a_{LY}Y}{a_{LX}X + a_{LY}Y}w_Y = w_Z \\ &\Leftrightarrow (w_Z - w_Y)a_{LY}Y = (\overline{w}_X - w_Z)a_{LX}X \end{aligned} . \tag{13.7}$$

Then, we obtain three types of skilled-unskilled wage inequality: (a) wage inequality between skilled labor and sector X, $w_{SX} = w_S – \overline{w}_X$; (b) wage inequality between skilled labor and sector Y, $w_{SY} = w_S - w_Y$; and (c) wage inequality between skilled labor and sector Z, $w_{SZ} = w_S - w_Z$. Similarly, we obtain three types of urban-rural wage inequality: (a) wage inequality between sector X and sector Y, $w_{XY} = \overline{w}_X – w_Y$; (b) wage inequality between sector X and sector Z, $w_{XZ} = \overline{w}_X – w_Z$; and (c) wage inequality between sector Y and sector Z, $w_{ZY} = w_Z - w_Y$.

According to Eq. (13.7), w_Y is even lower than w_Z; thus, we assume that laborers' income in sector Y can only meet their basic living needs, and no surplus is repatriated in the form of rural subsidies. However, rural-urban migrants employed in sector X will remit part of their wages to their rural homes, and then the amount of remittance transferred to rural areas is as follows:[4]

$$k = \theta \overline{w}_X a_{LX} X, \tag{13.8}$$

where θ $(0 \leq \theta \leq 1)$ is the remittance-wage ratio of rural-urban migrants in sector X (hereafter called the "remittance rate").

13.3 Sector-Specific Capital Case

In this section, we consider the case where capital is specific to a sector and cannot move between sectors. In this case, K_X and K_Z are fixed as the capital employed in sector X and sector Z, respectively. Then the capital market-clearing condition is as follows:

$$a_{KX} X = K_X, \tag{13.9}$$

$$\frac{a_{KZ}}{g(k)} Z = K_Z. \tag{13.10}$$

In particular, from Eqs. (13.1), (13.5), and (13.9), we can discern that X, w_S, and r_X will be unaffected by θ. This is to say, the production and factor inputs of sector X are not affected. Therefore, rural-urban migrants' remittances, k, increase on the same scale as the remittance rate, θ, does (Eq. 13.8). The complete differentiation of Eqs. (13.2), (13.3), (13.4), (13.6), (13.7), and (13.10) can be reorganized as follows:[5]

$$\begin{bmatrix} a & -(a+b) \\ \lambda_{LY} c & -\lambda_{LY}(a+b) - \lambda_{LZ} d \end{bmatrix} \begin{bmatrix} \widehat{w}_Y \\ \widehat{w}_Z \end{bmatrix} = \begin{bmatrix} -e \\ -\varepsilon \lambda_{LZ} d \end{bmatrix} \widehat{\theta}, \tag{13.11}$$

where $a = w_Z/(w_Z - w_Y) > 0$, $b = w_Z/(\overline{w}_X - w_Z) > 0$, $c = w_Y/(w_Z - w_Y) > 0$, $d = \left(\varepsilon_{KL}^Z + \varepsilon_{LK}^Z\right)/\theta_{KZ} > 0$, $e = k/(p_X X - k) > 0$,[6] $\varepsilon = g' k/g > 0$, $\lambda_{LY} = a_{LY} Y/L$, $\lambda_{LZ} = a_{LZ} Z/gL$, $\theta_{KZ} = r_Z a_{KZ}/g$, $\varepsilon_{KL}^Z = (\partial a_{KZ}/\partial w_Z)(w_Z/a_{KZ}) > 0$, and $\varepsilon_{LK}^Z = (\partial a_{LZ}/\partial r_Z)(r_Z/a_{LZ}) > 0$. By denoting Δ_1 as the determinant of the coefficient matrix in Eq. (13.11), we have

---

[4] We do not consider the transaction costs of currency transfers. In fact, rural-urban migrants usually send money through unofficial channels that rarely involve remittance costs.

[5] Detailed derivation is presented in Appendix 1.

[6] Note that e denotes the ratio of rural-urban migrants' remittances to disposable income (total income minus the remittance) in sector X. Because most developing countries suffer from uneven development and increasing income disparities between rural and urban areas, the amount of rural-urban migrants' remittances is huge but the value of e is still small.

Table 13.1 Effect of an increase in θ on wage inequality for the capital-specific case

Variable	Sign
$\widehat{w}_{SX}/\widehat{\theta}$	0
$\widehat{w}_{SY}/\widehat{\theta}$	−
$\widehat{w}_{SZ}/\widehat{\theta}$	−
$\widehat{w}_{XY}/\widehat{\theta}$	−
$\widehat{w}_{XZ}/\widehat{\theta}$	−
$\widehat{w}_{ZY}/\widehat{\theta}$	\
$\widehat{w}_{SY}/\widehat{\theta}-\widehat{w}_{XY}/\widehat{\theta}$	0
$\widehat{w}_{SZ}/\widehat{\theta}-\widehat{w}_{XZ}/\widehat{\theta}$	0

Note: $\widehat{w}_{ZY}/\widehat{\theta}=\{\varepsilon\lambda_{LZ}d[(a+b)c-a^2]-ce(\lambda_{LZ}d+\lambda_{LY}b)\}/\Delta_1$, its sign is ambiguous

Source: Authors' own elaboration

$$\Delta_1=-\lambda_{LY}(a+b)-\lambda_{LZ}ad<0.$$

According to the definition of e, we might assume it satisfies $e<\lambda_{LZ}d(a+b)\varepsilon/[\lambda_{LZ}d+\lambda_{LY}(a+b)]$. By solving Eq. (13.11) with Cramer's rule, we can obtain the following:

$$\frac{\widehat{w}_Y}{\widehat{\theta}}=\frac{\lambda_{LZ}ed+\lambda_{LY}(a+b)e-\varepsilon\lambda_{LZ}(a+b)d}{\Delta_1}>0, \tag{13.12}$$

$$\frac{\widehat{w}_Z}{\widehat{\theta}}=\frac{\lambda_{LY}ce-\varepsilon\lambda_{LZ}da}{\Delta_1}>0. \tag{13.13}$$

An increase in θ also increases w_Y and w_Z. To specify this mechanism, note that increasing the remittance rate (or the amount of rural-urban migrants' remittances) raises labor productivity in rural areas through the purchase of machines, equipment, and fertilizer needed for rural production. Thus, w_Z increases, thereby attracting some laborers in sector Y to return to rural areas. This produces a higher w_Y.

Turning to wage inequality, we consider the impact of the remittance rate on wage inequality. The results are reported in Table 13.1.

In accordance with Table 13.1, we present Propositions 1 and 2.

Proposition 1 *Consider a small, open country where capital is immobile between sectors. When rural-urban migrants raise their remittance rate, it will not affect wage inequality between skilled labor and the urban formal sector,* w_{SX}*, but it will generate the following impacts on other skilled-unskilled wage inequalities:*

- *Wage inequality between skilled labor and the urban informal sector,* w_{SY}*, narrows.*
- *Wage inequality between skilled labor and the rural sector,* w_{SZ}*, narrows.*

Proposition 2 *Consider a small, open country where capital is immobile between sectors. When rural-urban migrants raise their remittance rate, it will generate the following impacts on urban-rural wage inequalities:*

- *Wage inequality between the urban formal sector and the urban informal sector,* w_{XY}*, narrows.*
- *Wage inequality between the urban formal sector and the rural sector,* w_{XZ}*, narrows.*

As for wage inequality between sector Y and sector Z, conventional wisdom regards it as a direct comparison of the change between the two wage rates (Chaudhuri and Yabuuchi 2007; Chao et al. 2016). In this study, we can calculate that$\widehat{w}_Z/\widehat{\theta} < \widehat{w}_Y/\widehat{\theta}$. However, when w_Z is much higher than w_Y, notwithstanding the fact that $\widehat{w}_Z/\widehat{\theta} < \widehat{w}_Y/\widehat{\theta}$, the increase of w_Z might be larger than the increase of w_Y, leading to a larger w_{ZY}. Therefore, we believe that the effect on w_{ZY} is ambiguous. Finally, with the unaffected w_S and exogenous $\overline{w}_X$, w_{SY} and w_{SZ} decrease by the same percent as do w_{XY} and w_{XZ}, respectively.

13.4 Mobile Capital Case

In this section, we examine the case where capital can move freely between sector X and sector Z. Then, the capital market-clearing condition becomes the following:

$$a_{KX}X + \frac{a_{KZ}}{g(k)}Z = K, \tag{13.14}$$

where K is the endowment of capital in the economy. Due to the perfectly sectoral mobility of capital, we have $r_X = r_Z = r$.

In the mobile capital case, we focus on the main difference of impacts on wage inequality from the specific capital case. The comparison of substitutions of capital and skilled labor for unskilled labor in sector X plays an important role in the following discussion. Therefore, in this section, we make the following assumption:

Assumption 1

$$\tau_{LK}^X = \tau_{LS}^X.$$

Here, $\tau_{LK}^X = \varepsilon_{LK}^X/\theta_{KX} > 0$ and $\tau_{LS}^X = \varepsilon_{LS}^X/\theta_{SX} > 0$ are the Allen-Uzawa partial elasticities of factor substitution in sector X between unskilled labor and capital, and unskilled labor and skilled-labor, respectively; $\varepsilon_{LK}^X = (\partial a_{LX}/\partial r)(r/a_{LX}) > 0$, $\varepsilon_{LS}^X = (\partial a_{LX}/\partial w_S)(w_S/a_{LX}) > 0$, $\theta_{KX} = ra_{KX}/p_X$, and $\theta_{SX} = w_S a_{SX}/p_X$. The complete differentiation of Eqs. (13.1)–(13.8) and (13.14) can be reorganized as follows:[7]

[7]Detailed derivation is presented in Appendix 1.

$$\begin{bmatrix} 0 & \theta_{LZ} & \theta_{KZ}+\varepsilon h \\ -a & a+b & 0 \\ \lambda_{LY} & \lambda_{LZ}\left(\varepsilon_{KL}^{Z}-\varepsilon_{LL}^{Z}\right) & A \end{bmatrix}\begin{bmatrix} \widehat{w}_Y \\ \widehat{w}_Z \\ \widehat{r} \end{bmatrix}=\begin{bmatrix} \varepsilon \\ e \\ -\lambda_{LY}e \end{bmatrix}\widehat{\theta}, \tag{13.15}$$

where $A=h(\lambda_{LX}+\lambda_{LY}-\lambda_{LZ}\lambda_{KX}/\lambda_{KZ})+j\lambda_{LZ}\lambda_{KX}/\lambda_{KZ}-\lambda_{LZ}\left(\varepsilon_{LK}^{X}-\varepsilon_{KK}^{X}\right)$, $h=\varepsilon_{SK}^{X}-\varepsilon_{SS}^{X}\theta_{KX}/\theta_{SX}>0$, and $j=\varepsilon_{KK}^{X}-\varepsilon_{KS}^{X}\theta_{KX}/\theta_{SX}<0$. In developing countries, relative to the rural sector Z, the urban formal sector X is generally capital-intensive, that is, $\lambda_{KX}/(\lambda_{LX}+\lambda_{LY})>\lambda_{KZ}/\lambda_{LZ}$. Therefore, we can conclude that $A<0$. We defined the determinant of the matrix in Eq. (13.15) as Δ_2 and calculated Δ_2 to obtain the following:

$$\Delta_2=-\left[a\lambda_{LZ}\left(\varepsilon_{KL}^{Z}-\varepsilon_{LL}^{Z}\right)+\lambda_{LY}(a+b)\right](\theta_{KZ}+\varepsilon h)+a\theta_{LZ}A<0.$$

Given a small enough value of $e(e<\min\{e_1,e_2\})$,[8] solving Eq. (13.15) using Cramer's rule yields the following:

$$\frac{\widehat{w}_Y}{\widehat{\theta}}=\frac{\varepsilon(a+b)A+e\left\{(\theta_{KZ}+\varepsilon h)\left[\lambda_{LZ}\left(\varepsilon_{KL}^{Z}-\varepsilon_{LL}^{Z}\right)+\lambda_{LY}(a+b)\right]-\theta_{LZ}A\right\}}{\Delta_2}>0, \tag{13.16}$$

$$\frac{\widehat{w}_Z}{\widehat{\theta}}=\frac{c\lambda_{LY}e(\theta_{KZ}+\varepsilon h)+aA\varepsilon}{\Delta_2}>0, \tag{13.17}$$

$$\frac{\widehat{r}}{\widehat{\theta}}=-\frac{a\varepsilon\lambda_{LZ}\left(\varepsilon_{KL}^{Z}-\varepsilon_{LL}^{Z}\right)+\lambda_{LY}\theta_{LZ}ec+\varepsilon(a+b)\lambda_{LY}}{\Delta_2}>0. \tag{13.18}$$

Substituting Eq. (13.16) into Eq. (13.2) results in $\widehat{p}_Y/\widehat{\theta}=\widehat{w}_Y/\widehat{\theta}>0$;[9] substituting Eq. (13.18) into Eqs. (13.1), (13.5), and (13.8) then yields $\widehat{w}S/\widehat{\theta}=-(\theta_{KX}/\theta_{SX})\widehat{r}/\widehat{\theta}<0$, $\widehat{X}/\widehat{\theta}=-h\widehat{r}/\widehat{\theta}<0$, and $\widehat{k}/\widehat{\theta}=1-h\widehat{r}/\widehat{\theta}>0$; completely differentiating Eqs. (13.4) and (13.6), one obtains $\widehat{Y}/\widehat{\theta}<0$ and $\widehat{Z}/\widehat{\theta}>0$. To specify this mechanism, note that an increase in θ also increases k, improving the production environment in sector Z. This increases the marginal productivity of factors in sector Z and then increases their prices, that is r_Z and w_Z. Because capital moves freely between sector X and sector Z, a higher r_Z attracts urban capital into sector Z. An increase in w_Z results in a reflow of labor into sector Z. As a result, sector Z expands while sector X scales back production. Thus, the wage rate of skilled labor, for a given S, decreases. Similarly, sector Y shrinks too, leading to an increase in its wage rate. As for the amount of rural-urban migrants'

[8] The exact expressions for e_1 and e_2 are as follows:
$e_1=\frac{-(a+b)A\varepsilon}{(\theta_{KZ}+\varepsilon h)\left[\lambda_{LZ}\left(\varepsilon_{KL}^{Z}-\varepsilon_{LL}^{Z}\right)+\lambda_{LY}(a+b)\right]-\theta_{LZ}A}>0$, and $e_2=-\frac{aA\varepsilon}{c\lambda_{LY}(\theta_{KZ}+\varepsilon h)}>0$.

[9] This result differs from that of Li and Wang (2015), who take rural-urban migrants' remittance as given.

Table 13.2 Effect of an increase in θ on wage inequality for the mobile capital case

Variable	Sign
$\widehat{w_{SX}}/\widehat{\theta}$	−
$\widehat{w_{SY}}/\widehat{\theta}$	−
$\widehat{w_{SZ}}/\widehat{\theta}$	−
$\widehat{w_{XY}}/\widehat{\theta}$	−
$\widehat{w_{XZ}}/\widehat{\theta}$	−
$\widehat{w_{ZY}}/\widehat{\theta}$	\
$\widehat{w_{SY}}/\widehat{\theta} - \widehat{w_{XY}}/\widehat{\theta}$	−
$\widehat{w_{SZ}}/\widehat{\theta} - \widehat{w_{XZ}}/\widehat{\theta}$	−

Note: $\widehat{w_{ZY}}/\widehat{\theta} = \{[a^2 - c(a+b)]\varepsilon A + e\{c\theta_{LZ}A - (\theta_{KZ} + \varepsilon h)[\lambda_{LZ}c(\varepsilon_{KL}^Z - \varepsilon_{LL}^Z) + \lambda_{LY}[a + a^2 - (a+b)c]]\}\}/\Delta_2$, its sign is ambiguous

Source: Author's own elaboration

remittances, note that the employment of unskilled labor in the urban formal sector decreases. This means that the amount of rural-urban migrants' remittances, in the mobile capital case increases on a smaller scale than that in the capital-specific case because $0 < \widehat{k}/\widehat{\theta} < 1$.

Turning to wage inequality, we consider the impact of the remittance rate on wage inequality, which is shown in Table 13.2.

In accordance with Table 13.2, we obtain Propositions 3 and 4.

Proposition 3 *Consider a small, open country where capital is mobile between the urban formal sector and the rural sector. When rural-urban migrants increase their remittance rate, the wage inequality between skilled labor and the urban formal sector narrows.*

Proposition 4 *Consider a small, open country where capital is mobile between the urban formal sector and the rural sector. When rural-urban migrants increase their remittance rate, each of the skilled-unskilled wage inequalities, w_{SY} and w_{SZ}, decreases by a larger percent than the urban-rural wage inequalities, w_{XY} and w_{XZ}, do separately.*

In the mobile capital case, when rural-urban migrants increase their remittance rate, w_{SY} and w_{SZ} both decrease and w_{XY} and w_{XZ} both narrow, which is the same as the effects in the capital-specific case. However, considering the rate of change in wage inequalities, there are some differences between the effects in the two cases. Proposition 3 is different from the result in Proposition 1; meanwhile, Proposition 4 is different from the results indicated in Table 13.1. These reflect that capital plays a different role in different cases. In the capital-specific case, the output level of each sector depends on its labor pool. The amount of skilled labor is given, and $\overline{w}_X$ is downwardly rigid; thus, a change in θ does not affect production of sector X. Hence, w_S remains unaltered by changes in θ. However, in the mobile capital case, capital moves freely between sectors X and Z. This may cause a new mechanism, wherein an increase in θ improves the production environment in sector Z and raises the marginal productivity of factor inputs, causing higher factor prices and so attracting a flow of factor into sector Z. Thus, sector Y shrinks, resulting in a slowdown in demand for skilled labor and then a lower wage rate. Therefore, in the mobile capital case, the wage inequalities between skilled labor and the other sectors diminish by a larger percent than those in the capital-specific case do.

13.5 Numerical Simulation Analysis

To examine whether the model presented in this paper correctly explains the impacts of rural-urban migrants' remittances on wage inequality, we use related economic data from China to calibrate the parameters of the model, and then we use the general algebraic modeling system (GAMS) to perform numerical simulations. Finally, we carry out a sensitivity analysis to test the robustness of the model's conclusions.

13.5.1 Calibration of Parameters

We set up the production functions of three sectors as a Cobb-Douglas form:

$$X = S^{\alpha_1} L_X^{\alpha_2} K_X^{\alpha_3}, \quad Y = \beta L_Y, \quad Z = g(k) L_Z^{\gamma_1} K_Z^{\gamma_2}, \tag{13.19}$$

where α_1, α_2, α_3, γ_1, and γ_2 are the respective output elasticities of the associated factors; β is the effective labor parameter in sector X; and $g(k)$ is the external effect function of remittance on rural production. According to the model, let $g(k)$ be represented as $g(k) = 1 + k^{\sigma}$, where σ is the externality parameter of rural-urban migrants' remittances on rural production.

Based on the three strata of industry in National Bureau of Statistics of China (2017b), let the primary industry be the rural sector Z and the secondary and tertiary industries be the urban formal sector X. As for the urban informal sector Y, we define labor employed in sector Y as including both the economically active population excluding employed persons, as well as rural-urban migrants who provide hotel and catering services, services to households, repair services, and other services. Turning to rural-urban migrants' remittances, according to National Bureau of Statistics of China (2017a), the total number of rural-urban migrants in China was about 281.71 million, and their average monthly wage was about US$487.23. According to some Chinese survey data,[10] we can calculate that the rural-urban migrants' remittances were about US$363,414 million. As for the interest rate, it was calculated as being 6.9% according to the benchmark 1-to-5-year lending rate announced by China's

[10]For details, see Appendix 2.

Table 13.3 Calibration of parameter values to Chinese data

Parameter	Description	Calibration value
α_1	Share of skilled labor in urban formal sector	0.131
α_2	Share of unskilled labor in urban formal sector	0.304
β	Effective parameter of labor in urban formal sector	1.441
γ_1	Share of unskilled labor in rural sector	0.442
σ	Externality parameter of rural-urban migrants' remittances on rural production	0.209
θ	Remittance rate	0.118
ϕ	Proportion of their budget for labor in urban sectors spend on urban informal products	0.009

Source: Authors' own elaboration

central bank in 2016. Generally, in developing countries, the interest rate in the rural sector is higher than that of other sectors, which is 10.35% (=1.5 × 6.9%).

We used the economic data described above to calibrate the parameters. The results are summarized in Table 13.3.[11]

13.5.2 Numerical Simulation

Based on the parameter calibration, we conducted a numerical simulation to test whether the conclusions of the model with realistic economic data are consistent with the results of comparative static analysis.

Numerical Simulation for the Capital-Specific Case

The numerical simulation results for the capital-specific case are shown in Fig. 13.1. According to Fig. 13.1, as the remittance rate, θ, increases, the wage rate of skilled labor, w_S, remains unchanged, but the wage rates in sector Y and Z, w_Y and w_Z, both increase. Therefore, w_{SX} remains unchanged, but the skilled-unskilled wage inequalities, w_{SY} and w_{SZ}, both decrease and the urban-rural wage inequalities, w_{XY} and w_{XZ}, both decrease as well. This is consistent with the numerical characteristics of Propositions 1 and 2.

Numerical Simulation for the Mobile Capital Case

The numerical simulation results for the mobile capital case are shown in Fig. 13.2. According to Fig. 13.2, as θ increases, w_{SX} decreases, which is consistent with the

[11] The process of parameters calibration is discussed in greater detail in Appendix 2.

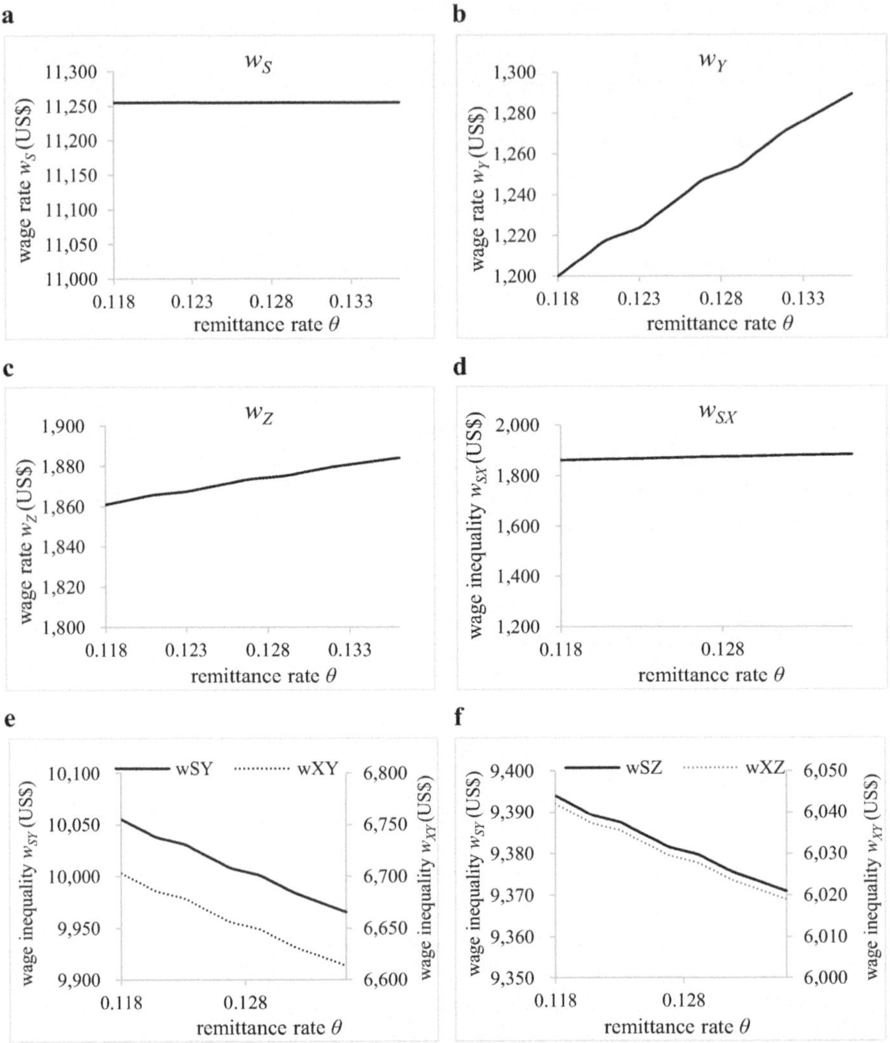

Fig. 13.1 The numerical simulation results for the capital-specific case (unit: US$). (**a**) The wage rate of skilled labor, w_S. (**b**) The wage rate in sector *Y*, w_Y. (**c**) The wage rate in sector *Z*, w_Z. (**d**) The wage inequality between skilled labor and sector *X*, w_{SX}. (**e**) The wage inequalities w_{SY} and w_{XY}. (**f**) The wage inequalities w_{SZ} and w_{XZ}. (Source: Authors' own elaboration)

numerical characteristics of Proposition 3. In addition, the skilled-unskilled wage inequalities, w_{SY} and w_{SZ}, decrease by a larger scale than the corresponding urban-rural wage inequalities, w_{XY} and w_{XZ}, respectively. This is consistent with the numerical characteristics of Proposition 4. However, in Fig. 13.1, w_{SY} decreases by the same percentage as w_{XY}, while w_{SZ} decreases by the same percentage as w_{XZ}, which is different from Fig. 13.2.

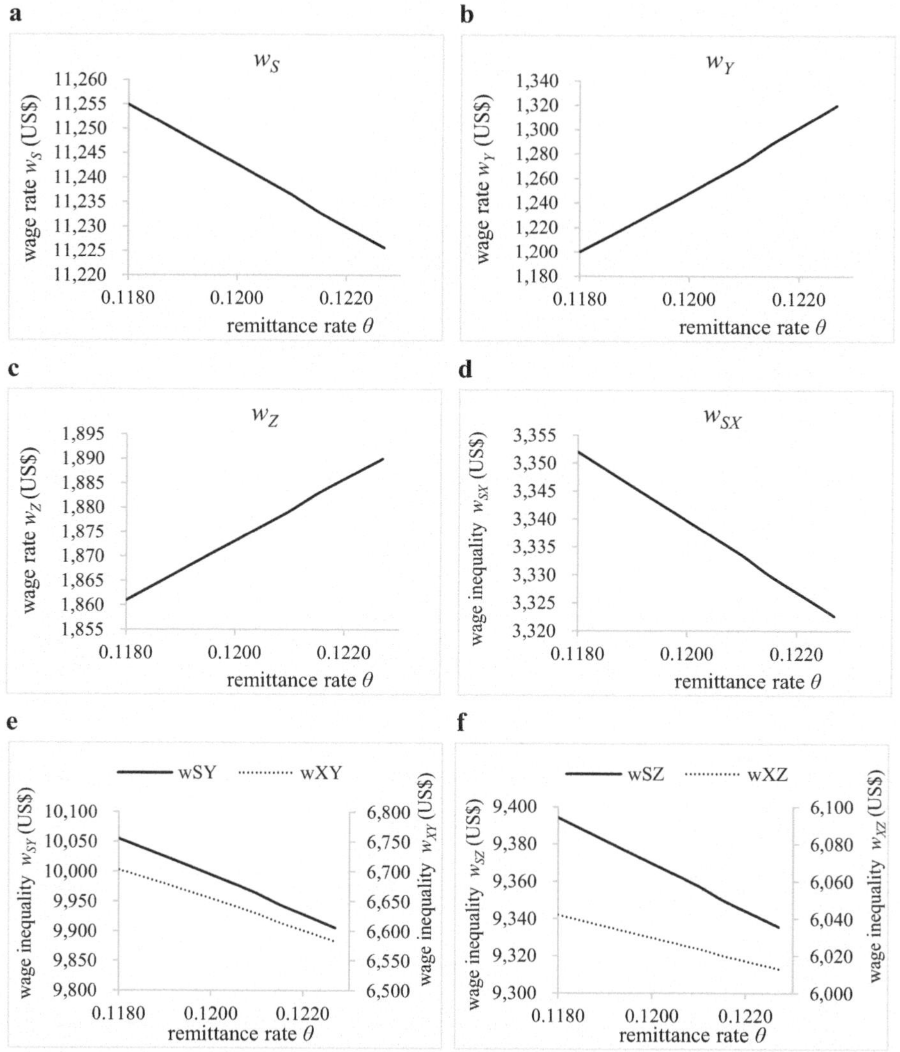

Fig. 13.2 The numerical simulation results for the mobile capital case (Unit: US$). (**a**) The wage rate of skilled labor, w_S. (**b**) The wage rate in sector Y, w_Y. (**c**) The wage rate in sector Z, w_Z. (**d**) The wage inequality between skilled labor and sector X, w_{SX}. (**e**) The wage inequalities w_{SY} and w_{XY}. (**f**) The wage inequalities w_{SZ} and w_{XZ}. (Source: Authors' own elaboration)

Sensitivity Analysis

In the economy of China, the cost of rural capital varies in different regions and seasons. Thus, the rural interest rate, r_Z, cannot be reflected by a single rate. Therefore, we determined whether different values of r_Z could have a significant impact on our conclusions. In the analysis presented in the previous section, we set

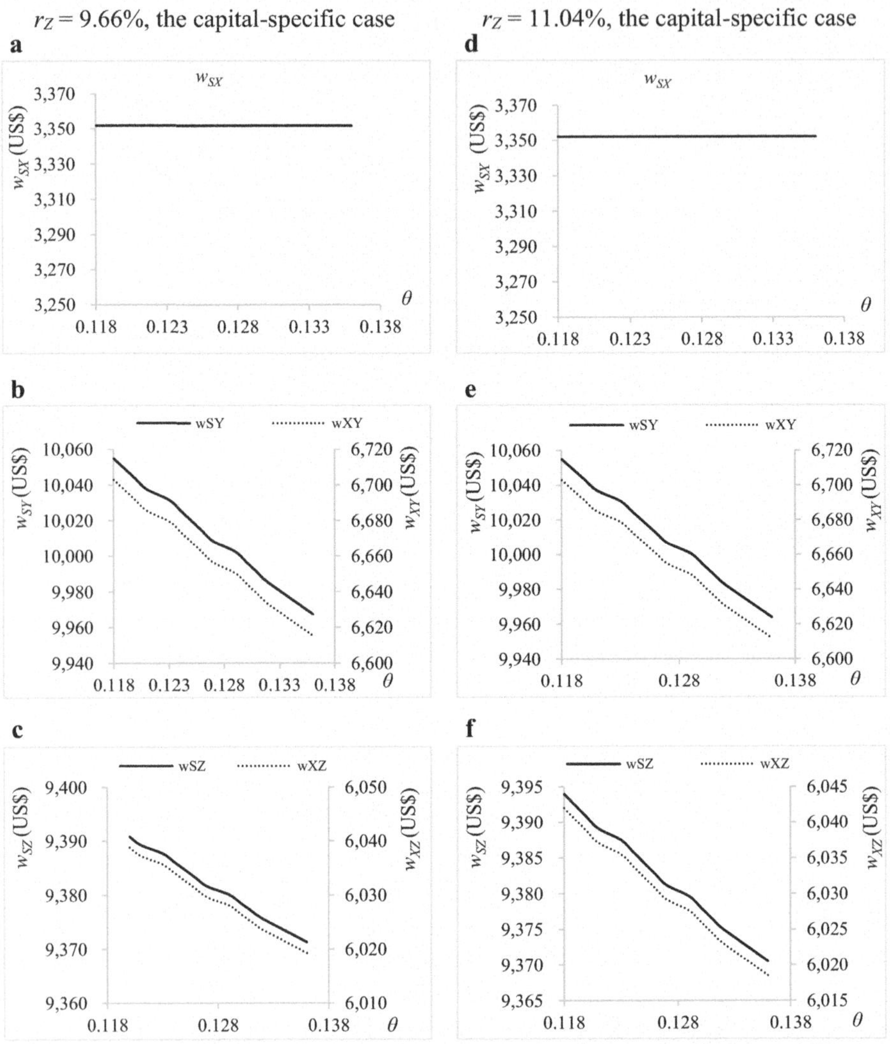

Fig. 13.3 The numerical simulation results using different rural interest rates (unit: US$). (**a**) The wage rate of skilled labor, w_S, (**b**) the wage inequalities w_{SY} and w_{XY}, (**c**) the wage inequalities w_{SZ} and w_{XZ} when $r_Z = 9.66\%$ in the capital-specific case; (**d**) the wage rate of skilled labor, w_S, (**e**) the wage inequalities w_{SY} and w_{XY}, (**f**) the wage inequalities w_{SZ} and w_{XZ} when $r_Z = 11.04\%$ in the capital-specific case; (**g**) the wage rate of skilled labor, w_S, (**h**) the wage inequalities w_{SY} and w_{XY}, (**i**) the wage inequalities w_{SZ} and w_{XZ} when $r_Z = 9.66\%$ in the mobile capital case; (**j**) the wage rate of skilled labor, w_S, (**k**) the wage inequalities w_{SY} and w_{XY}, (**l**) the wage inequalities w_{SZ} and w_{XZ} when $r_Z = 11.04\%$ in the mobile capital case. (Source: Authors' own elaboration)

r_Z at 1.5 times the urban interest rate, r_X; here, we will use 1.4 times (9.66%) and 1.6 times (11.04%). Using different values of r_Z, we recalibrated σ: when r_Z is 9.66%, σ is 0.206, and when r_Z is 11.04%, σ is 0.212. As seen in Fig. 13.3, differences in r_Z had no influence on our conclusions. Thus, the numerical simulation was robust.

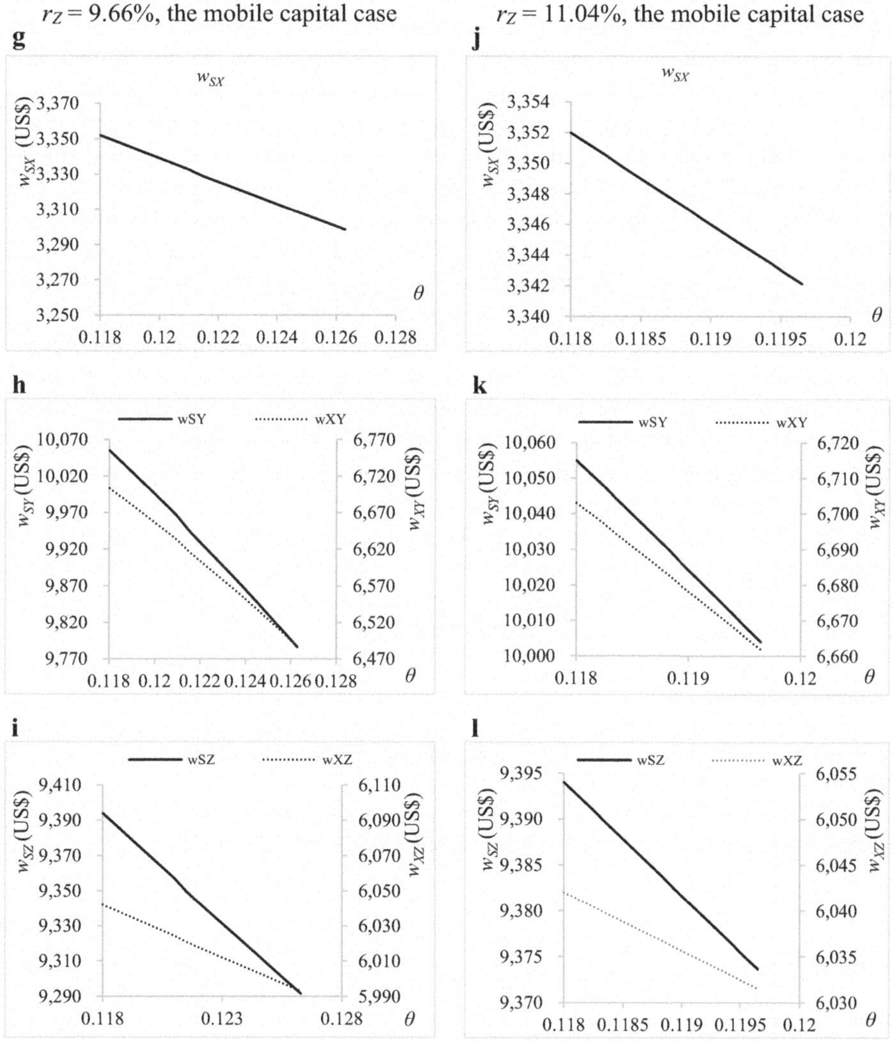

Fig. 13.3 (continued)

13.6 Conclusions

In this study, we used a general equilibrium model of endogenous remittances from rural-urban migrants and positive externality on agriculture, with which one can examine the effects of remittance rate on wage inequality in a small open economy. Similar to the findings of Quibria (1997), we find that an increase in rural-urban migrants' remittance volume (or rate) raises the wage rate in rural areas (labor-outsourcing region). Note that the main concern of Quibria (1997) is with international remittance. Furthermore, we take urban-rural wage inequality into consideration and hence complement those studies that only focused on the skilled-unskilled wage inequality, such as Li and Zhou (2013). It is shown that rural-urban migrants' remittances could help ease the wage inequalities between urban and rural areas. Further, dividing labor into skilled and unskilled labor makes our model different from those used by Li and Wang (2015). In this study, an increased remittance rate increases the low wage rate (w_Y), but does not affect or even reduces the high wage rate (w_S), in urban areas. That is to say, an increased remittance rate also improves the wage inequalities within urban areas. However, in Li and Wang (2015), the effects hinge on whether capital is sector-specific or mobile.

These conclusions are not only of academic value, but also of practical significance for relevant economic policies. Using the parameters calibrated with Chinese macroeconomic data, we perform numerical simulations and find that the results support the theoretical analysis. Consequently, in a developing country, encouraging rural-urban migrants to raise their remittance rate would be an effective policy alternative for reducing wage inequality.

It should be noted that the results for the mobile capital case are dependent on the assumption of factor substitution in urban formal sector. It is clear that further analysis should be done with this assumption relaxed. Obviously, taking rural skilled labor into account is also a good avenue for future research.

Competing Interests

Funding This work was supported by the Humanities and Social Sciences of the Ministry of Education, China, Project No. 17JJD630002.

Disclosure Statement No potential conflict of interest was reported by the authors.

Appendix

Appendix 1

Total differential of Eqs. (13.1)–(13.10) is the following:

$$\theta_{SX}\widehat{w}_S + \theta_{KX}\widehat{r}_X = 0, \tag{13.20}$$

$$\widehat{p}_Y = \widehat{w}_Y, \tag{13.21}$$

$$\theta_{LZ}\widehat{w}_Z + \theta_{KZ}\widehat{r}_Z - \varepsilon\widehat{k} = 0, \tag{13.22}$$

$$\widehat{p}_Y + \widehat{Y} - (1+e)\widehat{X} + e\widehat{k} = 0, \quad (13.23)$$

$$\widehat{X} + \varepsilon^X_{SS}\widehat{w}_S + \varepsilon^X_{SK}\widehat{r}_X = 0, \quad (13.24)$$

$$\lambda_{LX}\left(\widehat{X} + \varepsilon^X_{LS}\widehat{w}_S + \varepsilon^X_{LK}\widehat{r}_X\right) + \lambda_{LY}\widehat{Y} + \lambda_{LZ}\left(\widehat{Z} + +\varepsilon^Z_{LL}\widehat{w}_Z + \varepsilon^Z_{LK}\widehat{r}_Z - \varepsilon\widehat{k}\right) = 0, \quad (13.25)$$

$$\varepsilon^X_{LK}\widehat{r}_X + \varepsilon^X_{LS}\widehat{w}_S + \widehat{X} - \widehat{Y} + c\widehat{w}_Y - (a+b)\widehat{w}_Z = 0, \quad (13.26)$$

$$\widehat{X} + \varepsilon^X_{LS}\widehat{w}_S + \varepsilon^X_{LK}\widehat{r}_X + \widehat{\theta} = \widehat{k}, \quad (13.27)$$

$$\widehat{X} + \varepsilon^X_{KS}\widehat{w}_S + \varepsilon^X_{KK}\widehat{r}_X = 0, \quad (13.28)$$

$$\widehat{Z} + \varepsilon^Z_{KL}\widehat{w}_Z + \varepsilon^Z_{KK}\widehat{r}_Z - \varepsilon\widehat{k} = 0. \quad (13.29)$$

According to Eq.(13.20), we have $\widehat{r}_X = -\theta_{SX}/\theta_{KX}\widehat{w}_S$, then Eqs. (13.24) and (13.28) become, respectively: $\widehat{X} + \left(\varepsilon^X_{SS} - \varepsilon^X_{SK}\theta_{SX}/\theta_{KX}\right)\widehat{w}_S = 0$ and $\widehat{X} + \left(\varepsilon^X_{KS} - \varepsilon^X_{KK}\theta_{SX}/\theta_{KX}\right)\widehat{w}_S = 0$. Thus, X, w_S, r_X will be unaffected by θ. Therefore, we have $\widehat{\theta} = \widehat{k}$ in Eq. (13.27), $c\widehat{w}_Y - (a+b)\widehat{w}_Z = \widehat{Y}$ in Eq. (13.26), $\widehat{r}_Z = -\theta_{LZ}/\theta_{KZ}\widehat{w}_Z + \varepsilon/\theta_{KZ}\widehat{\theta}$ in Eq. (13.22), and $\widehat{Z} = -\varepsilon\left(\varepsilon^Z_{KK}/\theta_{KZ} - 1\right)\widehat{\theta} - \left(\varepsilon^Z_{KL} - \varepsilon^Z_{KK}\theta_{LZ}/\theta_{KZ}\right)\widehat{w}_Z$ in Eq. (13.29). By Eq. (13.21) and $c\widehat{w}_Y - (a+b)\widehat{w}_Z = \widehat{Y}$, and $\widehat{Z} = -\varepsilon\left(\varepsilon^Z_{KK}/\theta_{KZ} - 1\right)\widehat{\theta} - \left(\varepsilon^Z_{KL} - \varepsilon^Z_{KK}\theta_{LZ}/\theta_{KZ}\right)\widehat{w}_Z$, we have $a\widehat{w}_Y - (a+b)\widehat{w}_Z = -e\widehat{\theta}$ in Eq. (13.23), and $c\lambda_{LY}\widehat{w}_Y - [\lambda_{LY}(a+b) + \lambda_{LZ}d]\widehat{w}_Z = -\lambda_{LZ}\varepsilon d\widehat{\theta}$ in Eq. (13.25). Therefore, we obtain Eq. (13.11).

Solving Eq. (13.11) with Cramer's rule, we can obtain the following:

$$\begin{aligned}\frac{\widehat{w}_Y}{\widehat{\theta}} &= \frac{1}{\Delta_1}\begin{vmatrix} -e & -(a+b) \\ -\varepsilon\lambda_{LZ}d & -\lambda_{LY}(a+b) - \lambda_{LZ}d \end{vmatrix} \\ &= \frac{1}{\Delta_1}\{[\lambda_{LY}(a+b) + \lambda_{LZ}d]e - \varepsilon\lambda_{LZ}d(a+b)\},\end{aligned} \quad (13.30)$$

$$\frac{\widehat{w}_Z}{\widehat{\theta}} = \frac{1}{\Delta_1}\begin{vmatrix} a & -e \\ \lambda_{LY}c & -\varepsilon\lambda_{LZ}d \end{vmatrix} = \frac{1}{\Delta_1}(\lambda_{LY}ce - \varepsilon\lambda_{LZ}da). \quad (13.31)$$

As for the mobile capital case, total differential of Eqs. (13.1)–(13.8) and (13.14) is the following:

$$\theta_{SX}\widehat{w}_S + \theta_{KX}\widehat{r} = 0, \quad (13.32)$$

$$\widehat{p}_Y = \widehat{w}_Y, \quad (13.33)$$

$$\theta_{LZ}\widehat{w}_Z + \theta_{KZ}\widehat{r} - \varepsilon\widehat{k} = 0, \quad (13.34)$$

$$\widehat{p}_Y + \widehat{Y} - (1+e)\widehat{X} + e\widehat{k} = 0, \quad (13.35)$$

$$\widehat{X}+\varepsilon_{SS}^{X}\widehat{w}_S+\varepsilon_{SK}^{X}\widehat{r}=0, \tag{13.36}$$

$$\lambda_{LX}\left(\widehat{X}+\varepsilon_{LS}^{X}\widehat{w}_S+\varepsilon_{LK}^{X}\widehat{r}\right)+\lambda_{LY}\widehat{Y}+\lambda_{LZ}\left(\widehat{Z}++\varepsilon_{LL}^{Z}\widehat{w}_Z+\varepsilon_{LK}^{Z}\widehat{r}-\varepsilon\widehat{k}\right)=0, \tag{13.37}$$

$$\varepsilon_{LK}^{X}\widehat{r}+\varepsilon_{LS}^{X}\widehat{w}_S+\widehat{X}-\widehat{Y}+c\widehat{w}_Y-(a+b)\widehat{w}_Z=0, \tag{13.38}$$

$$\widehat{X}+\varepsilon_{LS}^{X}\widehat{w}_S+\varepsilon_{LK}^{X}\widehat{r}+\widehat{\theta}=\widehat{k}, \tag{13.39}$$

$$\lambda_{KX}\left(\widehat{X}+\varepsilon_{KS}^{X}\widehat{w}_S+\varepsilon_{KK}^{X}\widehat{r}\right)+\lambda_{KZ}\left(\widehat{Z}+\varepsilon_{KL}^{Z}\widehat{w}_Z+\varepsilon_{KK}^{Z}\widehat{r}-\varepsilon\widehat{k}\right)=0. \tag{13.40}$$

According to Eqs. (13.32) and (13.36), we have $\widehat{w}_S=-\theta_{KX}/\theta_{SX}\widehat{r}$, $\widehat{X}=-h\widehat{r}$. By Assumption 1, we have $\widehat{k}=-h\widehat{r}+\widehat{\theta}$ in Eq. (13.39), $\widehat{Y}=-\widehat{w}_Y-h\widehat{r}-e\widehat{\theta}$ in Eq. (13.35), $\widehat{Z}=-\left[\varepsilon_{KK}^{Z}+\varepsilon h+(j-h)\lambda_{KX}/\lambda_{KZ}\right]\widehat{r}-\varepsilon_{KL}^{Z}\widehat{w}_Z+\varepsilon\widehat{\theta}$ in Eq. (13.40). Thus, we have $\theta_{LZ}\widehat{w}_Z+(\theta_{KZ}+\varepsilon h)\widehat{r}=\varepsilon\widehat{\theta}$ in Eq. (13.34), $\lambda_{LY}\widehat{w}_Y+\lambda_{LZ}\left(\varepsilon_{KL}^{Z}-\varepsilon_{LL}^{Z}\right)\widehat{w}_Z+A\widehat{r}=-\lambda_{LY}e\widehat{\theta}$ in Eq. (13.37), $-a\widehat{w}_Y+(a+b)\widehat{w}_Z=e\widehat{\theta}$ in Eq. (13.38). Therefore, we obtain Eq. (13.15).

Solving Eq. (13.15) using Cramer's rule yields the following:

$$\frac{\widehat{w}_Y}{\widehat{\theta}}=\frac{1}{\Delta_2}\begin{vmatrix}\varepsilon & \theta_{LZ} & \theta_{KZ}+\varepsilon h\\ e & a+b & 0\\ -\lambda_{LY}e & \lambda_{LZ}\left(\varepsilon_{KL}^{Z}-\varepsilon_{LL}^{Z}\right) & A\end{vmatrix}$$
$$=\frac{1}{\Delta_2}\left\{\varepsilon A(a+b)+e\begin{bmatrix}(\theta_{KZ}+\varepsilon h)\lambda_{LZ}\left(\varepsilon_{KL}^{Z}-\varepsilon_{LL}^{Z}\right)\\ +\lambda_{LY}(a+b)(\theta_{KZ}+\varepsilon h)-\theta_{LZ}A\end{bmatrix}\right\}, \tag{13.41}$$

$$\frac{\widehat{w}_Z}{\widehat{\theta}}=\frac{1}{\Delta_2}\begin{vmatrix}0 & \varepsilon & \theta_{KZ}+\varepsilon h\\ -a & e & 0\\ \lambda_{LY} & -\lambda_{LY}e & A\end{vmatrix}=\frac{1}{\Delta_2}[c\lambda_{LY}e(\theta_{KZ}+\varepsilon h)+aA\varepsilon], \tag{13.42}$$

$$\frac{\widehat{r}}{\widehat{\theta}}=\frac{1}{\Delta_2}\begin{vmatrix}0 & \theta_{LZ} & \varepsilon\\ -a & a+b & e\\ \lambda_{LY} & \lambda_{LZ}\left(\varepsilon_{KL}^{Z}-\varepsilon_{LL}^{Z}\right) & -\lambda_{LY}e\end{vmatrix}$$
$$=-\frac{1}{\Delta_2}\left[\varepsilon a\lambda_{LZ}\left(\varepsilon_{KL}^{Z}-\varepsilon_{LL}^{Z}\right)+\varepsilon(a+b)\lambda_{LY}+\lambda_{LY}ec\theta_{LZ}\right]>0. \tag{13.43}$$

Appendix 2

Based on the three strata of industry in National Bureau of Statistics of China (2017b), let the primary industry be the rural sector *Z*, and the secondary and tertiary industries be the urban formal sector *X*

- In the primary industry, the value-added was US$905,397.23 million, the number of employed persons was 214.96 million people, and the per capita disposable income of rural households was US$1861. We can then calculate the output elasticity in the rural sector.
- In the secondary industry, the value-added was US$4,464,533.37, and the number of employed persons was 223.5 million people. In the tertiary industry, the value-added was US$5,771,704.08 million, and the number of employed persons was 337.57 million people. Let urban labor with junior college or above degree represent skilled labor, while urban labor with technical secondary school or less represents unskilled labor of the urban formal sector.[12] According to the Chinese Household Income Project Survey in 2014 (CHIP 2013),[13] there were 19,887 individuals in the survey sample of urban households. Among them, there were 5711 individuals with a college degree or above, whose average annual wage income was US$8862. The average annual wage income of other individuals with a lower degree was US$6223. According to National Bureau of Statistics of China (2017b), in 2016, the number of urban employed persons was 414.28 million people, and the per capita disposable income of urban households was US $5061; in 2013, the number of urban employed persons was 382.4 million people, and the per capita disposable income of urban households was US$3985. Thus, we can approximate that skilled labor in 2013 was 109.81 million people. Based on the growth rate of the number of urban employed persons, skilled labor in 2016 was 118.97 million people. With the growth rate of the per capita disposable income of urban households, the average annual wage income of skilled labor in 2016 was US$11,255, while that of unskilled urban labor was US$7903. From the above, we can calculate the output elasticity in the urban formal sector.
- As for the urban informal sector, note that the wage rate of this sector is lower than that of the rural sector, and labor transfers to this sector in order to wait for employment opportunities in the urban formal sector, and goods and services produced by this sector can only be provided to urban residents. Therefore, we define labor employed in the urban informal as including both the economically active population excluding employed persons, which was calculated as being 30.91 million people,[14] as well as rural-urban migrants who provide hotel and

[12] Chinese workers' income is directly related to their education level, and a junior college diploma is the level above which one is considered to have higher education.

[13] Available at http://www.ciidbnu.org/chip/chips.asp?year=2013&lang=EN.

[14] According to National Bureau of Statistics of China (2017b), in 2016, the number of economically active population in China was 806.94 million persons, and the number of employed persons was 776.03 million persons.

catering services, services to households, repair services, and other services, which was calculated as being 47.89 million people.[15] According to the Statistical Report of the People's Republic of China on the Development of Social Service in 2016 issued by Ministry of Civil Affairs,[16] the average standard of urban subsistence allowances in China was US$893.5 (US$74.46 monthly) per person, which provides an urban household with the minimum food requirements. Considering the minimum cost of housing for rural-urban migrants, the wage rate of the urban informal sector was estimated to be US$1200. Since the output of the informal sector is missed in official statistics, we used accounting method for China's informal economy suggested by Hu (2015) as well as the definition of China's informal employment suggested by Hu and Zhao (2006), and calculated the ratio of the output for China's informal economy to the income of China's informal employment. In this way, we calculated the effective labor parameter in the urban informal sector.

Turning to rural-urban migrants' remittances, according to National Bureau of Statistics of China (2017a), the total number of rural-urban migrant workers in China was about 281.71 million, and their average monthly wage was about US$493; Li et al. (2008) found that about 25% of rural-urban migrants did not send money back home. Meanwhile, a new generation of migrant workers born since 1980 has become an important part of rural-urban migrant, accounting for 49.7% of the national total in 2016 (National Bureau of Statistics of China 2017a); Liu and Sun (2014) found that remittance-wage ratio of the new generation is about 80.14% of that of the older generation of migrant workers. Therefore, we can calculate that the internal remittance k was about US$363,414 million.

As for the interest rate, it was calculated as being 6.9% according to the benchmark 1-to-5-year lending rate announced by China's central bank in 2016. Because capital cannot flow freely from urban areas to rural areas in developing countries—and China is not an exception—it is reasonable to consider that the interest rate in the rural sector is higher than that of other sectors, which is 10.35% ($=1.5 \times 6.9\%$).

We used the economic data described above to calibrate the parameters. The results are summarized in Table 13.3. Since the unskilled labor allocation mechanism in Eq. (13.7) only has considered the relationship between wage rates, the effect of unconsidered factors on unskilled labor allocation is depicted by the migration parameter, 3.647, which is derived from the initial equilibrium of Eq. (13.7).

[15] According to National Bureau of Statistics of China (2017a), we obtained the industrial distribution of Chinese migrant workers.

[16] Available at https://www.mca.gov.cn/n156/n189/c93379/content.html (accessed March 28, 2024).

References

Ball CP, Lopez C, Reyes J (2013) Remittances, inflation and exchange rate regimes in small open economies. World Econ 36(4):487–507. https://doi.org/10.1111/twec.12042

Beladi H, Chaudhuri S, Yabuuchi S (2008) Can international factor mobility reduce wage inequality in a dual economy? Rev Int Econ 16(5):893–903. https://doi.org/10.1111/j.1467-9396.2008.00751.x

Chao CC, Nabin M, Nguye X, Sgro PM (2016) Wage inequality and welfare in developing countries: privatization and reforms in the short and long run. Int Rev Econ Financ 42:474–483. https://doi.org/10.1016/j.iref.2015.10.023

Chatterjee S, Turnovsky SJ (2018) Remittances and the informal economy. J Dev Econ 133:66–83. https://doi.org/10.1016/j.jdeveco.2018.02.002

Chaudhuri S, Banerjee D (2010) Foreign capital inflow, skilled-unskilled wage inequality and unemployment of unskilled labour in a fair wage model. Econ Model 27(1):477–486. https://doi.org/10.1016/j.econmod.2009.10.015

Chaudhuri S, Yabuuchi S (2007) Economic liberalization and wage inequality in the presence of labour market imperfection. Int Rev Econ Financ 16(4):592–603. https://doi.org/10.1016/j.iref.2005.12.004

Das SP (2002) Foreign direct investment and the relative wage in a developing economy. J Dev Econ 67(1):55–77. https://doi.org/10.1016/S0304-3878(01)00177-8

Djajic S (1998) Emigration and welfare in an economy with foreign capital. J Dev Econ 56(2):433–445. https://doi.org/10.1016/S0304-3878(98)00073-X

Fang CR, Huang LH, Wang MC (2008) Technology spillover and wage inequality. Econ Model 25(1):137–147. https://doi.org/10.1016/j.econmod.2007.05.002

Harris JR, Todaro MP (1970) Migration, unemployment and development: a two-sector analysis. Am Econ Rev 60(1):126–142. https://www.jstor.org/stable/1807860

Hu H (2015) Study on the measurement of output of informal economy in China. Stat Decis 18:22–25. (in Chinese). https://doi.org/10.13546/j.cnki.tjyjc.2015.18.006

Hu AG, Zhao L (2006) Informal employment and informal economy in the economic transformation in the process of urbanization in China (1990-2004). J Tsinghua Univ (Philos Soc Sci) 3:111–119. (in Chinese) https://kns.cnki.net/kcms2/article/abstract?v=Ma1nt2RbXajhRxtJn8Qd7irBPpFF28XlcviNKWt4Nofn2LKowKkw1HkCR42OepaxBI5UCBxpRDmJUY9zd-oNSG8SgzJu-NlLzmGRlzM27-8br0xxgAtGe9Z4qPo0BCpJ&uniplatform=NZKPT&language=CHS

Kar S, Beladi H (2004) Skill formation and international migration: welfare perspective of developing countries. Jpn World Econ 16(1):35–54. https://doi.org/10.1016/j.japwor.2002.10.001

Li X, Wang D (2015) The impacts of rural–urban migrants' remittances on the urban economy. Ann Reg Sci 54:591–603. https://doi.org/10.1007/s00168-015-0668-y

Li X, Zhou Y (2013) An economic analysis of remittance of unskilled migration on skilled–unskilled wage inequality in labor host region. Econ Model 33:428–432. https://doi.org/10.1016/j.econmod.2013.04.034

Li X, Zhou J (2015) Environmental effects of remittance of rural–urban migrant. Econ Model 47:174–179. https://doi.org/10.1016/j.econmod.2015.02.023

Li Q, Mao XF, Zhang T (2008) Analysis of decision making, quantity, and utilization of remittances by migrant workers. China Rural Surv 3:2–12. (in Chinese) https://kns.cnki.net/kcms2/article/abstract?v=Ma1nt2RbXajoy4DerGZwGiV9PD26cYa9etmLAQ-lpGpKx5owIsG6inuWGDTH5ZjBGxek1i67yUwGWtTRSKS7x1cl4bFSk7sb3nkyRId9G-nEeJ3oH7sMvCKDPH4syFDT&uniplatform=NZKPT&language=CHS

Liu JP, Sun YF (2014) Income levels, consumption behavior, and changing trends of the new generation of migrant workers in China. Reform Econ Syst 4:95–99. (in Chinese) https://kns.cnki.net/kcms2/article/abstract?v=Ma1nt2RbXaiu9zFdcBbJjE9_zzJ88-Nvkl949ByjEGpAM9QDWLRsDh9kDKtq0AWXFZuxXuk0b2Mh-FYhE2UxEPSrc1nY0bh5bvgVMOQCmI8U-j5c0GGBpqDtdXjoM3Ly&uniplatform=NZKPT&language=CHS

Lundahl M (1985) International migration, remittances and real incomes: effects on the source country. Scand J Econ 87(4):647–657. https://doi.org/10.2307/3439977

Moore MP, Ranjan P (2005) Globalisation vs skill-biased technological change: implications for unemployment and wage inequality. Econ J 115(503):391–422. https://doi.org/10.1111/j.1468-0297.2005.00994.x

National Bureau of Statistics of China (2017a) Migrant workers monitoring survey report 2016. https://www.stats.gov.cn/sj/zxfb/202302/t20230203_1899495.html (in Chinese). Accessed 28 Mar 2024

National Bureau of Statistics of China (2017b) China statistical yearbook 2016. China Statistics Press, Beijing. https://www.stats.gov.cn/sj/ndsj/2017/indexeh.htm

Pradhan G, Upadhyay M, Upadhyaya K (2008) Remittances and economic growth in developing countries. Eur J Dev Res 20:497–506. https://doi.org/10.1080/09578810802246285

Quibria MG (1997) International migration, remittances and income distribution in the source country: a synthesis. B Econ Res 49(1):29–46. https://doi.org/10.1111/1467-8586.00025

Rozelle S, Taylor JE, deBrauw A (1999) Migration, remittances, and agricultural productivity in China. Am Econ Rev 89(2):287–291. https://doi.org/10.1257/aer.89.2.287

Taylor JE, Wyatt TJ (1996) The shadow value of migrant remittance, income and inequality in a household-farm economy. J Dev Stud 32(6):899–912. https://doi.org/10.1080/00220389608422445

Wang D (2019) Manufacturing and agricultural pollution, private mitigation and wage inequality in the presence of pollution externalities. Agric Econ-Czech 65(2):51–58. https://doi.org/10.17221/79/2018-AGRICECON

Chapter 14
Foreign Investment and Environment in Developing Countries: A Perspective from Agricultural Subsidy with Foreign Capital Taxation

Abstract It is often difficult to improve the environment when attracting foreign investment in developing countries. Therefore, this paper develops a policy concept of subsidizing agriculture financed by foreign-capital income tax in developing countries, and explores whether it can improve the environment while increasing the inflow of foreign capital. To this end, we propose a general-equilibrium model comprising the characteristics of developing countries and, account for the economic and environmental effects of this policy by using that model. It shows that both wage subsidy and interest subsidy, whether in the long run or in the short run, improve the environment and promote the welfare conditionally. Most importantly, in the long run, the inflow of foreign capital can be increased under certain conditions.

Keywords Foreign investment · Environment · Agricultural subsidy · Foreign capital tax

14.1 Introduction

The foreign investment is an important tool for developing countries to boost the economy. Foreign investment, despite promoting the economic growth, is often accompanied by environmental deterioration in developing countries. Also, many developing countries, for economic development, have adopted economic prioritized policy in environmental protection and economic development, and have become the "Pollution Havens." Therefore, some pollution-intensive industries in developed countries relocate to developing countries with less stringent regulation through foreign direct investment (FDI), making the latter's environment problems more seriously. Many scholars have proved the negative effects of FDI on the environmental quality of developing countries from both theoretical and empirical standpoints:[1] Jorgenson (2006, 2009) demonstrated that FDI can cause water and air

[1] There are also studies arguing that FDI can contribute to a cleaner environment, for example, Demena and Afesorbor (2020), which is observed from the perspective of positive effects of the technological upgrading on the environment.

X. Li, Y. Wu, *Research on Characteristic Issues in Current Developing Economies*, New Frontiers in Regional Science: Asian Perspectives 80,
https://doi.org/10.1007/978-981-97-7284-1_14

Table 14.1 Industrial structure of foreign-funded enterprises at the end of 1992 (Huang 1994)

	Number of enterprises (Unit)	Amount of foreign investment (US$ million)	Proportion of enterprises (%)	Foreign investment proportion (%)
Primary industry	2168	1390	2.57	2.02
Secondary industry	70,232	45,908	83.24	66.84
Tertiary industry	11,973	21,390	14.19	31.14
TOTAL	84,373	68,688	100.00	100.00

pollution in less-developed countries; Cole et al. (2011) suggested that the output of foreign-owned firms increases several pollutants in China; Shahbaz et al. (2015) showed that the increase of FDI in the long run leads to environmental degradation.

Grossman and Krueger (1991, 1995) point out that environmental quality is related to the scale of economic activity, the techniques of production, and the composition of economic activity. Here, the expansion of economic activity damages the environment, the technological progress improves the environment, while the effect of economic structure changes on the environment depends on the trend of change. For developing countries, foreign investment has negative impacts on the environment not only by expanding the scale of economic activity, but also by altering the composition of economic activity. Most early foreign investment was concentrated in the secondary industry. Taking China as an example, according to Table 14.1, by the end of 1992, the number of foreign-funded enterprises and the amount of foreign investment in the secondary industry accounted for 83.24% and 66.84%, respectively. This is because at the stage of economic takeoff, the market has a low level of demand for services, and the secondary industry is mostly in areas where advanced infrastructure is relatively densely equipped, therefore, for foreign capital, investment in the secondary industry has the advantages of small investment and quicker results.

Here, we focus on the environmental pollution path of Copeland and Taylor (1999), which is the main mode of current theoretical research on environmental pollution, that is, the production of the industrial sector causes emissions of pollutants that harm the environment. The harmful substance emitted, such as waste gas, waste residue, and wastewater, pollutes water and soil for agricultural use through atmosphere, rivers, and other media. Hence, the product efficiency of the agricultural sector decreases. Accordingly, foreign investment would expand the scale of industrial production, reduce the efficiency of agricultural production, and inevitably tilt economic resources toward the secondary industry, thereby reducing environmental quality by changing the economic structure.

Facing the environmental degradation, governments in developing countries can adopt measures to restrict pollution-intensive foreign investment. For instance, since 1997, China has revised the "Catalogue for the Guidance of Foreign Investment

Industries"[2] 10 times, and each revision highlights environmental protection. However, restrictions on foreign investment in domestic projects that have high degrees of pollution would slow down foreign-capital inflows, and even lead to foreign-capital outflow, resulting in economic losses. So, is there a certain kind of economic policy can attract foreign-capital inflow while protecting the environment? For developing countries, this is an extremely important topic. If there is such a policy, economic growth and environmental improvement can be realized at the same time in developing countries. This can not only change the trend of the environmental Kuznets curve (EKC) at low levels of national income, but also enrich and develop the development policy of developing countries.

In order to provide a theoretical foundation for finding such a policy, this paper considers the policy of subsidizing agriculture with foreign capital income tax, and explore whether this policy can take the environmental protection as well as the economic growth into consideration. There are three reasons why the agricultural subsidization policy should be considered:

- Developing countries have always one-sidedly emphasized economic development and neglected environmental protection, and there is an urgent need for policies that take both into account, to change the backward economic development model of "Treatment after Pollution" and improve the efficiency of economic development.
- Under the environmental pollution path of Copeland and Taylor (1999), the impact of foreign investment-induced pollution on agricultural production cannot be ignored.
- Agricultural subsidy policies are the most basic and most commonly used ones, which are familiar to both the government and the public, and convenient to use.

But none of the aforementioned researches that investigates the environmental effects of foreign investment is related to agricultural subsidization policy. Numerous achievements have been made in studying the economic effects of agricultural subsidies: Bhagwati and Srinivasan (1974) and Basu (1980) analyzed the two-sector unified wage subsidies or agricultural production subsidies coordinated with the manufacturing-wage subsidies, they found that in the two-sector model, these policies could achieve optimal welfare goals. In recent years, there are also some theoretical economists who investigate the impact of subsidies on the topics such as vendor location decisions and rural economic development. Related studies include Haufler and Wooton (2006), Dwibedi and Chaudhuri (2014), etc. Current empirical research focuses mainly on the application of agricultural subsidy policies in specific countries, particularly the evolution and reform of the agricultural subsidy system, and on the impact of such policies on the country's grain output, food safety, economic growth, and sustainable development, see Harrigan (2003), Vitalis

[2] It is the catalog of industries where foreign investment is encouraged or restricted, and has been released by the National Development and Reform Commission of the People's Republic of China and the Ministry of Commerce of the People's Republic of China.

(2007), Dorward and Chirwa (2011), and so on. However, the common problem with these achievements is that they have not combined agricultural subsidies to the problem of foreign capital-induced pollution. In addition, with regard to foreign capital income tax, the existing research mainly focuses on the relevant discussion of host-country tax incentives, such as Haufler and Wooton (1999). However, Gupta (1995) considered the destination of foreign-capital income tax—subsidizing urban sector wages, and analyzed its economic impacts. Chao and Yu (1997) considered the welfare effects of foreign investment taxes. But none of them considered agricultural subsidies or environmental pollution.

Based on the above literature review, we assert that there is still a lack of theoretical research combining foreign investment, environment problems, and agricultural subsidies in developing countries, but there is no lack of scenarios where the three interact in actual economic activities. Therefore, this paper studies what kinds of changes will happen to the inflow of foreign capital and the environmental quality when developing countries subsidize agriculture based on foreign capital income tax. To this end, we develop a general-equilibrium model comprising the characteristics of developing countries and examine the economic and environmental effects of this policy by using that model. This paper chooses the model wage subsidy and interest subsidy in the agricultural subsidy policies. We find that with the wage subsidies and interest subsidies in the agricultural sector, whether in the long run or in the short run, environmental quality would improve, and the economy grows conditionally. In the long run particularly, the inflow of foreign capital can be increased under certain conditions. This conclusion is innovative and can provide a theoretical basis for developing countries in their efforts to formulate relevant policies.

The rest of this paper is organized as follows: in Sect. 14.2, we set up the theoretical model; in Sect. 14.3, we analyze the effect of the wage subsidization policy; the effect of the interest subsidization policy is presented in Sect. 14.4; the welfare effects of wage subsidies and interest subsidies in Sect. 14.5; and we draw conclusions in Sect. 14.6.

14.2 Model

Consider a developing country with a small open economy, which consists of two sectors: urban (U), producing import-competing manufactured products, and rural (R), producing export-competing agricultural products. Each sector utilizes two factors of production, labor (L) and capital (K), and diminishing returns to scale (DRS) technology; factors are assumed to exhibit positive but diminishing marginal products and positive cross-partial derivatives. This paper follows the model considered by Copeland and Taylor (1999), which means the production in the urban sector will generate pollution, which injures the environment, while the production procedure of rural sector depends on environmental factors. Thus, the production functions in the urban sector and rural sector are given separately by

$$X_U = F^U(L_U, K_U), \tag{14.1}$$

$$X_R = g(E)F^R(L_R, K_R). \tag{14.2}$$

Here, X_i, L_i, and K_i are the level of output, employment, and capital stock of the ith sector, for $i = U, R$. Function F^i is concave, subscripts to F^i denote the first or second derivative with respect to production factors indicated.[3] We assume that foreign capital entering into the urban sector only. Therefore, here K_U contains foreign capital inflows, K_F. Denote that E is the quality of environment after pollution. $g(E)$, with the properties $0 < g < 1$, $g' > 0$, $g'' < 0$, represents the effect of environment on agricultural productivity. Let $\overline{E} > 0$ to represent environment endowment when there is no pollution in the economy. μ $(0 < \mu < 1)$ is the pollution that the urban sector discharges in producing one unit of goods. Thus, the environmental quality can be represented as:

$$E = \overline{E} - \mu X_U. \tag{14.3}$$

To maximize the profit of each sector, we have the following equations:

$$p_U F_L^U(L_U, K_U) = \overline{w}_U, \tag{14.4}$$

$$p_U F_K^U(L_U, K_U) = r_U, \tag{14.5}$$

$$g(E)F_L^R(L_R, K_R) = w_R - s_w, \tag{14.6}$$

$$g(E)F_K^R(L_R, K_R) = r_R, \tag{14.7}$$

where p_U is the relative price of the urban product in terms of the rural sector, which is fixed world price; r_U and r_R are the interest rates in the urban sector and the rural sector, respectively; $\overline{w}_U$ and w_R are the wage rate in the urban sector and the rural sector, respectively. Due to institutional reasons, such as union resistance and government requirements, the urban sector's wage rate shows downward rigid, so $\overline{w}_U$ is an exogenous variable. The wage rate of the rural sector is flexible, which satisfies $w_R < \overline{w}_U$. s_w stands for the subsidy given to the rural sector per unit of employment (hereinafter referred to as "wage subsidy") and this is financed by taxing the foreign capital income otherwise repatriated.

Let λ be the ratio of urban unemployment to the urban employment, which means the unemployment rate. Rural labor moves to urban regions until the expected urban wage equals the actual rural wage (see Harris and Todaro 1970). Thus, the labor allocation mechanism between sectors can be shown as follows:

---

[3] $F_{LL}^i F_{KK}^i - F_{LK}^i F_{KL}^i > 0$ because DRS is assumed.

$$(1+\lambda)w_R = \overline{w}_U. \tag{14.8}$$

The equilibrium condition for labor demand and supply in the economy can be written as

$$(1+\lambda)L_U + L_R = \overline{L}, \tag{14.9}$$

where $\overline{L}$ is the exogenously given labor endowment in the economy.

With the wage subsidy financed by a tax on foreign capital, the government's balanced budget constraint is

$$s_w L_R = tK_F. \tag{14.10}$$

Furthermore, the supply of foreign capital is a positive function of its net rate of return, that is, the excess of the interest rate over the tax rate denoted by t. Foreign capital and domestic capital are perfect substitutes, and the equation describing equilibrium in the international capital market is

$$r_U - t = \overline{r}_F, \tag{14.11}$$

where $\overline{r}_F$ is the given rate of interest in the international market, which is interpreted as the opportunity cost of foreign capital.

In the short run, domestic capital stock in each sector is exogenously given, but in the long run capital is perfectly mobile.[4] For the short run, full-utilization of the capital stock in each sector leads to the following equation:

$$K_U = \overline{K}_U + K_F, \quad K_R = \overline{K}_R, \tag{14.12}$$

where $\overline{K}_i (i = U, R)$ is the domestic capital stock in the ith sector. And in the long run, we have

$$K_U + K_R = \overline{K} + K_F, \tag{14.13}$$

where $\overline{K} = \overline{K}_U + \overline{K}_R$ is the stock of domestic capital of the economy, which is exogenously given. Due to the perfectly sectoral mobility of capital, we have $r_R = r_U = r$ in the long run. Because capital can move freely between sectors, the foreign-capital in the urban sector also participates in the inter-sector movement of capital in the long run.

In the short-run case, we have 12 equations, Eqs. (14.1)–(14.12), which determine 12 endogenous variables X_U, X_R, E, L_U, L_R, K_U, K_F, w_R, r_U, r_R, t, and λ. In this

[4]In developing countries, institutional barriers and capital distortions impede capital mobility between urban and rural areas. With economic development, these hindrances gradually subside, promoting increased capital mobility and integration between urban and rural sectors.

case, there are nine exogenous variables $\overline{L}$, $\overline{K}_U$, $\overline{K}_R$, $\overline{E}$, μ, p_U, $\overline{w}_U$, $\overline{r}_F$, and s_w. However, in the long-run case, the general equilibrium model consists of the 12 equations, which are the Eqs. (14.1)–(14.11) and (14.13). They determine 12 endogenous variables X_U, X_R, E, L_U, L_R, K_U, K_R, K_F, w_R, r, t, and λ. In this case, there are eight exogenous variables $\overline{L}$, $\overline{K}$, $\overline{E}$, μ, p_U, $\overline{w}_U$, $\overline{r}_F$, and s_w.

14.3 Effect of Wage-Subsidy Policy for the Rural Sector

14.3.1 Short-Run Analysis

Let $s_w = 0$ at the initiation of the subsidy policy, it can be easily shown from Eqs. (14.10) and (14.11) that

$$\mathrm{d}r_U = \mathrm{d}t = \frac{L_R}{K_F}\mathrm{d}s_w. \tag{14.14}$$

Then, substituting Eq. (14.4) into Eq. (14.5), we obtain $\mathrm{d}K_U/\mathrm{d}r_U < 0$ and $\mathrm{d}L_U/\mathrm{d}r_U < 0$, and this implies $\mathrm{d}X_U/\mathrm{d}r_U < 0$, $\mathrm{d}E/\mathrm{d}r_U < 0$, and $\mathrm{d}K_F/\mathrm{d}r_U < 0$ according to Eqs. (14.1), (14.3), and (14.12). Therefore, we have

$$\frac{\mathrm{d}E}{\mathrm{d}s_w} = \frac{\mu\left(F_L^U F_{LK}^U - F_K^U F_{LL}^U\right)L_R}{p_U\left(F_{KK}^U F_{LL}^U - F_{KL}^U F_{LK}^U\right)K_F} > 0, \tag{14.15}$$

$$\frac{\mathrm{d}K_F}{\mathrm{d}s_w} = \frac{F_{LL}^U L_R}{p_U\left(F_{KK}^U F_{LL}^U - F_{KL}^U F_{LK}^U\right)K_F} < 0. \tag{14.16}$$

When the government subsidizes the rural sector, it is inevitable to raise the foreign-capital income tax as the source of subsidies, hence t rises. If $\overline{r}_F + t$ becomes higher than r_U, an outflow of foreign capital takes place and this decrease in K_F raises the urban sector's marginal productivity of capital. So r_U increases and Eq. (14.11) is reestablished. Since $F_{LK}^U > 0$, the marginal product of employed labor in the urban sector declines, in the case of wage rigidity in the urban sector, the employment of labor in the urban sector, L_U, also decreases. This lowers the marginal productivity of capital in the urban sector, so r_U falls again. But because DRS is assumed, r_U becomes higher in the new equilibrium and K_F becomes lower. As K_F is decreases, Eq. (14.1), with a given $\overline{K}_U$ and a lower L_U, implies that the production scale of urban sector shrinks, and the quality of the environment is improved.

This mechanism can also be illustrated by Fig. 14.1. Figure 14.1 shows the situation when the government increases the wage subsidy. The left half of the horizontal axis is the urban-sector output, X_U, and its right half represents the wage subsidy, s_w. The right side of the upper half of the vertical axis is the foreign-capital stock, K_F, its left side represents the environmental quality, E, and the lower half of

Fig. 14.1 The effect of wage subsidy in the short run

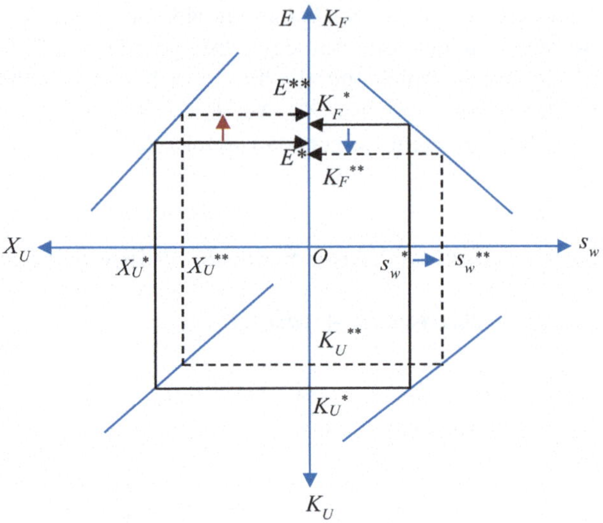

the vertical axis is the capital employment in the urban sector, K_U. The bivariate relationships shown in each quadrant are derived from the general equilibrium model. Starting from the wage subsidy s_w^* toward the first and fourth quadrants, respectively, we can obtain the foreign capital stock K_F^* and environmental quality E^* at equilibrium. When the wage subsidy increases to s_w^{**}, then it is found that the foreign capital stock decreases to K_F^{**} and the environmental quality improves to E^{**} in the new equilibrium.

Turn to the rural sector, differentiating Eq. (14.6), we obtain

$$\mathrm{d}w_R = g' F_L^R \mathrm{d}E + g F_{LL}^R \mathrm{d}L_R + \mathrm{d}s_w \tag{14.17}$$

and then, from Eqs. (14.8) and (14.9), we have

$$\mathrm{d}L_R - \frac{(1+\lambda)L_U}{w_R}\mathrm{d}w_R = -(1+\lambda)\mathrm{d}L_U. \tag{14.18}$$

Combining Eqs. (14.17) and (14.18), we obtain

$$\frac{\mathrm{d}L_R}{\mathrm{d}s_w} = \frac{(1+\lambda)L_U}{w_R - (1+\lambda)L_U g F_{LL}^R} - \frac{(1+\lambda)w_R}{w_R - (1+\lambda)L_U g F_{LL}^R}\frac{\mathrm{d}L_U}{\mathrm{d}s_w} + \frac{(1+\lambda)L_U g' F_L^R}{w_R - (1+\lambda)L_U g F_{LL}^R}\frac{\mathrm{d}E}{\mathrm{d}s_w} > 0, \tag{14.19}$$

Table 14.2 The effect of wage subsidy in the short run

	E	K_F	L_U	L_R	r_U	r_R	w_R	t	λ	X_U	X_R
s_w	+	−	−	+	+	+	+[1]	+	−[1]	−	+

Note: "+" and "−" mean that the change of s_w causes the corresponding endogenous variables to change in the same or opposite directions; "[1]" means the corresponding symbol can only be determined when the Assumption 1 is established

$$\frac{\mathrm{d}w_R}{\mathrm{d}s_w} = \frac{g w_R}{w_R - (1+\lambda) L_U g F^R_{LL}} + \frac{w_R g' F^R_L}{w_R - (1+\lambda) L_U g F^R_{LL}} \frac{\mathrm{d}E}{\mathrm{d}s_w} - \frac{w_R (1+\lambda) g F^R_{LL}}{w_R - (1+\lambda) L_U g F^R_{LL}} \frac{\mathrm{d}L_U}{\mathrm{d}s_w}. \quad (14.20)$$

As $\mathrm{d}L_U/\mathrm{d}s_w < 0$, $\mathrm{d}E/\mathrm{d}s_w > 0$, so we will get $\mathrm{d}L_R/\mathrm{d}s_w > 0$ by Eq. (14.19), and this implies $\mathrm{d}X_R/\mathrm{d}s_w > 0$ and $\mathrm{d}r_R/\mathrm{d}s_w > 0$ according to Eqs. (14.2) and (14.7), respectively. Wage subsidy lowers the unit cost of rural employment, reduces urban employment, and improves environmental quality and production conditions in the rural sector. With the combined effect of these channels, the rural sector increases labor employment and thus its interest rate and output.

The increase in L_R lowers the rural sector's marginal productivity of labor, but the improvement of the environmental quality can promote the productivity at the same time. From Eq. (14.20), it can be found that the change in w_R at this time cannot be determined. In order to determine the sign of the derivative $\mathrm{d}w_R/\mathrm{d}s_w > 0$, we make the following assumption:

Assumption 1 $\varepsilon_E/\varepsilon^R_{LL} > a$,[5] where $\varepsilon_E = g' E/g$ is the externality elasticity of environment to the production in the rural sector and, $a = (1+\lambda) E F^U_{LK} / \mu L_R (F^U_L F^U_{LK} - F^U_K F^U_{LL}) > 0$.

When the Assumption 1 is established, we obtain $\mathrm{d}w_R/\mathrm{d}s_w > 0$, and thus, from Eq. (14.8), we have $\mathrm{d}\lambda/\mathrm{d}s_w < 0$. Assumption 1 implies that the positive effect of environmental improvements on rural productivity exceeds the impact of the increase in L_R. At this time, the rural sector's wage rate rises. Because the urban-sector wage is downward rigid, this leads to a transfer of urban labor to the rural sector and a decline in unemployment rate.

Summarizing the results, we establish Table 14.2 as follows (see Appendix 1 for details):

According to Table 14.2, we can establish Proposition 1 as follows:

Proposition 1 *In the short run, wage subsidization for the rural sector financed by tax on the foreign-capital income otherwise repatriated will (a) improve the*

[5] $\varepsilon^h_{ij}(>0)$ is the partial elasticity of substitution between factors i and j in the hth sector, for example, $\varepsilon^R_{LL} = -F^R_{LL} L_R / F^R_L$ and $\varepsilon^U_{LK} = F^U_{LK} K_U / F^U_L$.

environmental quality, (b) decrease the foreign-capital inflow, and (c) lower the unemployment rate if $\varepsilon_E/\varepsilon_{LL}^R > a$.

In general, the wage rate and labor employment in a sector cannot change in the same direction, see Li and Zhou (2015) and Li and Wang (2015). In this model, however, the rise of wage rate and the increase of labor employment in the rural sector appear simultaneously. This is because of the establishment of Assumption 1 that allows the improvement of environmental quality has a considerable positive effect on agricultural production. This indicates that the environmental effects of wage subsidies financed by foreign-capital income tax can have a positive impact on the rural economy.

14.3.2 Long-Run Analysis

In the long-run analysis, Eq. (14.14) is replaced by

$$\frac{\mathrm{d}r}{\mathrm{d}s_w} = \frac{L_R}{K_F} > 0. \tag{14.21}$$

Same as in the short run, wage subsidy raises the foreign capital income tax, and the equilibrium of the international capital market at this moment is broken. In the long-run case, the foreign-capital inflow in the urban sector also participates in the inter-sector movement of capital, and therefore, through capital reallocation, the interest rate in the domestic capital market, r, rises, and the international capital market reaches equilibrium again. The mechanisms of capital reallocation are analyzed below.

First, as r rises, capital utilized by the urban sector declines; and as in the short-run analysis, this leads to lower labor employment L_U, lower output X_U, and therefore an improved environment E. Moreover, the rise in r also tends to reduce the capital input in the rural sector; however, the environmental improvement makes the production conditions in the rural sector better, and wage subsidy lowers its unit cost of labor, so the rural sector can hire more capital. Therefore, the amount of capital utilized by the rural sector K_R is determined by the combination effect of the capital market, the environment and the labor market.

Using Eqs. (14.6)–(14.9), we can obtain

$$\begin{bmatrix} gF_{LL}^R & gF_{LK}^R & -1 \\ gF_{KL}^R & gF_{KK}^R & 0 \\ 1 & 0 & -\dfrac{(1+\lambda)L_U}{w_R} \end{bmatrix} \begin{bmatrix} \mathrm{d}L_R \\ \mathrm{d}K_R \\ \mathrm{d}w_R \end{bmatrix} = \begin{bmatrix} -g'F_L^R\mathrm{d}E - \mathrm{d}s_w \\ -g'F_K^R\mathrm{d}E + \mathrm{d}r \\ -(1+\lambda)\mathrm{d}L_U \end{bmatrix}. \tag{14.22}$$

Define the determinant of square matrix in Eq. (14.22) as Δ and calculate Δ to obtain

$$\Delta = g\left[F_{KK}^{R} - \frac{(1+\lambda)L_U}{w_R} g\left(F_{LL}^{R}F_{KK}^{R} - F_{KL}^{R}F_{LK}^{R}\right)\right] < 0.$$

In order to facilitate the calculations, we make the following assumption:

Assumption 2 $\varepsilon_E >$ max $\{b_1, b_2, b_3\}$, where $b_1 = \frac{E\left(F_{KK}^{U}F_{LL}^{U} - F_{KL}^{U}F_{LK}^{U}\right)}{\mu F_{K}^{U}\left(F_{L}^{U}F_{LK}^{U} - F_{K}^{U}F_{LL}^{U}\right)} > 0$, $b_2 = -\frac{(1+\lambda)EF_{LK}^{U}\left(F_{KK}^{R}F_{LL}^{R} - F_{LK}^{R}F_{KL}^{R}\right)}{\mu F_{KK}^{R}F_{L}^{R}\left(F_{L}^{U}F_{LK}^{U} - F_{K}^{U}F_{LL}^{U}\right)} > 0$, and $b_3 = -\frac{F_{LL}^{U}E\left[(1+\lambda)L_U\left(F_{LL}^{R}F_{KK}^{R} - F_{KL}^{R}F_{LK}^{R}\right) - F_{KK}^{R}F_{L}^{R}\right]}{\mu(1+\lambda)L_U F_{KL}^{R}F_{L}^{R}\left(F_{L}^{U}F_{LK}^{U} - F_{LL}^{U}F_{K}^{U}\right)} > 0.$

Assumption 2 implies that the externalities of the environment on agricultural production are sufficiently large. When $\varepsilon_E > b_1$, there is $g'F_K^R(\mathrm{d}E/\mathrm{d}s_w) - (\mathrm{d}r/\mathrm{d}s_w) > 0$, that is, the positive effect of environmental improvement on rural production can offset the negative effect of rising interest rate on rural production. At this point, by solving Eq. (14.22), we can obtain $\mathrm{d}L_R/\mathrm{d}s_w > 0$ and $\mathrm{d}K_R/\mathrm{d}s_w > 0$, indicating that the wage subsidy increases labor and capital inputs in the rural sector. Substituting this outcome into Eq. (14.2) reveals an increase in X_R. When $\varepsilon_E >$ max $\{b_1, b_2\}$, there is $\mathrm{d}w_R/\mathrm{d}s_w > 0$, and we can derive a decrease in λ by substituting into Eq. (14.8). Subsequently, introducing these results into Eq. (14.13) yields

$$\frac{\mathrm{d}K_F}{\mathrm{d}s_w} = \frac{1}{\Delta}\left\{\begin{array}{l} g\left[F_{KK}^{R} - \frac{(1+\lambda)L_U}{w_R} g\left(F_{LL}^{R}F_{KK}^{R} - F_{KL}^{R}F_{LK}^{R}\right)\right]\frac{\mathrm{d}K_U}{\mathrm{d}s_w} + (1+\lambda)gF_{KL}^{R}\frac{\mathrm{d}L_U}{\mathrm{d}s_w} \\ -\left[1 - \frac{(1+\lambda)L_U}{w_R} gF_{LL}^{R}\right]\left(g'F_K^R\frac{\mathrm{d}E}{\mathrm{d}s_w} - \frac{\mathrm{d}r_R}{\mathrm{d}s_w}\right) + \frac{(1+\lambda)L_U}{w_R} gF_{KL}^{R}\left(-g'F_L^R\frac{\mathrm{d}E}{\mathrm{d}s_w} - 1\right) \end{array}\right\}. \quad (14.23)$$

If $\varepsilon_E >$ max $\{b_1, b_3\}$, there is $\mathrm{d}K_F/\mathrm{d}s_w > 0$, that is, wage subsidy increases the foreign-capital inflow.

Summarizing the results, Proposition 2 and Table 14.3 can be obtained as follows.

Proposition 2 *In the long run, wage subsidization for the rural sector financed by tax on the foreign-capital income improves the quality of environment, and leads to an increase in the inflow of foreign capital and a decrease in the unemployment rate under* Assumption 2.

Table 14.3 The effect of wage subsidy in the long run

	E	K_F	K_U	K_R	L_U	L_R	w_R	t	λ	X_U	X_R	r
s_w	+	+[2]	−	+[2]	−	+[2]	+[2]	+	−[2]	−	+[2]	+

Note: "+" and "−" mean that the change of s_w causes the corresponding endogenous variables to change in the same or opposite directions; "[2]" means the corresponding symbol can only be determined when the Assumption 2 is established. See Appendix 3 for details

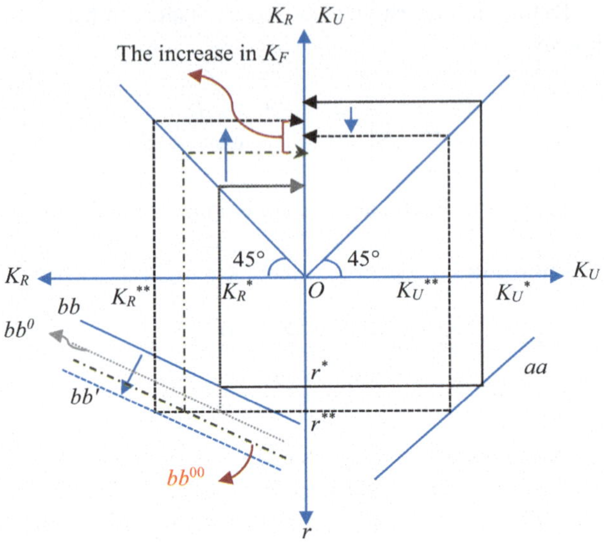

Fig. 14.2 The effect of wage subsidy in the long run

According to Propositions 1 and 2, the most obvious difference between the short-term and long-term effects of wage subsidy lies in the flow of foreign capital. The rise in interest rate caused by wage subsidy reduces capital used in the urban sector. Hence, the foreign capital inflows should decrease. However, in the long run, changes in foreign-capital inflows depend upon changes in capital demand between the rural and urban sectors, which in turn depend on the sensitivity of production in the rural sector to the environment. Therefore, even if wage subsidy pushes up interest rate, due to the effects of wage subsidy and environmental improvement, the rural sector still expands its employment of capital when the environmental externality on agricultural output surpass a certain threshold; and when the environmental externality is large enough, the amount of capital transferred into the rural sector is greater than the decrease in capital employment in the urban sector, leading to an increase in international capital demand, and consequently, an increase in foreign-capital inflows.

The effects can also be illustrated by Fig. 14.2. Figure 14.2 shows the situation when the government increases the wage subsidy. The left side of the upper half of the vertical axis is K_R, and its right side represents K_U. According to Eq. (14.13), the sum of the changes of the two is equal to the change in K_F. The interest rate r is inversely related to K_U as well as K_R, which are represented by curves aa and bb, respectively. The increase in r caused by wage subsidy reduces K_U. On the other hand, wage subsidy raises the marginal productivity of capital in the rural sector, leading to an outward shift of the curve bb because wage subsidy causes an environmental improvement and a lower labor unit cost in the rural sector.

- When the curve bb shifts outward beyond bb^0, the positive effect of marginal productivity gains on capital input is greater than the inverse effect of rising r on capital input, and thus the capital input in the rural sector increases.

- When the curve bb shifts outward beyond bb^{00}, the increase in K_R outweighs the decrease in K_U, and thus K_F increases.

From Proposition 2, it can be known that with rural wage subsidies, the increase of foreign capital inflows and environmental improvement can coexist. It is also noted that in this paper, the impact mechanism of wage subsidies on the environment is achieved primarily through its financial source, that is, the foreign-capital income tax, to affect the international capital market, rather than through subsidies to environmentally sensitive sectors to affect the return gap of factors between sectors, change the allocation of factors, and reduce the production of polluting sectors. Arguably, the direct cause of environmental improvement in this paper is the foreign capital income tax. If the inflow of foreign capital is increased, this tax source will be further enriched, the subsidies will be stronger, and then the environmental quality will be improved to a greater extent. In this sense, the inflow of foreign capital is the basis of environmental improvement.

14.4 Effect of Interest-Subsidy Policy for the Rural Sector

This section analyzes the interest subsidy given to the rural sector and this is also financed by taxing the foreign-capital income otherwise repatriated (hereinafter referred to as "interest subsidy"). In the section, we focus on the comparison of effects caused by interest subsidy with those caused by wage subsidy, particularly the effect on the environmental quality, the inflow of foreign capital and the unemployment rate.

Whether in the short run or the long run, interest subsidy only affects the Eqs. (14.6), (14.7), and (14.10). These equations are replaced by the following:

$$g(E)F_L^R(L_R, K_R) = w_R, \tag{14.24}$$

$$g(E)F_K^R(L_R, K_R) = r_R - s_r, \tag{14.25}$$

$$s_r K_R = tK_F, \tag{14.26}$$

where s_r stands for the rural subsidy per unit of capital, the rest of the symbols have the same meaning as in the wage subsidy model. The other equations in the interest subsidy case are the same as those in the wage subsidy case in Sect. 14.2.

In the short run, the calculations are similar to those in Sect. 14.3 and are summarized in Table 14.4 (see Appendix 2 for details).

Table 14.4 The effect of interest subsidy in the short run

	E	K_F	L_U	L_R	r_U	r_R	w_R	t	λ	X_U	X_R
s_r	+	−	−	+	+	+	+[1]	+	−[1]	−	+

Note: The meanings of the signs are same as those in Table 14.2

In the long run, differentiating equations in the model and writing in matrix notation, we can obtain the following equation:

$$\begin{bmatrix} gF^R_{LL} & gF^R_{LK} & -1 \\ gF^R_{KL} & gF^R_{KK} & 0 \\ 1 & 0 & -\dfrac{(1+\lambda)L_U}{w_R} \end{bmatrix} \begin{bmatrix} \mathrm{d}L_R \\ \mathrm{d}K_R \\ \mathrm{d}w_R \end{bmatrix} = \begin{bmatrix} -g'F^R_L\mathrm{d}E \\ -g'F^R_K\mathrm{d}E + \mathrm{d}r - \mathrm{d}s_r \\ -(1+\lambda)\mathrm{d}L_U \end{bmatrix}. \quad (14.27)$$

The value of the determinants of square matrix in Eq. (14.27) is the same as that of Eq. (14.22). By solving Eq. (14.27) with Cramer's rule and substituting the result into the model, we can obtain Table 14.5 (see Appendix 4 for details).

From the above calculation results, it can be seen that after changing the subsidy type, in both the short-run and long-run cases, the sign of the derivative of each endogenous variable value in the model has not changed. The mathematical reason is that the change of the subsidy type has a limited impact on the composition of the equations in the model, and there are few equations that have changed, so it is difficult to make the calculation results change directionally.

Compare the calculation results of the two kinds of subsidy policies, when the total amount and the change rate of subsidy are the same, it is easy to know that the wage subsidization and the interest subsidization have the same effect on the environment. The effects on foreign capital flows, unemployment rate, and agricultural production need to be discussed separately in the short and long terms. In the short run, since the domestic capital stock in each sector is fixed, wage subsidies and interest subsidies have the same effect on foreign capital inflows, while wage subsidies have a more direct impact on the labor market and therefore have a greater impact on agricultural production and unemployment rate. And in the long run, the effect of wage subsidies on the unemployment rate is more pronounced when $\varepsilon^R_{KK}/\varepsilon^R_{KL} > 1$, whereas interest subsidies have a greater impact on the foreign-capital inflow when $L_R/[(1+\lambda)L_U] > (\varepsilon^R_{LK} - \varepsilon^R_{LL})$, and on the output in the rural sector when $F^R_K + g\frac{(1+\lambda)L_U}{w_R}\left[F^R_L\left(F^R_{LK} + \frac{K_R}{L_R}F^R_{KK}\right) + F^R_K\left(-F^R_{LL} - \frac{K_R}{L_R}F^R_{KL}\right)\right] > 0$.

In summary, the following proposition can be obtained.

Proposition 3 *In the long run, the wage subsidy policy and the interest subsidy policy have the same effect on the environment, but different effects on foreign capital inflows. If a subsidy is given to the rural sector, the increase in foreign capital inflow caused by wage subsidy is smaller than that caused by interest subsidy when* $L_R/[(1+\lambda)L_U] > \varepsilon^R_{LK} - \varepsilon^R_{LL}$.

Table 14.5 The effect of interest subsidy in the long run

	E	K_F	K_U	K_R	L_U	L_R	w_R	t	λ	X_U	X_R	r
s_r	+	+[2]	–	+[2]	–	+[2]	+[2]	+	–[2]	–	+[2]	+

Note: The meanings of the signs are same as those in Table 14.3

The condition in Proposition 3 is actually the magnitude relationship between the ratio of rural to urban labor and a specific value $\left(\varepsilon_{LK}^{R} - \varepsilon_{LL}^{R}\right)$. In developing countries, the ratio of rural to urban labor tends to be relatively high. Additionally, due to the lower wage rates in the rural sector, the elasticity of wages with respect to factors is relatively small. Therefore, we consider the condition where $L_R/[(1+\lambda)L_U] > \varepsilon_{LK}^{R} - \varepsilon_{LL}^{R}$.

14.5 Welfare Effects of Wage Subsidies and Interest Subsides

In this section, we discuss the welfare effects of agricultural subsidies. The demand side of the economy can be represented by an expenditure function, $e(p_U, 1, u) = \min\,(p_U C_U + C_R)$ with the respect to the demand for the two commodities, C_U and C_R, subject to a strictly quasi-concave utility function $u(C_U, C_R) \geq u$.

As the subsidies are financed by a tax on foreign capital-income which is otherwise repatriated, the economy's budge constrain can be written as

$$e(p_U, 1, u) = p_U X_U + X_R - (r_U - t)K_F. \tag{14.28}$$

Using Eqs. (14.8), (14.9), and (14.12) or (14.13), and totally differentiating Eq. (14.28) at the initiation of the subsidy policy, we obtain the welfare change as (see Appendix 5 or details)

$$e_u \mathrm{d}u = -w_R L_U \mathrm{d}\lambda + g' F^R \mathrm{d}E, \tag{14.29}$$

where $e_u = \partial e/\partial u > 0$. The equation above shows that the urban unemployment has a negative impact on social welfare, while environmental quality exhibits a positive association with social welfare. It is noteworthy that both wage subsidies and interest subsidies, whether in the long run or in the short run, improve the environment with $\mathrm{d}E/\widehat{s}_w = \mathrm{d}E/\widehat{s}_r$. Moreover, in the short run, $|\mathrm{d}\lambda/\widehat{s}_w| > |\mathrm{d}\lambda/\widehat{s}_r|$, and we have $\mathrm{d}\lambda/\mathrm{d}s_w < 0$, $\mathrm{d}\lambda/\mathrm{d}s_r < 0$ under Assumption 1; in the long run, $\mathrm{d}\lambda/\mathrm{d}s_w < 0$, $\mathrm{d}\lambda/\mathrm{d}s_r < 0$ under Assumption 2. Consequently, in the short run, $\mathrm{d}u/\widehat{s}_w > \mathrm{d}u/\widehat{s}_r$, along with $\mathrm{d}u/\mathrm{d}s_w > 0$, $\mathrm{d}u/\mathrm{d}s_r > 0$ if Assumption 1 holds; in the long run, when Assumption 2 is valid, $\mathrm{d}u/\mathrm{d}s_w > 0$ and $\mathrm{d}u/\mathrm{d}s_r > 0$. In other words, when ε_E is sufficiently large, both in the short and long run, subsidy policy in the rural sector, if financed by a tax on foreign-capital income, can enhance social welfare.

In conclusion, it is worth noting that wage subsidies, in comparison to interest subsidies, demonstrate a more favorable impact on social welfare in the short term. In the long run, rural subsidies can increase the stock of foreign capital, improve the environment, and ultimately enhance social welfare, which is a sustainable development path.

14.6 Conclusion

In this paper, we investigate the impacts of agricultural subsidies that are financed by foreign-capital income tax on the inflow of foreign capital and the environmental quality, which has rich practical significance for developing countries. We find that in the long run, while improving the environment, agricultural subsidies can also lead to increased foreign capital inflows when certain corresponding conditions are satisfied. In addition, we find that unemployment rate and welfare can also improve conditionally.

But it should be pointed out that we cannot guarantee that this policy is a perfect strategy that only wins but not loses. The main reason is that the agricultural subsidy based on foreign-capital income tax in this paper has caused the output of the urban sector to decline and the output of the rural sector to rise. If the rising value of agricultural output can offset the decline of industrial output, then this policy has more important practical significance. For developing countries, such a policy can break through the constraints of the EKC and is an environmentally friendly measure to economic development.

Similarly, we do not deny the environmental problems caused by foreign investment because of the conclusions of this paper, nor does it mean that with this kind of countermeasures, the damage on the environment of foreign capital should be taken lightly. We also have reason to believe that the economic policy of agricultural subsidies financed by foreign capital tax is not the only policy that can promote both the introduction of foreign investment and environmental protection. It is our future research direction to explore similar economic mechanisms and pathways.

Competing Interests

Funding This work was supported by the Jiangsu Planned Project for Postdoctoral Research Funds, China, Project No. 2021K027A and the Yuxiu Postdoctoral School of Nanjing University.

Disclosure Statement No potential conflict of interest was reported by the authors.

Appendix

Appendix 1: The Effect of Wage Subsidy in the Short Run

$$\frac{\mathrm{d}K_F}{\mathrm{d}s_w} = \frac{\mathrm{d}K_U}{\mathrm{d}s_w} = \frac{L_R F^U_{LL}}{K_F p_U\left(F^U_{KK}F^U_{LL} - F^U_{KL}F^U_{LK}\right)} < 0,$$

$$\frac{\mathrm{d}L_U}{\mathrm{d}s_w} = -\frac{L_R F^U_{LK}}{K_F p_U\left(F^U_{KK}F^U_{LL} - F^U_{KL}F^U_{LK}\right)} < 0, \frac{\mathrm{d}E}{\mathrm{d}s_w} = -\frac{\mu L_R\left(F^U_K F^U_{LL} - F^U_L F^U_{LK}\right)}{K_F p_U\left(F^U_{KK}F^U_{LL} - F^U_{KL}F^U_{LK}\right)} > 0,$$

$$\frac{\mathrm{d}L_R}{\mathrm{d}s_w} = \frac{-(1+\lambda)w_R}{w_R - (1+\lambda)L_U g F^R_{LL}}\frac{\mathrm{d}L_U}{\mathrm{d}s_w} + \frac{(1+\lambda)L_U g' F^R_L}{w_R - (1+\lambda)L_U g F^R_{LL}}\frac{\mathrm{d}E}{\mathrm{d}s_w} + \frac{(1+\lambda)L_U}{w_R - (1+\lambda)L_U g F^R_{LL}} > 0,$$

$$\frac{\mathrm{d}r_R}{\mathrm{d}s_w} = g' F_K^R \frac{\mathrm{d}E}{\mathrm{d}s_w} + g F_{KL}^R \frac{\mathrm{d}L_R}{\mathrm{d}s_w} > 0,$$

$$\frac{\mathrm{d}w_R}{\mathrm{d}s_w} = \frac{w_R L_R \left[F_{LK}^U (1+\lambda) g F_{LL}^R - \mu\left(F_K^U F_{LL}^U - F_L^U F_{LK}^U\right) g' F_L^R\right]}{\left[w_R - (1+\lambda) L_U g F_{LL}^R\right] K_F p_U \left(F_{KK}^U F_{LL}^U - F_{KL}^U F_{LK}^U\right)} + \frac{w_R g}{w_R - (1+\lambda) L_U g F_{LL}^R}.$$

Appendix 2: The Effect of Interest Subsidy in the Short Run

$$\frac{\mathrm{d}K_F}{\mathrm{d}s_r} = \frac{\mathrm{d}K_U}{\mathrm{d}s_r} = \frac{K_R F_{LL}^U}{K_F p_U \left(F_{KK}^U F_{LL}^U - F_{KL}^U F_{LK}^U\right)} < 0, \qquad \frac{\mathrm{d}L_U}{\mathrm{d}s_r} = -\frac{K_R F_{LK}^U}{K_F p_U \left(F_{KK}^U F_{LL}^U - F_{KL}^U F_{LK}^U\right)} < 0,$$

$$\frac{\mathrm{d}E}{\mathrm{d}s_r} = -\frac{\mu K_R \left(F_K^U F_{LL}^U - F_L^U F_{LK}^U\right)}{K_F p_U \left(F_{KK}^U F_{LL}^U - F_{KL}^U F_{LK}^U\right)} > 0, \quad \frac{\mathrm{d}L_R}{\mathrm{d}s_r} = \frac{-(1+\lambda) w_R}{w_R - (1+\lambda) L_U g F_{LL}^R} \frac{\mathrm{d}L_U}{\mathrm{d}s_r} + \frac{(1+\lambda) L_U g' F_L^R}{w_R - (1+\lambda) L_U g F_{LL}^R} \frac{\mathrm{d}E}{\mathrm{d}s_r} > 0,$$

$$\frac{\mathrm{d}r_R}{\mathrm{d}s_r} = g' F_K^R \frac{\mathrm{d}E}{\mathrm{d}s_r} + g F_{KL}^R \frac{\mathrm{d}L_R}{\mathrm{d}s_r} + 1 > 0, \quad \frac{\mathrm{d}w_R}{\mathrm{d}s_r} = \frac{w_R K_R \left[(1+\lambda) g F_{LL}^R F_{LK}^U - g' F_L^R \mu K_R \left(F_K^U F_{LL}^U - F_L^U F_{LK}^U\right)\right]}{K_F p_U \left(F_{KK}^U F_{LL}^U - F_{KL}^U F_{LK}^U\right)\left[w_R - (1+\lambda) L_U g F_{LL}^R\right]}.$$

In the short run, wage subsidies and interest subsidies affect the environmental quality, foreign capital inflows, and the other endogenous variables in the same direction. When the total amounts of wage subsidy and interest subsidy are the same, the rate of change of subsidy has the following relationship: $\frac{\widehat{s_w}}{s_r} = \frac{\mathrm{d}s_w/s_w}{\mathrm{d}s_r/s_r} = \frac{\mathrm{d}s_w}{\mathrm{d}s_r}\frac{L_R}{K_R}$, therefore, at a 1% change in the subsidy, interest subsidies and wage subsidies have the same degree of impact on the environmental quality E and the foreign capital inflows K_F, as well as r_U, t, L_U, K_U, and X_U. While wage subsidies have a greater impact on L_R, X_R, w_R, and unemployment rate λ, interest subsidies have a greater impact on r_R if $L_R/[(1+\lambda)L_U] > \varepsilon_{LK}^R - \varepsilon_{LL}^R$.

Appendix 3: The Effect of Wage Subsidy in the Long Run

$$\frac{\mathrm{d}K_U}{\mathrm{d}s_w} = \frac{L_R F_{LL}^U}{K_F p_U \left(F_{KK}^U F_{LL}^U - F_{KL}^U F_{LK}^U\right)} < 0, \qquad \frac{\mathrm{d}E}{\mathrm{d}s_w} = -\frac{\mu L_R \left(F_K^U F_{LL}^U - F_L^U F_{LK}^U\right)}{K_F p_U \left(F_{KK}^U F_{LL}^U - F_{KL}^U F_{LK}^U\right)} > 0,$$

$$\frac{\mathrm{d}L_R}{\mathrm{d}s_w} = -\frac{g}{\Delta}\left\{\frac{(1+\lambda)L_U}{w_R}\left[F_{LK}^R\left(g' F_K^R \frac{\mathrm{d}E}{\mathrm{d}s_w} - \frac{\mathrm{d}r}{\mathrm{d}s_w}\right) - F_{KK}^R g' F_L^R \frac{\mathrm{d}E}{\mathrm{d}s_w} - F_{KK}^R\right] + F_{KK}^R (1+\lambda) \frac{\mathrm{d}L_U}{\mathrm{d}s_w}\right\},$$

$$\frac{\mathrm{d}K_R}{\mathrm{d}s_w} = \frac{1}{\Delta}\left\{\begin{array}{l} -\left[1 - \dfrac{(1+\lambda)L_U}{w_R} g F_{LL}^R\right]\left(g' F_K^R \dfrac{\mathrm{d}E}{\mathrm{d}s_w} - \dfrac{\mathrm{d}r}{\mathrm{d}s_w}\right) + (1+\lambda) g F_{KL}^R \dfrac{\mathrm{d}L_U}{\mathrm{d}s_w} \\ + \dfrac{(1+\lambda)L_U}{w_R} g F_{KL}^R \left(-g' F_L^R \dfrac{\mathrm{d}E}{\mathrm{d}s_w} - 1\right) \end{array}\right\},$$

$$\frac{\mathrm{d}X_R}{\mathrm{d}s_w} = g' F^R \frac{\mathrm{d}E}{\mathrm{d}s_w} + \frac{g}{\Delta}\left\{\begin{array}{l} -\left[F_K^R + \dfrac{(1+\lambda)L_U}{w_R} g\left(F_L^R F_{LK}^R - F_K^R F_{LL}^R\right)\right]\left(g' F_K^R \dfrac{\mathrm{d}E}{\mathrm{d}s_w} - \dfrac{\mathrm{d}r}{\mathrm{d}s_w}\right) \\ +(1+\lambda) g\left(F_K^R F_{KL}^R - F_L^R F_{KK}^R\right)\dfrac{\mathrm{d}L_U}{\mathrm{d}s_w} - \dfrac{(1+\lambda)L_U}{w_R} g g' F_L^R \left(F_K^R F_{KL}^R - F_L^R F_{KK}^R\right)\dfrac{\mathrm{d}E}{\mathrm{d}s_w} \\ + \dfrac{(1+\lambda)L_U}{w_R} g\left(F_L^R F_{KK}^R - F_K^R F_{KL}^R\right) \end{array}\right\},$$

$$\frac{\mathrm{d}w_R}{\mathrm{d}s_w} = \frac{g}{\Delta}\left\{\begin{array}{l} \dfrac{1}{F_{LL}^U}\left[(1+\lambda) g F_{LK}^U \left(F_{KK}^R F_{LL}^R - F_{LK}^R F_{KL}^R\right) + g' \mu F_L^R F_{KK}^R \left(F_L^U F_{LK}^U - F_K^U F_{LL}^U\right)\right]\dfrac{\mathrm{d}K_U}{\mathrm{d}s_w} \\ -F_{LK}^R \left(g' F_K^R \dfrac{\mathrm{d}E}{\mathrm{d}s_w} - \dfrac{\mathrm{d}r}{\mathrm{d}s_w}\right) + F_{KK}^R \end{array}\right\},$$

$$\frac{\mathrm{d}K_F}{\mathrm{d}s_w}=\frac{1}{\Delta}\left\{\begin{array}{l} g\left[F^R_{KK}-\frac{(1+\lambda)L_U}{w_R}g\left(F^R_{LL}F^R_{KK}-F^R_{KL}F^R_{LK}\right)-\frac{F^U_{LK}}{F^U_{LL}}(1+\lambda)F^R_{KL}+\mu\left(F^U_K-\frac{F^U_{LK}}{F^U_{LL}}F^U_L\right)\frac{(1+\lambda)L_U}{w_R}F^R_{KL}g'F^R_L\right]\frac{\mathrm{d}K_U}{\mathrm{d}s_w} \\ -\left[1-\frac{(1+\lambda)L_U}{w_R}gF^R_{LL}\right]\left(g'F^R_K\frac{\mathrm{d}E}{\mathrm{d}s_w}-\frac{\mathrm{d}r}{\mathrm{d}s_w}\right)-\frac{(1+\lambda)L_U}{w_R}gF^R_{KL} \end{array}\right\}.$$

Appendix 4: The Effect of Interest Subsidy in the Long Run

$$\frac{\mathrm{d}K_U}{\mathrm{d}s_r}=\frac{K_RF^U_{LL}}{K_Fp_U\left(F^U_{KK}F^U_{LL}-F^U_{KL}F^U_{LK}\right)}<0, \qquad \frac{\mathrm{d}E}{\mathrm{d}s_r}=-\frac{\mu K_R\left(F^U_KF^U_{LL}-F^U_LF^U_{LK}\right)}{K_Fp_U\left(F^U_{KK}F^U_{LL}-F^U_{KL}F^U_{LK}\right)}>0,$$

$$\frac{\mathrm{d}L_R}{\mathrm{d}s_r}=-\frac{g}{\Delta}\left\{\frac{(1+\lambda)L_U}{w_R}\left[F^R_{LK}\left(g'F^R_K\frac{\mathrm{d}E}{\mathrm{d}s_r}-\frac{\mathrm{d}r}{\mathrm{d}s_r}\right)-F^R_{KK}g'F^R_L\frac{\mathrm{d}E}{\mathrm{d}s_r}+F^R_{LK}\right]+(1+\lambda)F^R_{KK}\frac{\mathrm{d}L_U}{\mathrm{d}s_r}\right\},$$

$$\frac{\mathrm{d}K_R}{\mathrm{d}s_r}=\frac{1}{\Delta}\left\{\begin{array}{l} -\left[1-\frac{(1+\lambda)L_U}{w_R}gF^R_{LL}\right]\left(g'F^R_K\frac{\mathrm{d}E}{\mathrm{d}s_r}-\frac{\mathrm{d}r}{\mathrm{d}s_r}\right)+(1+\lambda)gF^R_{KL}\frac{\mathrm{d}L_U}{\mathrm{d}s_r} \\ -\frac{(1+\lambda)L_U}{w_R}gF^R_{KL}g'F^R_L\frac{\mathrm{d}E}{\mathrm{d}s_r}-\left[1-\frac{(1+\lambda)L_U}{w_R}gF^R_{LL}\right] \end{array}\right\},$$

$$\frac{\mathrm{d}w_R}{\mathrm{d}s_r}=\frac{g}{\Delta}\left\{\begin{array}{l} \frac{1}{F^U_{LL}}\left[(1+\lambda)gF^U_{LK}\left(F^R_{KK}F^R_{LL}-F^R_{LK}F^R_{KL}\right)+g'\mu F^R_LF^R_{KK}\left(F^U_LF^U_{LK}-F^U_KF^U_{LL}\right)\right]\frac{\mathrm{d}K_U}{\mathrm{d}s_r} \\ -F^R_{LK}\left(g'F^R_K\frac{\mathrm{d}E}{\mathrm{d}s_r}-\frac{\mathrm{d}r}{\mathrm{d}s_r}\right)-F^R_{LK} \end{array}\right\},$$

$$\frac{\mathrm{d}X_R}{\mathrm{d}s_r}=g'F^R\frac{\mathrm{d}E}{\mathrm{d}s_r}+\frac{g}{\Delta}\left\{\begin{array}{l} -\left[F^R_K-\frac{(1+\lambda)L_U}{w_R}gF^R_KF^R_{LL}+g\frac{(1+\lambda)L_U}{w_R}F^R_LF^R_{LK}\right]\left(g'F^R_K\frac{\mathrm{d}E}{\mathrm{d}s_r}-\frac{\mathrm{d}r}{\mathrm{d}s_r}\right) \\ +\left(F^R_KF^R_{KL}-F^R_LF^R_{KK}\right)(1+\lambda)g\frac{\mathrm{d}L_U}{\mathrm{d}s_r}+\left(F^R_LF^R_{KK}-F^R_KF^R_{KL}\right)\frac{(1+\lambda)L_U}{w_R}gg'F^R_L\frac{\mathrm{d}E}{\mathrm{d}s_r} \\ -F^R_K\left[1-\frac{(1+\lambda)L_U}{w_R}gF^R_{LL}\right]-gF^R_L\frac{(1+\lambda)L_U}{w_R}F^R_{LK} \end{array}\right\},$$

$$\frac{\mathrm{d}K_F}{\mathrm{d}s_r}=\frac{1}{\Delta}\left\{\begin{array}{l} g\left[F^R_{KK}-\frac{(1+\lambda)L_U}{w_R}g\left(F^R_{LL}F^R_{KK}-F^R_{KL}F^R_{LK}\right)-\frac{F^U_{LK}}{F^U_{LL}}(1+\lambda)F^R_{KL}+\mu\left(F^U_K-\frac{F^U_{LK}}{F^U_{LL}}F^U_L\right)\frac{(1+\lambda)L_U}{w_R}F^R_{KL}g'F^R_L\right]\frac{\mathrm{d}K_U}{\mathrm{d}s_w} \\ -\left[1-\frac{(1+\lambda)L_U}{w_R}gF^R_{LL}\right]\left(g'F^R_K\frac{\mathrm{d}E}{\mathrm{d}s_r}-\frac{\mathrm{d}r}{\mathrm{d}s_r}\right)-\left[1-\frac{(1+\lambda)L_U}{w_R}gF^R_{LL}\right] \end{array}\right\}.$$

In the long run, wage subsidies and interest subsidies affect the environmental quality, foreign capital inflows, and the other endogenous variables in the same direction. When the total amounts of wage subsidy and interest subsidy are the same, at a 1% change in the subsidy, interest subsidies and wage subsidies have the same degree of impact on the environmental quality E, as well as r, t, L_U, K_U, and X_U. While wage subsidies have a greater impact on L_R, w_R, and unemployment rate λ when $-F^R_{KK}K_R>L_RF^R_{LK}$, interest subsidies have a greater impact on K_R and foreign capital inflows K_F when $1-\frac{(1+\lambda)L_U}{w_R}g\left(\frac{K_RF^R_{KL}}{L_R}+F^R_{LL}\right)>0$, and on X_R when $F^R_K+g\frac{(1+\lambda)L_U}{w_R}\left[F^R_L\left(F^R_{LK}+\frac{K_R}{L_R}F^R_{KK}\right)+F^R_K\left(-F^R_{LL}-\frac{K_R}{L_R}F^R_{KL}\right)\right]>0$.

Appendix 5: The Derivation of Eq. (14.29)

Totally differentiating Eq. (14.28) at the initiation of the subsidy policy, we obtain the welfare change as in the short run

$$\begin{aligned} e_u \mathrm{d}u &= p_U \mathrm{d}X_U + \mathrm{d}X_R - (r_U - t)\mathrm{d}K_F - K_F \mathrm{d}(r_U - t) \\ &= \overline{w}_U \mathrm{d}L_U + r_U \mathrm{d}K_U + w_R \mathrm{d}L_R + r_R \mathrm{d}\overline{K}_R + g' F^R \mathrm{d}E - r_U \mathrm{d}K_F, \end{aligned}$$

or in the long run

$$e_u \mathrm{d}u = \overline{w}_U \mathrm{d}L_U + r\mathrm{d}K_U + w_R \mathrm{d}L_R + r\mathrm{d}K_R + g' F^R \mathrm{d}E - r\mathrm{d}K_F.$$

Using Eq. (14.12) or (14.13), the above two equations can be written as

$$e_u \mathrm{d}u = \overline{w}_U \mathrm{d}L_U + w_R \mathrm{d}L_R + g' F^R \mathrm{d}E.$$

Using Eqs. (14.8) and (14.9), we have $\overline{w}_U \mathrm{d}L_U + w_R \mathrm{d}L_R = -w_R L_U \mathrm{d}\lambda$. Therefore, we obtain Eq. (14.29) in the text.

References

Basu KC (1980) Optimal policies in dual economies. Q J Econ 95(1):187–196. https://doi.org/10.2307/1885356

Bhagwati JN, Srinivasan TN (1974) On reanalyzing the Harris-Todaro model: policy rankings in the case of sector-specific sticky wages. Am Econ Rev 64(3):502–508. https://www.jstor.org/stable/1808907

Chao CC, Yu ESH (1997) Foreign-investment tax and tariff policies in developing countries. Rev Int Econ 5(1):47–62. https://doi.org/10.1111/1467-9396.00038

Cole MA, Elliott RJR, Zhang J (2011) Growth, foreign direct investment, and the environment: evidence from Chinese cities. J Reg Sci 51(1):121–138. https://doi.org/10.1111/j.1467-9787.2010.00674.x

Copeland BR, Taylor MS (1999) Trade, spatial separation, and the environment. J Int Econ 47(1):137–168. https://doi.org/10.1016/S0022-1996(98)00020-8

Demena BA, Afesorbor SK (2020) The effect of FDI on environmental emissions: evidence from a meta-analysis. Energy Policy 138:111–192. https://doi.org/10.1016/j.enpol.2019.111192

Dorward A, Chirwa E (2011) The Malawi agricultural input subsidy programme: 2005/06 to 2008/09. Int J Agric Sustain 9(1):232–247. https://doi.org/10.3763/ijas.2010.0567

Dwibedi JK, Chaudhuri S (2014) Agricultural subsidy policies fail to deal with child labour under agricultural dualism: what could be the alternative policies? Res Econ 68(3):277–291. https://doi.org/10.1016/j.rie.2014.05.003

Grossman GM, Krueger AB (1991) Environmental impacts of a north American free trade agreement. NBER working papers no. 3914. National Bureau of Economic Research, Inc. https://EconPapers.repec.org/RePEc:nbr:nberwo:3914

Grossman GM, Krueger AB (1995) Economic growth and the environment. Q J Econ 110(2):353–377. https://doi.org/10.2307/2118443

Gupta MR (1995) Tax on foreign capital income and wage subsidy to the urban sector in the Harris-Todaro model. J Dev Econ 47(2):469–479. https://doi.org/10.1016/0304-3878(95)00021-H
Harrigan J (2003) U-turns and full circles: two decades of agricultural reform in Malawi 1981–2000. World Dev 31(5):847–863. https://doi.org/10.1016/S0305-750X(03)00019-6
Harris JR, Todaro MP (1970) Migration, unemployment and development: a two-sector analysis. Am Econ Rev 60(1):126–142. https://EconPapers.repec.org/RePEc:aea:aecrev:v
Haufler A, Wooton I (1999) Country size and tax competition for foreign direct investment. J Public Econ 71(1):121–139. https://doi.org/10.1016/S0047-2727(98)00055-3
Haufler A, Wooton I (2006) The effects of regional tax and subsidy coordination on foreign direct investment. Eur Econ Rev 50(2):285–305. https://doi.org/10.1016/j.euroecorev.2004.07.006
Huang J (1994) An empirical analysis of China's foreign-invested enterprises (in Chinese). Manage World 1:145–151. https://doi.org/10.19744/j.cnki.11-1235/f.1994.01.020
Jorgenson AK (2006) The transnational organization of production and environmental degradation: a cross-national study of the effects of foreign capital penetration on water pollution intensity, 1980–1995. Soc Sci Q 87(3):711–730. https://doi.org/10.1111/j.1540-6237.2006.00405.x
Jorgenson AK (2009) Foreign direct investment and the environment, the mitigating influence of institutional and civil society factors, and relationships between industrial pollution and human health: a panel study of less-developed countries. Organ Environ 22(2):135–157. https://doi.org/10.1177/1086026609338163
Li X, Wang D (2015) The impacts of rural-urban migrants' remittances on the urban economy. Ann Reg Sci 54(2):591–603. https://doi.org/10.1007/s00168-015-0668-y
Li X, Zhou J (2015) Environmental effects of remittance of rural-urban migrant. Econ Model 47: 174–179. https://doi.org/10.1016/j.econmod.2015.02.023
Shahbaz M, Nasreen S, Abbas F, Anis O (2015) Does foreign direct investment impede environmental quality in high, middle and low-income countries? Energy Econ 51:275–287. https://doi.org/10.1016/j.eneco.2015.06.014
Vitalis V (2007) Agricultural subsidy reform and its implications for sustainable development: the New Zealand experience. Environ Sci 4(1):21–40. https://doi.org/10.1080/15693430601108086

The manufacturer's authorised representative in the EU is Springer Nature Customer Service Centre GmbH, Europaplatz 3, 69115 Heidelberg, Germany. If you have any concerns regarding our products, please contact ProductSafety@springernature.com

Printed and bound by CPI Group (UK) Ltd, Croydon, CR0 4YY
01/10/2026
02225966-0011